*Hi!* Ron Bishop

*Merry TubaChristmas and
Happy 30th TubaBirthday!
Thank you for your participation in
Cleveland TubaChristmas 2003.*

*Frederick Fennell*

11/30/03           Frederick Fennell

# ffortissimo

*A Bio-Discography of*

# frederick fennell

*the first forty years
1953 to 1993*

Roger E. Rickson

PUBLISHING CO., INC.
557 EAST 140th STREET
CLEVELAND, OHIO 44110-1999

# ACKNOWLEDGMENTS

Without the help of the following people, this publication would not be possible. I recognize these people and I sincerely say thank you to —

Brad Hinkson, Dr. Tony Mazzaferro, John F. Maltester, Monte LaBonte, Larry Martin, Bill Muntz, Gregory Taylor and Michael Ridgway for their help in research and the difficult process of proofreading the manuscript, checking detail after detail — time after time. I also thank them for their valuable suggestions and comments.

Elizabeth Ludwig Fennell for her tireless efforts in the preparation of the final product, which I hope will live up to the fine reputation of Ludwig Music Publishing.

Donald Schmeer of Byron Hoyt Sheet Music [San Francisco, CA] for his devotion to music education and his knowledge of the published music available on these many recordings.

MAC, my faithful longtime, efficient and silent digital companion in the preparation and formulation of the data that follows.

Donald Hunsberger, Wilma Cozart Fine and David Hall for their continued interest and devotion to the Maestro, Frederick Fennell.

Louis Ouzer, Kosei Publishing Co., William L. Decker, Telarc International, Reference Recordings, G. Leblanc Corporation, Edward Pettengill, David Speckman, Harold Lawrence and Mary Morris Lawrence for permission to use their photographs.

Judy for her patience and understanding during this almost life-long project.

Frederick Fennell, without his total dedication, commitment and love for all music genre, this would not have happened. Thanks, Fred.

**ISBN 1-57134-000-9**
© copyright 1993 by

ROGER E. RICKSON
LUDWIG MUSIC PUBLISHING CO., INC.
Cleveland Ohio 44110-1999

International Copyright Secured
All rights reserved

**FIRST EDITION**

No part of this publication may be reproduced, stored in a retrieval system or transmitted in any form by any means, electronic, mechanical, photocopying, recording or otherwise without prior written permission of the publisher.

# TABLE of CONTENTS

Introduction ................................................................................................. i

Theme – Variations I & II – Development ................................................. iii - xii

Section I – Album Reference .................................................................... page 1

Section II – Composer Index ..................................................................... page 175

Section III – Title Index ............................................................................. page 197

Section IV – Eastman Wind Ensemble Personnel and Programs .............. page 219

Section V – Numerical Album Index .......................................................... page 253

Section VI – Fennell Narrative ................................................................... page 259

Section VII – Appendices ........................................................................... page 299

    Eastman Wind Ensemble Recording Dates
    Eastman Wind Ensemble 45 RPM Singles and Reel-to-Reel Tapes
    Frederick Fennell Mercury Records Recording Contracts
    Complete Recording Dates of Frederick Fennell [1953-1993]
    Where Are They Now?  EWE Personnel 1952-1962
    Study/Performance Essays and Articles by Frederick Fennell
    Music Editions/Arrangements/Compositions by Frederick Fennell

© 1993  Roger E. Rickson
Ludwig Music Publishing Co., Inc.

# INTRODUCTION

This book started innocently forty years ago as I entered college. I was first introduced to the Eastman Wind Ensemble and Frederick Fennell by a marvelous musician/teacher, C. Paul Oxley, my band director. Paul asked me to conduct *Psalm for Band* by Persichetti for the graduation ceremonies and he recommended that I listen to the only recording available at that time. Naturally it was the recently released La Fiesta Mexicana recording of May 1954. This would be record number one in my collection which has grown to over 300 records, tapes and compact discs.

This innocent beginning was soon to become an obsession. I had to find everything I could that concerned Frederick Fennell and the Eastman Wind Ensemble. But it didn't stop there, because Fred didn't stop there. Soon there were recordings with the Eastman-Rochester "Pops" Orchestra. Then came the London "Pops", the Fennell Symphonic Winds, the Frederick Fennell Orchestra, the Empire Brass Quintet and Friends, the MusiCrafters Orchestra, the Cleveland Symphonic Winds, the London Symphony Orchestra with Doc Severinsen, and now the massive collection with the Tokyo Kosei Windorchestra.

Fred's first label, Mercury, didn't help my collecting habit. They continued to re-issue his recordings in unlimited re-couplings. Not just re-coupling but a plethora of 'sampler' albums – all of which had to be in my collection. A friend then introduced me to all of the re-issues of the Eastman Wind Ensemble from Japan and then the numerous Golden Imports, many of which were issued on both LP and cassette.

Mercury Records made my collecting job even more difficult by changing covers, numbers, colors, logos, liner notes, label variations and photos changed from full color to black and white on future releases. For a number of years these great recordings were issued in both mono and stereo and each release was a little different. In 1991, under the personal supervision of Wilma Cozart Fine, the first of the Living Presence compact discs appeared. Still more to collect.

I put the beginnings of this discography together in the early seventies. A skimpy fourteen page document. This changed rapidly when I first met Fred in the mid-seventies, and his study/performance articles in The Instrumentalist began to appear. Now I had to have not only the recordings, but all of the writings by and about Frederick Fennell.

The organization of all of this information took various forms over the past few years. I tried many computer programs to help me with this large compilation of materials. I finally settled on two programs for this book, one for data management and one for page layout. My project began to take shape and to grow.

Through a long series of letters, faxes, telephone conversations, personal visits and taped interviews, Fred and I developed what follows. At first it was going to stop with the listing of all of the recordings, but we felt that further information was necessary to complete the project.

Dr. Tony Mazzaferro of Fullerton College volunteered to help with proofreading and suggested that I include more background on Fred. This suggestion became a series of cassette narratives by Fred speaking about his life and experiences. These have been transcribed, preserving his unique style, later in the book.

I have attempted to organize all of this information in a manner that will allow the reader to connect the various facets of not only the recordings, but the personnel of the Eastman Wind Ensemble for the years 1952-1962, and an up-to-date "Where Are They Now", provided by Fred. In a recent visit to their home in Siesta Key, Florida, Fred shared many rare photographs, most of which have not been seen before. These have been placed throughout the publication.

Section One is the listing of each recording and related background information. It naturally begins with the recordings of the Eastman Wind Ensemble and continues to the latest recording with the Dallas Wind Symphony. I have tried to provide all of the pertinent information for each recording.

Section Two lists all selections by composer and Section Three provides a cross-reference, title by title, over 600.

Section Four provides information on Eastman Wind Ensemble personnel and a collection of programs tracing Fred's history from 1935 to 1962. Section Five lists the collection by album number.

Section Six contains the exciting recollections and photographs that will help to chronicle the life of the Maestro.

Section Seven, the Appendices, will provide technical information on the recordings and publications of Frederick Fennell.

What began with Fred, Dr. Howard Hanson, David Hall, C. Robert Fine, the Eastman Wind Ensemble and Mercury Records Classical Division, continues to entertain, impress the audio specialists and inspire countless future performers and educators. Frederick Fennell has provided a vast legacy of historic recordings – authoritative articles, books, repertory editions, clinics and symposiums. It is our good fortune that many of these definitive examples are still available.

I hope that this publication will not only educate but provide a challenge for others to search out these items and in so doing, trace the development of the Maestro. I also hope that all will develop an appreciation for his enthusiasm to teach and inspire.

I look forward to the next forty years !

Roger E. Rickson
Corona, California
August 1993

# THEME

The founding of the Eastman Wind Ensemble in 1952 by Frederick Fennell has become the most important development in wind performance during the second half of the 20th century. This has occurred primarily through Fred's emphasis on the importance of original compositions for the wind band and the style of performance that he espoused from the very first days of the program. It is interesting to contemplate what else he might have done in the early 1950's had he not taken this course. Although much of his basic experiences were orchestral, his wind experience most probably would have led him to continue in the large symphony band trend and attempt to develop or polish that entity.

I first met Frederick Fennell during the winter of 1950 in Hazleton, Pennsylvania at the All-State Band, where I was a high school senior playing trombone, and he was the Festival Guest Conductor. The next occasion was as an Eastman freshman at the first rehearsal of the Eastman Symphony Band in the Annex Rehearsal Room where I was one of thirteen trombonists in the 1950-51 edition of that ensemble. It is interesting that although our paths first crossed in a group, which at that time was the desired goal of most band directors – the large 100-120 peopled symphonic band – now, forty-two years later, we are each still continuing to build upon the principles he established for the wind ensemble/wind orchestra, both in repertoire development and in performance practices. The directions he set for the Ensemble have indeed revolutionized the wind world and the recordings have continued to provide leadership and guidance for succeeding generations. The past years have been unique for me personally, as I have had the opportunity to be an integral part of this unique development, and especially through our forty-three year friendship.

If I may offer some insight into the paths leading toward that development from the perspective of an insider, perhaps this will further enhance the vast amount of information already contained in this book. Of course, anyone who has known Fred over these many decades is aware of his highly developed note taking, information-gathering, minutiae-splitting, ultimate "packrat" approach to every happening in every day of his life! Thus, it should come as no surprise to anyone that all the enclosed information is contained in one Boosey and Hawkes date book or another. [Frequently I have called him with a particular question regarding repertoire or a performer and he has drawn the facts from his small sized digest and further amplified it from his incredible memory].

The question has been asked many times: "What did it feel like on September 20, 1952, to be part of the original EWE in its first rehearsal?" Truthfully, the importance of that date and of what was to occur of such great impact over the following four decades, was far beyond our scope of thinking at that moment. At that time, the Eastman Symphony Band was held in varying degrees of regard within the ranks of many of the students, as most of the performers at Eastman [and still the same today] were being trained in orchestral techniques for a career in that direction. Many of the students in the late 1940's and early '50's, were discharged veterans of the Armed Forces who were not overly thrilled with traditional band literature or performance, even though Fred's programming was constantly seeking out original works for the band in deference to the standard transcriptions and popular style occasional fare that was the norm for the bands of America. Thus, the opportunity to perform in a singly-instrumented ensemble [two B-flat clarinets to a part] was a welcome change that complemented the orchestral experience.

During his ten concert seasons with the EWE, Fred molded and shaped the Ensemble into an International concert image through the programming of works ranging from Gabrieli and Pezel through Mozart, Stravinsky, to the Hindemith *Symphony*. Chamber music works were presented, as well as were the Annual Concert of Marches programs. Much of this original music programming had already been a pattern that Fred began to develop following his return from WW II, as his repertoire had already begun to move into the small, but significant, reservoir of original works for the wind band by the latter part of the 1940's decade.

Following the war, his first year's programming for the Eastman Symphony Band contained a total of thirty-four works; ten original works including the Barber *Commando March*, Norman Cazden *Elegy Before the Dawn*, Henry Cowell *Schoonthree*, Holst *Suite in E-flat*, Jacob *William Byrd Suite*, Gardner Read *Prayers of Steel* from "Sketches of the City", Wallingford Riegger *Passacaglia and Fugue*, San Juan *Yoroba Song*, and Burnett Tuthill *Suite for Band* in addition to twenty-one transcriptions of Bach, Borodin, Grieg, Handel, Holst, Rimsky-Korsakov, Tchaikowsky and Wagner, plus three Sousa marches.

This ration of original works to transcriptions was already significant for the day. It may be difficult for many to examine those programs of the late 40's and the 50's and see anything special, for much of what Fred programmed then has become standard repertoire for bands of all sizes and caliber today; however, at that time, the programming of so much original music, and especially entire programs as Fred did throughout the ten year period he guided the EWE, was considered highly revolutionary!

During the middle of my first year at Eastman, Fred performed a program in Kilbourn Hall that really pointed the way toward his future programs and recordings. When one examines the contents of this concert [see following page], you can see how the development of the Ensemble became not only a natural happening, but also a necessary one. The concert was called:

## CONCERT OF MUSIC FOR WIND INSTRUMENTS
### Performed by Students from the Orchestral Department
### Under the Direction of
## FREDERICK FENNELL

During the next season, 1951-52, the year before the birth of the Ensemble, this same ratio of transcribed to original works [exclusive of marches] became nineteen transcriptions and seventeen original works, including the fabulous march *Pieces of Eight* by Eastman composition students Joe Jenkins and Jerry Neff. Among the original compositions were: *Fourth of July* [Gould], *Symphony in B-flat* [Hindemith], *Music for a Festival* [Jacob], *Solemn Prelude* [Kay], *Canzona* [Mennin], *Symphony No. 19 in E-flat* [Miakovsky], *Suite Francaise* [Milhaud], *Divertimento for Band* [Persichetti], *Tunbridge Fair* [Piston], *Russian Christmas Music* [Reed], *Processional, Passacaglia and Fugue* [Riegger], *Theme and Variations, Op. 43a* [Schoenberg], *George Washington Bridge* [Schuman] and *Crown Imperial March* [Walton].

Now, it is necessary for anyone who still has any lingering doubts remaining concerning the importance of the programming of this original repertoire during this season to check the copyright and publication dates of these works.

This was new music performance right up to the minute! A balance of original works to this extent was not standard practice throughout the bands of America at this time and firmly establishes the need for the next step, the actual founding of the Ensemble in September 1952.

Our first repertoire that Fall semester in the new EWE was a series of new publications plus some standard fare that was to be performed for radio broadcasts for the New York State School Music Association over the Rural Radio Network; also works were read for future programming. Unfortunately, the repertoire for these radio broadcasts was not of overly high level or quality and it

# EASTMAN SCHOOL OF MUSIC
*Of The University of Rochester*

## Kilbourn Hall

CONCERT OF MUSIC FOR WIND INSTRUMENTS

Performed by Students from the Orchestral Department

*Under the Direction of*

FREDERICK FENNELL

---

### Program

| | |
|---|---|
| Ricercare for Wind Instruments (1559) | ADRIAN WILLAERT (1480-1562) |
| Canzon XXVI (Bergamasca) for Five Instruments | SAMUEL SCHEIDT (1587-1654) |
| Motet: Tui Sunt Coeli for Eight-voice Double Brass Choir | ORLANDO DI LASSO (1532-1594) |
| Sonata pian e forte<br>Canzon Noni Toni a. 12 from *Sacre Symphoniae* (1597) | GIOVANNI GABRIELI (1557-1612) |

Suite No. 2 for Brass Instruments (Turmmusik) (1685) — JOHANN PEZEL (1639-1694)
    Courante
    Intrada
    Bal
    Sarabande
    Gigue

Three Equale for Four Trombones (1812) — LUDWIG VAN BEETHOVEN (1770-1827)
    Andante
    Poco adagio
    Poco sostenuto
    Played by 25 trombone students from the class of Emory Remington

### INTERMISSION—*ten minutes*

Serenade No. 10 in B flat major for Wind Instruments (K. V. 361) (1781) — WOLFGANG AMADEUS MOZART (1756-1791)
    Largo—Allegro molto
    Menuetto
    Adagio
    Menuetto—Allegretto
    Romanze—Adagio
    Thema mit Variationen—Andante
    Rondo—Allegro molto

### INTERMISSION—*five minutes*

| | |
|---|---|
| Serenade in E flat major, Opus 7 (1881) for Thirteen Wind Instruments | RICHARD STRAUSS (1864-1949) |
| Angels, from "Men and Angels" (1921) for multiple Brass Choir | CARL RUGGLES (1876- ) |
| Symphonies for Wind Instruments (1920) In Memory of Claude Debussy | IGOR STRAVINSKY (1882- ) |

At 8:15 o'clock, Monday
February 5, 1951

was not until after February 8 in the second semester, when the Premiere Concert was performed with the Mozart *Serenade No. 10 in B-flat, K. 361*, the Wallingford Riegger *Nonet for Brass* and the *Symphony for Band* of Paul Hindemith [composed only three years earlier], did a feeling of something special begin to be felt. Then, in May, when the Mercury recording truck appeared on Swan Street behind the Eastman Theatre to set up to record the Eastman Rochester Orchestra under Howard Hanson and the EWE under Frederick Fennell, did a true feeling of importance and professionalism begin to develop. [As an early devotee of technical apparatus in film projection and sound reinforcement from high school days, I was totally overwhelmed to be permitted to sit in the recording truck and hear that fabulous Mercury sound that we had just heard in their recording of *Pictures At An Exhibition* recorded by the Chicago Symphony, and especially the experimental use of binaural recording techniques being tested by Bert Whyte. Although the first recording was released in monaural sound, stereo techniques were not very far down the road].

It takes an examination of all the repertoire that the Eastman Wind Ensemble performed under Frederick Fennell's direction in the ten year period of 1952-53 through 1961-62 to totally assess how the recording material fit into each performing season. Such a listing will be part of the entire forty years of programs of the Ensemble contained in the book THE EASTMAN WIND ENSEMBLE, A Celebration of 40 Years Activity to be published by the University of Rochester Press in 1994.

The typical concert season included about seven concerts in addition to the mandatory public performance of the recording material [a rule of the American Federation of Musicians in order to record on Symphonic Scale instead of Commercial Scale] which was included on each disc. Always, there were appearances on the Annual Festival of American Music which Howard Hanson had begun in the middle 1920's to feature and support new and rediscovered works by American composers. Thus, the remainder of the school year was spent in programming numerous works on a schedule that permitted approximately three to four weeks between each concert on the schedule of four fifty-minute rehearsals per week.

Howard Hanson is mentioned frequently in Fred's comments. Unless you had the opportunity to work or perform with him, it is highly difficult to accurately assess the influence that he had on everyone who was part of the Eastman School. Brilliant in many directions, shrewd and even crafty in his decision-making, he always set goals and a standard of excellence for others to follow. It was Fred's fortune to have had the opportunity to work with Dr. Hanson from the early 1930's until he left Eastman in 1962. [Dr. Hanson retired in 1964 and the Eastman-Mercury relationship disintegrated shortly following that]. In addition to Dr. Hanson, Fred had three friends with whom he ate lunch on almost a daily basis. Here, planning, examination of repertoire or just ruminating over future programming and all types of development occurred in the small room off the Eastman Ensemble Library with Litchard Toland – Ensemble Librarian, Lyndol Mitchell – ESM composer and theorist, and Everett Gates, the Chairman of the Music Education Department. The ability to bounce ideas off these trusted friends provided a comfort and sounding board to Frederick Fennell, for the Ensemble Department functioned somewhat independently of other departments of the School. Perhaps, the greatest influence over the years for Fred may well have been Emory Remington and his wife Laura, each of whom possessed wisdom, very high standards and compassion for the students at ESM.

In 1958, upon finishing a four year hitch in the U.S. Marine Band as trombonist and Chief Staff Arranger, I was offered an Assistantship with Fred in the Ensemble Department. This was also the year he was President of the College Band Directors National Association which required much traveling, guest conducting and work for C.B.D.N.A. This absence provided me the opportunity to fill in for him in rehearsal and to study further in depth the procedures and manner in which he prepared works for performance and recording. It was an invaluable opportunity not only to prepare music in the manner in which he performed it, but also to start stretching some very young conducting wings.

In various areas in Fred's narrative you will find reference to a "living room floor" period during the preparation of a composition for rehearsal. This meant that he literally spread all the individual parts of a manuscript work or publication, which did not possess a full score, out across the floor and studied each and every part to learn the individual performer's outlook on the composition. In addition, the ability to discern and match different articulations and phrasings [especially important in marches, where turn-of-the-century publication proofreading process left much to be desired] led to meticulously marked parts [always in a fine point red pen] which enabled each section to perform stylistically together. This attention to detail has been one of his trademarks and now may be seen by all in the many march editions, chamber works and especially the *Lincolnshire Posy* full score edition published through Ludwig Music Publishing Company.

From the performer's point of view, these corrected parts relieved everyone in the rehearsal of much discussion and questioning. Compared to many wind band conductors or directors in the middle decades of the century, Fred did not speak excessively in rehearsals but rather relied upon the skills and teachings of the Eastman wind faculty to set styles or individual instrumental performance. There was always an emphasis upon orchestral performance techniques and direct correlations drawn between classical composers of all periods and the techniques necessary to perform their works. There was never a direction toward or definition of a "Band Sound", it was always a classical orchestral approach to playing wind instruments.

In the Fall of 1960 Fred began a new program of chamber music at Cutler Union, a large building located next to the Memorial Art Gallery on the University of Rochester's Prince Street Campus. Although the Ensemble had performed concerts of mixed size instrumentations in both Kilbourn Hall and the Eastman Theatre since its inception, this new series drew attention to the flexible chamber side of the Ensemble who was becoming more and more known nationally in its full instrumentation recordings. Programs from this series will be seen in the Personnel section of this book.

Thus, in these many ways, the vision and forward thinking of one individual has shaped much of the wind world during the second half of the 20th Century. While variations of these beginnings are practiced daily in wind bands throughout the world, the basic principles that Fred created are still the guiding underpinnings of contemporary wind practices.

Frederick Fennell and the Eastman Wind Ensemble never set out to change the world or to unravel existing wind programs, but over the past forty-plus years much of this has taken place as a natural part of growth and through the seeking of higher planes and standards. I'm certain that what is in this book will not only provide fascinating reading, but inspiration as well. I'm only grateful that I have had the opportunity to be a part of it throughout all these years. So, from each of us everywhere — Thanks, Fred for all you have provided for musicians everywhere.

Donald Hunsberger, Conductor
Eastman Wind Ensemble
August 1993

Eastman Wind Ensemble, 1954. Photo courtesy of Louis Ouzer

# VARIATION I

Recording with Frederick Fennell has been an ongoing and meaningful part of my life since 1953. His talent, his dedication, his intimate knowledge of every detail of his craft and his skill at conveying this information to others – as well as the fire from within which drives him – were inspiring from the start. Through his recordings with the Eastman Wind Ensemble, he has been an outstanding leader and teacher, not only for the group itself, but also for thousands of collectors for whom his recordings served as musical revelations. Those recordings have influenced and informed band and wind ensemble directors and players both here and abroad.

He has introduced his legions of admirers to music and composers they might not otherwise have known, to sound they might not otherwise have heard, and commissioned new works from composers who might not otherwise have written them. He has directly touched the lives of wind players, young and old, on an international scale.

His commitment to young people is well-known and his vitality and enthusiasm are infectious. Something magical happens when he steps up to the podium before a group of young musicians. People often comment about the "electricity" which is heard and felt in his recordings with the Eastman Wind Ensemble.

He and the Wind Ensemble were always meticulously prepared for any eventuality which could be foreseen before the scheduled sessions. Anticipation ran high and work proceeded efficiently and enthusiastically in a taut yet informal atmosphere of charged excitement. Needless to say, all who participated vividly remember those intense hours of music-making and camaraderie.

The massive effort by Fennell, the Eastman School of Music, and Mercury Records to record the two volumes of THE CIVIL WAR – ITS MUSIC AND ITS SOUNDS, could not have been realized without Fred's family background, his musical expertise, sense of history, and his total dedication to the project. Five years in the making, this recorded documentation of that period is one of Fennell's and Mercury's proudest legacies.

Whether working with the Wind Ensemble or with an orchestra, Fred's experienced leadership and definitive performances have captivated and endeared him to audiences everywhere.

It is fortunate, indeed, that Fred's career has spanned so many years and that his present-day commitment to new projects, performance, and teaching remains firm and strong. He has been honored many times, in many ways, worldwide, but I think his greatest tribute is the deep-seated gratitude, devotion, and loyalty felt by the several generations for whom _his_ musical experience has become _their_ musical experience. His musical talent and personality have expanded, enlightened, and enriched their world of music.

His distinguished career is a great gift to us all.

Wilma Cozart Fine
Former Vice-President,
Mercury Records Corporation
Producer, Mercury Living Presence
July 1993

# VARIATION II

I have presented three separate papers in as many years, in various aspects of the Mercury Records Classical Division. I think it's a good idea to include some nuts-and-bolts information on recording techniques "from the horse's mouth", so to speak.

In 1952, Mercury Records undertook a major American Music recording program with the Eastman School of Music Director, Howard Hanson, conducting the Eastman-Rochester Symphony Orchestra. Since the 1920's, Dr. Hanson had presented, each spring at Eastman, an annual Festival of American Music. The recording program carried out at Eastman, initially by RCA Victor, by Columbia Records, and culminating in the Mercury Series, was a natural outgrowth.

A totally new twist took shape within a year after Mercury's entrance on the scene – the development of a full scale band and wind music program. The vehicle for this was the newly organized Eastman Wind Ensemble conducted by Frederick Fennell. This was a compact group of forty-five musicians, which, in its composition and finesse of execution, virtually revolutionized the performance of wind band music in this country – chiefly through the medium of the Mercury recordings.

How did we go about recording at Eastman? For one thing, the Eastman Theatre at that time was acoustically one of the best recording venues in the country. This I became aware of back in 1938 from the RCA Victor 78 rpm discs from Eastman.

By good fortune, when engineer, C. R. "Bob" Fine and myself did the first symphonic recordings for Mercury with the Louisville Orchestra in 1950, we found ourselves at one in insisting on the use of a single microphone for the job – and we had at our disposal the Telefunken U-47 condenser microphone, then a very new and scarce item in the United States. In my days as a member of the production staff for Toscanini's NBC Symphony Orchestra, both the NBC engineer, Bob Johnston and the broadcast producer, Richard Leonard, pointed out the importance of leaving control of the orchestral balance in the hands of the conductor, *not* in those of the engineer.

So we had a fine auditorium and the most technically refined microphone in the business – and we had our own self-contained recording van that we could simply park at the rear of the auditorium, run cables from our tape machines, and thereby be operating in very short order.

Stage and microphone set-up, both in the early 1950's monophonic recordings and later for stereo, were essentially the same. The set-up, whether a single mic for mono or the minimum of two needed for stereo, called for use of suspension rather than stands, which tend to produce extraneous resonance in climactic musical passages.

The stage was essentially bare and care was taken not to seat low register instruments on risers – also to prevent extraneous resonance. A basic concept underlying all this was the use of the stage floor as the fundamental reflecting surface.

In all Mercury recording sessions, general practice was to go for long takes – two complete playthroughs of a given movement or short work, followed, if necessary, by a patch or two to cover us for any musically doubtful spots.

During my tenure at Mercury, up through mid-1956, in the days before high-tech automation, I also undertook any necessary tape editing and personally supervised the transfers from master tape to the lacquer disc that eventually was processed to a finished LP.

David Hall
Castine, Maine
July 1993

# DEVELOPMENT

Among life's simple truths is to say what you mean and mean it; you never know, somebody just might be listening. Roger Rickson was when he decided to come back for a second time to my Conducting Symposium at Saddleback College in Orange County, California. But it wasn't until his third appearance that I developed the distinct feeling that I was both being listened-to and watched. Conversations, dropped remarks began to add a third dimension: <u>questions</u>! When was I going to make another record for Telarc with the Cleveland Winds, was there anything yet un-released from Mercury, when are you going to get into Video? – all knowing, even more than probing inquiries.

And I was happy to unload whatever seemed appropriate. The Symposium vanished with what once was ready California cash; friendships remained. After a time the Rickson I had observed sent a large bundle of ideas carefully thought-out for the assembly of a discography – something that I always thought was quite a bit down the road. But not Roger. He was computerized and ready to go.

The first ample three-ring binder that came was impressive in its detailed information, much of which was news to me. He is consumed by a passion for sleeves, art work, liners, labels, technical details, etc. As the project continued to grow, he wanted personal information by exchange of my answers to his questions. These are part of the final format, which emerged when he came to visit Elizabeth and me at our home on Siesta Key off mainland Sarasota, Florida in February, '93. The walls of study areas there are covered with photographs he simply had to have, moving the discography beyond recordings to include all those other writer compilations present in his Bio-Discography. And all of this grew from his love for the music contained on every disc.

The simple listing of composers and the titles of repertory they created is, of itself a considerable task – and when I finally saw it, is impressive, too! And Rickson was faithful to the facts of a recording's production as published on the sleeves and his questions. What he could not know is the totally unique manner in which our Mercury records – ALL Mercury records were planned.

It should be well-known by now that the Eastman Wind Ensemble's participation in the University of Rochester/Eastman School of Music/Mercury Records alliance began with the contract that was negotiated with the School's Director, Dr. Howard Hanson in 1950 as the microgroove recording era began. In conversations, David Hall mentioned band music as repertory items of interest to Mercury in addition to the Hanson series of American Festival Recordings with the Eastman-Rochester Orchestra that prompted the Mercury interest in the first place. Mercury and Eastman became a heaven-made marriage of ideas, with repertory not duplicated on any major label. At that level of the industry, the process of producing a recording probably is so fragmented that total workings are known to no single person.

Such was not the case with the Classical Division of Mercury Records, where, from humble beginnings, Wilma Cozart was in charge since 1950, working in modest offices on floor two above the Buick agency at 1733 Broadway, New York. With her was David Hall, whose encyclopedic knowledge of recorded music and performance made him a pioneer in the industry. After six years of brilliant and imaginative recordings jointly produced, first in Chicago, then Minneapolis and Rochester, he withdrew his participation in favor of other interests. My last recordings with him are <u>The Spirit of '76</u> and <u>Ruffles and Flourishes</u>, and it all began with <u>American Concert Band Masterpieces</u> in May, 1953.

Having worked so closely with all facets of Mercury Classical's metamorphosis from monaural to stereo, Wilma Cozart soon was to become Vice President of Mercury Records in charge of the Classical Division. Unlike the afore-mentioned corporate labyrinth, Miss Cozart constantly wove the Mercury team and its common functions together, finding Harold Lawrence – a superb choice to assume the work David Hall had done with such success from the early Mercury Classical days.

And Wilma was in charge of it all. Getting Clair Van Ausdall to sign-on from Eastman with his special talents for music and with the just-right words to go with it, plus his thoughts tastefully artistic. She had it all from artist relations with individuals and ensembles, long-term planning of their repertory, copyright clearance, public relations, art work for sleeves, liner notes, coordination of schedules – on and on. For the Division's Special Projects, such as <u>The Civil War – Its Music and Its Sounds</u> and my New York Studio Sessions for <u>Gershwin</u>, <u>Porter</u> and <u>Herbert</u>, she had to promote those out-of-budget funds, too. All of this also came along with her critical presence, LISTENING for everything as it went down on the tape at every session, re-listening as she mixed the center channel to the two outer signals; then Harold Lawrence made final edits from his immaculately-kept session data of takes and preferences, on to the transfer from tape to master disc by George Piros for stereo and John Johnson for mono. No corporate hang-ups here.

Then came Wilma's critical listening to every test for all those blemishes to which she is so allergic! And she became party to all the technical "insiderie" when she and the great engineer, C. Robert Fine were married. Fine's electronics engineering genius for phonograph recording had already made him famous. It was a remarkable partnership and it worked for many reasons; among them was the unusual fact that Fine had his own business and Mercury hired him, from its classical beginnings, to make their recordings.

The success of our association flowed from Wilma's single purpose to plan it all the way with everybody's input, let the artists deliver their signal to engineering, then oversee every movement to eventual release and tasteful promotion. The quality of product now transferred to compact disc by the same Wilma Cozart Fine extends us all, these many decades later, into this present sonic dimension. She began on floor two and carried Mercury Living Presence Records to the very top floor of the profession and its industry.

Frederick Fennell
Siesta Key, Florida
July 1993

FF in lecture demonstration at West Coast
Conducting Symposium, 1973.
Photo courtesy of Monte LaBonte

# SECTION I

# ALBUM REFERENCE

1960 magazine advertisement courtesy William F. Ludwig II and Ludwig Industries

| | |
|---|---|
| **ALBUM TITLE:** | <u>American Concert Band Masterpieces</u> |

**LABEL:** Mercury   **MONO** MG 40006 / 50079   **STEREO** No stereo release

**GOLDEN IMPORTS  SRI** 75086   **ALBUM REFERENCE NO.** 1

**COVER ART:** See notes   **LINER NOTES:** David Hall

**ENGINEER:** C.R. Fine   **TAPE TRANSFER:** George Piros

**RECORDING DATE:** May 14, 1953   **PERSONNEL LIST:** #1

## PROGRAM
\* = Premier recording

* George Washington Bridge - William Schuman
* Divertimento For Band - Vincent Persichetti
* Ballad For Band - Morton Gould
* Suite of Old American Dances - Robert Russell Bennett
* Tunbridge Fair - Walter Piston
* Commando March - Samuel Barber

## NOTES

American Music Festival Series, Volume 7.  This series of recordings for Mercury Records was initiated by Dr. Howard Hanson.  Title of album suggested by David Hall, who also wrote the liner notes

MG 40006 has brown cover with fair, carnival scene. Gold label, Golden Lyre logo. MG 50079 has blue cover with photo of George Washington Bridge. Red label, Olympian with Mercury logo. Golden Imports cassette MRI 75086. Japanese Philips release, PC-1621 (mono), same cover as MG 50079 (better detail on photo of bridge).

FF: Tape transfers were done in the C.R. Fine studio usually by assistant, George Piros, a master of tape transfer and cutting of the master disk.  Recorded in a two-hour session with a mandatory (and wise) 20 minute break in each hour.  Testing and recording time = 80 minutes. Repertory time: 43 minutes. Less time than two takes each title. The Eastman Wind Ensemble always recorded under the AF of M symphonic rate for a 2 hour session, with additional recording as overtime by half hours. 24 hours had to pass between the mandatory concert and the recording session. Players, all members of local 66 AF of M, Rochester Musicians Association, were paid scale by the Eastman School of Music.

FF: **NO FACULTY WERE EVER USED IN THE EASTMAN WIND ENSEMBLE RECORDINGS.**   As of this note (9/6/86) 32 years and 11 months after its release, this beautiful music/recording is still available. The debut concert of the Eastman Wind Ensemble took place on 8 February 1953 in Kilbourn Hall, with the following program: *Nonet for Brass* by Wallingford Riegger, *Symphony in B-flat for Concert Band* by Paul Hindemith and *Serenade No. 10 in B-flat, K. 361* by Wolfgang Amadeus Mozart.

Music Supervisor: David Hall
Recording Director: David Hall
Recording Site: Eastman Theatre, Eastman School of Music, University of Rochester. Rochester, New York
Group listed as Eastman Symphonic Wind Ensemble. The first recording by Eastman Wind Ensemble.

First rehearsal of
Eastman Wind Ensemble.
Eastman Theatre –
September 1952
Courtesy of FF.

# American Concert Band Masterpieces

## "How it all Began"
Conversation with Frederick Fennell
Siesta Key, Florida
17 August 1991

RR: How did this all begin? What led to this first recording?

FF: I had no idea of the extent of the Eastman contract with Mercury Records until I met David Hall. I went to the MENC meeting in Philadelphia in April of 1952, and that's where I had an appointment to meet David Hall. I met him on the eighth floor of the Bellevue-Stratford Hotel and we quickly went to Horn and Hardart across the street where, in the front booth, we sat and literally talked about the whole future of the Eastman Wind Ensemble [not yet born], and I think at that time we laid out what was to be the basic repertory, because he told me then, that when the contract was made with Dr. Hanson, he had told him the prime thing was to record the Eastman Festival Series with the Eastman Rochester Orchestra, but, he also wanted to record the whole school. Everything, including faculty. He had also told Dr. Hanson that he wanted band music and the Holst Suites. From then on, I carried a slip of paper with this exact recorded repertory on it in my wallet. Dr. Howard Hanson finally invited the Eastman Wind Ensemble to join him in the Mercury Records project in the American Music Festival Series. I never had any other music in mind for this recording. After I told him the above repertory, there was a long contemplative silence while he stroked his goatee. He finally said, "You know, Fred, you won't sell ten of them. But, we can always give them to the alumni." That's the statement from him that I will long remember. I said, "That's not my purpose in making this recording. This should be a statement of where original music for the wind band by American composers is in May of 1953."

RR: This first recording was very ambitious for the first season.

FF: Yes, but everybody, especially the kids playing in the group - and I say 'kids' affectionately - they knew that we had something to offer that was just a little bit different.

RR: Did you do all the auditioning personally?

FF: There were no auditions. I just chose them. I had three auditions altogether in the ten years that I was conductor of the Eastman Wind Ensemble. Two were for bass trombone and one was for piccolo. There were so many good trombone players and Joe Mariano had so many great flute players. But that was it. I just chose them because I had known most of them before they came to Eastman and I knew what they were doing after they got there and the kids just fell into their natural slots. It worked very well. I knew where they belonged and I never had any problem about that from anybody.

RR: Would you talk about the rehearsal schedule for the Eastman Wind Ensemble?

FF: It was always the same. It was never five days a week, always four days a week - Monday, Tuesday, Thursday and Friday. Wednesday was the Symphony Band one hour rehearsal. Rehearsals were always 50 minutes long - 10 past one until 2 o'clock. We couldn't have rehearsed any time longer than that. It was so intense. For those 50 minutes, those players in those groups gave, and thought and listened and concentrated. That was the hottest 50 minutes that you can imagine. We were into style, all the time style - and not only style. I tried, even then, to say to the players, look - I don't think we should think about rehearsing for performances. I think we should rehearse to learn to play together. That's a difficult thing for a lot of people to understand. Normally you are rehearsing for the concert. But the concert is only the result of how the group plays together. How they think about each other. More than anything, when I went to Tokyo, I said the same thing. My first day there we had a concert - but in my rehearsal I needed to know that we know what we are doing musically between each other, and that's why they're playing the way they are today. We don't really rehearse a concert. We rehearse sound and playing together. We rehearse to become, every time, an ensemble. And the Eastman kids, they jumped into that concept right away.

RR: Did you have any contact with these composers during this premier season?

FF: None whatsoever. None at all. I, first of all, as long as he lived, never met Samuel Barber. Sorry to say. He wasn't very happy about *Commando March* that he had written, and he denied it as a matter of fact, as a piece of his. It was something that I did during the War, and it wasn't really one of my pieces, he has told everybody. I met William Schuman sometime later. Persichetti, I met later and Gould and I had met before. I knew Morton before the *Ballad* was recorded and only because of his visits to Rochester as guest of the Rochester Civic Orchestra and once he conducted the New York All State Band, when he played a great deal of wonderful Percy Grainger music, as well as his own. That was my first meeting with Morton, and after that I got to know him a little bit better after we made this first recording. I only got to know Russell Bennett after this recording and Walter Piston, I met only once in Boston.

There was no big rush from everybody, except sometime later, some people would say, "that was very good." The composers didn't react very strongly to it, which I thought was a little strange. But again, as I said in the beginning of these conversations, nobody gives a damn about the band, so, I'm not surprised that I could present them with a sales figure that they couldn't believe, and that they were beginning to get royalties that they hadn't had before. But again, that didn't seem to make an impression on anybody.

RR: Do you have any sales figures for this first release?

FF: Not really. Well, of course when it came time for payment for this recording, and I had talked about this with Eric Leinsdorf, who was the conductor of the Rochester Philharmonic at this time, and it was his advice to take a payment and run. He said, "Nobody makes any money in the record business."

Maybe his advice was very valid. I, however, didn't take it. Dr. Hanson said very much the same thing, and I said, "Dr. Hanson, let's make it this way. I'll only get my percentage of royalties when the school has gotten all its money back on the recordings that we make. Each record. Not accumulative, but each record. And then, how about one-third of everything the school gets?" Dr. Hanson thought that was very fair, and that's the contract that is still in effect between the University of Rochester and me.

RR: Any other comments?

FF: Yes. I have always felt that people didn't really pick up on Gould's *Ballad* as they should have. Not even recently. Morton feels the same way. Looking at the repertory of this album, we opened with *George Washington Bridge*, which is a real block-buster and then *Divertimento for Band*, which diverted everybody - their listening - the wonderful pieces by themselves. Then we needed the contrast that was the *Ballad*. That was a great contrast. Then the *Suite of Old American Dances*, which is totally a unique piece of music. *Tunbridge Fair*, by a man who nobody really related to anything of the band. He was a great chamber music composer and composer of many works for the symphonic scene. He was a Harvard professor and a leading composer of his time. And, of course, Samuel Barber. But, as I said to you earlier, he didn't think much of the *Commando March*. But people who bought the recording and those still buying and programming the music, do think a great deal of it.

RR: This is a monumental recording of great historical significance, the effect of which is still to be felt in many circles of music education, and all of this great music is still available.

FF: Exactly. That's the point. I felt that these were exemplary pieces. I have a photograph in that pile right to your left shoulder there, of the release of this, our very first album. It was on 19 October 1953 at Levis Music Store in Rochester. Don Hunsberger, John Krance, myself and a few other members of the Ensemble were there for the photo with the distributors who came in from Buffalo.

Note: An excellent discussion of this period is contained in the booklet, <u>The Wind Ensemble</u> by Frederick Fennell. 1988. Delta Publications. Distributed by Southern Music Co., San Antonio, TX

## C. Robert Fine Mobile Recording Van

## "How it all Began"
Correspondence from
Frederick Fennell
28 April 1987

Frederick Fennell wrote the following on the reverse side of one of the large Mercury Records cardboard easel stands displayed in record stores in the 50's and 60's. The front shows a photo by Mary Morris in the C. Robert Fine Studio - the Ballroom of the old Great Northern Hotel on 57th Street, New York.

"Jerome Hill, president of the Great Northern Railroad was Bob's ticket to his success as a recording engineer, for he commissioned Bob to build a recording truck, self reliant for power, so J.H. could record the sights and sounds on film of the great railroads of Europe and the North American Continent. When that long and fascinating project was completed, Hill made Bob a present of the truck. Every recording [except Broadway Marches, Cole Porter, Gershwin and Herbert] was made in that truck ... not just for me, but for Dorati, Hanson, Paray, all the Russian records, too!

I confess that I had a special lump the first time I saw this promo easel. It is quite a road, long and winding, from the drum majorship of the John Adams High School Band to seeing this in Sam Goody's - Broadway - New York.

In Bob Fine's recording truck prior to the first recording session. At the back is David Hall, the originator of the Mercury Classical Catalog and great recording authority on all music. Bob Fine in middle. The machines are the Fairchilds that Bob had personally built. Bob began his life in audio and electronics at Fairchild while he was in high school. Photo courtesy of William L. Decker

| | | | |
|---|---|---|---|
| **ALBUM TITLE:** | **Marches** | | |
| **LABEL:** Mercury | **MONO** MG40007 / 50080 | **STEREO** No stereo release | |
| **GOLDEN IMPORTS   SRI** | | **ALBUM REFERENCE NO.** 2 | |
| **COVER ART:** See notes. | | **LINER NOTES:** David Hall | |
| **ENGINEER:** C.R. Fine | | **TAPE TRANSFER:** George Piros | |
| **RECORDING DATE:** November 21, 1953 | | **PERSONNEL LIST:** #2 | |

## PROGRAM
\* = Premier recording

**John Philip Sousa:**  Fairest of the Fair, Manhattan Beach, Black Horse Troop, *Daughters of Texas, Rifle Regiment, Corcoran Cadets, Hands Across the Sea, Semper Fidelis.
* Pieces of Eight - Joseph Wilcox Jenkins/Jerome Neff
* March Carillon, Op. 19, No. 2 - Howard Hanson, arr. Rob Roy Perry/Erik Leidzen
  Cheerio - Edwin Franko Goldman
  His Honor - Henry Fillmore
  Our Director - Frederick Ellsworth Bigelow
* Glory of the Gridiron - Harry L. Alford
* Pride of the Illini - Karl L. King
  National Emblem - Edwin Eugene Bagley

## NOTES

American Music Festival Series, Volume 8.

MG 40007 has Art deco cover in green and gold. Gold label and Golden Lyre logo. MG 50080 has different cover with miniature marching band figures on green background. Red label with Olympian and Mercury logo. FF: "Wilma Cozart's tasty idea and among the first used with inanimate objects. She and I regret the hasty disappearance of all of the figures."
Japanese Philips release PC-1628 (mono) with Mercury logo. Issued with same cover as MG 50080 on blue paper (US issue on green paper). These sixteen marches were recorded in an 80 minute session, and includes Fennell's favorite march, *National Emblem*.

RR: One of my copies of this album must have been fabricated in a local zoo - the opening is on the left side and the liner notes are printed up-side down which creates a real challenge.

FF: Hold on to it; like the upside-down airplane on the stamp, it may be worth a few bucks someday.

RR: There is an excellent short biography of Frederick Fennell and a statement of purpose in the organization of the Wind Ensemble concept .... "A native of Cleveland, Ohio, Frederick Fennell is a graduate of the Eastman School of Music. Since 1939 he has been on the Eastman School conducting faculty, save for a brief period during World War Two when he was National U.S.O. Music Advisor. Fennell's work in the wind ensemble and band field began in earnest during his very first year as a student at Eastman, when he took the marching band he had organized at the University of Rochester and persuaded Dr. Hanson to let him transform it into the Eastman School Symphony Band. The years of work with the Symphony Band resulted in Fennell's becoming one of the nation's foremost experts in band and wind music and a conductor whose services have been sought everywhere. The founding of the Eastman Wind Ensemble arose from a need, from Mr. Fennell's point of view, for an instrumental group of virtuoso caliber which could be called upon to play every type of music written for wind instruments from the chamber wind serenades of Mozart to the massed sonorities of a full band. Mr. Fennell has expressed his aims for the Eastman Wind Ensemble in a letter directed to composers throughout the United States "I submit this widely diversified grouping of wind-brass sonorities to you as a medium which I hope will be attractive enough to interest you as a composer. While the outlines of the contemporary wind band are obvious in the instrumentation, I trust you will be so objective as to lay aside whatever 'unpleasant' connotations the term 'band' may bring to your mind. It is my earnest hope that you will consider this a wind-brass-percussion sonority resource which will afford you a far from limited instrumental palette worthy of your consideration."

Recording Director: David Hall
Producer: David Hall
Recording site: Eastman Theatre
Group listed as Eastman Symphonic Wind Ensemble [This is interesting, especially with the above quote].

RR: The marching figures are "Pershing's Own Band" and were probably produced by Britains. Contact Dan Patterson of Jack Scruby's Soldier Factory, PO Box 1658, Cambria CA 93428 for information on availability of miniature band figures. 805-927-3805.

## Marches by Sousa and Others

## "How it all Began"
Conversation with Frederick Fennell
Siesta Key, Florida
18 August 1991

RR: Do you have a count of marches recorded by you and the Eastman Wind Ensemble?

FF: I will have to do that. I think with Eastman, not including the many marches within the Civil War album, I think it was sixty-eight marches. Again I haven't been keeping books on that. That will have to come when I'm weak and feeble and can't get out of the chair.

RR: The march albums by the Eastman Wind Ensemble have been issued and re-issued 24 different times, not including the Civil War albums.

FF: Nobody else was doing them like that. Nobody still is doing them like that. Nobody records marches like the Eastman Wind Ensemble and of course, now the Tokyo Kosei Windorchestra, because most conductors just do not approach them as pieces that interest them as pieces of music, and of course we're in a period now that bleeds over from the orchestra and the system of playing on original instruments without string vibrato and the like, and conducted by conductors who feel that they must go way back to the original conditions and original tempi, and that's a big thing now that has come over to us now in John Philip Sousa's repertory because there are many people who would like to have a complete Sousa discography, which we originally started out to do, but I wasn't at Eastman to finish that project, and I wasn't so sure that after I'd finished it, that anybody would really go for the whole thing. But in the meantime, there have been attempts in a Sousa concert to emulate him, dressed and coiffured the same, confining conductor motions to those associated with his style. Sgt. Frank Byrne of the Staff of the United States Marine Band, together with Assistant Conductor Timothy Foley have put their energy into the offering of Sousa's marches, played and recorded as Sousa may have played them, based upon the memory of men who performed them with him, altering dynamics, instrumentation, register, nuance and emphases at his will and rarely written into the parts. It becomes, in this practice, an adventure in orchestration - or re-orchestration; it is not an endeavor to play them only as he wrote and published them.
I was never aware until high school of Sousa as a conductor even though my father took me to what was the first performance of his great march, *Black Horse Troop*. When it was time for that, up on the stage came these beautiful horses, and I thought after that when I went to a band concert, where are the horses? I was ten at the time. I didn't have any sophisticated musical input to all of that. I just have to play the marches as I feel them. I am sure that they are not all that welcome to all people, but to many others, they are very welcome. Those are the people for whom I record them, I guess. It's always stated that these are my opinions, that I didn't learn this from somebody else. This is how I feel it.

RR: One might assume that over the years, the march albums have been purchased more by the lay public rather than our profession.

FF: I don't know, but it could well be that way. Of course, as you well know, we played them, both because I loved them and wanted to record them, but they were also our oranges for the banana ... those perishable bananas of Persichetti, Schuman, Hindemith, Stravinsky and Schoenberg ... they need some propping up on sales, and of course a good album of good marches always put us in the black. I guess to this day, that fund must be rather OK and I hope it's there for Hunsberger to use in all the good ways he uses it.

RR: Do you have a favorite march on this album?

FF: *National Emblem.* All my life it's been my favorite march. And there is a long history to my admiration for this march. Allow me to quote from my article in BD Guide from 1990: At home in Cleveland, we lived a half mile from John Adams High. I couldn't just put one foot in front of the other to get there - *I had to march.*, singing and whistling as I covered the ground to school. One day I found myself making conductor-like motions; they felt *so* good. And so began my school day "research" into march styles. I'd not be surprised to know that some housewife along my line of march had taken to saying, "...well, here he comes again, that crazy kid with the marching feet and those funny motions." But while this [or worse] might have been whispered into the curtains, I was saying out loud: "Now, Fennell, when you get your gang, *this* is how we are going to play *National Emblem*!" A lifetime later I don't think there is anything special about my continual interest in these wonderful little pieces of music. I just play them like everything else, to the best of my ability as a musician, to the top of my imagination as a conductor, and with enthusiasm for this frequently underplayed and mostly underprivileged music literature. ... As a performer, I've never forgotten what a fabulous experience it can be, to play a great march with a band that swings, from a conductor who loves what's being done. Years behind all the cymbals and the drums, in the heat, cold and slop, helped me to know what I had to do.

It had been a wonderful concert - and for a dream audience - that the Tokyo Kosei Windorchestra had just played in the Rodahal at the 1989 World Music Concours/Kerkrade, Netherlands. On my way back to the podium for the first encore, my morning marchings to high school came crashing back, and as I walked - a lifetime later - I said it out loud: "Now Fennell, *this* is how we're going to play *National Emblem*!" And this for me was an absolutely great moment in my life.

RR: This passage was written by Frederick Fennell on 22 September 1989 for the article in March/April 1990, <u>BD Guide.</u>

FF: You know, you're not supposed to play marches at that festival. Nobody told me that, but if they had, that's exactly why I would have played one. The audience was on its feet all night long. It's hard to say what is my favorite march. But if I had to, I'd have to say *National Emblem*.

**LISTEN** - Rehearsal in old annex hall - 1959-60. Alec Wilder is seated with legs crossed, listening to rehearsal which inspired him to eventually compose *Entertainment I*. Photo courtesy of Louis Ouzer.

**ALBUM TITLE:** <u>La Fiesta Mexicana</u>

**LABEL:** Mercury  **MONO** MG40011 / 50084  **STEREO** No stereo release

**GOLDEN IMPORTS  SRI**  **ALBUM REFERENCE NO.** 3

**COVER ART:** George Maas  **LINER NOTES:**

**ENGINEER:** C.R. Fine / Aaron Nathanson  **TAPE TRANSFER:** George Piros

**RECORDING DATE:** May 12, 1954  **PERSONNEL LIST:** #2

### PROGRAM
\* = Premier recording

* La Fiesta Mexicana - H. Owen Reed
* Canzona - Peter Mennin
* Psalm for Band - Vincent Persichetti
* A Solemn Music - Virgil Thomson
* Chorale and Alleluia - Howard Hanson

### NOTES

American Music Festival Series, Volume 12.

MG 40011 has Golden Lyre logo with gold label.  MG 50084 has Olympian logo with Mercury red label.
Japanese Philips release #PC 1622 (mono) with same cover as US release.

FF: We made this (the third recording) on very short notice at Howard Hanson's request when his mother had died and he could not face recording his *Cherubic Hymn* scheduled for this date; Mercury could not afford to come to Rochester for less than six sides; these were #5 and 6. The recording really introduced the BBb contrabass clarinet to the sound world and to record listeners. The *La Fiesta* opening is played by Gerald Corey on the new Leblanc contrabass clarinet. These five selections were recorded in a two and one-half hour session.

RR: The very first Eastman album I purchased. Over the past thirty-five years I have been searching for what we are working on today. I graduated from high school in 1955 and attended our local community college, San Bernardino Valley College, where my conductor, C. Paul Oxley, provided me a conducting opportunity for the 1957 graduation ceremony. My assignment was *Psalm for Band* and this recording was my model. A better model I could not have had.

FF: Well, we didn't start out to make them as models, but that's what they became. We did them just because that's what had to be done. What the world was going to do with them, we couldn't control anyhow. We just made the best recordings we could make, chose the music carefully and that's the most we could do.

Recording Director: David Hall
Musical Supervisor: David Hall
Recording site: Eastman Theatre
Group listed as Eastman Symphonic Wind Ensemble

Recording Director, David Hll at home in
Castine, Maine – August 1991.
Photo by FF

**ALBUM TITLE: British Band Classics**

**LABEL:** Mercury  **MONO** MG40015 / 50088  **STEREO** SR 90388

**GOLDEN IMPORTS SRI** 75011  **ALBUM REFERENCE NO.** 4

**COVER ART:** See notes  **LINER NOTES:** David Hall quoting Fennell

**ENGINEER:** Aaron Nathanson  **TAPE TRANSFER:** Aaron Nathanson

**RECORDING DATE:** May 10, 1955  **PERSONNEL LIST:** #3

### PROGRAM
\* = Premier recording

* Suite No. 1 in E-flat for Military Band, Op. 28a - Gustav Holst
* Suite No. 2 in F for Military Band, Op. 28b - Gustav Holst
* Toccata Marziale - Ralph Vaughan Williams
* Folksong Suite - Ralph Vaughan Williams

### NOTES

Recording date as listed on album back is April 23, 1955. The above listed date is correct.
Golden Imports cassette release MRI 75011. Title of album chosen by Frederick Fennell.

RR: Cover art: MG 40015 shows "Household Cavalry", courtesy of British Travel Association. Golden lyre logo and gold label. MG 50088 (first re-issue) has Olympian Mercury logo with red label with same cover design as MG 40015. Japanese re-releases the same as SR 90388: PC 1601 (1975) and PC 18-110 (1980).

Recording Director: David Hall
Music Supervisor: David Hall
Recording site: Eastman Theatre
Group listed as Eastman Symphonic Wind Ensemble

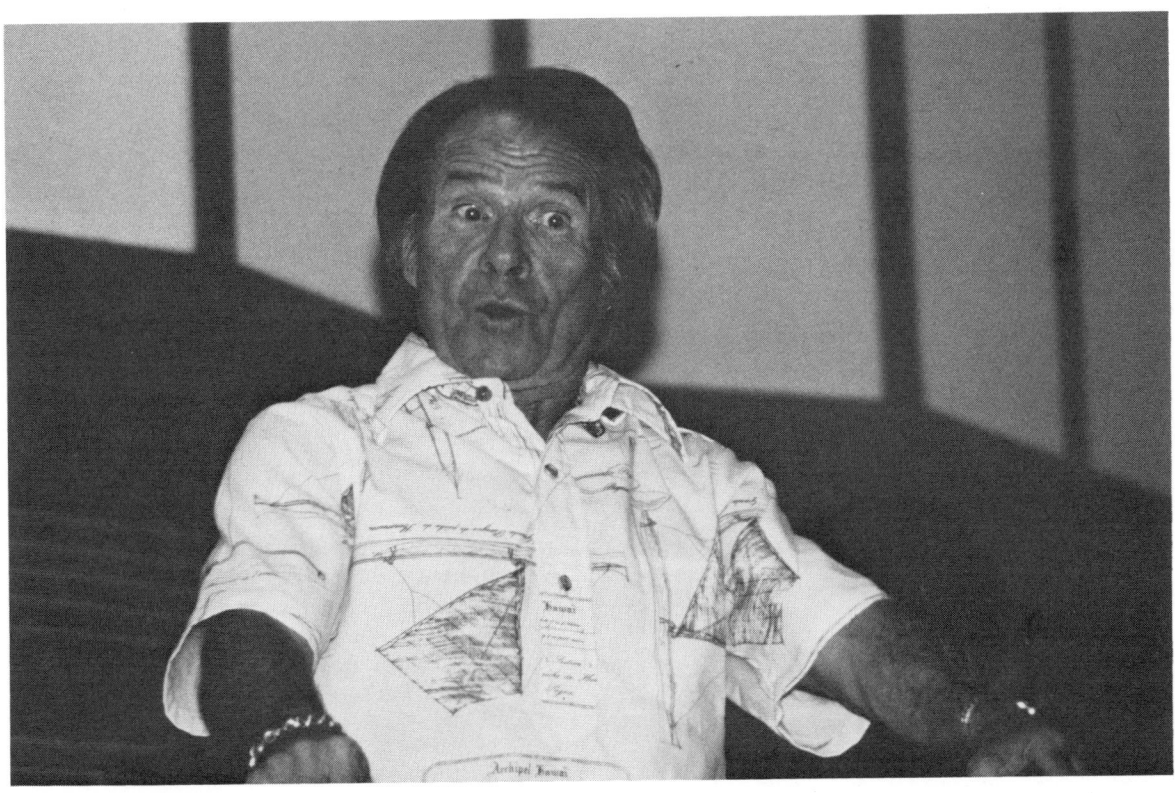

Frederick Fennell at California State University, San Bernardino – January 1981.
Photo by Roger E. Rickson

**ALBUM TITLE: British Band Classics**

**LABEL:** Mercury  **MONO** MG40015 / 50088  **STEREO** SR 90388

**GOLDEN IMPORTS  SRI** 75011  **ALBUM REFERENCE NO.** 5

**COVER ART:** See notes  **LINER NOTES:** David Hall quoting Fennell

**ENGINEER:** Aaron Nathanson  **TAPE TRANSFER:** Aaron Nathanson

**RECORDING DATE:** May 10, 1955  **PERSONNEL LIST:** #3

### PROGRAM
\* = Premier recording

* Suite No. 1 in E-flat for Military Band, Op. 28a - Gustav Holst
* Suite No. 2 in F for Military Band, Op. 28b - Gustav Holst
* Toccata Marziale - Ralph Vaughan Williams
* Folksong Suite - Ralph Vaughan Williams
* Hill Song No. 2 - Percy A. Grainger (included only on SR 90388 and SRI 75011)\*\*

### NOTES

\*\* Hill Song No. 2 was added to SR 90388 [album reference number 5] and SRI 75011 by Wilma Cozart for the re-issue program. Hill Song No. 2 was also issued on "promo" tape from TRN Music Publisher for their 1985/1986 release of this title.

Recording date as listed on album back is April 23, 1955. The above listed date is correct.
Golden Imports cassette release MRI 75011. Title of album chosen by Frederick Fennell.

SR 90388 cover is by George Maas, a combination of what appears to be British folklore woodcuts. [The liner notes on SR 90388 have been re-arranged and expanded to include Hill Song No. 2, with an added technical note describing the electronically created stereo version from the original mono only recording.] MG 50088 (first re-issue) has Olympian Mercury logo with red label with same cover design as MG 40015. Japanese re-releases the same as SR 90388: PC 1601 (1975) and PC 18-110 (1980). A recoupling was issued on English Philips (GL 5840) which included Holst's *Hammersmith* from Volume II (SR 90197) -- the liner notes are virtually the same as SR 90388. Cover on the Japanese 18PC-110 shares the close-up picture of instruments, not unlike the familiar and boring covers of THE INSTRUMENTALIST, as appear on some of the Golden Imports release.

Recording Director: David Hall
Music Supervisor: David Hall
Recording site: Eastman Theatre
Group listed as Eastman Symphonic Wind Ensemble

Fred at home with drum set. Two real Chinese cymbals, tom toms, four tuned cowbells, sock cymbal and 36" bass drum. Last such photograph at drum set. June 1933. Courtesy of FF.

| ALBUM TITLE: | _Marching Along_ | | |
|---|---|---|---|
| LABEL: Mercury | | MONO MG 50105 | STEREO SR 90105 |
| GOLDEN IMPORTS SRI 75004 | | | ALBUM REFERENCE NO. 6 |
| COVER ART: Photo by Ormond Gigli | | | LINER NOTES: Frederick Fennell |
| ENGINEER: C.R. Fine | | | TAPE TRANSFER: George Piros |
| RECORDING DATE: January 20, 1956 | | | PERSONNEL LIST: #4 |

## PROGRAM
\* = Premier recording

JOHN PHILIP SOUSA: U.S. Field Artillery, The Thunderer, The Washington Post, King Cotton, El Capitan, The Stars and Stripes Forever.
American Patrol - Frank W. Meacham
On The Mall - Edwin Franko Goldman
Lights Out - Earl E. McCoy
Barnum and Bailey's Favorite - Karl L. King
Colonel Bogey - Kenneth J. Alford
The Billboard - John N. Klohr

## NOTES

The fifth recording by the EWE and the first in **STEREO**. Album title chosen by Frederick Fennell from John Philip Sousa's autobiography, _Marching Along_.

FF: The cover photo is reproduced backwards. I have always looked on the "A" on the band uniforms as signifying "anonymous band", which it is, thank God! ... it was not my choice.

Golden Imports cassette MRI 75004; Japanese Philips PC 1612 (same cover and contents as US issue). The Hi-Fi Facts on the liner notes on MG 50105 and SR 90105 differ slightly from each other. SR 90105 states .."was made on three channel tape machines, and tape to disc transfer was done from the original three channel tape." Both notes include "For those who glory in superb mass drum impact, we recommend the "break" strains of **King Cotton !** " The SR version also includes a part of the four-color photo from the cover, the famous Anonymous Band. It is again interesting to note that a mention of the Eastman Wind Ensemble is still accompanied by "Symphonic" on the cover, but not on the back notes. The earlier mono release [MG 50105] includes the short article including Eastman Wind Ensemble, but both front and back covers include "Symphonic" in the group listing. Mercury reel-to-reel tape release, MWS5-14, contains only the selections by John Philip Sousa. The tape contains the slogan "A MERCURY LIVING PRESENCE "SEEING EAR" STEREOPHONIC TAPE RECORDING. List price for this tape was $6.95. Lp release date: 12 May 1956.

Recording Director: David Hall
Music Supervisor: David Hall
Recording site: Eastman Theatre
Group listed as Eastman Symphonic Wind Ensemble

Howard Hanson at Interlochen, 1931
Notice the plus-fours, the vest and coat,
and of course, at this time for him,
the inevitable pipe.
Photo courtesy of FF.

| **ALBUM TITLE:** | **The Spirit of '76** | | |
|---|---|---|---|
| **LABEL:** Mercury | | **MONO** MG 50111 | **STEREO** SR 90111 |
| **GOLDEN IMPORTS  SRI** 75048 | | **ALBUM REFERENCE NO.** 7 | |
| **COVER ART:** See notes * | | **LINER NOTES:** Frederick Fennell | |
| **ENGINEER:** C.R. Fine | | **TAPE TRANSFER:** George Piros | |
| **RECORDING DATE:** May 6, 1956 | | **PERSONNEL LIST:** #4 | |

### PROGRAM
\* = Premier recording

**MUSIC FOR FIFES AND DRUMS BASED UPON THE FIELD MUSIC OF THE U.S. ARMY:**
Traditional Marching Tunes for Fifes and Drums : Yankee Doodle, Sergeant O'Leary, The Belle of the Mohawk Vale, Gary Owen, Dixie , Sentry Box, Rally 'round the Flag , Bonnie Blue Flag [Harry McCarty], The White Cockade.

**THE CAMP DUTY OF THE U.S. ARMY:** The Three Camps, The Slow Scotch, The Austrian, Dawning of the Day, The Hessian, Dusky Night, The Prussian, The Dutch, The Quick Scotch, The Three Camps.

**TRADITIONAL MUSIC FOR FIFES AND DRUMS:** The Breakfast Call, The Dinner Call, Wrecker's Daughter-Quickstep, Hell on the Wabash, Downfall of Paris.

**DRUM SOLOS**: Connecticut Half-time ; Fancy 6/8

Dixie composed by Daniel Decatur Emmett
Fancy 6/8 composed by William F. Ludwig, Sr.
Rally 'Round the Flag composed by G. S. Root
Bonnie Blue Flag composed by Harry McCarty
Connecticut Half-time adapted by J. Burns Moore

**ALL SELECTIONS ARE PREMIER RECORDINGS**. The music is traditional and public domain. Drum parts written by Frederick Fennell, copyright 1956 by Eastman School of Music of the University of Rochester. Published by Eastman School of Music. Agents: Carl Fischer, Inc. *The Drummers Heritage,* compiled by Frederick Fennell. Frederick Fennell's distinguished signature was added to the cover of later printings.

### NOTES

\*The cover "Spirit of '76" by Archibald M. Willard. Permission granted by The Selectmen, to reproduce the painting which hangs in the Gallery at Abbot Hall, Marblehead, Mass. Back liner photo of Fennell in rehearsal by Radford Bascome is included only on the mono release [MG 50111]. With the limited instrumentation listed below, the group is listed as members of the Eastman Symphonic Wind Ensemble. The personnel is listed on the liner notes of both issues. Golden Imports cassette MRI 75048.

FF: I had to go to the Abbot Hall to ask their permission, and I did! The painting has deteriorated to a dull brown mass. Willard was a wagon painter of scenes of one's farms, dog, wife, barn, etc. on the side of wagons below the seat. He used the same kind of paint for "Spirit of '76", so it cannot be restored. The Camp Zeke Fife and Drum Corps in its '76 uniforms [in the sesquicentennial year, 1926]. My father and I played for the re-dedication of a plaque on the building in downtown Cleveland, where, in a loft, Willard painted the picture, which is life-size. I saw the plaque on Sunday, 8 February 1987.
This was recorded in a three and one-half hour session.

Instrumentation requires only the following:
Piccolo: David Gilbert, Shelley Gruskin, Barbara Eklund, Harold Mueller. Drums: Frederick Fennell, Gordon Peters, Mitchell Peters, Theodore Frazeur [field drums], Kenneth Wendrich [bass drum].

Recording Director: David Hall
Musical Supervisor: David Hall
Recording site: Eastman Theatre
Group listed as Members of the Eastman Symphonic Wind Ensemble.

| | |
|---|---|
| **ALBUM TITLE:** <u>Ruffles and Flourishes</u> | |
| **LABEL:** Mercury     **MONO** MG 50112 | **STEREO** SR 90112 |
| **GOLDEN IMPORTS**   SRI   75034 | **ALBUM REFERENCE NO.** 8 |
| **COVER ART:** See notes | **LINER NOTES:** Frederick Fennell |
| **ENGINEER:** C. R. Fine | **TAPE TRANSFER:** George Piros |
| **RECORDING DATE:** May 6, 1956 | **PERSONNEL LIST:** #4 |

### PROGRAM
\* = Premier recording

**MUSIC FOR FIELD TRUMPETS AND DRUMS BASED UPON THE FIELD MUSIC OF THE U.S. ARMED FORCES FROM THE REVOLUTIONARY WAR TO THE PRESENT DAY.**

**TRADITIONAL MARCHES AND INSPECTION PIECES:** General Dooley, The Old Guard, The American Flag, The Cavaliers, Old Six-eight, I've Got Three Years To Do This In, Hens and Chickens, No Slum Today, Holy Joe, Soapsuds Row, The Colonel's Daughter, The Prisoner, Rip Van Winkle, The Garrison Belle, General Burt, You're In The Army Now, Spanish Guard Mount, The Red Hussars, A-hunting We Will Go, Payday, Double Time, The President's March, [Each group is introduced by 'Sound Off'].

**MUSIC FOR RENDERING HONORS:** Ruffles and Flourishes, General's March, To The Color, Funeral March

**BUGLE CALLS OF THE U.S. ARMY:** Ruffles and Flourishes, Assembly, Adjutant's Call, Church Call, Drill Call, General Call, Mail Call, Mess Call, Retreat, Call to Quarters, Reveille, Tattoo, Taps

**DRUM SOLOS:** Swinging Down the Street (William G. Street); Connecticut Half-time.

### NOTES

On MG 50012, the original issue, the back cover has a photo of Frederick Fennell by Radford Bascome. Stereo release, SR 90112 has no photo]. Cover photo by Sgt. Joney Williams, courtesy of U.S. Marine Corps. Mercury reel-to-reel tape MS5-13. [Ten titles missing on the reel-to-reel tape.] List price: $8.95. Golden Imports cassette MRI 75034.

The *Star Spangled Banner* performed by full EWE (48). Omitted on the first SR release but is included on the SRI re-issue. Arrangement of *Star Spangled Banner* made by Frederick Fennell during WW II. Key is Ab major. All selections are premier recordings except for the Star Spangled Banner. See note regarding drum parts for "Spirit of '76" - *The Drummer's Heritage*, compiled by Frederick Fennell.

Valuable historical information on the use of trumpets and drums are included in the notes by Frederick Fennell. Title of album selected by Frederick Fennell.

Instrumentation requires only the following personnel: Trumpet: Thomas Hohstadt, James Austin, David Johnson, Ruth Still; Percussion: Frederick Fennell, Gordon Peters, Mitchell Peters, Theodore Frazeur [field drum], Kenneth Wendrich [bass drum], James Dotson [cymbals].

Seventh recording by EWE and David Hall's final recording with the ensemble.
FF: David left after this album. In the early fall he took his family to Denmark on a Fulbright He severed all relationship to any recording company [still his policy] But without him at the start, we'd probably had no Mercury relationship, and I, no career in recording.

Recording Director: David Hall
Musical Supervisor: David Hall
Recording site: Eastman Theatre
Group listed as Members of the Eastman Symphonic Wind Ensemble.

## The Spirit of '76 and Ruffles and Flourishes

## "How it all Began"
### Conversation with Frederick Fennell
### Siesta Key, Florida
### 18 August 1991

This record was born in my brain one very beautiful, bright, sunny afternoon. We went up to Interlochen for a little holiday. I rented a cottage, and one afternoon I was out laying on one of those little rubber rafts on Green Lake. I was just taking in some sun, thinking about nothing and everything - my first real chance to "goof-off" for half an hour in months. But, of course, what to record next had become such a part of daily life, that thoughts drifted to my first music experiences at old Camp Zeke and that great fife and drum corp. Of course, what else? A little 45 rpm - those great tunes that would have absolutely NO competition in the market. So I splashed off of the float, dried off, got dressed and went to the public phone at Bud's Gas Station next to the Post Office at Interlochen, and called Wilma Cozart. I told her that something had just occurred to me, out of my past, that we should talk about the next time she came to Rochester.

My family had a fife and drum corps, and there were a lot of great tunes that they played. Wilma said: "Maybe putting it together with the bugle music and bugle calls of the Army we could have a very good low-budget project that would be worth it. The next time we come to Rochester, let's talk about this".

We had just completed the recording of the day, "Marching Along", and I was in the garage with the truck with Wilma and Bob. Bob was looking for something that had blown. A gassy tube or something, and he was having a hard time finding it and we were just visiting while he was exploring. Wilma said, "Fred, why don't you tell us what this business is about fifes and drums that you called me about?". I talked about it for awhile, but the more I talked, the more I thought, this won't do. I went back into the theatre, 'cause everybody had gone home, where backstage was one of the field drums with a sling and some sticks. I brought that over into the garage. It was cold and I had on my heavy winter coat with the drum slung around my neck, and I was marching up and down the garage whistling the fife parts and playing the drum. Bob Fine came to the door of the truck and said, "Wilma, we've just got to record this."

One morning in April, during Spring break, I sat down on the floor in Indian fashion, with a little foot stool that we had, my drum sticks and a blank pad of paper, and by seven o'clock that night I had written "Ruffles and Flourishes" and the "Spirit of '76". All the drum parts.

I wrote the two records that day because I knew all these tunes, all my life, and I bought them from the government [for five cents], the manual for the bugle and the drum. I got a copyright on all the drum parts because that had never ever been done by anybody.

I got my fee as a conductor of the two sessions. A fee as a performer on both sessions, and I wrote and published a book of this called, <u>The Drummers Heritage</u>. It's the only smart thing I ever did in my life.

The two albums together cost us $902.00, for both, and they sold like jazz.

I used to get phone calls from Generals who hadn't heard this music since they were at West Point, and all that kind of stuff. We knew we had hit something. Mothers were using this recording to get their kids to move in the morning and march around the table. It was very successful, I'm glad to say. It was just something out of Camp Zeke in Cleveland, Ohio.

These two recordings were done in three and one-half hours of recording - both sessions. It didn't cost the school much to make, but they paid for a lot of other things.

Left to right: Jim Dotson, Kenneth Windrich, Mitchell Peters, Gordon Peters, FF, Theodore Frazeur, David Hall [the Everything for this session] with my Camp Zeke bass drum beater and William Street. Photo courtesy of William L. Decker.

| | | |
|---|---|---|
| **ALBUM TITLE:** | **Marches For Twirling** | |
| **LABEL:** Mercury | **MONO** MG 50113 | **STEREO** No stereo release |
| **GOLDEN IMPORTS** SRI | | **ALBUM REFERENCE NO.** 9 |
| **COVER ART:** See notes | | **LINER NOTES:** Frederick Fennell |
| **ENGINEER:** | | **TAPE TRANSFER:** |
| **RECORDING DATE:** | | **PERSONNEL LIST:** #2 and #4 |

### PROGRAM
\* = Premier recording

This is a recoupling of other recordings [MG 50080 and MG 50105]

His Honor - Henry Fillmore
The U.S. Field Artillery - John Philip Sousa
Glory of the Gridiron - Harry L. Alford
Pride of the Illini - Karl L. King
The Stars and Stripes Forever - John Philip Sousa
Our Director - Frederick E. Bigelow
The Billboard - John N. Klohr
Semper Fidelis - John Philip Sousa
Barnum and Bailey's Favorite - Karl L. King
Manhattan Beach - John Philip Sousa
National Emblem - Edwin Eugene Bagley

### NOTES

Liner notes by Frederick Fennell may be the first and only source published of the background for the Drum Major and the emergence of the baton twirler.

FF: It was my idea to issue this recoupling and slant it toward the 'twirling world'. It sold very well and helped to pay for other things, specifically the Hindemith session. The wholesome looking majorette on the cover was my choice, but Mercury's sales head said we'd probably have sold more if we'd had some legs and one of those skin-tight jobs on the cover.
Title of album selected by Frederick Fennell.

RR: What about the cover photo ?   FF: from one of those pools of them ... that was done by the NY office.
Olympian-Mercury label.  RR: It was only issued in mono. No stereo [SR] release of this recording.

RR: Fred do you have information on the release date of this album:

FF: Can't give exact release date, but it first shows in my Boohawks for May 9, 1956 as I selected the titles from MG 50080 and MG 50105 on that day for Wilma Cozart. I believe it preceded the release of "Spirit" and "Ruffles" to hit the High School fall marching band kids ... say July. Stereo or mono wasn't a factor, just something to twirl by! It sold pretty well. "Marching Along", from which tunes were taken for the "Twirlers" was released on 12 May 1956. I also find an entry for "Twirling" on 17 May 1956 with MG 50113 number. Guess: release mid July to August 1st of same year.

Group listed as Eastman Symphonic Wind Ensemble

Joseph Maddy, founder of Interlochen – standing next to one of the great pines. Summer 1931. Photo courtesy of FF.

**ALBUM TITLE:** <u>**Hindemith - Schoenberg - Stravinsky**</u>

**LABEL:** Mercury   **MONO** MG 50143   **STEREO** SR 90143
**GOLDEN IMPORTS  SRI** 75057   **ALBUM REFERENCE NO.** 10
**COVER ART:** Radford Bascome **   **LINER NOTES:** Frederick Fennell
**ENGINEER:** C.R. Fine   **TAPE TRANSFER:** George Piros
**RECORDING DATE:** March 24, 1957   **PERSONNEL LIST:** #5

### PROGRAM
* = Premier recording

* Symphony in B-flat for Concert Band - Paul Hindemith
* Theme and Variations, Op. 43a - Arnold Schoenberg
Symphonies of Wind Instruments - Igor Stravinsky

### NOTES

FF: Dr. Hanson turned me down on this recording on 2 May 1956, and this was recorded less than a year later. Roger, I believe we did predate Paul Hindemith's recording of Symphony in B-flat with Berlin Philharmonic Orchestra Winds, but you might ask somebody who has that disk to check it. I sent a copy of this recording to Paul Hindemith and his response was to send me a photograph of himself.
I also sent a copy, the first stereo copy, to Igor Stravinsky as a gift to him on his 75th birthday, 17 June 1957. He responded with a photograph, the famous one on the cover of his own recording of the symphony, inscribed as follows: "To Frederick Fennell and the Eastman Wind Ensemble, my very best wishes for their birthday wishes and their good recording of my Symphony for Wind Instruments. Most sincerely, I. Strawinsky." December 1957." Note that he did not refer to the work as Symphonies of Wind Instruments and signed his name I. StraWinsky. Another interesting note is that in the printed score, he said the duration of the piece is 12 minutes. Our recording lasts 8:36, and then when Stravinsky recorded it with the Toronto players, the CBC, his timing was 8:36. How is it possible that a man of Stravinsky's passion for accuracy to either miscalculate this to the extent that he did or to allow such an error as this be published. How could he allow that? The man who had complete control of everything.

RR: I did check the Hindemith recording, and it is dated 1957, but no month listing - so I am opting to leave the premier recording to Fennell, who is usually ahead of his time anyway.

FF: ** Cover photo of instruments by Radford Bascome "courtesy of C.G. Conn, Ltd. (trombone and horn); H. & A. Selmer, Inc. (alto saxophone) ; and G. Leblanc Co. (flugelhorn and contra clarinet). The flugel was played in the Schoenberg and I carried both to NYC for the photo session.
This is the first **Wilma Cozart** session as Recording Director with **Harold Lawrence** as the Music Supervisor. Wilma bought me the red tie to pick up that color in the paper background.

RR: Was it Mercury's idea to use "Symphonic" in the group listings?

FF: Yes, but Dr. Hanson along with David Hall and their concern for sales of the first record, I guess.

Japanese release, [Philips] PC-1607, has same cover and contents as US release .

RR: "Beguine for Band" [Glenn Osser] and "Prom Night" [Ralph Hermann] were recorded during this session. Both were released on "Curtain UP - Fennell and the POPS - SR 90340. FF: The session began at 9:00 AM and "Prom Night" was recorded at 9:10 AM and "Beguine for Band" followed the Schoenberg at 11:02 AM"

Title of album selected by Frederick Fennell.

Recording Director: Wilma Cozart
Musical Supervisor: Harold Lawrence
Recording site: Eastman Theatre
Group listed as Eastman Wind Ensemble.

**FIRST RELEASE AS EASTMAN WIND ENSEMBLE** without Symphonic attached, five years after the organization of the Ensemble. FF: By now, both Dr. Hanson and Wilma Cozart had been convinced of my only name for the group: The Eastman Wind Ensemble. Sales and National recognition had done their part, too.

See next page for Stravinsky personnel.

# PERSONNEL

## "Symphonies of Wind Instruments"

### Igor Stravinsky

### Eastman Wind Ensemble

### Frederick Fennell, Conductor

**FLUTE**
David Gilbert
Barbara Eklund
Elizabeth Bruner

**OBOE**
Daniel Stolper
Vivian Brooks
Bernard Rubenstein, English Horn

**CLARINET**
Robert Gauldin
Joseph Carlucci
Mitchell Weiss

**BASSOON**
Alan Brown
Richard Hall
Glen Williams, Contra-Bassoon

**HORN**
Barry Benjamin
Aubrey Bouck, assistant
Kenneth Schultz
Waldo Comfort
William Bommelje

**TRUMPET**
James Austin
Manuel Alvarez
Gary Smith

**TROMBONE**
Porter Poindexter
Frederick Halt
Jonathan Clark

**TUBA**
Roger Bobo

**Stravinsky Wind Symphonies**

```
  O O O↓O O O O
  └trumpets┘ └trombones┘ tuba

     O O O O O
     └─ Horns ─┘

  O O O  O O O
  └Bassoons┘ └clarinets┘

  O O  O  O  O O
  └flutes┘  └oboes┘
```

**Mozart Serenade X · B♭**

```
   O O O O
   └─ Horns ─┘        O — Contrabass clarinet

   O O  O O           O — Contra Bassoon
   └Clarinet┘ └Bassoons┘
   O O  O O           O — String contrabass
   └oboes┘ └Basset
            horns┘
```

Strauss Serenade in E♭, opus 7
Same as above, without the
Basset horns, and plus flutes
at the left of the set.

| | | |
|---|---|---|
| **ALBUM TITLE:** | **March Time** | |
| **LABEL:** Mercury | **MONO** MG 50170 | **STEREO** SR 90170 |
| **GOLDEN IMPORTS  SRI** 75055 | **ALBUM REFERENCE NO.** 11 | |
| **COVER ART:** Photo by Henry Ries | **LINER NOTES:** Frederick Fennell | |
| **ENGINEER:** C.R. Fine | **TAPE TRANSFER:** George Piros | |
| **RECORDING DATE:** October 19, 1957 | **PERSONNEL LIST:** #6 | |

### PROGRAM
\* = Premier recording

Bugles and Drums - Edwin Franko Goldman
\* Illinois March - Edwin Franko Goldman
Children's March - Edwin Franko Goldman
\*The Interlochen Bowl - Edwin Franko Goldman
Onward-Upward - Edwin Franko Goldman
\* Boy Scouts of America - Edwin Franko Goldman
Americans We - Henry Fillmore
Officer of the Day - Robert Browne Hall
March Grandioso - Roland Forrest Seitz
Second Regiment Connecticut National Guard March - David Wallis Reeves
The Mad Major - Kenneth John Alford
\* Guadalcanal March from "Victory at Sea" - Richard Rodgers [arr. Erik Leidzen]

### NOTES

Frederick Fennell played the traps on "Children's March" by Goldman.
Cover photo of instruments supplied by C.G. Conn, Ltd. and Ludwig Drums.
Japanese Philips release PC-1614 - same contents and cover. Also issued on reel-to-reel tape MWS5-29.

"March Time" was issued with "Screamers" on a Mercury Living Presence CD in 1991. The CD cover reproduces the original cover of "Screamers". Original liner notes are preserved in the CD issue. The group is listed as the Eastman Wind Ensemble on this release.

Robert Browne Hall, composer of "Officer of the Day" is listed in the liner notes as Robert Bruce Hall. This error is corrected on the Living Presence compact disc release.

Holland cassette on Classette [yes, Classette] Label issued by PolyGram - 412-300-4. Black and white cover does not match the Golden Imports packaging.

Also recorded at this session were "Christmas Festival" by Leroy Anderson and "The Beachcomber" by Norman Richardson. "The Beachcomber" is the only unreleased title recorded by the Eastman Wind Ensemble.

FF: We did this in three hours of recording and that was after only sixteen hours of being together as a group. At the conclusion of this session we recorded *The Beachcomber* by Norman Richardson. I was in Boosey-Hawkes on 57th Street one day, waiting for Martha Baxter, to take her to lunch. She was their Educational Representative, a very terrific young lady, whom I enjoyed very much. I was looking through a stack of octavos, and I found *The Beachcomber* and said now that's an attractive title. So, I spent some time looking at it, and when Martha came out of a conference, I said "can I have a set of this?" So, they had to order it from England, and eventually I received a set and our librarian, Litchard Toland, put it in the Wind Ensemble folders and we read it. The Ensemble said "hey, this is really cute. Let's make this." So I kept it in the books until the three minutes came along. A very delightful piece and it is the only unreleased recording by the Eastman Wind Ensemble. The only one. Every other thing was released. They forgot about it, I guess. And, of course, you know, the people in this business are so busy, and they just forgot about this title. I'm glad that this was done and that I have a copy and now you have a copy.

Recording Director: Wilma Cozart
Musical Supervisor: Harold Lawrence
Recording site: Eastman Theatre
Group listed as Eastman Symphonic Wind Ensemble [reverting to the use of Symphonic]

**ALBUM TITLE: Winds in Hi-Fi**

**LABEL:** Mercury  **MONO** MG 50173  **STEREO** SR 90173
**GOLDEN IMPORTS SRI** 75093  **ALBUM REFERENCE NO.** 12
**COVER ART:** See notes  **LINER NOTES:** Frederick Fennell
**ENGINEER:** C. R. Fine  **TAPE TRANSFER:** George Piros
**RECORDING DATE:** March 2, 1958  **PERSONNEL LIST:** #6

### PROGRAM
\* = Premier recording

* Lincolnshire Posy - Percy A. Grainger
* Three Japanese Dances - Bernard Rogers
* Suite Francaise - Darius Milhaud
* Serenade in E - flat, Op. 7 - Richard Strauss

### NOTES

FF: The wind version of *Three Japanese Dances* by Bernard Rogers was written for the Eastman Wind Ensemble and was premiered in 1954. When I suggested a wind version, Rogers responded with considerable enthusiasm. Bernard Rogers was an unusual man and held in highest esteem at Eastman by his pupils as a superb teacher of composition. It was never easy to satisfy him with any performance, and I rarely did that among a substantial list of his pieces for chamber orchestra, for instance. He was never interested in writing anything for the Symphony Band even though I began to ask him to as early as 1935. But the E.W.E. interested him, hence this re-setting of one of his most successful orchestral works. Original works came later for Donald Hunsberger.

See following page for personnel on Strauss Serenade in E - flat, Op. 7. Seating chart on page 18.

Original cover has red lettering with red logo. Re-issue, same number, has white lettering with blue logo.

Japanese Philips re-release [1975] PC-1604, same cover without the "Winds in Hi-Fi" title, and contents.
Golden Imports cassette: MRI 75093. The release date for this LP was 15 October 1958.

**SPECIAL MERIT:** This album received the *STEREO REVIEW* award, July 1977, as one of the fifty best recordings of the first century of the phonograph 1877-1977. David Hall selected the recording of Grainger's "Lincolnshire Posy" from over 500,000 possibilities.

Recording Director: Wilma Cozart
Musical Supervisor: Harold Lawrence
Recording site: Eastman Theatre
Group listed as Eastman Wind Ensemble

Winds in Hi-Fi session in Eastman Theatre, March 1958
Photo courtesy of William L. Decker.

## PERSONNEL

**Richard Strauss "Serenade in E - flat, Op. 7"**
**Wolfgang A. Mozart "Serenade No. 10 in B - flat, K. 361"**

**Eastman Wind Ensemble**

**Frederick Fennell, Conductor**

| Serenade in E - flat, Op. 7 | Serenade No. 10 in B -flat, K. 361 |
|---|---|
| **FLUTE**<br>David Gilbert<br>Joanne Dickinson | **OBOE**<br>Daniel Stolper<br>William Harrod<br>Bernard Rubenstein |
| **OBOE**<br>Daniel Stolper<br>Bernard Rubenstein | **CLARINET**<br>Robert Gauldin<br>Elsa Ludewig |
| **CLARINET**<br>Robert Gauldin<br>Elsa Ludewig | **BASSET HORN**<br>Rolf Legband<br>Eugene Zoro |
| **BASSOON**<br>Alan Brown<br>Richard Campbell | **BASSOON**<br>Alan Brown<br>Richard Campbell |
| **CONTRA-BASSOON**<br>Glenn Williams | **CONTRA-BASSOON**<br>Glenn Williams |
| **CONTRA-BASS CLARINET**<br>James Badalato | **CONTRA-BASS CLARINET**<br>James Badalato |
| **STRING CONTRABASS**<br>Marie Mann | **STRING CONTRABASS**<br>Marie Mann |
| **HORN**<br>Aubrey Bouck<br>Norman Schweikart<br>Steven Seiffert<br>Esther Sweigart<br>Kenneth Schultz | **HORN**<br>Aubrey Bouck<br>Steven Seiffert<br>Esther Sweigert<br>Kenneth Schultz |

# THE EASTMAN WIND ENSEMBLE
# ON MERCURY RECORDS

By Frederick Fennell
Eastman School of Music
Rochester, New York
1 August 1959

A new and exciting era in the recording art began on 1 October 1953 when MERCURY RECORDS and the Eastman School of Music released THE AMERICAN CONCERT BAND MASTERPIECES album for sale to the public. It was the era of long-playing records, however, that was new and exciting -- not the idea of a recording of band music, even though this medium of music as a listening pleasure had been virtually untouched by all record labels since the earliest years of the recording industry. In those days of cylinder-discs and thick, single-faced platters, recording engineers had been quick to realize that the directional focus of tonal resource in most of the winds made them ideal for recording. Within the limitations of those recording processes in use before the invention of vacuum tubes and power-driven microphones, the famous wind bands of the early 20th century shared with clog dancers, comedians, and great voices a prominent place in the catalogs of labels that still dominate the industry. Indeed, the infant art of recording might never have grown as rapidly or so healthily without this initial reliance on the band's traditional marches, novelties, and virtuoso solo pieces, which, together, with its generous borrowing from the opera pit, music hall, and concert stage, were staple items in the earliest catalogs of recorded music.

In the formation of the Eastman School's new instrumental group, which I have chosen to call the EASTMAN WIND ENSEMBLE, it became our simple purpose to pick up the threads of those beginnings in recording -- but this time to explore the whole of the broad field of wind music from its earliest beginning in 16th century brass music, through the Mozart serenades to the unprecedented creative activity of today.

Our primary concern in the first-dozen recordings in this long-range series has been that music conceived for and written to the sonorities of wind instruments plus percussion. The second dozen in the series will also be devoted exclusively to original literature of a similarly broad nature of interest, designed to couple an historical perspective with the pleasurable listening that is granted by the best in performance and engineering.

The advent of the stereophonic disc as an added dimension in recorded sound within the grasp of interested record buyers was anticipated by Mercury Records long before it became a practical reality. For this we are all indebted to our renowned and incomparable chief engineer, C. Robert Fine. It is his vision and true genius that is responsible for Mercury's superior single-microphone technique in monaural recording. Fine's remarkable sensitivity to sound and his unfettered administration of the Mercury engineering department has made possible the dual recording in "mono" and "stereo" of all of our sessions since 1956, beginning with MARCHING ALONG.

Several of our nine albums thus recorded and already released monaurally will be issued as stereo disc in the ensuing months. Our program thus continues to unfold as time, resources, and listener interest will allow.

Wilma Cozart, Vice-President of Mercury Records in charge of the Classical Division, and a long-time friend and enthusiastic counselor to Eastman recording activity has asked me to assure our patrons that no monaural LP record released thus far in this series will be withdrawn as long as present demands for it will continue.

The Eastman School esteemed Director, Howard Hanson, likewise has assured me that our efforts shall continue to have the full support of the Eastman School of Music which joins with Mercury Records in the presentation of this unique series of recordings. Dr. Hanson has devoted a life-time of enthusiastic leadership to the support of a variety of pioneer projects that have become a casual part of American music life. He also provided the initial artistic effort that brought the American composer to commercial recordings.

The players of the Eastman Wind Ensemble join me to thank our friends and patrons whose enthusiastic acceptance of these recordings has assured their continuance and expansion.

The attached listings of recordings and other pertinent information may, I trust, be of interest to you.

Conducting Symposium at Saddleback College – June 1982
Photo by Roger E. Rickson

| | | | |
|---|---|---|---|
| **ALBUM TITLE:** | **Mozart Serenade No. 10 in B - flat, K. 361** | | |
| **LABEL:** Mercury | **MONO** MG 50176 | | **STEREO** SR 90176 |
| **GOLDEN IMPORTS   SRI** | | **ALBUM REFERENCE NO.** 13 | |
| **COVER ART:** Henry Ries * | | **LINER NOTES:** Frederick Fennell | |
| **ENGINEER:** C. R. Fine | | **TAPE TRANSFER:** George Piros | |
| **RECORDING DATE:** March 3, 1958 | | **PERSONNEL LIST:** #6 | |

### PROGRAM
* = Premier recording

Serenade No. 10 in B - flat, K. 361

### NOTES

Also released as Mercury MG 50412/SR 90412 which is coupled with Eine Kleine Nachtmusik, K. 525 with the London Symphony Orchestra, Antal Dorati, Conducting.  Liner notes on this release are by Edward Downes.

FF: "This is the best recording I've ever made; I wanted to live long enough to record this great music.  It was this, the Strauss, Gabrieli, the Stravinsky Symphonies and Hill Song No. 2 that convinced me to start the Eastman Wind Ensemble.  The Mozart and the selections on Winds in Hi-Fi were done in a two day session.  On Sunday, 2 March 1958 we recorded the Milhaud, Grainger, Strauss and Rogers.  Monday, 3 March we did the Mozart.

FF: *"Original cover:  I laid the instruments out on the marble floor at the entry hall of George Eastman's house on East Avenue.  The brass strips were so shiny because a rubber mat had covered the walk trod by countless visitors to the house, which was a museum of photography.   That is the old Eastman School of Music contra and my Bassett horn."  [Bassett horn by G. Leblanc]

See page 21 for personnel on this recording and seating chart will be found on page 19.
Also issued on Mercury reel-to-reel tape ST 90176 distributed by Bel Canto.

Recording Director: Wilma Cozart
Musical Supervisor: Harold Lawrence
Recording site: Eastman Theatre
Group listed as Eastman Wind Ensemble

Eastman Wind Ensemble first recording session in our usual set-up
in Eastman Theatre.   Photo courtesy of William L. Decker.

| | | | |
|---|---|---|---|
| **ALBUM TITLE:** | **British Band Classics, Vol. II** | | |
| **LABEL:** Mercury | | **MONO** MG 50197 | **STEREO** SR 90197 |
| **GOLDEN IMPORTS** SRI 75028 | | **ALBUM REFERENCE NO.** 14 | |
| **COVER ART:** Henry Ries * | | **LINER NOTES:** Frederick Fennell | |
| **ENGINEER:** C. R. Fine | | **TAPE TRANSFER:** George Piros/John Johnson | |
| **RECORDING DATE:** November 21, 1958 | | **PERSONNEL LIST:** #7 | |

### PROGRAM
\* = Premier recording

* Suite: William Byrd - Gordon Jacob
* Hammersmith: Prelude and Scherzo, Op. 52 - Gustav Holst
Crown Imperial: A Coronation March - William Walton, arr. W. J. Duthoit
   [Premier recording of band transcription]

### NOTES

FF: Crown Imperial was done in one take at the recording session. I made the organ part from the band condensed score for Andrea Toth. We worked it out together. The new CD really brings it out! During this take we had the feeling from everyone that it is going to be something. As we finished, and after the decay and the silence, the light flicked on for the telephone. At the other end was Harold Lawrence, saying in a very demure tone of voice ... "that was fine Fred, but could we have it again?" I said "Hell, NO! "- The Wind Ensemble cheered. That was a great moment in our work together.

Crown Imperial is included on Mercury CD 432 009-2 "British and American Band Classics."

From the liner notes: About this Recording ... Dr. Fennell refers, in his mention of William Walton's *Crown Imperial*, to its "ample breadth of sound," and certainly wind music like that on this disc demands an equal breadth of sound in the auditorium where it is to be played. Fortunately, the Eastman Theatre in Rochester, New York, is possessed of some of the finest natural resonance to be found anywhere in the world. In preparation for the recording sessions, the large stage was stripped of sets and other encumbrances, so that the forty-five players who constitute the Eastman Wind Ensemble had the stage to themselves, and the acoustics of the hall could blend perfectly with the music.

* Life Guard's Helmet, courtesy of British Travel Association.

Golden Imports Cassette: MRI 75028
Tape transfer: George Piros [stereo] - John Johnson [mono]
Recording Director: Wilma Cozart
Musical Supervisor: Harold Lawrence
Recording site: Eastman Theatre
Group listed as Eastman Wind Ensemble

First recording session in Eastman Theatre. David Hall sitting on podium with Telefunken directly above my head.
Photo courtesy of William L. Decker

| | | |
|---|---|---|
| **ALBUM TITLE:** | **Hands Across The Sea** | |
| **LABEL:** Mercury | **MONO** MG 50207 | **STEREO** SR 90207 |
| **GOLDEN IMPORTS** SRI 75099 | | **ALBUM REFERENCE NO.** 15 |
| **COVER ART:** Henry Ries | | **LINER NOTES:** Frederick Fennell |
| **ENGINEER:** C. R. Fine | | **TAPE TRANSFER:** George Piros/John Johnson |
| **RECORDING DATE:** November 23, 1958 | | **PERSONNEL LIST:** #7 |

## PROGRAM
\* = Premier recording

Hands Across the Sea - John Philip Sousa **
\* Inglesina - Davide Della Cese
Knightsbridge March - Eric Coates, arr. Paul Yoder.
Old Comrades - Carl Teike
Father of Victory - Louis Ganne
\* Valdres March - Johannes Hanssen
\* Golden Ear - Mariano San Miguel
\* March, Op. 99 - Serge Prokofiev, arr. Paul Yoder from the original Russian instrumentation.

## NOTES

The liner notes contain excellent Hi-Fi facts on Eastman Theatre set-up. From the liner notes: "Whenever recording sessions by the Eastman Wind Ensemble take place, the entire stage of the Eastman Theatre in Rochester is stripped of sets and any other unnecessary fixtures. The Wind Ensemble is then arranged on the stage in its normal concert placement. A single extremely sensitive omni-directional microphone is hung in the precise focal point of the auditorium. At this point, Mercury engineers have learned through endless experimentation and testing, the musical sound attains its full "bloom" and is further enhanced by the natural resonance of the hall.
When the recording session begins, several level checks are taken, during which the ensemble plays loud and soft passages from the music to be recorded. From that time on no electronic compression, no monitoring, no boosting, no changes in volume level are ever permitted to intrude upon the flow of the music, and the listener thus hears it just as Dr. Fennell wished him to hear it. All these aspects of the session are carefully and constantly checked by members of the classical staff, who are listening on a playback system installed in another room of the theatre."

FF: Original release labels/both sides were badly screwed-up! Never knew by whom or why.

RR: Any other stories about this album?

FF: Yes, regarding *The Golden Ear*. I had been invited to guest conduct the Navy Band; the guest of Charles Brendler, who was an elegant individual and a very successful conductor of the Navy Band. We became very good friends. He liked the recordings we were making and he liked our approach to music and he invited me to come and guest conduct a concert with the Navy Band. We were having dinner in the Officers Club there and he said: "What's up - What are your plans?" I said: "I'm trying to put things together really for an international album of marches which I am going to call Hands Across the Sea." "What Spanish march are you going to play?" he asked. "I've already recorded *Amparito Roca* with orchestra and I don't think I will record that again," I replied. "There's only one march for you to do - only one. I'll send it to you." He did and that was the basis of the edition which Elizabeth and I published through Ludwig Music.

** Hands Across the Sea was re-recorded in stereo for this release, not taken from MG 40007.
Japanese Philips release: PC-1615 with same cover and contents as US release.

Tape transfer: George Piros [stereo] - John Johnson [mono]
Recording Director: Wilma Cozart
Musical Supervisor: Harold Lawrence
Recording site: Eastman Theatre
Group listed as Eastman Wind Ensemble

## Frederick Fennell on "Inglesina"
## Recorded: 23 November 1958
## Article: 19 August 1984
## Tokyo, Japan

In the mid 1950's I was invited to be guest conductor by the host of the Pennsylvania All-State Band, held at Clairton. His interesting Italian name began my association with this superb symphonic march. He was Rotillio Rotilli, conductor of the band at Clairton High School; he was short and stout, with his large head sitting almost on his shoulders. The students at Clairton affectionately called him "teach."

Friday night, after a rehearsal, he had his staff and the P.M.E.A. officials for All-State and me to his house for a great spaghetti dinner. I had the test for Marching Along SR 90105, with me and he asked me to bring it to the party. We all enjoyed listening to the really wonderful playing of the Eastman Wind Ensemble.

On the drive back to my hotel, Rotillio said he knew of a "great-a Italiana Marcha I had-da-to record." ... when I asked him the name of it, he said very enthusiastically "INGALAZEENA," and that he would send it to me after he went "... homa ta Roma ..." in the summer. I thanked him for the great spaghetti, wine and the fellowship.

Many people have said they would send me their favorite march to record, but really none ever came [but one later from George Way of Leedy Drums, who sent *In Storm and Sunshine*] so I forgot about Rotilli's idea. But come September, a package came from him with the set that is still at Eastman; Litchard Toland, Eastman librarian, put it in the books, and from the first reading we all knew it was the great march that it is.

It was recorded as the Italian entry on our album Hands Across the Sea, which introduced it to the American band world, thanks to "Teach" Rotilli who kept his word to send it, and thanks as well to the Eastman players who had so impressed him.

Frederick Fennell
Tokyo, Japan
19 August 1984

| | |
|---|---|
| ALBUM TITLE: | **American Masterpieces for Concert Band** |

**LABEL:** Mercury  **MONO** MG 50220  **STEREO** SR 90220
**GOLDEN IMPORTS SRI** See notes   **ALBUM REFERENCE NO.** 16
**COVER ART:** Henry Ries **   **LINER NOTES:** Frederick Fennell
**ENGINEER:** C. R. Fine   **TAPE TRANSFER:** John Johnson/George Piros
**RECORDING DATE:** May 3, 1959   **PERSONNEL LIST:** #7

### PROGRAM
\* = Premier recording

- \* West Point Symphony - Morton Gould  [included on Golden Imports SRI 75094]
- \* Autumn Walk - Julian Work [edited by FF]
- \* Symphonic Songs for Band - Robert Russell Bennett
- \* Fanfare and Allegro - Clifton Williams [included on Golden Imports SRI 95094]
  [edited by FF for this release and again for the future release by Tokyo Kosei]

### NOTES

Japanese Philips PC - 1634 includes West Point Symphony, Autumn Walk and Concerto for 23 Winds by Hartley. Same cover as SR 90220 [1976 release]
The title "American Masterpieces for Concert Band" was not the choice of FF.
** Cover photo of cadet at West Point by Henry Ries.

FF: I did not hear the *West Point Symphony* when I went to West Point for some observations. I heard the one by Roy Harris, which was not a successful work. But, I heard a performance of this by the Oberlin Symphony Band at the CBDNA in Chicago, and I thought it was an outstanding work. *Symphonic Songs for Band* - this was a commission by Kappa Kappa Psi, for their Annual Intercollegiate Band, and some people told me that it was an outstanding work, and I did get a hold of it. We were rehearsed and ready to go with the recording and Russell Bennett wrote me and told me he was changing the ending of the first movement. It's too hard. I think I have the only copy in the world of the original ending. I don't think it is that much more difficult. I think the ending is difficult enough. I have a note here in my score which reads ...At the Rochester concert, to which Russell came, he decided that the last seven bars were going to be too tough for school bands and for the publication he made the now familiar change to twelve rather than the original seven measures.
*Fanfare and Allegro*. I knew it was going to be a smashing publication and I was quite sure it was going to win the ABA. No question about it. The ending is slightly changed by me, with his signature. I also changed it again for the TOKWO recording. The marching feet of the Eastman School Symphony Band for Gould's *West Point Symphony* were recorded on 5 May 1959. It was arranged that Bob Fine put the tape on the machine and gave me some earphones. So, I had the Wind Ensemble playing that part of *West Point Symphony* while I was conducting the marchers.

Tape transfer: George Piros [stereo] - John Johnson [mono]
Recording Director: Wilma Cozart
Musical Supervisor: Harold Lawrence
Recording site: Eastman Theatre
Group listed as Eastman Wind Ensemble

Putnam Farm on Miles Avenue in what was then called Newburg, Ohio. Small building is Betsy Ross Cottage. Circa 1913.
Photo courtesy of FF.

| | | | |
|---|---|---|---|
| **ALBUM TITLE:** | *Diverse Winds* | | |
| **LABEL:** Mercury | **MONO** MG 50221 | | **STEREO** SR 90221 |
| **GOLDEN IMPORTS SRI** See notes | | **ALBUM REFERENCE NO.** 17 | |
| **COVER ART:** George Maas/Henry Ries ** | | **LINER NOTES:** Frederick Fennell | |
| **ENGINEER:** C. R. Fine | | **TAPE TRANSFER:** John Johnson/George Piros | |
| **RECORDING DATE:** May 4, 1959 | | **PERSONNEL LIST:** #7 | |

### PROGRAM
\* = Premier recording

* Symphony No. 6 for Band - Vincent Persichetti [included on Golden Imports SRI 75094]
* Concerto for 23 Winds - Walter Hartley
* Hill Song No. 2 - Percy A. Grainger [included on Golden Imports SRI 75011]
* Armenian Dances - Aram Khachaturian, arr. Ralph Satz - ed. by FF [included on Golden Imports SRI 75094]

### NOTES

Japanese Philips PC - 1603 [1975] replaces Grainger's Hill Song No. 2 with Robert Russell Bennett's Symphonic Songs for Band [listed as Symphonic Song for Band].

RR: Regarding the editing of the Khachaturian, Fennell used some euphonium doubling not indicated in the score and parts. A welcome edit for the clarity of the melodic lines.

FF: Yes. I felt that was necessary. Wilma Cozart had a big thing because I couldn't give her anything about the Khatchaturian movements. I said there are only two, and that's how they are booked. It just says I and II and doesn't say anything except possible tempos. She has to have it absolutely 100 percent correct when these things go out. Excellent title suggested by Clair W. Van Ausdall

**Cover art work of weather vein on chair by George Maas with photo by Henry Ries.

Tape transfer: George Piros [stereo] - John Johnson [mono]
Recording Director: Wilma Cozart
Musical Supervisor: Harold Lawrence
Recording site: Eastman Theatre
Group listed as Eastman Wind Ensemble.

Frederick in study of Betsy Ross Cabin after Interlochen, Summer 1933. Study was added by Frederick in 1929. Photos on desk show Bill Ludwig and his father. Philco radio where he first heard the National High School Orchestra. Photo courtesy of FF.

## PERSONNEL

## Walter Hartley - "Concerto for 23 Winds"

## Eastman Wind Ensemble

## Frederick Fennell, Conductor

**FLUTE**
Gerald Carey
Joanne Dickinson
Joanna Tousey

**OBOE**
Alice Gordon
Sandra Flesher
Thomas Stacy

**CLARINET**
Elsa Ludewig
Larry Combs
Richard Webster

**BASSOON**
Alan Brown
Vernon Read
Bruce Degan

**HORN**
Norman Schweikert
Stephen Seiffert
John Covert
Robert Sheldon
Carol Ladrach

**TRUMPET**
James Austin
Joel Koplin
Ralph Montgomery
Roger Sherman

**TROMBONE**
George Osborn
David Fetter
Robert Gillespie
David Richey

**TUBA**
Roger Bobo

**PERCUSSION**
Joel Thome

| ALBUM TITLE: | **_Music of Andrea and Giovanni Gabrieli_** | |
|---|---|---|
| LABEL: Mercury | MONO MG 50245 | STEREO SR 90245 |
| GOLDEN IMPORTS SRI 75130 | | ALBUM REFERENCE NO. 18 |
| COVER ART: see notes ** | | LINER NOTES: Egon Kenton |
| ENGINEER: C.R. Fine/R. Eberenz | | TAPE TRANSFER: George Piros/John Johnson |
| RECORDING DATE: May 6, 1961 | | PERSONNEL LIST: #9 |

## PROGRAM
\* = Premier recording

Music of Andrea and Giovanni Gabrieli

\*Aria Della Battaglia - **Andrea Gabrieli**, transcribed by Ghedini

**Giovanni Gabrieli**
Sonata Octavi Toni
Sonata Pian e Forte
Canzon Duodecimi Toni
Canzon Noni Toni
Canzon Septimi Toni, No. 1
Canzon Quarti Toni

## NOTES

FF: Egon Kenton is a musicologist; from my ESM faculty friend and professor of musicology - Charles Warren Fox - also editor of the Journal of the American Musicological Society [AMS], I knew that Kenton was about to present a very learned piece on the Gabrieli's; hence he was a natural for the liner notes, which he wrote at my request. This is the first and only time we recorded out of the Eastman Theatre. We had great cooperation from Christ Church. I have prepared a seating arrangement for you . Added to all of our other recordings, we were crossing all the areas of music. We were not stuck in one scene at all. These are the only completely panoramic view by a wind group.

RR: The original issue cover includes three color close-ups of one angel on back cover but these photos have been deleted on future printings. Both issues contain an excellent description of the 35mm film recording technique.

\*\* Cover Art: "Three Angels" [probably Italian, late 15th or early 16th century] Gold and enamel courtesy of Metropolitan Museum of Art. A gift of J. Pierpoint Morgan, 1917.

\*\*FF: Discovered by Clair W. Van Ausdall who had become a member of the Mercury New York staff for all the top writing, research, ideas, artist relations, etc. I sort of edged him into leaving his job as concert manager at ESM into the Mercury organization. Clair was keyboards in the original Eastman Wind Ensemble, 1952/53.

Japanese Philips: PC 1623 - Mercury Logo - no Philips logo - same cover and contents as US release.

Tape transfer: George Piros [stereo] - John Johnson [mono]
Recording Director: Wilma Cozart
Musical Supervisor: Harold Lawrence
Recording Site: Christ Church, Rochester, New York
Group listed as Eastman Wind Ensemble.

See following pages for personnel and seating chart for recording.

## PERSONNEL

### Andrea and Giovanni Gabrieli

### Eastman Wind Ensemble

### Frederick Fennell, Conductor

**CORNET**
John Thyhsen
Ralph Montgomery
Albert MacKinnon
George Cavanagh
John Landis

**HORN**
Norman Schweikert
Bette Allison
John Covert
Robert Sheldon
Stephen Seiffert

**TROMBONE**
David Fetter
Early Anderson
Robert Gillespie
David Richey

**CONTRA-BASS TROMBONE**
Roger Bobo

**VIOLA**
Tosca Kramer

**ORGAN**
Anne Labounsky

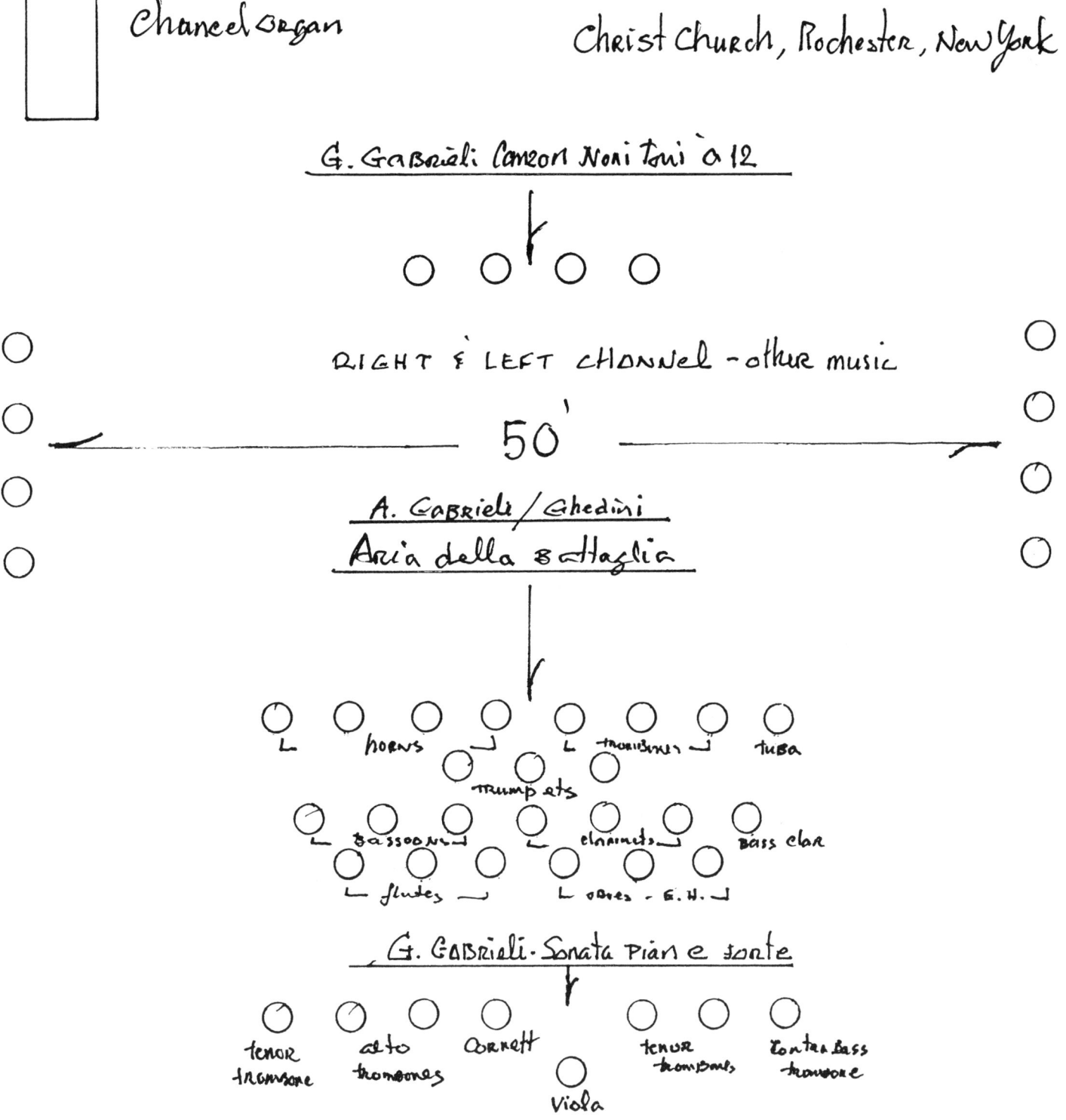

| ALBUM TITLE: | **Ballet for Band** | | |
|---|---|---|---|
| LABEL: Mercury | MONO MG 50256 | STEREO SR 90256 | |
| GOLDEN IMPORTS SRI 75138 | | ALBUM REFERENCE NO. 19 | |
| COVER ART: George Maas/Henry Ries | | LINER NOTES: Frederick Fennell | |
| ENGINEER: C. R. Fine | | TAPE TRANSFER: John Johnson/George Piros | |
| RECORDING DATE: October 24, 1959 | | PERSONNEL LIST: #8 | |

### PROGRAM
\* = Premier recording

* La Boutique Fantasque - Gioacchino A. Rossini, arr. Dan Godfrey
* Ballet Music from "Faust" - Charles Gounod, arr. William Winterbottom
* Pineapple Poll - Arthur Sullivan/Charles Mackerras, arr. W. J. Duthoit

Premier recordings of the band transcriptions.

### NOTES

Cover art by George Maas with photography by Henry Ries.

Japanese Philips PC - 1606 [1975] same contents as US release but sides have been reversed.

RR: Album title selected by Frederick Fennell. The album covers are an interesting study. Original album SR 90256 was designed with the assistance of Clair W. Van Ausdall - "French Horn"; SRI 75138 - "Ballet Shoes"; Japanese Philips PC 1606 - a combination of ballet shoes and French horn". The US mono cover does not have the close-up picture of horn on back as does the stereo release.

Tape transfer: George Piros [stereo] - John Johnson [mono]
Recording Director: Wilma Cozart
Musical Supervisor: Harold Lawrence
Recording site: Eastman Theatre
Group listed as Eastman Wind Ensemble

FF: Recording of this album and "Wagner for Band" SR 90276, took place on 23 - 24 October 1959 - 10:00 AM - 2:30 PM each date. On the 23rd we recorded all of the Wagner, except *Entry of the Gods*. On the 24th we recorded that, *Pineapple*, *La Boutique* and the *Faust*.

On the stage of Interlochen Bowl in 1941. Paul Whiteman [left] and his Band had been invited, somewhat at Fred's suggestion to T.P. Giddings. Joe Maddy [middle] had given Fred the business of seating them in the middle of the High School Orchestra and Band. Photo by Dorothy Fennell.

| | |
|---|---|
| **ALBUM TITLE:** Sound Off ! | |
| **LABEL:** Mercury   **MONO** MG 50264 | **STEREO** SR 90264 |
| **GOLDEN IMPORTS  SRI** 75047 | **ALBUM REFERENCE NO.** 20 |
| **COVER ART:** Photo: Henry Ries ** | **LINER NOTES:** Frederick Fennell |
| **ENGINEER:** C.R. Fine/Robert Eberenz | **TAPE TRANSFER:** John Johnson/George Piros |
| **RECORDING DATE:** May 2, 1960 | **PERSONNEL LIST:** #8 |

### PROGRAM
* = Premier recording

**Marches of John Philip Sousa:**

Sound Off
Sabre and Spurs
Our Flirtations
The Invincible Eagle
The Liberty Bell
Solid Men to the Front
Nobles of the Mystic Shrine
The Picadore
The High School Cadets
Bullets and Bayonets
Riders For the Flag
The Gallant Seventh

### NOTES

** Cover shows a Turkish Crescent, courtesy of JenCo Musical Products.

FF: I carried this [Turkish Crescent] to New York, in my wife Dorothy's shoe and hat box, polished all the bells and the German silver tents (pavilions). If you look very closely at the largest tent, directly, you will see Hank Ries' camera pointed right at the scene, distorted of course by the concave shape of the pavilion.

FF: Many of the EWE players expressed to me that they thought this to be our best album of marches.

Title chosen by FF from the march title and the bugle call and the WWII cadence-count in training camp.

FF: [from the liner notes] All the marches recorded on this disc were played by the full instrumentation of the Eastman Wind Ensemble from the published editions. Sousa's Marine Band of 1891 contained 49 players [26 reeds, 20 brasses, 3 percussion]. The Eastman Wind Ensemble personnel lists 52 players: 25 reeds, 19 brasses, 6 percussion, harp, and string contrabass .

RR: String contrabass listed as contra<u>brass</u> on the mono edition. The stereo issue is listed correctly  The technical information found on the mono edition is omitted on the stereo release.

Tape transfer: George Piros [stereo] - John Johnson [mono]
Recording Director: Wilma Cozart
Musical Supervisor: Harold Lawrence
Recording site: Eastman Theatre
Group listed as Eastman Wind Ensemble

**ALBUM TITLE:** <u>**Wagner for Band**</u>

**LABEL:** Mercury  **MONO** MG 50276  **STEREO** SR 90276
**GOLDEN IMPORTS  SRI** 75096  **ALBUM REFERENCE NO.** 21
**COVER ART:** George Maas and Henry Ries  **LINER NOTES:** Frederick Fennell
**ENGINEER:** C. R. Fine/Robert Eberenz  **TAPE TRANSFER:** George Piros/John Johnson
**RECORDING DATE:** October 23, 1959  **PERSONNEL LIST:** #8

### PROGRAM
\* = Premier recording

* Prelude to Act III, and Bridal Chorus from "Lohengrin" - arr. Frank Winterbottom
* Entry of the Gods into Valhalla from "Das Rheingold" - arr. Dan Godfrey
* Elsa's Procession to the Cathedral from "Lohengrin" - arr. Lucien Cailliet
* Overture to "Rienzi" - arr. Victor Grabel
* Good Friday Music from "Parsifal" - arr. Dan Godfrey

\* premier recording of the band transcriptions.

### NOTES

FF: I agreed to make three albums of transcriptions, this was number 2. [Ballet was number 1]. The Bach never got done by the Eastman Wind Ensemble, but was recorded by the Tokyo Kosei Windorchestra. Title of album was my choice.

RR: Japanese Philips PC - 1605 [1976] with same cover and contents as US release. Issued on Golden Imports both in LP and cassette MRI 75096. Another Japanese release, 18PC-111 contains *Elsa's Procession to the Cathedral, Overture to Rienzi, Prelude to Act III* on side one. Side two contains Gounod: *Faust Ballet Music*, Coates: *Knightsbridge March* and Prokofiev: *March, Op. 99*. The original stereo release SR90262 has a full color back, while a subsequent re-issue is black and white only.

FF: Recording of this album and "Ballet for Band" SR 90256, took place on 23-24 October 1949 - 10:00 AM - 2:30 PM each date.

Liner notes completed by Frederick Fennell in November of 1960.
Tape transfer: George Piros [stereo] - John Johnson [mono]
Recording Director: Wilma Cozart
Musical Supervisor: Harold Lawrence
Recording site: Eastman Theatre
Group listed as Eastman Wind Ensemble

Wilma Cozart Fine
Photo courtesy of
Harold Lawrence

| ALBUM TITLE: | **Sousa on Review** | | |
|---|---|---|---|
| LABEL: Mercury | | MONO MG 50284 | STEREO SR 90284 |
| GOLDEN IMPORTS SRI 75064 | | | ALBUM REFERENCE NO. 22 |
| COVER ART: George Maas, Henry Ries | | | LINER NOTES: Frederick Fennell |
| ENGINEER: C.R. Fine/Robert Eberenz | | | TAPE TRANSFER: George Piros/John Johnson |
| RECORDING DATE: May 5, 1961 | | | PERSONNEL LIST: #9 |

## PROGRAM
\* = Premier recording

The Rifle Regiment
The Black Horse Troop
The Pride of the Wolverines
The Glory of the Yankee Navy
Sesquicentennial Exposition
Manhattan Beach
\*New Mexico March
Ancient and Honorable Artillery Company
The National Game
\*The Gridiron Club
\*The Kansas Wildcats
Golden Jubilee

## NOTES

FF: Album title is my choice. This was a very successful release. After the release of this album, I received a letter from the office of the Governor of New Mexico asking me if I had written some special piece for the State of New Mexico. I replied, no, Mr. Sousa had written it. The trio, the last thing is "Oh, Fair New Mexico." *Rifle Regiment* is Sousa's longest march. *Black Horse Troop* - I saw the premier of this march - Troop "A" riding team with all of those splendiforous trappings, beautiful horses, etc.
*Bullets and Bayonets* is a piece you have to come to grips with. When he wrote this, at the time of WWI, those were a very real part of everyday life for hundreds of thousands of Americans on the Western front. So Sousa didn't have any reluctance putting it in the title of his march. Many people think this could be Sousa's best composed march. I think *Freelance* is the best composition, as well as *Corcoran Cadets*. As a piece of composition - variety - extending his ideas - having it be unmistakably his - *Freelance* is a high candidate.
[from liner notes] ... All the marches recorded on this disc were played by the full instrumentation of the Eastman Wind Ensemble from the standard published editions. With these twelve titles, 31 of the 128 published marches by Sousa are now available in our Mercury Record[s] repertory as part of our Sousa march anthology.

[Again from the liner notes] ... The decision to record every one of John Philip Sousa's marches was arrived at almost by accident, following the release of the album SOUND OFF!, which was to become the first volume of the collection. Both Frederick Fennell and Mercury Records were nearly overwhelmed with messages of congratulation and thanks from delighted listeners who, it would seem, simply can't get enough of Sousa and his particular brand of genius. "Give us more, give us more," said these letters - so many times that it was finally decided to give, eventually, everything in the way of a march that Sousa wrote. The twelve marches in this volume were all recorded in one long session on Friday, May 5, 1961.

Stereo release SR 90284 continues the trumpet color photo on the back cover. Omitted on the mono release MG 50284.
Cassette version on Golden Imports: MRI 75064

Tape transfer: George Piros [Stereo], John Johnson [Mono].
Recording Director: Wilma Cozart
Musical Supervisor: Harold Lawrence
Recording site: Eastman Theatre
Group listed as Eastman Wind Ensemble

## "…. From Long Distilled Thoughts"

## "How it all Began"
### Frederick Fennell

FF: I wrote this for Charles Riker in 1961 for the supplement to <u>The Eastman School of Music, Its First Half Century</u>. Riker published it with no credit to me. It is my best statement about the Eastman Wind Ensemble.

The Eastman Wind Ensemble was organized in the Fall of 1952. Our decision to establish this new group grew out of twenty years of careful study and performance by the Eastman School Symphony Band of the significant musical literature for the wind band, original and transcribed; vital though these experiences had been to our decision, they were not the whole reason for the action that followed. This, then, is how the Wind Ensemble idea grew from our work with the Symphony Band and from a long and varied association with the chamber and symphony orchestra. There was our awareness of that sprawling but significant musical literature for assorted combinations of wind instruments in ensemble that did not fall into the pattern of the traditional wind quintet but which was performed only rarely mostly because there existed no ensemble which considered its performance to be a part of the repertory.

A few decades of industry on the part of some composers and a few bandmasters had stimulated genuine interest in the creation of contemporary music for the wind band, but the mere existence of this music did not guarantee its performance, proper or otherwise. It was my concern that, for want of proper performance, this hard-won interest by composers of our time would be lost, thus robbing the wind-band medium of its greatest chance for artistic acceptance and survival. These observations seemed to call for a new kind of ensemble. There was the unique American gift for artistry of the highest calibre on the wind and percussion instruments and our incredibly well-organized systems for attracting the youth of the land to the teaching of these instruments. The unprecedented participation of millions of school children in band activity was both system and result. This vast and churning activity, consuming the daily musical thought of millions of people, seemed in need of a fresh, imaginative, and responsible approach. It was our further conviction that matters of instrumentation have always been the province of composers rather than committees; the music to be played would be the only factor to govern the choice of instruments that would be assembled.

It is from this premise that I chose the instruments which would constitute the group: 25 reeds, 18 brass, 8 percussion, harp, etc. The resulting instrumental force had as its basis an instrumentation which permitted the performance of the exemplary music written for the wind band; these forces when reduced to those required for the performance of music which in no way lies within the band medium offered a group capable of performing a rich and neglected musical literature. Our instrumental fabric could, therefore, be flexible and minimum, it being our further desire to eliminate the multiple doubling of the players on a part that had become so consistent a liability to the large wind band. We were to dedicate our work to the exclusive study and performance of original music for the wind medium. As our purpose was a clear concern for the artistic elevation of the wind instruments in ensemble, our choice for a name which would set our work and its purpose apart from all that had gone before was the obvious one: WIND ENSEMBLE. I submitted these plans to the Director.

The result of these long-digested thoughts was Dr. Howard Hanson's approval for the establishment of the Eastman Wind Ensemble as part of the courses in ensemble study under the School's Instrumental Ensemble Department. From the outset we held it imperative that this new group was in no way to supplant the work of or to impair the further development of the School's Symphony Band.

In the 40th Anniversary year of this School in which so many fertile ideas have first been fashioned into reality, the Eastman Wind Ensemble completes its 10th year of activity. In this decade the School has continued to project its traditional spirit of high musical adventure and its solid conscience of educational responsibility into vast areas of the broad musical life of our country. The Wind Ensemble has become a part of this. Its purposes remain a daily achievement. Additional to its concerts here at School which have also produced an endless succession of premiere performances of music, past and present, the Eastman Wind Ensemble has become a long arm of the University of Rochester, extended across the world by means of recordings.

It was at the conclusion of our first season of work that Dr. Hanson invited us to join him in the School's unique and imaginative program of recording exemplary music by American composers, a pioneer activity which he had undertaken many years previously with remarkable success and which he was then expanding under a new agreement with the then little-known but dynamically promising firm of Mercury Records. In the ten years during which we have contributed 23 discs to the Eastman-Mercury catalog, the recorded repertory of American music has been expanded and documented to include wind music from the period of the Revolution to today; school bands have found an example to follow in all aspects of performance; composers everywhere have been offered the fact of a challenging facet of musical art which they may now accept or reject from knowledge rather than ignorance; the virtuoso performer on a wind instrument may hear that there exists yet another exciting and challenging opportunity for performance in an ensemble that demands and permits his time-honored role of individuality. We have been honored with the compliment of adoption of our name and purpose by countless schools across the nation.

To me the greatest reason for its success has always been the students of the Eastman School who have filled its chairs -- and it has always been composed exclusively of students. Each fall since 1952 this personnel has changed and in recent years the turnover has been 50%. They have always been selected on a strict merit system, no seniority governing our choice; membership is open to any student in the School.

But behind their admission to School and before their interest in coming must be counted the presence of an incomparable faculty of artist teacher-performers who beckon them to Rochester. It is these teachers who, by their great example as performers, set and keep them on the paths of purpose and artistic achievement, and who, together with their colleagues of the Eastman community prepare them for a whole life of teaching and playing, for their participation in the Eastman Wind Ensemble is but one part of their education. It is an experience, however, which now includes the Wind Ensemble, a contribution to education and musical life which is a distinct and unique achievement of the Eastman School of Music of the University of Rochester.

RR: This essay became the basis for "The Wind Ensemble, Inception -- From Long Distilled Thoughts" published in The Instrumentalist, February 1972.

| | | |
|---|---|---|
| **ALBUM TITLE:** | **Curtain Up! Sousa Favorites** | |
| **LABEL:** Mercury | **MONO** MG 50291 | **STEREO** SR 90291 |
| **GOLDEN IMPORTS** SRI | | **ALBUM REFERENCE NO.** 23 |
| **COVER ART:** Photo Wm. F. Ludwig Drum Co. | | **LINER NOTES:** not credited |
| **ENGINEER:** | | **TAPE TRANSFER:** |
| **RECORDING DATE:** | | **PERSONNEL LIST:** |

### PROGRAM
\* = Premier recording

John Philip Sousa

The U.S. Field Artillery
The Liberty Bell
El Capitan
Manhattan Beach
Hands Across the Sea
Bullets and Bayonets
Washington Post
Sabre and Spurs
King Cotton
Black Horse Troop
Riders for the Flag
Kansas Wildcats

### NOTES

Cover photo of marching band supplied by William F. Ludwig Drum Company.
All recordings are a recoupling of previously released material.
Liner notes [limited] are by an anonymous writer.
"Curtain Up" generic with gold tassels. There is also another re-issue with the generic cover with drawing by Robert Day.

Group listed as Eastman Wind Ensemble

Eastman Wind Ensemble on Swan Street "Circus Day". Spontaneously planned and executed parade prior to concert that lead to the <u>Screamers</u> recording. Lead trumpet on left is the great Boyde Hood.
Photo courtesy of Louis Ouzer.

| | | | |
|---|---|---|---|
| **ALBUM TITLE:** | **Screamers! - A Collection of Exciting Marches from the Circus Ring** | | |
| **LABEL:** Mercury | **MONO** MG 50314 | | **STEREO** SR 90314 |
| **GOLDEN IMPORTS SRI** 75087 | | **ALBUM REFERENCE NO.** 24 | |
| **COVER ART:** George Maas - see notes | | **LINER NOTES:** Frederick Fennell | |
| **ENGINEER:** Robert Eberenz/C.R. Fine | | **TAPE TRANSFER:** George Piros/John Johnson | |
| **RECORDING DATE:** May 6, 1962 | | **PERSONNEL LIST:** #10 | |

## PROGRAM
\* = Premier recording

Screamers! A Collection of Exciting Marches from the Circus Ring

\* In Storm and Sunshine  - John C. Heed
Invictus - Karl L. King
Bones Trombone  - Henry Fillmore
The Circus Bee  - Henry Fillmore
Thunder and Blazes  -  Entry of the Gladiators - Julius Fucik
\*Circus Days  -Karl L. King
The Squealer  - Will Huff
\*Bennett's Triumphal  -  John H. Ribble
\*Whip and Spur  - Thomas S. Allen
\*The Big Cage  - Karl L. King
Them Basses  - Getty H. Huffine
\*The Screamer  - Fred Jewell
Robinson's Grand Entree  - Karl L. King
Bombasto  - Orion R. Farrar
Rolling Thunder  - Henry Fillmore
\*Bravura  - Charles E. Duble

## NOTES

FF: The last recording made with Frederick Fennell and the Eastman Wind Ensemble

RR: Were you aware that this would be the last session? Was the EWE aware?

FF: Yes, I knew I was going, but I didn't allow an announcement of that until long after the session.  The EWE had no idea of it.

RR: Would you make some comments on this session?

FF: The players picked up on a comment I made at rehearsal about a circus concert. We always had to play a public concert of the repertory under the symphonic rate, 24 hours before the recording. They [the EWE] really made it a circus which began with the group leading a parade around the four streets surrounding the school in funky "uniforms" -- leading the people to the annex rehearsal room above the garage, now demolished.  There they found what was always a very drab room turned into a "circus tent" - with saw-dust, peanuts, popcorn, balloons, clowns, --- the works! This took place at our regular rehearsal hour, 1:10 - 2:00 pm. The carnival atmosphere was euphorias  and they played with their always super way.  It simply was a great occasion and it is very clearly part of the recording.  I was about ready  to come apart,  but saved that until I got back up to my studio in 621.  Then it all came out.  This was my final time to be in that rehearsal room where I  really learned what little I know about being a conductor.  If I had to go, this concert was the ultimate way out.  When I was invited back for the 25th anniversary of the EWE, Hunsberger, knowing how much a sentimental slob I really am ... had saved the clock in that rehearsal room when they tore the building down, had it electrified, and presented it to me as the "30 year watch" I didn't get from the Eastman Administration.  It is on the wall in my super two-car garage in Siesta Key, where with all that wallspace I can do it and all those plaques of honor that house space does not allow.   I sure hope the plaques will taper to nothing pretty soon.  I  have a few pix of the parade someplace; but moving is disastrous for such things when there is so little time to pack it all carefully.  Written on board Northwest Flight #1204 - Sarasota/Detroit, 25 January 87.

Cover design was suggested to George Maas by Clair W. Van Ausdall. Album title was suggested by FF.  Chief engineer for this session was Robert Eberenz
"Screamers" was issued with "March Time" on Mercury Living Presence CD in early 1991.  Original liner notes and "Screamers" cover art are faithfully reproduced on the CD issue.  Re-release was coordinated by Wilma Cozart Fine from the original master tapes.  Also issued on Japanese Philips PC-1616 with original cover and contents.
Tape transfer:  George Piros [stereo] - John Johnson [mono]
Recording Director:  Wilma Cozart

Musical Supervisor: Harold Lawrence
Recording site: Eastman Theatre
Group listed as Eastman Wind Ensemble

---

**ALBUM TITLE: Curtain Up! More March Favorites**

| | |
|---|---|
| **LABEL:** Mercury   **MONO** MG 50325 | **STEREO** SR 90325 |
| **GOLDEN IMPORTS   SRI** | **ALBUM REFERENCE NO.** 25 |
| **COVER ART:** Joan Drew | **LINER NOTES:** not credited |
| **ENGINEER:** | **TAPE TRANSFER:** |
| **RECORDING DATE:** | **PERSONNEL LIST:** |

### PROGRAM
\* = Premier recording

**Eastman Wind Ensemble:**
 The Golden Ear - Mariano San Miguel
 Crown Imperial - A Coronation March - William Walton

**Eastman-Rochester POPS Orchestra**
 Children's March - Percy A. Grainger

### NOTES

A re-coupling of previously released material.

Cover art: original serigraph "Neighbors All" by Joan Drew. A very attractive horizontal format. It is interesting to note that some of the houses have flags and other have TV antennas.

---

**ALBUM TITLE: Curtain Up! Music and Plunk, Tinkle, Ting-A-Ling**

| | |
|---|---|
| **LABEL:** Mercury   **MONO** MG 50388 | **STEREO** SR 90388 |
| **GOLDEN IMPORTS   SRI** | **ALBUM REFERENCE NO.** 26 |
| **COVER ART:** Robert Day | **LINER NOTES:** not credited |
| **ENGINEER:** | **TAPE TRANSFER:** |
| **RECORDING DATE:** | **PERSONNEL LIST:** |

### PROGRAM
\* = Premier recording

**Eastman Wind Ensemble:**
 Nobles of the Mystic Shrine - John Philip Sousa
 New Mexico March - John Philip Sousa

**Frederick Fennell Orchestra:**
 My Heart Belongs To Daddy - Cole Porter

**Eastman-Rochester POPS Orchestra:**
 The Typewriter - Leroy Anderson
 Brazilian Sleigh Bells - Percy Faith
 Sandpaper Ballet - Leroy Anderson
 Children's March - Percy A. Grainger

### NOTES

Cover Art: A great Robert Day caricature of a "POPS" orchestra. Champagne popper [apparently filled with his instrument], typewriter player, trash can lid clasher, conductor, sandpaper player and [Brazilian] sleigh bells player, who even has bells on his toes.

| ALBUM TITLE: | **Curtain Up! Gala Favorites** | |
|---|---|---|
| **LABEL:** Mercury | **MONO** MG 50339 | **STEREO** SR 90339 |
| **GOLDEN IMPORTS** SRI | | **ALBUM REFERENCE NO.** 27 |
| **COVER ART:** Robert Day | | **LINER NOTES:** Anonymous |
| **ENGINEER:** | | **TAPE TRANSFER:** |
| **RECORDING DATE:** | | **PERSONNEL LIST:** |

### PROGRAM
\* = Premier recording

**Eastman Wind Ensemble:**
 Golden Jubilee - John Philip Sousa

**Eastman-Rochester POPS Orchestra:**
 Belle of the Ball - Leroy Anderson

### NOTES

Another great cover by Robert Day. Dancers of all shapes and sizes. Square Dancers, Ballet Artists, Flamenco Dancers and many more. A MUST SEE COVER.

| ALBUM TITLE: | **Curtain Up! Bravos in Brass** | |
|---|---|---|
| **LABEL:** Mercury | **MONO** MG 50360 | **STEREO** SR 90360 |
| **GOLDEN IMPORTS** SRI | | **ALBUM REFERENCE NO.** 28 |
| **COVER ART:** 19th Century Print * | | **LINER NOTES:** Clair W. Van Ausdall |
| **ENGINEER:** | | **TAPE TRANSFER:** |
| **RECORDING DATE:** | | **PERSONNEL LIST:** |

### PROGRAM
\* = Premier recording

**Eastman Wind Ensemble:**
 Thunder and Blazes - Entry of the Gladiators - Julius Fucik
 Second Regiment Connecticut National Guard - David Wallace Reeves
 Sesqui-Centennial Exposition - John Philip Sousa
 The Picadore - John Philip Sousa
 Inglesina - Davide Della Cese
 Solid Men to the Front - John Philip Sousa
 Onward-Upward - Edwin Franko Goldman
 In Storm and Sunshine - John Clifford Heed
 Colonel Bogey - Kenneth J. Alford
 The National Game - John Philip Sousa
 The Mad Major - Kenneth J. Alford
 Old Comrades - Carl Tieke

### NOTES

This is a recoupling of previously released material.

*The cover art "A View of the Battle Between the Austrian and French Armies", was published on June 27, 1809 by G. Thompson. A legend of the battle scene is printed on back liner notes.

The cover represents a fourth "generic" Curtain Up cover format.
Group listed as Eastman Wind Ensemble

**ALBUM TITLE:** <u>Curtain Up! Holidays Around The World</u>

**LABEL:** Mercury  **MONO** MG 50361  **STEREO** SR 90361

**GOLDEN IMPORTS SRI**  **ALBUM REFERENCE NO.** 29

**COVER ART:**  **LINER NOTES:** Clair W. Van Ausdall

**ENGINEER:**  **TAPE TRANSFER:**

**RECORDING DATE:**  **PERSONNEL LIST:**

### PROGRAM
\* = Premier recording

**Eastman Wind Ensemble:**
  Christmas Festival - Leroy Anderson
  Celebration from Symphonic Songs for Band - Robert Russell Bennett

**Eastman-Rochester POPS Orchestra:**
  The Bugler's Holiday - Leroy Anderson
  Wearing of the Green - Leroy Anderson

### NOTES

This is a recoupling of previously released material.
The cover art is a period piece [not identified on the liner notes] and there are excellent historical liner notes, again, no credits are provided on the album liner notes.

RR: Who was in charge of all of these "Curtain Up!" recouplings?

FF: Wilma started it all. They were carried on by Harold Lawrence, Clair W. Van Ausdall, Scott Mampe and Joseph R. Bott.

Broadway Marches session in Studio A [Ballroom] of the Great Northern Hotel. Visible are Harvey Phillips, tuba; Tony Mattola, guitar; John Barrows, horn; trumpets include Bernie Glow and Ray Crisarra. Photo courtesy of Mary Morris Lawrence.

| | | |
|---|---|---|
| **ALBUM TITLE:** _Broadway Marches_ | | |
| **LABEL:** Mercury | **MONO** MG 50390 | **STEREO** SR 90390 |
| **GOLDEN IMPORTS** SRI 75115 | | **ALBUM REFERENCE NO.** 30 |
| **COVER ART:** Ralph Steiner | | **LINER NOTES:** Stanley Green |
| **ENGINEER:** George Piros and C.R. Fine | | **TAPE TRANSFER:** |
| **RECORDING DATE:** May 19, 1964 | | **PERSONNEL LIST:** See notes |

### PROGRAM
\* = Premier recording

Strike Up The Band - George Gershwin
I Ain't Down Yet - Meredith Willson
There Is Nothin' Like a Dame - Richard Rodgers
Stouthearted Men - Sigmund Romberg
Broadway Minstrel Medley - John Krance\*\*
Consider Yourself - Lionel Bart
There's No Business Like Show Business - Irving Berlin
The March of the Siamese Children - Richard Rodgers
Seventy-Six Trombones - Meredith Willson
Give My Regards to Broadway - George M. Cohan
Wintergreen For President - George Gershwin
Get Me To The Church on Time - Frederick Loewe

### NOTES

\*\* Gunshots on Broadway Minstrel Medley were fired by John Krance.

This was recorded in a two-day session, 19 - 20 May 1964.
Cover photo by Ralph Steiner appears to be an 'out-of-focus' night shot of Times Square, New York
Also issued by Longines Symphonette Society as a single LP and part of a five record set entitled "John Philip Sousa On Parade." Album title selected by FF. From the liner notes ... "John Krance's association with Frederick Fennell dates back to 1952 when he played French horn in the Eastman Wind Ensemble, the celebrated wind-brass-percussion group founded by Fennell. It was at the Eastman School of Music that Krance received his formal musical training." In 1964 he was Music Director of Radio Station WPAT in New York City.

Recording Director: C.R. Fine
Musical Supervisor: Harold Lawrence
Recording Site: Fine Studio in the Ballroom of Great Northern Hotel, New York. Recorded by C.R. Fine studio staff with chief engineer George Piros.
Group listed as Fennell Symphonic Winds
Orchestral Contract #10

FF: All arrangements were made especially for this recording by John Krance

RR: With John Krance gone now, will any of these be published?

FF: I really don't believe so. John Krance didn't leave a will. No family. He was a man totally out of anything that would remotely resemble any connection with the world. John was in his own place and more strange as the days went by. And sadly so. He was a very talented man. The most important thing - John could not accept, on any single day, the world as it was presented to him. That's tragic. And all of us - whatever we got about our egos and our this's and that's - there comes a time when you have to accept the world, whether or not it accepts you. And obviously it didn't accept John, who blew more good jobs. A lot of his friends, myself included, did everything we could to try to get him on track.

PERSONNEL:
Reeds: Phillip Bodner, Romeo Penque, Albert Klink
Horns: John Barrows, James Buffington, Ray Alange, William Decker
Trumpets: Bernie Glow, Raymond Crisarra, Joseph Wilder
Trombones: ?
Tuba: Harvey Phillips
Banjo/Guitar: Tony Mattola
Organ/Accordion: ?
Percussion: Brad Spinney, Robert Swan

| | | | |
|---|---|---|---|
| **ALBUM TITLE:** | The Civil War - Its Music and Its Sounds, Volume 1 | | |
| **LABEL:** Mercury | **MONO** LPS 2-501 | | **STEREO** LPS 2-901 |
| **GOLDEN IMPORTS** | **SRI** 2-77011 | **ALBUM REFERENCE NO.** 31 | |
| **COVER ART:** George Maas | | **LINER NOTES:** Frederick Fennell | |
| **ENGINEER:** C.R. Fine/Robert Eberenz | | **TAPE TRANSFER:** George Piros/John Johnson | |
| **RECORDING DATE:** December 13, 1960 | | **PERSONNEL LIST:** #9 | |

### PROGRAM
\* = Premier recording

**Band Music of the Union Troops:** [Composed and/or arranged by C.S. Grafulla. Music for drums by Frederick Fennell]. Hail to the Chief (James Sanderson), Listen to the Mocking Bird (Alice Hawthorne), Palmyra Schottische (Rowlathem/Grafulla), Hail Columbia (Philip Philo), Freischutz Quickstep (C.S. Grafulla), Parade (C.S. Grafulla), Port Royal Galop (C.S. Grafulla), Nightingale Waltz (C.S. Grafulla), La Marseillaise (deLisle/Grafulla).

**Band Music of the Confederate Troops:** [Probably arranged by Julius Leinbach] Dixie (Daniel Emmett), Bonnie Blue Flag (Harry McCarthy), Cheer Boys, Cheer (Henry Russell), Luto Quickstep (unknown), Old North State (arr. Leinbach), Easter Galop (unknown), Come, Dearest, the Daylight is Gone (unknown), Maryland, My Maryland (unknown), Waltz No. 19 (unknown), Old Hundredth (Louis Bourgeois).

**Field Music of Union and Confederate Troops:** Camp, Garrison and Field Calls for Fifes and Drums: The Girl I Left Behind Me, The Recruiting Sergeant, Jefferson and Liberty, Old 1812, Carry Me Back, Liverpool Hornpipe, Newport, Gary Owen. Music for drums by Frederick Fennell.

**Cavalry Bugle Signals:** The General, Boots and Saddles, To Horse, Assembly, To Arms, To the Standard \*, March, The Charge, Reveille, Stable Call, Watering Call, Breakfast, Assembly of Guard, Rally, Orders, Assemble of Buglers, Retreat\*, Fatigue Call, Dinner Call, Distributions, Drill Call, Officers Call, Common Step\*, Cease Firing, Officers Take Place, Sick Call, Tattoo\*, Quick March
   \*Signals marked are played first without drums, then with drums, parade style. Music for drums by Frederick Fennell.

**The Sounds of Conflict: Fort Sumter to Gettysburg.** Martin Gabel, narrator.

### NOTES

Extensive research, photographs, and diagrams. The Reactivated Civil War Unit, Battery B, 2nd New Jersey Light Artillery. Martin Gabel, Narrator. The first edition with fold-out and tied covers issued with red labels. Volume I in gray and Volume II in brown with the lacquered photo alternated with the album title. The second release in boxed form reversed the colors for Volume I and Volume II and the photos are in the same perspective. The 35mm film logo changes from original issue to the subsequent re-issues.

Tape transfer: John Johnson [mono]; George Piros [stereo].
Recording Director: Wilma Cozart
Musical Supervisor: Harold Lawrence
Recording Technician: William L. Decker
Album Coordinator: Clair W. Van Ausdall
Script: Harold Lawrence
Photos: Henry Ries, William L. Decker, Harold Lawrence
Narrator: Martin Gable
Group listed as Eastman Wind Ensemble

Brass instruments used in these recordings are numbered and correspond to the personnel lists. This is true for volume one only, even though the same announcement appears in volume two. The numbers are not present next to the personnel in volume two. Restoration of the over-the-shoulder brass instruments by Robert Sheldon and Norman Schweikert.

RR: It is interesting to note that three of the original brass instruments [E-flat Sopranino Cornet, E-flat Alto Horn and E-flat Alto] were loaned from the private collection of Norman Schweikert and Robert Sheldon, two of the EWE members performing on these recordings.

Singing performed by the men of the Eastman Wind Ensemble with settings arranged by Frederick Fennell.

RR: Selections from this series were used in the 1990 PBS production of "The Civil War." Mercury Living Presence re-issued this set on compact disc on December 11, 1990, thirty years after the original recording. It is complete except for *Cape May Polka, Rachel Waltzes* and a single track of *The Star Spangled Banner*.

FF: Comments on these releases...

**Recording conditions**: As always, the superb Eastman Theatre provided the ideal chamber, and although I had to conduct downhill at the rear of the stage, I could hear everything that was possible, even with the signal going away from rather than to me.

**Original Instruments**: After the search and throughout Bob Sheldon's feverish work at restoration, there came that not-to-be-forgotten first play of them all together. I'd never hear a sound like that. It was mellow, dark, from another time, smooth, round, --- unforgettable. The comments in the booklets all say what it was, too.

**Accessibility of music**: That too is best expressed in the booklets. As usual, no score --- and the layout on the living room floor. Today we would have a 50% enlargement of these pages together with corrected century-old errors and omissions. All were manuscript.

**Recording process with the 35mm film**: That was Bob Fine's bailiwick. I only remember playback with less hiss and the ultimate in fidelity. The recording scenario was as follows: December 13 - record and listen; December 14 - record in two 2 and one-half hour sessions; December 15 - recording 10:00 am - 12:30 pm; December 16 - record singing with banjo

RR: If you still have the original seating arrangement that was posted .. it would be great to reproduce this in the publication. FF: I should have saved it, but I didn't. Damn it!.

RR: The original booklets of Volume I & Volume II in the listing of instruments and personnel of the Port Royal Band, the typesetter seems to have invented a new instrument, the E Flat Flat Bass. This error was corrected 30 years later with the release of the Mercury Living Presence Compact Disc. The CD booklet and cover do not show the 35mm logo as on the original LP version. All original 35mm notes are included in the booklet. CD produced and musically supervised by Wilma Cozart Fine. Mastering Engineer for CD: Dennis Drake. See issue 160.

The Civil War – the Union Army Band. I chose this set very carefully after considering all the possibilities and requirements. Just looking at that field of the bells of brass instruments pointing backwards over the shoulder, or in the case of Norman Schweikert and Linda Van Sickle, to the side. The three piccolos and four clarinets that were a part of the books of the Port Royal Band that we re-established, presented rather a large problem. The reeds had to face forward and the brass had to face backward and had to be raised on tiers the opposite way for me as the conductor. I was on the high end and I conducted downhill. As for the woodwinds, I solved their problem by going to an auto supply store and bought eight rearview mirrors that went under your visor. That's how they could see me.

It was completely my idea to use these mirrors. We had originally thought of using closed circuit TV but it created interference with the recording signal. Joel Thome is using my Civil War drum and John Galm, my Civil War wooden bass drum beater. Also visible are the great Elsa Ludewig and Charlie Bay and the unbelievable Mr. Chicago clarinet, Larry Combs. The brass players were unbelievable. Photo courtesy of William L. Decker, who, when he wasn't driving the truck for Bob Fine, was using his camera.

| | | | |
|---|---|---|---|
| **ALBUM TITLE:** | The Civil War - Its Music and Its Sounds, Volume 2 | | |
| **LABEL:** Mercury | **MONO** LPS 2-502 | | **STEREO** LPS 2-902 |
| **GOLDEN IMPORTS** SRI 2-77011 | | **ALBUM REFERENCE NO.** 32 | |
| **COVER ART:** | | **LINER NOTES:** Frederick Fennell | |
| **ENGINEER:** C.R. Fine/Robert Eberenz | | **TAPE TRANSFER:** John Johnson/George Piros | |
| **RECORDING DATE:** December 15, 1960 | | **PERSONNEL LIST:** #9 - see notes | |

### PROGRAM
\* = Premier recording

Introduction narrated by Martin Gabel.

**Band Music of the Union Troops:** Twinkling Stars Quickstep (J.P. Ordway), Old Kentucky, Kentucky (unknown), Cape May Polka (C.S. Grafulla), Rachel Waltzes (C.S. Grafulla), Come Where My Love Lies Dreaming (Stephen Foster), Un Ballo in Maschera Quickstep (G. Verdi, arr. Grafulla), St. Patrick's Day in the Morning (arr. Grafulla), Grafulla's Quickstep (C.S. Grafulla), Garry Owen (unknown), Cavalry Quickstep (C.S. Grafulla), Storm Galop (C.S. Grafulla), Star Spangled Banner (arr. Grafulla).

**Field Music of Union and Confederate Troops:** Bugle signals for the service of skirmishers, Forward, Halt, To the Left - To the Right, About - Rally on Chief, Trot - Galop, Commence Fire - Disperse, Change - Right, Change - Left, Recall, Retreat (short). **DRUM CALLS** [performed by Frederick Fennell]: Drummer's Call I and II, Assembly, Long Roll. **Camp and Field Duty Calls for Fifes and Drums:** Drill Call, Guard Mount, Retreat, Surgeon's Call, Adjutant's Call, Tattoo, Assembly, Fatigue.

**Band Music of the Confederate Troops:** Twenty-sixth Regiment Quickstep (J. Leinbach), Lulu's Gone (Stephen Foster), Tramp, Tramp, Tramp (G.F. Root), Juanita (unknown), Carry Me Back to Old Virginny's Shore (Charles T. White). **The Appomattox Bugle** (performed by Boyde Hood): Charge, Assembly, Taps.

**Songs of the Union and Confederate Soldiers:** We Are Coming, Father Abra'am (L.O. Emerson), Tenting Tonight on the Old Camp Ground (Walter Kittredge), Goober Peas (A.E. Blackmar), Marching Through Georgia (Henry C. Work), When Johnny Comes Marching Home (Patrick Gilmore), The Battle Hymn of the Republic (William Steffe).

**The Sounds of Conflict: Gettysburg to Appomattox**. Martin Gabel, narrator

### NOTES

Set produced by Wilma Cozart.

Cannon fire, musketry, small arms, horses and wagons, and other sounds were recorded at Gettysburg on 29 October 1960 using dry ammunition. All firing also recorded with live ammunition at the firing range, United States Military Academy, West Point, New York on 11 December 1960.

The premier issue of Volume I contained a coupon worth $1.00 on purchase of Volume II. In 1961 the two record set was priced at $8.98 [mono] and $9.98 [stereo]. I have two different releases of this two record set. The first issue was in a fold-out, tied package with gold labels. The second release was in a box format. Colors for the two issues were reversed with the fold-out set being issued in Gray and Brown and the box format issued in Brown and Gray for Volumes I and II respectively. There are also variations of the presentation of the 35mm logo for Stereo and Hi-Fi Monural.

Recording dates [December 14-16] as listed on album are incorrect. Frederick Fennell supplied the dates as December 13-16, 1960, plus the additional 'sound effects' dates as listed above. See issue 31 for information of 1990 Mercury Living Presence Compact Disc release.

RR: What can you tell us about the Civil War books?

FF: I got these books from the Library of Congress. I feel sure that the arrangement of the *Star Spangled Banner* is by Grafulla. The E-flat cornet book is the leaders book. There, of course, is no score. I had to make a book for Roger Bobo, as that book was not in existence.

All singing was done by the men of the Eastman Wind Ensemble using settings by Frederick Fennell.

# PERSONNEL OF
# THE PORT ROYAL BAND

**REEDS**
D FLAT FLUTE AND PICCOLO
Joanna Tousey, Susan Levitin, Doris Wilson
B FLAT CLARINET
Elsa Ludewig, Charles Bay, Larry Combs, Jerry Smith
**BRASSES**
E FLAT SOPRANINO CORNET
Boyde Hood, Joseph Koplin, David Greenhoe, Glen Bell
B FLAT SOPRANO CORNET
Albert MacKinnon, John Landis
E FLAT ALTO
Robert Sheldon, Herbert Spencer
Norman Schweikert, Linda Van Sickle
B FLAT TENOR  Robert Gillespie  E FLAT BASS Byron Hanson
B FLAT BASS
Larry Campbell, Early Anderson
E FLAT BASS
Roger Bobo, Paul Brown, Peter Phillips
SMALL DRUM  Joel Thome   LARGE DRUM  John Galm

# PERSONNEL OF REGIMENT BAND OF THE
# 26TH NORTH CAROLINA

E FLAT SOPRANINO CORNET
Boyde Hood
B FLAT SOPRANO CORNET
Albert MacKinnon, John Landis
E FLAT ALTO Norman Schweikert   B FLAT TENOR Byron Hanson
B FLAT BASS Larry Campbell   E FLAT BASS Roger Bobo
**BUGLERS**
Thomas Hohstadt, Joseph Koplin, Albert MacKinnon,
John Landis, Glen Bell, David Greenhoe
Appomattox Bugle: Boyde Hood
**FIFERS**
Joanna Tousey, Susan Levitin, Doris Wilson, Gerald Carey,
Mardele Johnson, Phillip Swanson
**DRUMMERS**
Joel Thome, John Galm, Norman Fickett, Dennis Kain,
Peter Webster, Frederick Fennell

Correspndence from Frederick Fennell - 12 December 1991

Musicians who perform as members of The Eastman Wind Ensemble in the two-volume [8 sides] Mercury Recordings LPS 2-901/LPS 902 recorded in the Eastman Theatre, Eastman School of Music, University of Rochester, 13,14,15 December 1960. All at this time, members of Local 66 AFM, listed alphabetically; all full-time students:

### Key to the columns at right which identify the music as it was recorded:

- A: 13 December - Afternoon session, music from the Union Army band books
- B: 14 December - Morning session, music from the Union Army band books, plus buglers & drummers
- C: 14 December - Afternoon session, music from the Confederate Army band books
- D: 15 December - Morning session, music from the Union Army band books, some fifes & drums
- E: 15 December - Morning session for piccolos [fifes] and drums only

| # | Name | Instrument | Sessions |
|---|---|---|---|
| 1. | Anderson, Early | B flat bass | A B D |
| 2. | Bay, Charles | B flat clarinet | A B D |
| 3. | Bell, Glen | E flat sopranino cornet & B flat bugle | A B D |
| 4. | Bobo, Roger | E flat bass | A B C D |
| 5. | Brown, Paul | E flat bass | A B D |
| 6. | Campbell, Larry | B flat bass | A B C D |
| 7. | Carey, Gerald | Piccolo | E |
| 8. | Combs, Larry | B flat clarinet | A B D |
| 9. | Fennell, Frederick | Solo and section drums | B D E |
| 10. | Fickett, Norman | Drummer | B D E |
| 11. | Galm, John | Drummer | A B D E |
| 12. | Gillespie, Robert | B flat tenor horn | A B D |
| 13. | Greenhoe, David | E flat sopranino cornet & B flat bugle | A B D |
| 14. | Hanson, Byron | E flat bass | A B C D |
| 15. | Hohstadt, Thomas | B flat bugle | B |
| 16. | Hood, Boyde | Solo sopranino cornet & B flat bugle | A B C D |
| 17. | Johnson, Mardele | Piccolo | E |
| 18. | Kain, Dennis | Drummer | E |
| 19. | Koplin, Joseph | E flat sopranino cornet & B flat bugle | A B D |
| 20. | Landis, John | B flat soprano cornet & B flat bugle | A B C D |
| 21. | Levitin, Susan | Piccolo | A B D E |
| 22. | Ludewig, Elsa | B flat clarinet | A B D |
| 23. | MacKinnon, Albert | B flat soprano cornet & B flat bugle | A B C D |
| 24. | Phillips, Peter | E flat bass | A B D |
| 25. | Schweikert, Norman | E flat alto horn | A B C D |
| 26. | Sheldon, Robert | E flat alto horn | A B D |
| 27. | Smith, Jerry N. | B flat clarinet | A B D |
| 28. | Spencer, Herbert | E flat alto horn | A B D |
| 29. | Swanson, Phillip | Piccolo | E |
| 30. | Thome, Joel | Drummer | A B D E |
| 31. | Tousey, Joanna | Piccolo | A B D E |
| 32. | Van Sickle, Linda | E flat alto horn | A B D |
| 33. | Webster, Peter | Drummer | E |
| 34. | Wilson, Doris | Piccolo | E |
| 35. | Frederick Fennell | Conductor, Music Director | A B C D E |

17. Mardele Johnson Marcellus, deceased
22. Elsa Ludewig Verdehr, married name
31. Joanna Tousey Parkes, married name
21. Susan Levitin, married name?
32. Linda Van Sickle, married name?
34. Doris Wilson, married name?

All of the above has been prepared from my personal records of these three days in December 1960

*Frederick Fennell*, Conductor
The Eastman Wind Ensemble
20 September 1952/6 May 1962

# FREDERICK FENNELL

## "How it all Began"
### General News Round-up of recent activities
### 14 August 1963

When the 60th season of the Minneapolis Symphony closed the first week in May, Frederick Fennell concluded his first season as the Orchestra's Associate Conductor. He conducted over thirty of its concerts covering every facet of the work of one of the country's important symphonic groups. Conductor Fennell found this year of acquaintance with a new community, after his long and distinguished residence at the Eastman School of Music, to be one of true adventure for him and his family. These new adventures included a busy schedule of speaking engagements before a variety of Twin City audiences. Continuing his interest in radio and television he was a frequent guest in those studios and began a nightly one-hour symphonic record program of his own for the Twin City Time-Life station WTCN.

January saw the release of SCREAMERS, the last album of recordings that Fennell made in his precedent-setting series of records for Mercury with the Eastman Wind Ensemble, which he founded in 1952. SCREAMERS is an album devoted to those exciting and fast-disappearing circus marches and it quickly established itself with his many enthusiastic record fans.

May found him once again in contact with youthful high school musicians of the country when he conducted a festival at the University of Maryland, sponsored by Lions International. This was followed by a pair of concerts in New Orleans at the end of June when he opened the 10th season of their summer concerts. The Fennell family then retreated to their summer home in the woods at Interlochen, Michigan, where all are enjoying their first extensive vacation together in many years.

Frederick Fennell's continuing interest and involvement in the music of the Civil War finds him as speaker at many functions around the country. His two volume record study of the music of the Civil War continues to bring forth the highest praise from critics in music, history, and the science and art of recording. Volume I captured the GRAMMY award of the National Academy of Recording Arts & Sciences in one of the engineering categories for 1963. Fennell also received the medal of the New York State Commission for the Centennial Observance and was the recipient of a glowing citation from Bruce Catton at the awarding of that medal. Honored by innumerable "buff" societies, including "The Confederate High Command", the first volume was joined by the second, released by Mercury Records in August. The national meeting of the Company of Military Historians elected Frederick Fennell a Fellow of The Company for his work in the field of military music.

August saw the beginning of a new series of radio programs for station WBEN in Buffalo, New York, a two-your Sunday evening musical program for which Fennell is commentator on recordings of his choice. For the January convocation of Macalester College in St. Paul, Minnesota, the faculty and students have invited Dr. Fennell to present an unusual evening in which he will rehearse members of the Minneapolis Symphony in an open session devoted to the challenges of performing one of the symphonies of Joseph Haydn.

A Twin City-wide High School Music Festival under his direction is planned for early summer, 1964, under the sponsorship of the Time-Life station, WTCN.

In the forthcoming concert season Dr. Fennell will continue his work with the Minneapolis Symphony, conducting its Sunday Series, its 20 concerts for young people, and special, subscription, and other events throughout the year. In January he will be the American conductor invited by Sir John Barbirolli, Conductor-in-Chief of the Houston Symphony, to help celebrate the Golden Anniversary of that Orchestra. Fennell will conduct a subscription pair.

**FREDERICK FENNELL RECORDS EXCLUSIVELY FOR MERCURY RECORDS**

Associate -   The Minneapolis Symphony Orchestra
              110 Northrop Memorial Auditorium
              University of Minnesota
              Minneapolis 14, Minnesota

14 August 1963

| | | | |
|---|---|---|---|
| **ALBUM TITLE:** | **Music of Leroy Anderson, Vol. 1** | | |
| **LABEL:** Mercury | **MONO** MG 50130 | **STEREO** SR 90009 ** | |
| **GOLDEN IMPORTS SRI** 75013 | | **ALBUM REFERENCE NO.** 33 | |
| **COVER ART:** Photo by Radford Bascome | | **LINER NOTES:** Alfred E. Simon | |
| **ENGINEER:** C.R. Fine | | **TAPE TRANSFER:** George Piros | |
| **RECORDING DATE:** October 25, 1956 | | **PERSONNEL LIST:** | |

### PROGRAM
*\* = Premier recording*

Sandpaper Ballet  
Serenata +  
Penny-Whistle Song  
Bugler's Holiday  
Forgotten Dreams  
Trumpeter's Lullaby  
Sleigh Ride +  
Irish Suite  

### NOTES

Color picture of Fennell on cover with glasses. [FF: My first glasses - awful pix!]

FF: This was the beginning of my personal contract with Mercury Records, and my first orchestral one. All of the Eastman Wind Ensemble records were made under the Eastman School of Music contract with Mercury and my only agreement for these records is with the ESM, of the University of Rochester. I accepted no payment from Eastman for any record until all of the money that had been invested in making it was returned to the ESM's revolving fund for records exclusively.
Leroy I was played by the Rochester Civic Orchestra, the pro orchestra of Rochester, 45 players, nucleus of the Rochester Philharmonic and the Eastman-Rochester Orchestra, which Hanson named when he began to record for Victor before WW II. We had two rehearsals for the throw-away public concert that we had to play under the symphonic recording rate. The Rochester Civic Music Association didn't really care for me, so they wouldn't book a regular concert and we played to about 100 people in Kilbourn Hall 24 hours before the session. This recording gave me a lot of exposure and is still played on FM these 30 years later. Of course, the Civic played these pieces and knew them like the great pros they were.

RR: I have four different copies of this release, each of which slightly different in the cover and jacket printing. The first is the mono MG 50130 was issued in two different covers. The first with the plain Olympian logo and the second with the Mercury Living Presence green diagonal band. The two stereo versions also differ from each other in the color of the 'STEREO' logo across the top and the diagonal Living Presence band. They also contain an additional color reproduction of the cover photo on the back liner. Recording information is also included only on the stereo releases. Both editions also include a short biography of Frederick Fennell .. each is different. ** One might also have anticipated that the usual SR 90130 would have been used for the stereo release. This never appeared. Oh, the joy of collecting.
Issued on Golden Imports cassette - MRI 75013

+ These two selections included on the 1992 Mercury CD "Frederick Fennell conducts the music of Leroy Anderson" 432 013-2 [see entry #165].

Recording Director: Wilma Cozart  
Musical Supervisor: Harold Lawrence  
Recording site: Eastman Theatre  
Group listed as Eastman-Rochester POPS Orchestra [plus winds and percussion. Total of 49]  
Orchestral contract #1.

| ALBUM TITLE: | **Music of Leroy Anderson, Vol. II** | |
|---|---|---|
| LABEL: Mercury | MONO MG 50043 | STEREO SR 90043 |
| GOLDEN IMPORTS SRI | | ALBUM REFERENCE NO. 34 |
| COVER ART: Photo by Henry Ries | | LINER NOTES: Clair W. Van Ausdall |
| ENGINEER: C. R. Fine | | TAPE TRANSFER: George Piros |
| RECORDING DATE: March 3, 1958 | | PERSONNEL LIST: Rochester Civic Orchestra |

### PROGRAM
\* = Premier recording

Belle of the Ball
The Waltzing Cat
Summer Skies
The Typewriter
The Girl in Satin
Sarabande
Horse and Buggy
Blue Tango
Song of the Bells
The Syncopated Clock
China Doll
Fiddle-Faddle

All selections included on Mercury CD "Frederick Fennell Conducts the Music of Leroy Anderson" 432 013-2

### NOTES

FF: Typewriter solo performed by Frederick Fennell - both survived. Both Leroy's were our shot at the Boston Pops market, where we did well. Hi Fi Ala Espanola helped a lot - then we came back with a convincing Leroy right down Arthur's alley.

Cover illustration, suggested by Clair W. Van Ausdall, depicts a clock pendulum, a stuffed cat and a toy typewriter on both the mono and stereo releases. Type setting is a little different for the mono release with a very large 2 after volume. Probably to gain the attention of the record buyer who already owns volume 1. The re-issue [second printing] of the stereo release changes the color reproduction to black and white and changes the Living Presence band from red to gray.

All three of the orchestral and the two TOKWO wind Anderson's recordings provide some of the finest of this great "Americana" composer.

Recording Director: Wilma Cozart
Musical Supervisor: Harold Lawrence
Recording site: Eastman Theatre
Group listed as Eastman-Rochester POPS Orchestra [plus extra winds and percussion. Total of 49]
Orchestral contract #3.

| | | |
|---|---|---|
| **ALBUM TITLE:** | Hi-Fi Ala Espanola | |
| **LABEL:** Mercury | **MONO** MG 50144 | **STEREO** SR 90144 |
| **GOLDEN IMPORTS** SRI 75097 | | **ALBUM REFERENCE NO.** 35 |
| **COVER ART:** Photo by George Pickow | | **LINER NOTES:** Frederick Fennell/H. Lawrence |
| **ENGINEER:** C. R. Fine | | **TAPE TRANSFER:** George Piros |
| **RECORDING DATE:** March 25, 1957 | | **PERSONNEL LIST:** |

### PROGRAM
\* = Premier recording

Brazilian Sleigh Bells - Percy Faith
Goyescas: Intermezzo - Enrique Granados
Batuque - Oscar Lorenzo Fernandez
El Amor Brujo - Ritual Fire Dance - Manuel de Falla
The Bullfighter's Prayer - Joaquin Turina
Andalucia - Ernesto Lecuona, arr. M. Gould
Malaguena - Ernesto Lecuona, arr. M. Gould
Jamaican Rumba - Arthur Benjamin
Amparito Roca - Jaime Texidor
\* Brazilian Dance - Camargo Mozart Guarnieri

FF: All of these are stocks, but like the marches, that's not the way I play them.

### NOTES

The liner notes on MG 50144 contain an excellent paragraph *Notes About Frederick Fennell and The Eastman-Rochester POPS* [quoted below], which is omitted on SR 90144. Cover type and colors are re-set from the original MG and the SR releases. The "STEREO Hi-Fi" top banner and Mercury Living Presence diagonal banner are included on the SR release.

**NOTES ABOUT FREDERICK FENNELL AND THE EASTMAN-ROCHESTER POPS** -- In MG 50130, The Music of Leroy Anderson, Frederick Fennell demonstrated, as Bert Whyte wrote in Radio and Television News, that "he knows how to handle strings as well as his beloved brass and percussion. His tempi are well-chosen, his phrasing and dynamics neatly expressive. Fennell is, above all, never heavy-handed and he lets the essential humor and grace of the works speak for themselves." The Music of Leroy Anderson marked the first release by the Eastman-Rochester POPS Orchestra. Fennell's previous recordings have been devoted to conducting the Eastman Symphonic Wind Ensemble, which the conductor formed in 1952. An exclusive Mercury artist, Fennell exhibits extraordinary versatility as an interpreter. His repertoire on Mercury Living Presence recordings ranges from the marches of John Philip Sousa (MG50080) to the concert band suites of Vaughan Williams and Holst (MG50088), the symphonic wind music of contemporary American composers (MG50079, MG50084), the orchestral scores of Spanish and Latin-American composers included in the present album, and other noteworthy releases.

Recording Director: Wilma Cozart
Musical Supervisor: Harold Lawrence
Guitar Soloist: Rolando Valdes-Blain
Recording site: Eastman Theatre
Group listed as Eastman-Rochester POPS Orchestra [plus extra winds, piano and percussion. Total of 50]
Orchestral contract #2.

| | |
|---|---|
| **ALBUM TITLE:** | <u>**Country Gardens & Other Favorites by Percy A. Grainger**</u> |

**LABEL:** Mercury  **MONO** MG 50219  **STEREO** SR 90219

**GOLDEN IMPORTS  SRI** 75102  **ALBUM REFERENCE NO.** 36

**COVER ART:** Photo by British Travel Association  **LINER NOTES:** Frederick Fennell

**ENGINEER:** C. R. Fine  **TAPE TRANSFER:** George Piros/John Johnson

**RECORDING DATE:** May 4, 1959  **PERSONNEL LIST:**

### PROGRAM
\* = Premier recording

Country Gardens
Colonial Song
The Immovable Do
Handel in the Strand
Spoon River
Molly on the Shore
Shepherd's Hey
Children's March
Mock Morris
Irish Tune from County Derry
My Robin is to the Greenwood Gone

### NOTES

FF: Only Stokowski had done PAG anything, so this was a new kid on the block recording, and to make it was Wilma Cozart's idea, which she told to me in a phone booth conversation at Bud's Gas Station, Interlochen, Michigan the previous summer. Percy could not believe that I wasn't going to ask him for money to pay for the recording! We used many of his personal sets of parts for this -- and he was really touched by my recording. I foolishly did not make copies of his parts before returning them !!!!.

RR: Liner notes on MG and SR release quote letters to Fennell from Grainger dated January 6 - August 6, 1959.
Also issued on Mercury WING [both stereo and mono] SRW 18060 and MGW 14060, which have a similar cover photo [cropped] and abbreviated liner notes [no credits to Fennell for notes], and Golden Imports cassette: MRI 75102. All selections issued on Mercury Living Presence CD 434 330-2, issue 169.

Tape transfer: George Piros [stereo] - John Johnson [mono]
Recording Director: Wilma Cozart
Musical Supervisor: Harold Lawrence
Site: Eastman Theatre
Group listed as Eastman-Rochester POPS Orchestra
Orchestral contract # 4.

Photo of Percy A. Grainger
by Frederick Fennell in
White Plains, New York
September 1958
© Frederick Fennell

| ALBUM TITLE: | POP Overs | | |
|---|---|---|---|
| LABEL: Mercury | | MONO MG 50222 | STEREO SR 90222 |
| GOLDEN IMPORTS SRI | | ALBUM REFERENCE NO. 37 | |
| COVER ART: George Maas/George Pickow | | LINER NOTES: Frederick Fennell | |
| ENGINEER: C.R. Fine | | TAPE TRANSFER: George Piros/John Johnson | |
| RECORDING DATE: May 5, 1959 | | PERSONNEL LIST: | |

### PROGRAM
\* = Premier recording

Polka and Fugue from "Schwanda" - Jaromir Weinberger
Procession of the Nobles - Nikolai Rimsky-Korsakov
Leibestraum - Franz Liszt
Hora Staccato - Gheorghe Dinicu
Prelude in G minor - Sergei Rachmaninoff
Russian Sailor's Dance - Reinhold Gliere
Clair de lune - Claude Debussy
Finlandia - Jean Sibelius
Love's Dream after the Ball - Alphons Czibulka
Polka from "The Golden Age" - Dmitri Shostakovich

### NOTES

FF: Wonderful repertory. Sad that it doesn't get played as it should - both in style and frequency. The music world is very snobbish!. Clair W. Van Ausdall came up with the title and the cover photo idea.

Back of album liner notes include great technical data on the recordings in Eastman Theatre. "Russian Sailors' Dance" is attributed to Glinka on back cover. I recently found another release of this album entitled "POPS" Favoritos with Orquesta Eastman-Rochester POPS. It was issued in Argentina by Philips. Fennell liner notes are translated and a new cover design with the familiar Mercury Living Presence banner.

Cover design by George Maas and photos of 'pop-overs' [the baked kind] by George Pickow.

Tape transfer: George Piros [stereo] - John Johnson [mono]
Recording Director: Wilma Cozart
Musical Supervisor: Harold Lawrence
Site: Eastman Theatre
Group listed as Eastman-Rochester POPS Orchestra [plus extra winds, percussion and organ. Total of 49]
Orchestral contract #5.

| ALBUM TITLE: | **Marches For Orchestra** | | |
|---|---|---|---|
| LABEL: Mercury | MONO MG 50271 | | STEREO SR 90271 |
| GOLDEN IMPORTS SRI | | ALBUM REFERENCE NO. 38 | |
| COVER ART: George Maas/Henry Ries | | LINER NOTES: Frederick Fennell | |
| ENGINEER: C.R. Fine/Robert Eberenz | | TAPE TRANSFER: George Piros/John Johnson | |
| RECORDING DATE: April 30, 1960 | | PERSONNEL LIST: | |

**PROGRAM**
\* = Premier recording

Orb and Sceptre - William Walton
Turkish March - Ludwig van Beethoven
Alla Marcia - Jean Sibelius
Tannhauser March - Richard Wagner
Marche Militaire - Franz Schubert
Homage March - Edvard Grieg
Prince Igor March - Alexander Borodin

**NOTES**

FF: Dr. Hanson, very protective of the School, allowed me to use the Eastman Philharmonia for this when, as previously mentioned, the Rochester Civic Music Association manager was short on appreciation of Frederick Fennell and could not find "schedule time", etc. So I did this. Of course, the winds and percussion were from the Eastman Wind Ensemble, and the larger string section of the Philharmonia, while young in experience, played with lots of conviction. A few faculty strings were added for this session.

Also issued on Mercury Wing WC 18069 [Compatible stereo/mono], with same cover, reduced in size to fit within a red rococo border. The SR version includes a vertical color pix of the cover cymbals, which is omitted from the MG release.

Tape transfer: George Piros [stereo] - John Johnson [mono]
Recording Director: Wilma Cozart
Musical Supervisor: Harold Lawrence
Recording Site: Eastman Theatre
Group listed as the Eastman-Rochester POPS [plus a few faculty strings].
Orchestral contract #6

| ALBUM TITLE: | **Curtain Up ! Orchestral March Favorites** | | |
|---|---|---|---|
| LABEL: Mercury | MONO MG 50292 | | STEREO SR 90292 |
| GOLDEN IMPORTS SRI | | ALBUM REFERENCE NO. 39 | |
| COVER ART: See notes | | LINER NOTES: | |
| ENGINEER: | | TAPE TRANSFER: | |
| RECORDING DATE: | | PERSONNEL LIST: | |

**PROGRAM**
\* = Premier recording

**Eastman-Rochester POPS Orchestra**
  Homage March - Edvard Grieg
  Turkish March - Ludwig van Beethoven

**NOTES**

Cover photo of Elizabethan marching unit courtesy of William F. Ludwig Drum Company

| ALBUM TITLE: | **Curtain Up ! Symphonic Dance Favorites** | | |
|---|---|---|---|
| **LABEL:** Mercury | **MONO** MG 50293 | | **STEREO** SR 90293 |
| **GOLDEN IMPORTS** SRI | | **ALBUM REFERENCE NO.** 40 | |
| **COVER ART:** See notes | | **LINER NOTES:** | |
| **ENGINEER:** | | **TAPE TRANSFER:** | |
| **RECORDING DATE:** | | **PERSONNEL LIST:** | |

**PROGRAM**
\* = Premier recording

**Eastman-Rochester POPS Orchestra**
Jamaican Rumba - Arthur Benjamin

**NOTES**

Cover photo of Sword Dancers is courtesy of William F. Ludwig Drum Company.

RR: What was the connection between Ludwig and Mercury?

FF: None, except when I used one of Bill's snare drums as on the cover of "March Time" or as in the cover of "Curtain Up", MG 50294.

| ALBUM TITLE: | **Curtain Up ! Fennell Favorites** | | |
|---|---|---|---|
| **LABEL:** Mercury | **MONO** MG 50294 | | **STEREO** SR 90294 |
| **GOLDEN IMPORTS** SRI | | **ALBUM REFERENCE NO.** 41 | |
| **COVER ART:** See notes | | **LINER NOTES:** | |
| **ENGINEER:** | | **TAPE TRANSFER:** | |
| **RECORDING DATE:** | | **PERSONNEL LIST:** | |

**PROGRAM**
\* = Premier recording

**Eastman-Rochester POPS Orchestra**
Hora Staccato - Gheorghe Dinicu
Marche Militaire - Franz Schubert
Country Gardens - Percy A. Grainger
Sleigh Ride - Leroy Anderson
Fiddle-Faddle - Leroy Anderson
Intermezzo from "Goyescas" - Enrique Granados
Polka and Fugue from "Schwanda" - Jaromir Weinberger
Clair de lune - Claude Debussy
Molly on the Shore - Percy A. Grainger
Blue Tango - Leroy Anderson
The Syncopated Clock - Leroy Anderson

**NOTES**

Cover photo of Fennell pictured with an array of his Mercury releases is courtesy of William F. Ludwig Drum Company.

RR: This photo would make a great frontispiece for the discography. How did it come about and is it available?

FF: Bill Ludwig arranged this [photo] in Chicago during a Midwest Clinic. I doubt they still have the negative, but I have a color copy, and it is available for use, if I can find it.

Recoupling of previously released material.
Group listed as Eastman-Rochester POPS Orchestra.

| ALBUM TITLE: | **Curtain Up! Musical Almanac** | |
|---|---|---|
| LABEL: Mercury | MONO MG 50337 | STEREO SR 90337 |
| GOLDEN IMPORTS   SRI | | ALBUM REFERENCE NO. 42 |
| COVER ART:   Robert Day | | LINER NOTES: |
| ENGINEER: | | TAPE TRANSFER: |
| RECORDING DATE: | | PERSONNEL LIST: |

**PROGRAM**
* = Premier recording

**Eastman Wind Ensemble**
  On The Mall - Edwin Franko Goldman
**Eastman-Rochester POPS Orchestra**
  Summer Skies - Leroy Anderson
  Last Rose of Summer - Leroy Anderson

**NOTES**

Recoupling of previously released material.
Another great cover by Robert Day.

| ALBUM TITLE: | **Curtain Up! Fennell And The "POPS"** | |
|---|---|---|
| LABEL: Mercury | MONO MG 50340 | STEREO SR 90340 |
| GOLDEN IMPORTS   SRI | | ALBUM REFERENCE NO. 43 |
| COVER ART:   Robert Day | | LINER NOTES: Anonymous |
| ENGINEER: | | TAPE TRANSFER: |
| RECORDING DATE: | | PERSONNEL LIST: |

**PROGRAM**
* = Premier recording

**Eastman Wind Ensemble**
  Spiritual from Symphonic Songs - Robert Russell Bennett
  *Prom Night - Ralph Hermann
  Provence from Suite Francaise - Darius Milhaud
  Pineapple Poll - Finale - Arthur Sullivan
  * Beguine for Band - Glenn Osser

**Eastman-Rochester POPS Orchestra**
  Mock Morris - Percy A. Grainger
  Liebestraum - Franz Liszt
  Malaguena - Ernesto Lecuona
  Love's Dream After the Ball - Alphons Czibulka

**Frederick Fennell Orchestra**
  Blow, Gabriel Blow - Cole Porter
  Streets of New York - Victor Herbert
  I Got Rhythm - George Gershwin

**NOTES**

* These two premier recordings were done on March 24, 1957, at the end of the Hindemith, Schoenberg and Stravinsky session. Personnel list #7. This is the first and only release of these two selections.
FF: Sunday, March 24, 1957 - my Boosey Hawkes lists the following: Session at 9:00 AM. "Prom Night" - 9:10 AM. "Beguine" recorded at 11:02 AM. Finish at 11:24 AM.

| ALBUM TITLE: | **Great Music by Russian Composers** | |
|---|---|---|
| **LABEL:** Mercury | **MONO** MG 50346 | **STEREO** SR 90346 |
| **GOLDEN IMPORTS** SRI | | **ALBUM REFERENCE NO.** 43a |
| **COVER ART:** | | **LINER NOTES:** Edward Downes |
| **ENGINEER:** | | **TAPE TRANSFER:** |
| **RECORDING DATE:** | | **PERSONNEL LIST:** |

**PROGRAM**
\* = Premier recording

**Eastman Wind Ensemble**
Armenian Dances - Aram Khachaturian, arr. Ralph Satz  from SR 90221

**Eastman-Rochester POPS Orchestra**
Polka from "The Age of Gold" - Dmitri Shostakovich from  SR 90222

**NOTES**

Recoupling of previously released material

Cover art: A reproduction of a colorful Russian festival by H. Tormkob 1933.
FF: This may be from a book of lacquer box art prints I purchased in Russia and possibly loaned to Mercury. These are called Palec, the name of the town where they are made.

| ALBUM TITLE: | **Music of Leroy Anderson, Volume III** | |
|---|---|---|
| **LABEL:** Mercury | **MONO** MG 50400 | **STEREO** SR 90400 |
| **GOLDEN IMPORTS** SRI | | **ALBUM REFERENCE NO.** 44 |
| **COVER ART:** George Maas | | **LINER NOTES:** Stanley Green |
| **ENGINEER:** Red Eberenz | | **TAPE TRANSFER:** John Johnson |
| **RECORDING DATE:** July 9, 1964 | | **PERSONNEL LIST:** |

**PROGRAM**
\* = Premier recording

Jazz Pizzicato +
The Bluebells of Scotland +
Plink, Plank, Plunk +
A Christmas Festival
Jazz Legato +
Chicken Reel +
Promenade +
Suite of Carols [Excerpts]
Song of Jupiter [George F. Handel] +
Pirate Dance
Phantom Regiment +
The First Day of Spring +

**NOTES**

FF: Members of the London Symphony who, though they would accept the date and the money, would not allow the name to appear on the record. See technical data on this and other London sessions on issue #45 "Frederick Fennell Conducts Music by Eric Coates"  + included on Mercury CD  432 013-2, released in 1992.

Recording Director: Harold Lawrence
Recording site: Town Hall, Watford, England
Group not identified. Frederick Fennell Conducting.
Orchestral contract #11.

| | |
|---|---|
| **ALBUM TITLE:** | <u>**Frederick Fennell Conducts Music by Eric Coates**</u> |

**LABEL:** Mercury     **MONO** MG 50439     **STEREO** SR 90439
**GOLDEN IMPORTS** SRI 75109     **ALBUM REFERENCE NO.** 45
**COVER ART:** Joan Stoliar     **LINER NOTES:** Stanley Green
**ENGINEER:** Henri de Fremery/Robert Eberenz     **TAPE TRANSFER:**
**RECORDING DATE:** July 19, 1965     **PERSONNEL LIST:**

### PROGRAM
\* = Premier recording

London Suite: Covent Garden, Westminster, Knightsbridge
Four Ways Suite: Eastwards, Northwards
The Three Elizabeths: Halcyon Days, Springtime in Angus, Youth of Britain

### NOTES

RR: Where was this album recorded, how much rehearsal time?

FF: Town Hall in Watford, England. There was no rehearsal time. Like all London sessions you just start working and the machines are running, then takes are called. We did this in two sessions on the above date and the following day [19-20 July 1965].

RR: Who are the London POPS ?

FF: The London Symphony Orchestra members, allowing their "use" -- just a hint at who they were.

RR: What can you tell me about the recording team?

FF: These were Philips engineers who came with a new "dehydrated" rig so small it fit in a little VW bug. Recording console was "miniature", Schoepps microphones, very straight forward people, like those of the C.R. Fine Studio. The transfer was probably in the Dutch studios. It was a VW bug, not a bus, that carried all the recording/playback equipment !! Things had so positively begun to change -- obviously a transistorized recording board. Being no real celebrity to Philips, they might have been using me and my sessions as guinea pigs. So what! It was an OK record, with which Mercury did absolutely nothing. Recording team included: Henk Jansen, Technical Director; Hans Lautenslager, Mixer; Henri de Fremery, Recording Engineer.

It is not easy to plumb the depths of the record business ... anytime. But this time comes back to me as transitory. Wilma's departure put Harold in charge and he did such a good job under what must have been tough pressure. My London dates used up the contract, kept me from going to any other label. I was not a record artist that Philips probably needed when they purchased Mercury in about 1960; what they did need was a going U.S. distributorship. With the Eastman-Rochester and Eastman Wind Ensemble catalogs they also acquired <u>singular</u> repertory not duplicated on any other label. My hope that they might pick me up with the many British and continental orchestras looking for work vanished when Philips went instead for compatriot Edo de Waart and <u>The Netherlands</u>, and for <u>St. Martin in The Fields</u>, and then for the "original instruments" sequence, which --- and remarkably The Eastman Wind Ensemble's two volume LP set of The Civil War preceded this now so busy "original instrument" scene by about 30 years --- research, instruments, manuscripts, style, historic significance, etc.

In 1965 the Mercury contract expired with my last London/Watford visit for the <u>Coates</u> and <u>Carousel Waltz</u> albums 19-20-21 July '65. I never kidded myself as to who played these sessions; probably being no accountable "maestro" to the mostly back-stands players of the L.S.O., the front players electing to pass. Same downbeat as in Rochester, OK results; nothing spectacular --- no surprise. When Harold Lawrence left Mercury to manage the L.S.O. he surely did his part to bring me for these sessions. When the L.S.O. came to Daytona Beach, FL., August 1968 for The Festival there, it was Alan Jenkins, the tuba player and executive secretary who asked for me as a guest for three concerts. Andre Previn (Chief) and Harold avoided me and my wife, Dorothy professionally and socially during the 10 days we were there, zero sympathy --- no surprise from Andre, if no pleasure, either. Chemistry, Roger is the stuff of the world of performance --- chemistry and respect. When your formula doesn't make it with theirs, there is no place to go; Daytona was the end of me and the L.S.O. for twelve years.

The continuing reward from energy expended where requested, needed, accepted sustains if questions pass across the mind. My energy still bumps the needle to the right. It goes these days to the Tokyo Kosei Windorchestra with which I hope to be until I drop. I'm not so sure they know how fine an ensemble they are.

As for the years of my time with recordings, I know that there are so many people "out there" who these recordings have reached, both by collection and repeated radio play. Sometimes I do meet them at concerts and professional gatherings then they come to say "hello" and "thanks". Many like you, Roger, are professional colleagues, and happily for me your Discography will be my file reference about it all. For those who want/need to know all those precise details which you have so patiently assembled, this book tells that story completely for the past forty-plus years.

Among the many friends who have helped to make it all happen I count David Hall, Bob and Wilma Fine, Harold

Lawrence, Red Eberenz, those great Eastman "kids", Dr. Hanson, Hunsberger, the ladies who married me, Larry Martin, Monte La Bonte, the whole Kosei Windorchestra --- and of course, you. And it all began because David Hall wanted to record the Holst Suites ! [24 July 91 & 12 February 92].

RR: On the lighter side, is there any significance to the pencil sketch of the lion with a baton?

FF: Yes, that's Frederick Fennell ruling Britannia!

Stanley Green also wrote the liner notes for "Broadway Marches" and "Leroy Anderson, III".
The Golden Imports SRI 75109, duplicates both cover and liner notes exactly as original issue.

Recording Director: Harold Lawrence
Musical Supervisor: Harold Lawrence
Recording dates: 19-20 July 1965
Recording Site: Town Hall, Watford, England
Group listed as London POPS Orchestra
Orchestral contract #12.

---

**ALBUM TITLE: Frederick Fennell Conducts Carousel Waltz**

**LABEL:** Mercury  **MONO** MG 50440  **STEREO** SR 90440

**GOLDEN IMPORTS SRI**  **ALBUM REFERENCE NO.** 46

**COVER ART:** Photo by Mary Morris Lawrence  **LINER NOTES:** Stanley Green

**ENGINEER:** Same team as Coates #45  **TAPE TRANSFER:**

**RECORDING DATE:** July 20, 1965  **PERSONNEL LIST:**

---

**PROGRAM**
* = Premier recording

Carousel Waltz - Richard Rodgers, arranged by Mark Walker
Le Cid Ballet - Jules Massenet [excerpts]
Minuet - Giovanni Bolzoni
Henry VIII Dances - Edward German
*Cotillon Suite - Arthur Benjamin
Passo a sei from William Tell - Gioacchino Rossini
Dance of the Tumblers - Nikolay Rimsky-Korsakov

**NOTES**

RR: This is a great photo with the crew cut hair. Who is the photographer?

FF: Mary Morris is the wife of our producer, Harold Lawrence, taken in C.R. Fine Studio, Great Northern Hotel.

RR: Any rehearsal time for this session?

FF: Same as the Coates session. We did these two discs over the three day period, 19-21 July 1965. The machines were running, etc.

RR: An important aside ...

FF: Upon returning to the Shed at Interlochen after these sessions -- that Saturday was the day I ceased to be a smoker. I survived and it stuck.

Stanley Green also wrote the liner notes for Broadway Marches, Eric Coates and Leroy Anderson, Vol. III.

Musical Supervisor: Harold Lawrence
Recording Site: Town Hall, Watford, England
Group listed as London POPS Orchestra
Orchestral contract # 13.

**ALBUM TITLE:** <u>**Fennell Spectacular: Musical Moods of Frederick Fennell**</u>

**LABEL:** Mercury  **MONO** MG 50510  **STEREO** SR 90510

**GOLDEN IMPORTS** SRI  **ALBUM REFERENCE NO.** 47

**COVER ART:** Photo montage - see notes  **LINER NOTES:** Eric Kisch

**ENGINEER:**  **TAPE TRANSFER:**

**RECORDING DATE:**  **PERSONNEL LIST:**

### PROGRAM
\* = Premier recording

**Fennell Symphonic Winds**
  Selections arranged by John Krance
  Seventy-Six Trombones - Meredith Willson
  March of the Siamese Children - Richard Rodgers
  Give My Regards to Broadway - George M. Cohan
  I Ain't Down Yet - Meredith Willson

**Eastman-Rochester POPS Orchestra**
  Andalucia - Ernesto Lecuona
  Belle of the Ball - Leroy Anderson
  Sarabande - Leroy Anderson
  Amparito Roca - Jaime Texidor
  Blue Tango - Leroy Anderson
  Serenata - Leroy Anderson

### NOTES

RR: Are the photos on front from Mercury files?

FF: No, they are by Louis Ouzer, Rochester photographer who took the principal one in rehearsal of the Eastman Chamber Orchestra, July 1953.

Note: Louis Ouzer's book, *Contemporary Musicians in Photographs.* Taken at the Eastman School of Music with text by Francis Crociata. Published by DOVER Publications, New York. 1979.

Leroy Anderson I – conference and adjustment prior to recording. To my left is Bob Fine. Over my right shoulder is concertmaster, Raymond Gniewek.
Photo courtesy of William L. Decker.

| | | | |
|---|---|---|---|
| **ALBUM TITLE:** | *Frederick Fennell Conducts George Gershwin* | | |
| **LABEL:** Mercury | **MONO** PPS 2006 | | **STEREO** PPS 6006 |
| **GOLDEN IMPORTS** SRI 75127 | | **ALBUM REFERENCE NO.** 48 | |
| **COVER ART:** See notes | | **LINER NOTES:** Rayburn Wright | |
| **ENGINEER:** C.R. Fine | | **TAPE TRANSFER:** George Piros | |
| **RECORDING DATE:** September 26, 1960 | | **PERSONNEL LIST:** See notes | |

### PROGRAM
\* = Premier recording

**George Gershwin**
I Got Rhythm - arr. Rayburn Wright
Love Walked In - arr. Dick Lieb
Bidin' My Time - arr. Rayburn Wright
Fascinating Rhythm - arr. Fred Karlin
Embraceable You - arr. Fred Karlin
Someone to Watch Over Me - arr. Rayburn Wright
Love Is Sweeping the Country - arr. Rayburn Wright
'S Wonderful - arr. Dick Lieb
Oh, Lady Be Good - arr. Rayburn Wright
Liza - arr. Rayburn Wright
The Man I Love - arr. Fred Karlin
But Not For Me - arr. Dick Lieb

### NOTES

Arrangements by Rayburn Wright, Fred Karlin and Dick Lieb [see above]
Recording dates: 26-27 September 1960
Liner notes by Rayburn Wright, Frederick Fennell and Edward Jablonski
Cover art by William Auerbach-Levy from LIFE Magazine. Picture of Frederick Fennell on inside cover by Harold Lawrence. FF: Harold took this photo just before the sessions.

PPS on label stands for **Perfect Presence Sound**

Recording Director: Wilma Cozart
Musical Director: Harold Lawrence
Orchestral contract # 7
Recording Site: FF: Ballroom, Great Northern Hotel on 57th Street, southside, between 6th and 7th avenue. Now demolished.
RR: Recording site listed on album as Studio A at Fine Recording Studios in New York City, with a generous volume of 76,000 cubic feet which were ideal for stereo recording techniques.

**Personnel:**
Violins: Eugene Orloff, Eugene Bergen, Peter Dimitriades, Paul Gersham, Harry Glickman, Max Hollander, Herold Kohon, Leo Kruczek, David Nadien, Tosha Samaroff, Julius Schacter, Sylvan Shulman
Violas: Walter Trampler, Sidney Brecher, Morris Sutow, Harry Zaratzian
Cellos: David Soyer, Alan Shulman, Harvey Shapiro, Charles McCracken
Basses: Homer Mensch, Reuben Jamitz
Woodwinds: Julius Baker [flute], Loren Glickman [bassoon], Philip Bodner [saxophone], Romeo Penque, Albert Klink [spelled Albent Klink on album], William Slapin, Harold Feldman [saxophone]
Horns: Fred Klein, Albert Richman
Trumpets: Carl Severinsen, Raymond Crisara, Joseph Wilder, Wilfred Roberts, Jr.
Trombones: Robert Alexander, Charles Small, William Elton, Ziskind Lieb, James Thompson
Tuba: Don Butterfield
Piano: Bernie Leighton, Jascha Zayde
Harp: Janet Remington
Drums: Robert Rosengarden
Percussion: Robert Swan
Guitar: Anthony Mottola

From correspondence dated December 1988: FF: The idea, the push to make the Gershwin - Herbert - Porter records came from Bob and Wilma Fine, he being "fed up with the garbage" being recorded, Wilma wishing to pick up on the absence of Kostelanetz from the scene, both wanting to put together a really quality product. This was all hashed out at a week-end meeting in their beautiful apartment at 1025 Park Avenue - really a home built by Reginald DeKoven. Things

were cooking. I had "The Civil War" on my mind, planning was completed and instruments assembled, so there was lots of room for Gershwin. Rayburn Wright was a camper at Interlochen, came to ESM to study trombone with Emory Remington, was interested in arranging even as a freshman. He did some Bach for me for the Symphony Band. He was with Fred Woolston's Band within the the U.S. Army Band, Washington during WWII, came out as sideman with the Miller Band and did charts for them, then became chief arranger for Radio City Music Hall. Dick Lieb, who was a trombone player at Eastman, and I encouraged his arranging interests by playing anything he brought to me the last ten minutes of Eastman rehearsals. After a hitch in the Air Force out in the field, he became a New York sideman and worked at the Music Hall where Ray was assembling a stable of good writers. The kettledrummer at the Music Hall was Robert L. Swan, also Eastman, and one of my closest friends there. He became contractor for the Hall. So, when Bob and Wilma wanted this record, I told them I wanted Wright, Lieb and Swan. Ray added Fred Karlin. We had a conference on the titles. Ray wanted to write "me" into the arrangements, which I feel they all achieved. Swan delivered the "famous fifty", New York's pros who played all the dates. I saw the scores for the first time in my hotel room the day before the first session. I was gassed by what I saw. The marking was done with a pack of Crayolas I bought at the drug store. All was arranged for stereo and slanted to the particular players like Severinsen, Mottola, Bodner, Alexander. Very Symphonic, lush virtuoso settings. We had decided to incorporate as many verses - and, the introduction to choruses to well known tunes like the masterful introduction Ray wrote for Janet Remington, harpist and daughter of Emory Remington, on *Lady Be Good*. These were her very first commercial sessions, and terrifically played. Dick Lieb's *Love Walked In* is a classic of the arranger's art. Ray's really incredible grasp of everything is present everywhere. He laid out the pace and character so we had the contrasts that are such a part of this very wonderful recording -- A Favorite !!
The playing at the start was just too much. We recorded right away. Ray, Dick [when not playing] and Fred were in the mix/record booth for everything.

RR: Who took care of the commissioning and the fees for these sessions?

FF: Of course, the costs of these sessions with my name on them were advanced by Mercury against my presumed ability to sell the records -- quite a bill !! -- But quite a recording!

Also released on Golden Imports cassette MRI 75127.

Broadway Marches playback. Left to right: John Krance, Harold Lawrence and FF. Photo courtesy of Mary Morris Lawrence.

| | | | |
|---|---|---|---|
| **ALBUM TITLE:** | <u>Frederick Fennell Conducts Victor Herbert</u> | | |
| **LABEL:** Mercury | **MONO** PPS 2007 | | **STEREO** PPS 6007 |
| **GOLDEN IMPORTS** SRI | | **ALBUM REFERENCE NO.** 49 | |
| **COVER ART:** see notes | | **LINER NOTES:** see notes | |
| **ENGINEER:** C.R. Fine | | **TAPE TRANSFER:** George Piros | |
| **RECORDING DATE:** October 4, 1960 | | **PERSONNEL LIST:** | |

## PROGRAM
\* = Premier recording

Victor Herbert - arrangements by Richard Hayman

The Streets of New York
I'm Falling In Love with Someone
Sweethearts
Italian Street Song
A Kiss in the Dark
Thine Alone
Habanera
March of the Toys
Ah, Sweet Mystery of Life
The Irish Have A Great Day Tonight
Romany Life
Kiss Me Again

## NOTES

Recording dates : 4-5 October 1960.

Re-issued in 1964 as Mercury MG 20954 and SR 60954 [album reference 90] with same basic liner notes but omitting the notes on the arrangements by Richard Hayman.
Personnel is similar to that of Gershwin [44 musicians] with a different harpist, different set percussion and Harvey Phillips on tuba.

FF: These were very easy settings and recording was straight forward.

Liner notes by Edward N. Waters, Richard Hayman and Frederick Fennell. Inside the PPS fold-out album contains a photo of Frederick Fennell by Mary Morris, wife of Harold Lawrence, our Musical Supervisor.

The cover illustration is by William Auerbach-Levy of LIFE Magazine.

Recording Director: Wilma Cozart
Musical Supervisor: Harold Lawrence
Recording Site: Studio A at Fine Recording Studios in New York City - [Ballroom of Great Northern Hotel] same as Gershwin.
Orchestral contract #8

| | | |
|---|---|---|
| **ALBUM TITLE:** | *Frederick Fennell Conducts Cole Porter* | |
| **LABEL:** Mercury | **MONO** PPS 2024 | **STEREO** PPS 6024 |
| **GOLDEN IMPORTS** SRI 75110 | | **ALBUM REFERENCE NO.** 50 |
| **COVER ART:** Henry Ries | | **LINER NOTES:** Nat Hentoff |
| **ENGINEER:** C.R. Fine | | **TAPE TRANSFER:** George Piros/John Johnson |
| **RECORDING DATE:** November 20, 1961 | | **PERSONNEL LIST:** |

## PROGRAM
* = Premier recording

Cole Porter - all arrangements by Rayburn Wright

Blow Gabriel Blow
So In Love
It's All Right With Me
Ridin' High
In the Still of the Night
Begin the Beguine
Night and Day
My Heart Belongs to Daddy
Anything Goes
I've Got You Under My Skin
It's Delovely
You'd Be So Nice To Come Home To

## NOTES

RR: Depending on the printing, the inside of fold-out jacket may be in color. The gold label replaces the normal blue of the PPS Series and the label may also contain the 35mm film logo, which was the recording format. The album back contains a seating diagram for the session and other technical information and short biographies of Frederick Fennell and Ray Wright. The cover photo of Fennell seated on a tall stool is by Henry Ries.

FF: Wilma bought me the shirt and blue velvesheen pull-over at Brooks Brothers on the way back to her office after lunch on the 19th. My favorite album. Superb arranging and best in playing.

Personnel as listed on album jacket:
Violins : Eugene Orloff, Eugene Bergen, Peter Dimitriades, Paul Gershman, Harry Glickman, Max Hollander, Leo Kruczek, David Nadien, Tosha Samaroff, Julius Schacter, Sylvan Shulman, Jesse Tyron
Violas: Walter Trampler, Arthur Granick, Ralph Hersh, Morris Sutow
Violoncellos: David Soyer, Seymour Barab, Charles McCracken, Alan Shulman, Marjorie Comstock, Ralph Oxman, Ray Schweitzer, Joseph Tekula, Avron Twerdowsky
Double Basses: Homer Mensch, Reuben Jamitz
French Horns: Albert Richman, Earl Chapin, Ralph Froelich, Richard Berg
Trumpets: Carl Severinsen, Raymond Crisara, Joseph Wilder, Wilfred Roberts
Woodwinds: Philip Bodner, Harvey Estrin, Harold Feldman, Albert Klink, Romeo Penque, William Slapin, Don Hammond, Al Howard
Bassoons: Loren Glickman, Arthur Weisberg
Trombones: Robert Alexander, Charles Small, James Thompson, Eddie Bert, Richard Hixson
Tuba: Don Butterfield
Pianos: Bernie Leighton, Morris Wechsler
Guitar: Mundell Lowe
Harps: Janet Putnam, Gloria Agostini
Percussion: Robert Rosengarden, Edwin Costa, Robert Swan

Recording Dates: 20-21 November 1961.
Recording Director: Wilma Cozart
Musical Supervisor: Harold Lawrence
Recording Site: Bayside Studio in Long Island which was part of the Fine Recording Company
Orchestral contract #9

Kilbourn Hall, University of Rochester, Eastman School of Music
Kilbourn Hall is a chamber music hall. Teak wood and ornate ceiling contribute to the marvelous acoustics. Grand piano, two chairs and lamps I can remember from the first day I went there. Seating capacity is 500.
Debut of Eastman Wind Ensemble was presented in this hall.
When the front row of seats are removed, the pit from which I produced a half-dozen operas was formed.
Built by Mr. Eastman in 1921 as a memorial to his mother, Maria Kilbourn.
Photo courtesy of Louis Ouzer

**ALBUM TITLE:** American Brass Band Journal - Revisited

**LABEL:** Sine Qua Non  **MONO**   **STEREO** SAS 2017

**GOLDEN IMPORTS   SRI**   **ALBUM REFERENCE NO.** 51

**COVER ART:** DAC Design   **LINER NOTES:** Jon Newsom

**ENGINEER:** Roger Byrd   **TAPE TRANSFER:**

**RECORDING DATE:** August 30, 1977   **PERSONNEL LIST:** see notes

## PROGRAM
\* = Premier recording

Music from the John F. Stratton Military Band Series

* You Naughty, Naughty Men Quickstep - G. Bicknell
* Souvenir Polka - Puffhold
* Farewell Waltzes - Joseph Gungl
* Review Quickstep - H.E. Crammatti
* Concertino for E-flat Cornet - Sachse [Rolf Smedvig, soloist]
* Liebling's Polka - Carl Faust
* Liebesgarten Duet - Robert Schumann
* Guard Mounting Quickstep - Henri E. Cramatte
* Adjutant's Call Quickstep - Henri E. Cramatte
* Dolores Schottische - Henry Yaeger
* Liebeshandel Duet - Grabeu-Hoffman
* Amor March - Strauss
* Familien-Gemalde Duet - Robert Schumann
* Frederic March - Joseph Gungl
* Doppelquartett: Auf dem See - Moritz Hauptmann
* Concordia March - Joseph Gungl

## NOTES

Producer: Judith Sherman
Recording dates: 30-31 August 1977
Recording site: Coolidge Auditorium, Library of Congress, Washington, D.C.
Group listed as Empire Brass Quintet and Friends.
First released in 1978

Musical arrangements are available from Sto-Art Publishing Co., Inc. 406 Malborough Street, Boston, MA. 02115
First US recording of above titles. First recording from the Library of Congress. H.E. Crammatti is the same as Henri E. Cramatte.

Personnel:
E-Flat trumpet: Rolf Smedvig, John DeWitt, David Flowers
B-Flat trumpet: David Flowers, Charles Lewis, Adel Sanchez
French Horn: David Ohanian, Edwin Thayer
Trombone: Norman Bolter, James Kraft
Baritone Horn: John Marcellus
Tuba: Samuel Pilafian
Percussion: Kenneth Harbison, Frank Ames

This recording has been issued in two different cassette versions:
[1] American Brass Band Premiers - SineQua Non [Chrome] 79032 [released in 1982] and
[2] Strike Up The Band - SineQua Non 5016-4 [released in 1985].

**ALBUM TITLE:** <u>Our Musical Past - A Concert for Brass Band, Voice and Piano</u>

**LABEL:** Library of Congress  **MONO**      **STEREO** OMP 101-102

**GOLDEN IMPORTS   SRI**     **ALBUM REFERENCE NO.** 52

**COVER ART:** see notes     **LINER NOTES:** Jon Newsom

**ENGINEER:** Library of Congress Staff   **TAPE TRANSFER:**

**RECORDING DATE:** September 27, 1974   **PERSONNEL LIST:** see notes

### PROGRAM
\* = Premier recording

All premier recordings:

Hunter's Chorus from *The Rose of Erin* - Sir Julius Benedict
O Summer Night from *Don Pasquale* - Gaetano Donizetti
Ah! May The Red Rose Live Alway - Stephen Foster
The Herdsman's Mountain Song - Adolf Fredrik Lindblad
Captain Shepherd's Quickstep - Claudio S. Grafulla
Captains Finch's Quickstep - Claudio S. Grafulla
Indiana Polka - Edmund Jaeger, arr. J. Schatzman
Old Memories - Stephen Foster
The Moonbeam Waltzes - Henry Farmer, arr. David L. Downing
La Fontaine - Charles-Samuel Bovy Lysberg
Upon A Summer's Day - Adolf Fredrik Lindblad
Slow March: Midnight - J.M. Noeren, arr. J. Schatzman
General Taylor Storming Monterey - Simon Knaeble
Lilly Bell Quickstep - G.W.E. Friederich
Door Latch Quickstep - George H. Goodwin
The Heart Bow'd Down - Michael William Balfe
Why, No One To Love? - Stephen Foster
Free and Easy - arr. by David L. Downing, ca. 1861

### NOTES

Cover art: "The Palace Garden Polka" by Thomas Baker [1858] Lithograph of Sarony, Major & Knapp, New York. Photos by Jon Newsom.
All music is performed on authentic mid-19th century instruments. Original instruments on loan from the Smithsonian and the private collection of Robert Sheldon, former member of the Eastman Wind Ensemble and formerly on the Smithsonian staff. He is currently curator, The Dayton C. Miller Collection, the Library of Congress. Also available on double cassette with booklet through Audio-Forum of Guilford, Connecticut. and on CD - OMP 101-102 Our Musical Past - Volume I - [1992]

Liner notes contain extensive historical data on early instruments and origin of recorded materials.

Personnel as listed on album jacket:
D-flat piccolo: Thomas Perazzoli
E-flat soprano saxhorn: Adel Sanchez, Lawrence J. Ferris, David M. Flowers
E-flat cornet: George Recker
B-flat cornet: David M. Flowers, G. Harrison Bowling
Trumpet: David M. Flowers
B-flat contralto saxhorn: Robert Brackman
E-flat tenorhorn: Thomas W. Murray, Richard Butler
B-flat tenorhorn: Roberts Isele
B-flat bass [baritone]: John Marcellus
B-flat bass: Robert H. Kraft
E-flat bass [tuba]: David Bragunier, Robert Eliason
Snare drum: James Stutsman
Bass drum: Nancy E. Stutsman
Soprano: Merja Sargon
Piano: Bernard Rose

Concert date: 26 September 1974, Coolidge Auditorium, Library of Congress.
Recording date: 27-28 September 1974
Recording site: Coolidge Auditorium, Library of Congress

**ALBUM TITLE:** <u>Our Musical Past - Volume 2</u>

**LABEL:** Library of Congress   MONO    **STEREO**   CD OMP-103

**GOLDEN IMPORTS   SRI**   **ALBUM REFERENCE NO.** 52a

**COVER ART:**   **LINER NOTES:** see notes

**ENGINEER:**   **TAPE TRANSFER:**

**RECORDING DATE:** May 1, 1984   **PERSONNEL LIST:** Included

### PROGRAM
\* = Premier recording

Two Silent Film Scores

Fall of a Nation - Victor Herbert
Gloria's Romance - Jerome Kern

### NOTES

FF: My favorite in this session is the Entr'acte: The Love Theme by Victor Herbert. A delightful and charming little piece.

Recording date:  1-2 May 1984
Recording site:  Coolidge Auditorium, Library of Congress
Producer:  Jon Newsom
Liner notes for "Fall of a Nation" by Wayne D. Shirley - for "Gloria's Romance" by John McGlinn
Instrumentation and personnel listed in liner notes.
Recording:  Motion Picture, Broadcasting and Recorded Sound Division
  Library of Congress, Washington, D.C.  20540
Also available on single cassette with booklet through Audio-Forum of Guilford, Connecticut.
Group listed as:  MusicCrafters Orchestra

Miscellaneous session – 1960-61. Notice the ensemble is far out
on the pit and the high emptiness of the Eastman Theatre.
Microphones are hung on clothesline, always in the same
position and at the same height from the floor.
Photo courtesy of William L. Decker

| | |
|---|---|
| **ALBUM TITLE:** | **The Cleveland Symphonic Winds** |

**LABEL:** Telarc  **MONO**  **STEREO** DG 5038/DG 10038 [CD]
**GOLDEN IMPORTS   SRI**  **ALBUM REFERENCE NO.** 53
**COVER ART:** Jack Renner  **LINER NOTES:** Frederick Fennell/H.A. Rogers
**ENGINEER:** Jack Renner  **TAPE TRANSFER:** Stan Ricker
**RECORDING DATE:** April 4, 1978  **PERSONNEL LIST:**

### PROGRAM
\* = Premier recording

**The Cleveland Symphonic Winds**
Suite No. 1 in E-flat for Military Band, Op. 28a - Gustav Holst
Suite No. 2 in F for Military Band, Op. 28b - Gustav Holst
Fantasia in G Major - Johann Sebastian Bach, transcription R.F. Goldman/Robert Leist
Music for the Royal Fireworks - George Frederick Handel, ed. Anthony Baines/Charles Mackerras

### NOTES

FF: This is a historic recording. This was the first symphonic recording made with the digital tape recorder in the United States. The bass drum, recorded so well, was an old Ludwig, 38" diameter by 18", very thick and old calf head, one sort of patched at the hoop, mounted on Alan Abel ring. Struck with my personal beater, the wood ball with two chamois, long bamboo handle, struck at optimum point of resonance. Stan Ricker and I chose that and at Stan's request, the bass drum was placed at the center of the set, very center. Its heads, which vibrate side to side, the drum was turned with the heads facing back-to-front to match the vibrating of the microphone diaphragm , so that the heads of the bass drum and the diaphragm of the microphone were in phase. This was Ricker's idea . What we should have had was a cut of the speakers sold to replace those that were blown by this when the owners failed to heed our "Surgeon General's" warning that the sound of the recording could endanger the health of your speakers.

There were no rehearsals, just run through and take. Of course, they played from my meticulously edited parts which were sent in my folders. All the Cleveland orchestra players had to do was open the folders and follow me. The extra players were the Cleveland Orchestra's and the many oboes and bassoons were pupils of the regular players.

Arriving at Severance Hall every early on the first day of recording, the Severance Hall stage manager asked me what kind of set I wanted. I suggested that all he needed to do was to push back all of the chairs for the strings - violins, violas, cellos - push them back to the walls of the permanent set, and to leave the chairs and stands of the winds and percussion as if they were recording the Mahler Eighth. The LP cover includes a photograph of this setting.

Recording dates:  4-5 April 1978.  Digital recording by Soundstream.
Recording site:  Severance Hall, Cleveland, Ohio
Producer:  Robert Woods.
Graphics:  Ray Kirschen Steiner
Jacket photos:  Corby Grubb, Nat Silverman
Digital editor:  Robert Ingebretsen
Digital engineers:  Thomas Stockham, Bruce Rothaar
Issued on Telarc Compact Disc:  CD 80038.  The CD booklet omits all the technical information regarding the digital recording process which is included on the LP versions.

Playback of first digital session. Left to right: Dr. Thomas Stockham, inventor of Soundstream digital recorder; Jack Renner, engineer and Frederick Fennell. Photo courtesy of Telarc International.

# BASIC PERSONNEL

## Cleveland Symphonic Winds
### Frederick Fennell, Conductor

**FLUTE**
Maurice Sharp
Martin Heylman
William Hebert

**PICCOLO**
William Hebert

**OBOE**
John Mack
Felix Kraus
Harvey McGuire
Vance Reger
Linda Strommen
Yvonne Powers
Patricia Grutzmacher
Patricia Taylor

**ENGLISH HORN**
Harvey McGuire

**E-FLAT CLARINET**
Theodore Johnson

**B-FLAT CLARINET**
Franklin Cohen
David Harris
Thomas Peterson *
Angelo Fortini
Joseph Lapinski
Richard Ingersoll

**BASS CLARINET**
Alfred Zetzer

**CONTRA-BASS CLARINET**
Errol Schlabach

**BASSOON**
George Goslee
Vaclav Laksar
Stanley Maret
Matthew Shubin
Britt Hebert
Ronald Phillips *
Lynette Cohen
Janis Jonap
Mark DeMio

**CONTRA-BASSOON**
Stanley Maret

**LIBRARIAN**
Ronald Whitaker

**SAXOPHONE**
Albert Blaser [alto]
Paul Cohen [alto]
Robert Gref [temor]
George Shernit [baritone]

**TRUMPET**
Bernard Adelstein
David Zauder
Charles Couch
James Darling
Robert Dolwick
Stephen Jeandheur

**CORNET**
David Zauder
James Darling
Charles Couch
Michael Suttle

**TROMBONE**
Robert Boyd
William Fay
Edward Zadronzny

**BARITONE**
Allen Kofsky
James DeSano

**HORN**
Richard Solis
Ralph Wagnitz
Albert Schmitter
Ernani Angelucci
Martin Morris

**TUBA**
Ronald Bishop *
John Olah

**STRING CONTRA-BASS**
Irving Nathanson

**TYMPANI**
Cloyd Duff

**PERCUSSION**
Richard Weiner
Robert Matson
Donald Miller
Joseph Adato
David Gooding

* = Former member of Eastman Wind Ensemble

# THE CLEVELAND SYMPHONIC WINDS
## America's Great New Wind Ensemble

### Frederick Fennell

It had been a long time between recording sessions. When Jack Renner and Bob Woods of Cleveland's TELARC RECORDS called to ask if I was interested in an association with them that would offer the winds of the Cleveland Orchestra as the group, I was more than ready to accept. Long known [and personally revered] as one of the great orchestras of the world, I was both grown-man and small-boy excited at the idea of making music with them.

Renner and Woods had gone to Ohio colleges earning degrees instrumental and vocal and both had teaching and professional performance experience. Renner started his personal service recording company in 1962 covering a large area where school and college performing groups awaited his musically-oriented skills as a recording engineer. Woods joined him in 1973 for the expansion that eventually led to the present company.

TELARC's initial thrust into the world of professional super-fi was a well-accepted direct-to-disc recording recently made with the Cleveland Orchestra led by Lorin Maazel, its Music Director and Conductor -- attractively titled DIRECT FROM CLEVELAND [Telarc #5020].

The direct disc process is as old as disc recording itself; it employs the standard micro-groove cutting lathe, the stylus of which receives the recording signal directly and cuts it into the vinyl master which -- as long as production allows it to last -- is then used to press the recordings played on everybody's turntable. Since there is no way to correct or to edit a disc, any mechanical playing error or extraneous noise in the music being recorded causes the entire disc to be scrapped, obliging the artists to start all over again. On occasion the no stop process has probably "scared" artists into delivering exciting performances; but at the dimension of a long-play record, both in time and its staggering costs, direct-to-disc recording is the ultimate form of musical Russian Roulette!

Even so, I felt comfortable in the secure thought that the superb artists who make up the Cleveland Orchestra winds would overcome all hazards. Repertory was settled: two titles I had not previously recorded along with two old and very dear friends. And just when I had accustomed myself to the direct disc idea, Renner and Woods called to say they had decided to abandon it in favor of a real and risky plunge into the use of the computer-based, or digital, tape recorder that had been developed by Dr. Thomas Stockham, Jr.

Stockham had spent some thirty years in the development of the SOUNDSTREAM digital tape recorder in his computer lab in Salt Lake City. One of three such processes known to the world, Stockham's was a proven success to them, and thus Renner, Woods, and their backer decided that it was time to be part of the first real change in the process of recording music since Thomas Edison recited "Mary Had a Little Lamb" into the first recording device a century ago.

I shall leave the finite technical data about digital tape recording to those experts in audio who are so considerate as not to try to tell me how to conduct. For us audio laymen, however, it is a simplicity, of course, to state that the digital tape recorder differs from the magnetic analog machine we know so well in that the digital tape recorder records numbers, not vibrations or "outlines of wave forms." To receive all of the frequencies in the music and to cover the range of its dynamic variation, to accommodate music's two principal properties -- sound and silence -- the computer technology employed by Dr. Stockham's digital tape recorder must sample 640,000 binary digits every second! When this information is played back, the numbers thus encoded "instruct" the playback equipment how to reconstruct the sound. And what is played back on this instruction ignores in the digital process everything that is not a number. This eliminates many of the old tape machine's bugaboos, such as "wow," "flutter," and distortion.

For the sessions, THE CLEVELAND SYMPHONIC WINDS were seated in the fashion I have used since the beginning of the Eastman Wind Ensemble. Their music was delivered to three conventional condenser microphones which fed their signal to a similarly conventional mixing console and then on to the SOUNDSTREAM equipment. Balances, nuances, and dynamics remained in my hands and ears; what you hear is what they played. Once the level check had established that ceiling, no devices stalked our performance.

Standing in front of that marvellous group was a joy. My own parts, critically edited, left nothing to chance and, of course, the players came fully prepared. They also brought along with them the Cleveland Orchestra attitude for what we were doing. Their professional and personal regard for the art and for each other added up to great music making.

We began to record as soon as seating and microphone placement satisfied all in the listening room and after a few minutes of get-acquainted playing. Among those who were listening was the man who would transfer whatever we put on tape to the master disc that either makes or breaks any recording session. This person was that master of the master disc, Stan Ricker, who was on our team by way of his position at Japanese Victor in Hollywood. Stan was very familiar with my end of the Eastman/Mercury series. As a graduate of the University of Kansas in music, he had been an experienced band director until his audio engineering gifts overpowered those pursuits. He also knew all about the remarkable pioneer engineering achievements of the audio genius, C. Robert Fine, who had engineered Mercury Records [and me] to an enviable advanced position in the world of quality recorded sound. The disc masters Ricker subsequently cut for us at the half-speed method are a love labor and a technical/artistic achievement of the first rank.

Representatives of Audio-Technica, who would distribute what I've grown to call DIGITAL/I, were there, too, as were writers from leading record and audio journals.

Stockham's SOUNDSTREAM equipment set out on a table in the listening room consisted of two very innocent-looking oblong objects about the size of two Farkas screw-bell model French horn cases placed one on top of the other. One received the signal from the microphones, encoding it in an ordinary data processor; the second object, placed to the left, decoded what the first had stored when playback was requested. Eventually this decoding process would deliver its reconstruction of the sound to an analog tape that in turn would be edited in the familiar fashion to assemble a master tape, free of the usual hassles, from which the master disc would be cut. Inasmuch as the digital master is never touched, never edited, endless master analog tapes can be made from the digital parent with no disintegration of this remarkable resource.

When we had made the first take, all the principal players joined me for playback in the listening room which was jam-packed by the time producer Bob Woods called for silence. We were all listening to silence and I was concentrating on the forth-coming hiss of the tape that heralds the arrival of analog recorded sound. In the midst of this silence -- suddenly the big G natural that begins the Bach *Fantasia* was coming out of Renner's speakers -- unheralded by hiss! My immediate, unguarded, and out-loud reaction was . . . "Wow!" a favorite expression for great occasions and, in audio parlance, a condition happily absent from the music as it continued to pour out of the speakers.

Reaction at the conclusion was unanimous: we were hearing recorded sound of unprecedented depth, clarity, and volume over the widest frequency range -- and totally without distortion or the wrong kind of wow. I was hearing it there as I had heard it on the Severance Hall stage, hearing it the way the guys had played it. We went back to the stage and did it again, just for luck, and in the four hours that flew by, we proceeded to finish up the Bach and to rehearse and record the two Suites for military band by Gustav Holst.

We all had great fun over the percussion sounds Tom Stockham's SOUNDSTREAM digital recorder had captured, particularly the ultimate sonority of the bass drum, an instrument I've been trying to bring out of the closet ever since my first recording.

We came back to Severance the next afternoon and spent three hours reading-down and recording George Frederick Handel's mighty contribution to wind literature, the Music for the Royal Fireworks. For this, my new entrepreneurs, Renner and Woods, had assembled 8 oboes and 8 bassoons in addition to the brass and percussion. It is difficult to imagine more beautiful and sensitive reed playing or more brilliant, virtuoso brass and percussion performance than one hears from these players.

We hope, for the CLEVELAND SYMPHONIC WINDS and TELARC RECORDS, that this may be but the beginning of what could be a whole new series of recordings of wind music in all its various manifestations. TELARC and the CLEVELAND players have confirmed this positive approach by following our first album with another recorded last December to be called MACHO MARCHES. It was recorded with the identical personnel and system in Severance Hall. There are eleven great ones here, including *Florentiner, Washington Grays, Marche Lorraine, Sea Songs* and *Radetzky*.

Our future depends, of course, on consumer response and thus far, at the premium price demanded by such an expensive undertaking, that has been sufficient to warrant the second album with plans for a third late this year. Critical and technical press response has been all that one could ask. Obviously, this is but the very beginning of the digital/computer/laser era that began in 1877 when bands with their direct "bell-front signal" were the principal recording ensembles, it is an interesting turn of circumstances that finds America's newest wind ensemble making the first symphonic recording in what bids to be known as the digital era of recording's second century.

The recording is available at audio stores and at some record shops. It does not require any new equipment to play it, although it is certain to offer its ultimate fidelity when played on a superior rig. Included under the dust cover is an audio "surgeon general's warning" that playing this recording at flat-response-volume may be dangerous to the health of your speakers -- particularly the woofers. I really hope you will enjoy it in many ways.

May 1978 Frederick Fennell
Unpublished

Close-up of first session in Severance Hall with the Cleveland Symphonic Winds.

Photo courtesy of Telarc International.

First session in Severance Hall. Photo includes three fromer members of the Eastman Wind Ensemble. Tom Peterson, clarinet; Ronald Phillips, bassoon, and Ronald Bishop, tuba.

Photo courtesy of Telarc International.

# HOW TO MAKE AN OFFICIAL BASS DRUM BEATER

## Frederick Fennell

from an interview with Quin Mathews
<u>Fanfare</u>
September-October, 1988

**Fanfare:** Let me ask you about the bass drum. It's become a famous "audiophile" bass drum, the one in the Holst suites. How do you feel about the way it came out?

**Fennell:** Well, it's a Bb bass drum, an ordinary bass drum. It's the one that the Cleveland Orchestra has always been using, all these many years. It had calf heads. It's about a 38-inch to 40-inch drum. Anybody who has that recording [in the LP form] and opens it up will see it at the back of the set. The thing about it, why the sound is so good on that recording is, first of all, I have my own bass drum beater, which is a kind of Irish shillelagh. It's not one of these nonsense powder-puff bass drum beaters that are so popular in Texas and everywhere else, where you're supposed to play bass drum, but nobody's supposed to hear it. That was happening all over the country and annoyed me no end wherever I went. So I carried my own beater with me. And when we got to this situation, Ricker and I spent some time tuning the bass drum with the players of the orchestra just to get the heads the way we thought they should be. Then of course, if you'll notice in that photograph, the bass drum is at the back of the set, and it's in the center of the set, and its heads, which vibrate in and out from having been struck on one side, vibrate in a sympathetic phase with the microphone, instead of jarring at it from some other side. I think it's that -- the position of the heads of the bass drum -- obviously the skill with which it was played, and the guaranteed no-nonsense bass drum beater that I take all around the world with me, which produce the sound -- directly.

**Fanfare:** Now tell me, what is this bass drum beater made of?

**Fennell:** As a matter of fact, it's one of those things that you stumble into. The head of it is a wood furniture ball, like you get in a lumber yard or a hardware store, that is the top ball when you make a set of shelves, with the separators in between. The one on top, you screw that down, and that's what holds your shelves together. I got the furniture ball and tube of epoxy glue. I had just made a whisker pole for the dinghy of my sailboat, and I had a length of bamboo left over, when I had cut the whisker pole to the right size. It's about 20 inches long. It just happened to fit right into the hole of the furniture ball, so I socked it in there, put the glue down, and waited for the next day. I started to hold it in my hand and play like I thought I was playing a bass drum, and I decided not to cut the handle short, which was my original intention. I left the handle long to have gravity on my side. And then I just covered the wood with two coverings of the ordinary chamois that you use to wash your automobile. And that's what the bass drum beater is. My friend Bob Zildjian, the cymbal maker, had given me a small roll of tape left over. I was up at his house playing tennis one summer, up in New Brunswick, and he had some of it left over, and so he gave it to me, and that's what I used to make the handle on the bass drum beater very solid like a tennis racket, so it wouldn't slip out of your hand. Aside from this, that's what that bass drum beater's all about, and that's where the legend grew. It's two things: How I feel about the bass drum, first of all; how Ricker felt about the bass drum, the man who was going to have to cut the master; the bass drum that the Cleveland Orchestra owned; and the bass drum beater. That's the story."

**ALBUM TITLE:** <u>Macho Marches</u>

**LABEL:** Telarc    **MONO**    **STEREO** DG 10043

**GOLDEN IMPORTS    SRI**    **ALBUM REFERENCE NO.** 54

**COVER ART:** see notes    **LINER NOTES:** Frederick Fennell

**ENGINEER:** Jack Renner    **TAPE TRANSFER:** Stan Ricker

**RECORDING DATE:** December 3, 1978    **PERSONNEL LIST:**

### PROGRAM
\* = Premier recording

**Cleveland Symphonic Winds**
  Commando March - Samuel Barber
  *Belgian Paratroopers - Pierre Leemans
  The Florentiner, Op. 214 - Julius Fucik [pronounced - Few Chik]
  *University of Pennsylvania Band March - Roland Seitz
  Barnum and Bailey's Favorite - Karl L. King
  Anchors Aweigh - Alfred Miles/Charles Zimmerman
  *Washington Grays - Claudio S. Grafulla
  Radetzky March - Johann Strauss
  *Sea Songs - Ralph Vaughan Williams
  Marche Lorraine - Louis Ganne
  The Stars and Stripes Forever - John Philip Sousa

### NOTES

The original title, MACHO MARCHES FF: this was my suggestion, that being a big, good word at the time. They [Telarc] got 'concerned' later and changed it.

RR: The album cover was also changed to a solo picture of Frederick Fennell. The original cover was a photo of the United States Marine Band with leader John Philip Sousa, taken during the Marine Band's first Pacific Coast Concert Tour in September, 1891 [courtesy of the American Bandmasters Association Research Center, University of Maryland, College Park, Maryland]. As much as I like the photo of Fennell on the re-issue, the photo of the Marine Band with Sousa made a great cover with historic value.

Recording date: 3 December 1978
Recording site: Severance Hall, Cleveland, Ohio
Jacket design: Timothy V. Hemsoth
Producer: Robert Woods
Digital editors: Jules Bloomenthal, Bob Ingebretsen, Bruce Rothaar, Thomas Stockham, Jim Youngberg
Personnel not listed on album. No photo credits are listed on album.

Seven of the above selections were re-issued on Telarc Compact Disc CD 80099 "Stars and Stripes" in 1984.

RR: When I was ready to purchase a compact disk player, I took this CD as my test. I successfully destroyed two sets of speakers in the audio stores when playing the final cut, "Shepherd's Hey" by Percy Grainger. A great 'test' piece.

The re-issue with the same catalog number keeps the same inside information, minus the MACHO MARCHES title. Both front and back covers have changed. The front is a full-front view of Fennell and the back, of course, is a back view of Fennell in a conducting stance. The record labels still include "Macho Marches". The inside jacket refers to "Classic Marches". All of the great photos are by Joel Marcus.

| ALBUM TITLE: | **The Cleveland Symphonic Winds** | | |
|---|---|---|---|
| **LABEL:** Telarc | **MONO** | **STEREO** | DG 10050 |
| **GOLDEN IMPORTS** SRI | | **ALBUM REFERENCE NO.** 55 | |
| **COVER ART:** Tim Hemsoth | | **LINER NOTES:** Frederick Fennell | |
| **ENGINEER:** Jack Renner | | **TAPE TRANSFER:** Bruce Leek | |
| **RECORDING DATE:** November 18, 1979 | | **PERSONNEL LIST:** | |

## PROGRAM
\* = Premier recording

**Cleveland Symphonic Winds**
  Three Fanfares for Brass and Percussion - Leo Arnaud
  Toccata Marziale - Ralph Vaughan Williams
  Lincolnshire Posy - Percy A. Grainger
  Shepherd's Hey - Percy A. Grainger

## NOTES

Recording date:  18 November 1979
Recording site:  Severance Hall, Cleveland, Ohio
Technical consultant:  Stan Ricker
Producer:  Robert Woods
Digital editing:  Dr. Thomas Stockham, Jules Bloomenthal, Jeff Ostler
Tape transfer:  Bruce Leek
Photography:  Joel Marcus, Don Snyder
Personnel is similar for all three TELARC releases.

Correspondence from Fennell dated 21 November 1979... FF:  I re-recorded the *Posy* last Sunday in Cleveland after much soul searching.  It was very difficult to do when the men -- however great, and they are great, had never played the piece before.  I had to get that, *Shepherd's Hey, Toccata Marziale*, and *Folk Song Suite* rehearsed and recorded in four hours, meaning 160 minutes of working time.  The release is expected as soon as possible, like February. ....  I spent 140 hours editing every bar of every part of *Posy* and I-II-III are finished in my Instrumentalist Series [50 pages typescript].

RR:  All of the above selections were released on Telarc compact disc CD 80099 along with seven selections from the MACHO MARCHES recording.

Percy A. Grainger – 20 February 1957. Inscribed on back: "To Dear Frederick, the perfect conductor and heroic champion of progressive music.  Admiringly from Percy".  Photo courtesy of FF

| ALBUM TITLE: | **The Compositions of Alec Wilder** | | |
|---|---|---|---|
| LABEL: Golden Crest | **MONO** | STEREO | ATH 5070 |
| GOLDEN IMPORTS   SRI | | ALBUM REFERENCE NO. | 56 |
| COVER ART: | | LINER NOTES: | Frederick Fennell/C. Galehouse |
| ENGINEER: Clark Galehouse/Keith Renman | | TAPE TRANSFER: | |
| RECORDING DATE: May 24, 1980 | | PERSONNEL LIST: | |

### PROGRAM
\* = Premier recording

**University of South Florida Wind Ensemble**
  * An Entertainment I
  * Concerto for Euphonium and Wind Ensemble, Brian Bowman, soloist
  * Concerto No. 2 for Trumpet, Flugelhorn and Wind Orchestra, Robert Levy, soloist

Dr. James Croft, Director
Dr. Frederick Fennell, Guest Conductor

### NOTES

One of a series of recordings issued on Golden Crest - THE AUTHENTICATED COMPOSERS SERIES.

No personnel list and no photo credits are listed.

Producer: Mack Wolfson
Recording dates: [listed on album] 24-25 May 1980

RR: Frederick Fennell lists dates of 24-26 May 1980. These are the correct recording dates

Recording site: Tampa Theatre, Tampa, Florida
Mastering & editing: Clark Galehouse and Keith Renman
Group listed as University of South Florida Wind Ensemble
Guest Euphonium soloist: Dr. Brian Bowman
Guest Trumpet soloist: Robert Levy
No cover photo credits.

RR: These premier recordings of the music of Alec Wilder are very important in the documentation of American Wind Music. This series has recently been discontinued as have most of this company's production. A great loss to music education.

| | | |
|---|---|---|
| ALBUM TITLE: | <u>John Philip Sousa on Parade</u> | |
| LABEL: Longines | MONO | STEREO |
| GOLDEN IMPORTS   SRI | | ALBUM REFERENCE NO. 57 |
| COVER ART: | | LINER NOTES: Jeremy Nader |
| ENGINEER: | | TAPE TRANSFER: |
| RECORDING DATE: | | PERSONNEL LIST: |

### PROGRAM
\* = Premier recording

**Eastman Wind Ensemble**

**John Philip Sousa:** Stars and Stripes Forever, King Cotton, New Mexico, Washington Post, Black Horse Troop, Rifle Regiment, Manhattan Beach, U.S. Field Artillery, Sound Off, Glory of the Yankee Navy, Pride of the Wolverines, The National Game, Ancient and Honorable Artillery Company, El Capitan, Nobles of the Mystic Shrine, Kansas Wildcats, Hands Across the Sea, Liberty Bell, Sesquicentennial Exposition, Sabre and Spurs, Gridiron Club, The Invincible Eagle, Our Flirtations, Riders for the Flag, High School Cadets, The Picadore, Golden Jubilee, The Gallant Seventh, The Thunderer

American Patrol - Frank W. Meacham
Thunder and Blazes - Entry of the Gladiators - Julius Fucik
Rolling Thunder - Henry Fillmore
Bones Trombones - Henry Fillmore
Whip and Spur - Thomas S. Allen
The Squealer - Will Huff
The Billboard - John N. Klohr
In Storm and Sunshine - John C. Heed
Robinson's Grand Entree - Karl L. King
Bombasto - Orion R. Farrar
Bravura - Charles E. Duble
On The Mall - Edwin Franko Goldman
Lights Out - Earl E. McCoy
The Screamer - Fred Jewell

### NOTES

This is a recoupling of forty-three of the marches recorded by the Eastman Wind Ensemble. Issued in two different versions by The Longines Symphonette Society.

The first edition, a "Limited Preview Edition", which appears on the front of box, contained the four records [with red labels] listed above. As a special bonus, a single album, "Broadway's Greatest Marches", which is the same as "Broadway Marches" with the Fennell Symphonic Winds [SR 90390].

The second edition was a five record set [black labels] including the bonus as part of the set. Both were very attractive packages with a great graphic of a parade band, and of course, the main focus was a Sousaphone. Both editions also include a short biography of Sousa and a short resume of some of the more familiar marches. A very attractive package and all of this for $11.00.

See entry #63 for contents of "Broadway's Greatest Marches".

| | |
|---|---|
| **ALBUM TITLE:** | **Longines Symphonette Society presents excerpts from Sousa on Parade** |
| **LABEL:** Longines     **MONO** | **STEREO** |
| **GOLDEN IMPORTS**    **SRI** | **ALBUM REFERENCE NO.** 57a |
| **COVER ART:** | **LINER NOTES:** |
| **ENGINEER:** | **TAPE TRANSFER:** |
| **RECORDING DATE:** | **PERSONNEL LIST:** |

### PROGRAM
\* = Premier recording

Eastman Wind Ensemble
Excerpts of ten marches from the five record set

### NOTES

A 7" floppy, one-sided, demonstration disc. "This is merely a demonstration disc, designed to give you a hint of the excitingly romantic sound that awaits you in the full, five record Treasury of JOHN PHILIP SOUSA ON PARADE. Each Gold Medal record in the five-record set is of full-weight, purest vinyl. We invite you to examine the Treasury for 10 days FREE.
LIVING SOUND STEREO *plays equally well on high fidelity, too!*"
This was accompanied with a red and white card-stock order form for the five record set.

| | |
|---|---|
| **ALBUM TITLE:** | **Great Music of the Classical Era** |
| **LABEL:** Mercury     **MONO** MG 50412 | **STEREO** SR 90412 |
| **GOLDEN IMPORTS**    **SRI** | **ALBUM REFERENCE NO.** 58 |
| **COVER ART:** see notes | **LINER NOTES:** Edward Downs |
| **ENGINEER:** | **TAPE TRANSFER:** |
| **RECORDING DATE:** | **PERSONNEL LIST:** |

### PROGRAM
\* = Premier recording

**Eastman Wind Ensemble**
Serenade No. 10 in B-flat Major, K. 361 - Wolfgang Amadeus Mozart

### NOTES

Recoupling of previously issued material.

Cover art: "Study for a Portrait of Mozart" by Joseph Solman

| | |
|---|---|
| **ALBUM TITLE:** Music for Musing | |
| **LABEL:** Mercury   **MONO** | **STEREO** SR 2-9132 |
| **GOLDEN IMPORTS**   SRI | **ALBUM REFERENCE NO.** 59 |
| **COVER ART:** | **LINER NOTES:** Eric Kisch |
| **ENGINEER:** | **TAPE TRANSFER:** |
| **RECORDING DATE:** | **PERSONNEL LIST:** |

**PROGRAM**
\* = Premier recording

**Eastman-Rochester POPS Orchestra**
 Irish Tune from County Derry - Percy A. Grainger
 Clair de lune - Claude Debussy

**NOTES**

A recoupling of earlier recordings.

RR: Two record set. Two different covers exist. The first has a ridiculous picture of an elephant head. The reason escapes me. The second issue has picture of swan on lake -- much more relaxing. No credits are provided on either issue. Inside is different on each, but contain the same liner information.

FF: I never saw this issue and don't have in my collection.

| | |
|---|---|
| **ALBUM TITLE:** Galaxy - Perfect Presence Sound Series | |
| **LABEL:** Mercury   **MONO** PPMD 3-12 | **STEREO** PPSD 3-12 |
| **GOLDEN IMPORTS**   SRI | **ALBUM REFERENCE NO.** 60 |
| **COVER ART:** | **LINER NOTES:** |
| **ENGINEER:** | **TAPE TRANSFER:** |
| **RECORDING DATE:** | **PERSONNEL LIST:** |

**PROGRAM**
\* = Premier recording

**The Frederick Fennell Orchestra**
 Streets of New York - Victor Herbert - from PPS 6007

**NOTES**

A recoupling and sampler album for the PPS series.

| ALBUM TITLE: | **Living Presence Galaxy** | | |
|---|---|---|---|
| LABEL: Mercury | MONO | STEREO | SRD - 10 |
| GOLDEN IMPORTS SRI | | ALBUM REFERENCE NO. | 61 |
| COVER ART: | | LINER NOTES: | |
| ENGINEER: | | TAPE TRANSFER: | |
| RECORDING DATE: | | PERSONNEL LIST: | |

**PROGRAM**
\* = Premier recording

**Eastman Wind Ensemble**
  Golden Jubilee - John Philip Sousa - from "Sousa On Review" SR 90284

**Eastman-Rochester POPS Orchestra**
  Trumpeter's Lullaby - Leroy Anderson - from Volume I SR 90009

**NOTES**

A recoupling and sampler of Mercury Living Presence. "Excerpts from a Decade of Distinguished Recordings 1951-1961."

| ALBUM TITLE: | **Mercury Living Presence High Fidelity Sampler** | | |
|---|---|---|---|
| LABEL: Mercury | MONO OLD - 6 | STEREO | |
| GOLDEN IMPORTS SRI | | ALBUM REFERENCE NO. | 62 |
| COVER ART: | | LINER NOTES: | |
| ENGINEER: | | TAPE TRANSFER: | |
| RECORDING DATE: | | PERSONNEL LIST: | |

**PROGRAM**
\* = Premier recording

**Eastman Symphonic Wind Ensemble**
  March from Suite No. 1 in E-flat for Military Band, Op. 28a - Gustav Holst

**NOTES**

A recoupling and sampler album of Mercury Living Presence Series [issued in mono only].
Picture [front lighted] of crew-cut Fennell. No picture or liner notes credits. List price stated on the album front was 98 cents.

| | | | |
|---|---|---|---|
| **ALBUM TITLE:** | **Broadway's Greatest Marches** | | |
| **LABEL:** Longines | **MONO** | **STEREO** LWS 143 | |
| **GOLDEN IMPORTS** SRI | | **ALBUM REFERENCE NO.** 63 | |
| **COVER ART:** | | **LINER NOTES:** | |
| **ENGINEER:** | | **TAPE TRANSFER:** | |
| **RECORDING DATE:** | | **PERSONNEL LIST:** | |

**PROGRAM**
\* = Premier recording

**Fennell Symphonic Winds**
Same as "Broadway Marches" Mercury SR 90390 with different arrangement of the twelve selections. All arrangements by John Krance.
  There's No Business Like Show Business
  Stouthearted Men
  Wintergreen for President
  Consider Yourself
  Get Me to the Church On Time
  Seventy-Six Trombones
  Strike Up the Band
  March of the Siamese Children
  There Is Nothing Like a Dame
  Give My Regards to Broadway
  Broadway Minstrel Medley
  I Ain't Down Yet

**NOTES**

This is a single issue preview album in conjunction with the Longines Symphonette Society release of the four record set entitled "John Philip Sousa On Parade", featuring Frederick Fennell and the Eastman Wind Ensemble. This single album was later included in a five record set.

| | | | |
|---|---|---|---|
| **ALBUM TITLE:** | **Joseph Wagner Works for Concert Band** | | |
| **LABEL:** Orion | **MONO** | **STEREO** ORS 73118 | |
| **GOLDEN IMPORTS** SRI | | **ALBUM REFERENCE NO.** 64 | |
| **COVER ART:** see notes | | **LINER NOTES:** unknown | |
| **ENGINEER:** | | **TAPE TRANSFER:** | |
| **RECORDING DATE:** | | **PERSONNEL LIST:** | |

**PROGRAM**
\* = Premier recording

**University of Miami Symphonic Wind Ensemble**
  A Festive Fanfare  - Joseph Wagner

**NOTES**

This is a very perplexing issue. The cover depicts a large photo of Joseph Wagner and ensemble photos of the various ensembles represented, including the University of Miami Symphonic Wind Ensemble with Frederick Fennell.

Picture of Fennell and the Miami Symphonic Wind Ensemble is on the cover. No photo or liner note credits. No recording information supplied on the album.

FF: Joseph Wagner was a most enterprising individual and he thought I was worth his time. I can't even remember doing this recording -- ever -- at all. He was such a hell of a promoter. I don't know where he got this. I knew nothing about it.

| | | |
|---|---|---|
| **ALBUM TITLE:** | **Demonstration of 35mm Magnetic Film Recording** | |
| **LABEL:** Mercury | **MONO** | **STEREO** SRD - 15 |
| **GOLDEN IMPORTS   SRI** | | **ALBUM REFERENCE NO.** 65 |
| **COVER ART:** | | **LINER NOTES:** |
| **ENGINEER:** | | **TAPE TRANSFER:** |
| **RECORDING DATE:** | | **PERSONNEL LIST:** |

**PROGRAM**
\* = Premier recording

**Eastman Wind Ensemble**
 Aria della Battaglia [excerpt] Gabrieli - from SR 90245

**Frederick Fennell Orchestra**
 My Heart Belongs to Daddy - Cole Porter - from PPS 6024

**NOTES**

A recoupling and sampler album of Mercury 35mm Magnetic Film recording.

| | | |
|---|---|---|
| **ALBUM TITLE:** | **Remember America** | |
| **LABEL:** Mercury-Wing | **MONO** | **STEREO** SRW 18113 |
| **GOLDEN IMPORTS   SRI** | | **ALBUM REFERENCE NO.** 66 |
| **COVER ART:**   See notes | | **LINER NOTES:**  Lois Hillman |
| **ENGINEER:** | | **TAPE TRANSFER:** |
| **RECORDING DATE:** | | **PERSONNEL LIST:** |

**PROGRAM**
\* = Premier recording

**Eastman Wind Ensemble**
 Yankee Doodle - Traditional
 Star Spangled Banner - John Stafford Smith
 Stars and Stripes Forever - John Philip Sousa
 Battle Hymn of the Republic - William Steffe
 American Patrol - Frank W. Meacham

**NOTES**

A recoupling issued on the 'budget' Mercury WING label. This would have been a great re-issue in 1976 for the Bicentennial.
The cover art is a collection of photos of American landmarks including Mt. Rushmore.
Executive A&R Director: Joseph R. Bott

| ALBUM TITLE: | **Music in Depth** | | |
|---|---|---|---|
| LABEL: Mercury | **MONO** PPMD 4-12 | **STEREO** PPSD 4-12 | |
| GOLDEN IMPORTS  SRI | | ALBUM REFERENCE NO. 67 | |
| COVER ART: | | LINER NOTES: | |
| ENGINEER: | | TAPE TRANSFER: | |
| RECORDING DATE: | | PERSONNEL LIST: | |

**PROGRAM**
\* = Premier recording

**Frederick Fennell Orchestra**
  So In Love - Cole Porter - from PPS 6024

**NOTES**

A recoupling sampler album. The album cover lists *Blow Gabriel Blow*, but the recording contains the above selection.

| ALBUM TITLE: | **Mercury Stereo Sampler  Volume 1** | | |
|---|---|---|---|
| LABEL: Mercury | **MONO** | **STEREO** SRD-1 | |
| GOLDEN IMPORTS  SRI | | ALBUM REFERENCE NO. 68 | |
| COVER ART: | | LINER NOTES: | |
| ENGINEER: | | TAPE TRANSFER: | |
| RECORDING DATE: | | PERSONNEL LIST: | |

**PROGRAM**
\* = Premier recording

**Eastman-Rochester POPS Orchestra**
  Sleigh Ride - Leroy Anderson - from SR 90009

**NOTES**

A recoupling sampler album containing popular, jazz and classical selections.

**ALBUM TITLE:** <u>**BOSE salutes the sound of ... MERCURY RECORDS**</u>

**LABEL:** Mercury Special   **MONO**     **STEREO** MB 1001

**GOLDEN IMPORTS**  SRI     **ALBUM REFERENCE NO.** 69

**COVER ART:**                **LINER NOTES:** Bert Whyte

**ENGINEER:**                 **TAPE TRANSFER:**

**RECORDING DATE:**           **PERSONNEL LIST:**

### PROGRAM
\* = Premier recording

**Eastman Wind Ensemble**
Armenian Dance No. 2 - Aram Khachaturian - from SR 90221
Celebration from Symphonic Songs for Band - Robert Russell Bennett - from SR 90220
Japanese Sword Dance - Bernard Rogers - from SR 90173

### NOTES

A product of Mercury Special Products for the BOSE Corporation. Demonstration record #1 (Classical).

The very interesting liner notes are by Bert Whyte. The selection listing contains a couple of errors. Armenian Dance #2 is listed as being from SR 50221 which is the stereo prefix and the mono number. Celebration by Bennett is listed as coming from Symphonic Dances not Symphonic Songs. Also included in the notes is a letter describing some of the technical aspects of the recording by Mercury Chief Engineer, John Eargle, with special mention of the Bernard Rogers and Robert Russell Bennett selections. It is interesting to note that these are the only two selections to receive such special mention in the letter.

**ALBUM TITLE:** <u>**Royal Pageant**</u>

**LABEL:** Philips          **MONO**     **STEREO** 6570 763

**GOLDEN IMPORTS**  SRI     **ALBUM REFERENCE NO.** 70

**COVER ART:** Keystone Press Photo   **LINER NOTES:**

**ENGINEER:**                **TAPE TRANSFER:**

**RECORDING DATE:**          **PERSONNEL LIST:**

### PROGRAM
\* = Premier recording

**Eastman Wind Ensemble**
Crown Imperial: A Coronation March - William Walton - from SR 90197

### NOTES

Cover photo by Keystone Press depicts a royal parade on horse back. Not a smile to be seen. Even the horses have bowed their heads for this procession.
This was issued in the United Kingdom only for the celebration of the Royal Wedding of Prince Charles and Lady Diane. The selection is followed by an asterisk to indicate this a 'stereo enhanced' version. This was recorded in stereo on SR 90197.

From liner notes ... Dr. Fennell states that for this recording he added to the normal military band score a part played on the large organ in the Eastman Theatre. This is perfectly legitimate, for the original orchestral score includes an organ part in the exciting and triumphant finale.

FF: In correspondence dated 7 August 1982 - I forgot to include this special release last Spring. I was so proud of the old EWE when somebody in Vienna told me he had seen a new recoupling of *Crown Imperial* for the Royal Wedding. When I got to London, it was all sold out at Chappell's. I got my copy courtesy of La Bonte when he went to London and I home. When I got home from Norway, a second copy came anonymously . I'll send it to you when I get home in September.

| | | | |
|---|---|---|---|
| **ALBUM TITLE:** | **Doc Severinsen Plays Modern Trumpet Concertos** | | |
| **LABEL:** Firstline | **MONO** | **STEREO** | FDLP 5002 |
| **GOLDEN IMPORTS** SRI | | **ALBUM REFERENCE NO.** | 71 |
| **COVER ART:** Jeffrey Weisel | | **LINER NOTES:** no credit | |
| **ENGINEER:** Keith Grant/Byron Scott | | **TAPE TRANSFER:** | |
| **RECORDING DATE:** September 26, 1979 | | **PERSONNEL LIST:** | |

### PROGRAM
\* = Premier recording

* Concerto for Trumpet and Orchestra - Allen Vizzutti and Jeff Tyzik
* Concerto No. 2 for Trumpet and Orchestra - Fisher Tull

### NOTES

Recording dates: 26-28 October 1979
Producer: Charles Underwood
Cover photo: Brian Sayer
Recording site: Olympic Studios, Barnes, England
Group listed as: London Symphony Orchestra

RR: The following was received from Frederick Fennell regarding this album. These were written "for Doc's London but did not get printed as part of the liners."

FF: In the late 1950's when The Eastman Wind Ensemble was making its now historic series of recordings for Mercury Records, I had a call one day from Wilma Cozart, its classical vice president asking me to make a fast trip to New York to listen critically on the equipment which we had just used to record the *Hindemith Symphony in B-flat*. It seemed that her husband Robert Fine, our incomparable recording engineer, had detected radio frequency in one of the tapes recorded on the dual machines making reel #1 unusable, but would I come and check out some other matters in the tape on machine #2.

All of the equipment always came to Rochester in Fine's famous truck and was then re-installed in his studios in the old Great Northern Hotel. I *had* to hear the playback *on that same* equipment. His studio was booked solid as usual, but there was tear down/set up time at 4:30 one afternoon. When I came into the control room a pop session was closing down, so we thought, but the conductor wanted a half hour more. I sat and listened. The band was obviously terrific if not all that interested in what was being recorded -- all that is, except for the first trumpet player. He blew everything like it was the greatest piece he'd ever played. I really concentrated on him for the rest of that session. I had hopes of expanding my repertory into the big studio orchestra and he, with no question *had* to be my first trumpet player. We didn't meet but I had no trouble finding out his name -- Carl something. Bob Fine told me he knew how to salvage our Hindemith session so I went back to Rochester.

Three years later that same trumpet player and I [and 49 of his terrific New York buddies] met in that same studio to begin the Mercury Studio Series [*Gershwin, Porter, Herbert, Broadway Marches*] and my friendship with Doc Severinsen began.

Some years later he asked if I could help him with conducting techniques when he knew Johnny Carson was about to announce him as conductor of the band in which he had played since the show's inception. At my home in Miami we worked out a few things for him, mostly to get him to forget about any conducting "problem" and to just continue "to play the trumpet" when he assumed the role of the conductor, using his brain, hands, face and body, when conducting in the same magnificent and incredibly disciplined manner that he had developed for playing his horn. This was achieved quickly when I got him in my pool where we substituted the resistance of the water for that remarkable way he handles the column of air in his instrument. Thus began Doc's career as a conductor and my interest in trying to teach this mostly unteachable art.

Doc has offered to give me trumpet lessons in return, but I'd most likely never find the right mouthpiece, so I'll forget the trumpet and continue to stand to his left when he plays, try to remember what I taught him about conducting, and be forever grateful that I've known and made music with an artist like Doc Severinsen.

### The Tokyo Kosei Windorchestra

## "How it all Began"
Correspondence with Frederick Fennell
Siesta Key, Florida
12 February 1992

The Tokyo Kosei Windorchestra was organized in 1960 as a professional group under the total sponsorship of the lay Buddhist Association, RISSHO KOSEI-KAI. Its 36 all-male, all Japanese members, function as a democratic ensemble; they have an annual contract with customary benefits. The players are in charge of the internal operation of the Orchestra.

During its twelve-month schedule, the Wind Orchestra has become a very busy recording ensemble; it travels the whole of the country as engaged, for special concerts, and it offers clinics of every fashion to the music youth and instructional profession of Japan. Its Tokyo services for the sponsor also include concerts in the city. The personnel is stable, affording a most extensive and ready repertory inclusive of a wide variety of western musical styles. Our 36 contract members are augmented from Tokyo's extensive pool of free-lance players according to the needs of a score.

RISSHO KOSEI-KAI also sponsors a traditional GAGAKU ensemble for the authentic performance of Japan's ancient music and dance while we serve music in the western tradition.

### Basic Instrumentation:

1 piccolo/flute, 1 flute, 1 oboe, 1 bassoon; E-flat clarinet, 6 B-flat/A clarinets, alto clarinet, bass clarinet, E-flat/BB-flat contra-bass clarinet; 4 saxophones [all play all]; 4 horns, 4 soprano brass [play all], 3 trombones, euphonium, 2 tubas, string contra-bass, kettledrums, 2 percussion.

American Day, July 1985. Tokyo Kosei Windorchestra was engaged by the American Embassy for a performance at the Great Japanese Electronics Fair in Tsukuba. We have just performed Copland's Fanfare for the Common Man.
Photo courtesy of Kosei Publishing

| | |
|---|---|
| **ALBUM TITLE:** | **<u>Frederick Fennell Conducts the Tokyo Kosei Wind Orchestra</u>** |

**LABEL:** Kosei  **MONO**    **STEREO** KOR 8130/KOCD 3503

**GOLDEN IMPORTS** SRI   **ALBUM REFERENCE NO.** 72
**COVER ART:** H. Hijikata   **LINER NOTES:** In Japanese
**ENGINEER:** S. Wakabayashi   **TAPE TRANSFER:** S. Wakabayashi
**RECORDING DATE:** March 23, 1982   **PERSONNEL LIST:** not listed

### PROGRAM
\* = Premier recording

The Florentiner March - Julius Fucik, edited by Frederick Fennell
Symphonic Suite - J. Clifton Williams, edited by Frederick Fennell
Symphonic Movement - Vaclav Nelhybel
Suite of Old American Dances - Robert Russell Bennett
Variations on a Korean Folk Song - John Barnes Chance

The following are added on compact disk KOCD 3503

First Suite in E-flat for Military Band, Op. 28a - Gustav Holst
Wedding Dance - Jacques Press, arr. Herbert N. Johnston

### NOTES

This is the first recording by Frederick Fennell with the Tokyo Kosei Windorchestra, which was to lead to his appointment as their first permanent conductor and music director.

FF: In correspondence dated 25 March 1982 ... You will surely have one of the best records I have ever made out of this visit to Tokyo, where the Kosei Windorchestra is totally sensational. We're getting along so well, they play so well, respond so fully, even though I speak NO Japanese ! It is the test of my technique - and it's passing the test! I'm treated like an Emperor here [with clothes -- old] of course, and live in luxury's lap on the 37th floor of a world class hotel facing Mt. Fuji on the horizon.

Recording dates: 23-24 March 1982
Recording site: Fumon Hall, Tokyo, Japan
Group listed as Tokyo Kosei Windorchestra
No personnel listing and liner notes are in Japanese.

I have just concluded, for me at this age, a triumphant performance of Connecticut Half-time, which is the most difficult piece in the rudimental drum repertory. I used my drum and, of course, my first pair of ebony sticks.
Photo courtesy of FF

| | |
|---|---|
| **ALBUM TITLE:** *Fanfare and Allegro* | |
| **LABEL:** Kosei    MONO | **STEREO** KOR 8411/KOCD 2811 |
| **GOLDEN IMPORTS**  SRI | **ALBUM REFERENCE NO.** 73 |
| **COVER ART:** S. Katoh | **LINER NOTES:** Frederick Fennell |
| **ENGINEER:** S. Wakabayashi/J. Itoh | **TAPE TRANSFER:** S. Wakabayashi |
| **RECORDING DATE:** March 24, 1984 | **PERSONNEL LIST:** |

## PROGRAM
\* = Premier recording

Fanfare and Allegro - J. Clifton Williams, edited by Frederick Fennell
Theme and Variations, Op. 43a - Arnold Schoenberg
Toccata Marziale - Ralph Vaughan Williams
Two Chorale Preludes, Opus 122 - Johannes Brahms, trans. Ralph Guenther, edited by Frederick Fennell
  I. Behold, A Rose is Blooming [No. 8], II. O, God, Thou Faithful God [No. 7]
Allerseelen [All Soul's Day] - Richard Strauss, arr. Albert O. Davis, edited by Frederick Fennell
"Elsa's Procession to the Cathedral" from Lohengrin - Richard Wagner, trans. Lucien Cailliet

## NOTES

Also released on compact disc KOCD 2811 with the same selections.

Became the first of 8 issues in the "Heart of the Wind Ensemble" Series by the Tokyo Kosei Windorchestra.

The LP liner notes by Frederick Fennell are printed in both Japanese and English, which is not true on the compact disc, which appear in Japanese only. The liner insert also includes a "physical set-up" of the TOKWO of 50 players. No personnel list is printed. Instrumentation list is included for each selection.

From the LP liner notes: FF: **ABOUT THE WIND ENSEMBLE**
The musical considerations which became my idea that led to the establishment of the Eastman Wind Ensemble in 1952 had been in my mind for many years prior to the founding of that now-legendary group. My musical experiences had been as broad as possible from an early age and the band was just part of a large musical profile. As I began my musical maturity I could see the need for a group that might play the band's literature but which would devote its principal energy to performing only the original works for winds, reducing the players from multiples on a part to one of each in the long-established tradition created by the composers of the orchestra's incomparable music. Wedding the two ideas, the Eastman Wind Ensemble reached back to the beginning of organized instrumental ensembles in the music of Giovanni and Andrea Gabrieli at the end of the 16th century and projected its work to music yet unwritten by principal composers of its day. It is a simple idea whose time has come.

RR: *Giovanni* is misspelled as *Giovannic* on the liner notes. Both LP and CD have a misspelling of Cailliet and the CD has a misspelling of Schoenberg. There is also a great history of the TOKWO included in the LP liner notes along with photos of Fennell and the ensemble in concert pose.

Recording dates: 24-25 March 1984
Recording site: Fumon Hall, Tokyo, Japan
Group listed as Tokyo Kosei Windorchestra
Issue date: 25 May 1984
Producers: S. Ikeda, T. Shibata
Cover photo: Noruyaki Kawamura

| | |
|---|---|
| **ALBUM TITLE:** <u>**Belle of the Ball**</u> | |
| **LABEL:** Kosei    **MONO** | **STEREO**   KOR/KOCD 8412/2812 |
| **GOLDEN IMPORTS   SRI** | **ALBUM REFERENCE NO.**  74 |
| **COVER ART:**   S. Katoh/M. Kajino | **LINER NOTES:**  no credits |
| **ENGINEER:**   S. Wakabayashi/J. Itoh | **TAPE TRANSFER:**  S. Wakabayashi |
| **RECORDING DATE:** December 19, 1984 | **PERSONNEL LIST:** not listed |

## PROGRAM
\* = Premier recording

**All selections by Leroy Anderson**

Belle of the Ball
Summer Skies , trans. Floyd E. Werle
The Penny-Whistle Song
Blue Tango
Bugler's Holiday, trans. M. Edwards
A Trumpeter's Lullaby, arr. Phillip J. Lang
Clarinet Candy
A Christmas Festival
Sleigh Ride
Song of the Bells
The Phantom Regiment
The Syncopated Clock, arr. Phillip J. Lang
The Typewriter, trans. Floyd E. Werle
Home Stretch

## NOTES

FF:  From correspondence dated 14 November 1982 [a postcard packed with the following information] - Get your magnifying glass.  Things are very busy here and my corresponds suffer.  Wish I had time to write you all the titles recorded, but just too busy!  POSY new edition gets what time there is.  Did 26 marches for King records, Sept., will do 32 Leroy Anderson with TOKWO after the Midwest, which attending.  Have signed on for '85 at 8 months.  Going to Australia in January, Sydney only, but hope a day at PAG [Grainger] Museum.  Have traveled extensively in valleys between No. & So. Japan Alps with TOKWO playing school concerts.  The work for sponsor strictly show biz with as much good music as can squeeze in.  They are not much for the 2nd half of 20th century, which I miss. ... Japan musicians are 100% pro; need leadership and they play anything.  Weakness is high brass while low is super.  Top percussion and dizzy fingers reeds.  TOKWO frequently plays with great brilliance, but they have boxed themselves into the trivia corner on repertory and are slaves to "pops".  They will go through big changes all next year.

All compositions by Leroy Anderson with arrangers/transcribers as listed.  Also released on compact disc KOCD 2812 with same selections.
Liner notes printed in both Japanese and English on the LP version only.

Recording date:  19-20 December  1984
Recording site: Fumon Hall, Tokyo, Japan
Issue date: 25 March 1985
Producer: T. Shibata
Cover/Back photos: Noruyaki Kawamura
Heart of the Wind Ensemble Series #2

| | | | |
|---|---|---|---|
| **ALBUM TITLE:** | _Serenata_ | | |
| **LABEL:** Kosei | **MONO** | **STEREO** | KOR/KOCD 8413/2813 |
| **GOLDEN IMPORTS   SRI** | | **ALBUM REFERENCE NO.** 75 | |
| **COVER ART:** S. Katoh | | **LINER NOTES:** not listed | |
| **ENGINEER:** S. Wakabayashi/J. Itoh | | **TAPE TRANSFER:** S. Wakabayashi | |
| **RECORDING DATE:** December 20, 1984 | | **PERSONNEL LIST:** not listed | |

### PROGRAM
\* = Premier recording

**All selections by Leroy Anderson**

Serenata
Forgotten Dreams
China Doll
Sandpaper Ballet
Horse and Buggy
The Bluebells of Scotland
The Waltzing Cat, trans. Phillip J. Lang
The Girl in Satin
The Irish Washerwoman
The Minstrel Boy
The Rakes of Mallow
The Girl I Left Behind me
The Golden Years
Promenade, arr. John Cacavas
Ticonderoga March

### NOTES

All compositions by Leroy Anderson with arrangers/transcribers as listed.  Also released on compact disc KOCD 2813

Liner notes printed in Japanese only.  CD liner notes include list of other Decca/MCA recordings by Leroy Anderson, but no listing of Fennell with the Eastman-Rochester POPS or the London POPS.   LP liner notes include a list of recorded selections by date of composition from 1939 through 1962 with publishers also cited.

Recording dates:  19-20 December 1984
Recording site:  Fumon Hall, Tokyo, Japan
Producer: T. Shibata
Cover/back photographs:  Noruyaki Kawamura
Heart of the Wind Ensemble Series #3

| | | | |
|---|---|---|---|
| **ALBUM TITLE:** | **La Fiesta Mexicana** | | |
| **LABEL:** Kosei | **MONO** | **STEREO** | KOR/KOCD 8414/2814 |
| **GOLDEN IMPORTS** SRI | | **ALBUM REFERENCE NO.** | 76 |
| **COVER ART:** S. Katoh/M. Kajino | | **LINER NOTES:** | |
| **ENGINEER:** S. Wakabayashi/J. Itoh | | **TAPE TRANSFER:** | S. Wakabayashi |
| **RECORDING DATE:** March 19, 1985 | | **PERSONNEL LIST:** | |

### PROGRAM
*\* = Premier recording*

La Boutique Fantasque - Rossini-Respighi, arr. Dan Godfrey
"Danzon" from Fancy Free - Leonard Bernstein, arr. John Krance
* "Rhapsodie" for Wind Orchestra - Yuzo Toyama/Genba Fujita [premier recording for winds]
"La Fiesta Mexicana" A Mexican Folk Song Symphony for Concert Band - H. Owen Reed

### NOTES

Liner notes on LP and CD in Japanese. LP release has English notes on Frederick Fennell and the TOKWO.

This is Frederick Fennell's second recording of selections #1 and #4.

Recording date: 19-20 March 1985
Recording site: Fumon Hall, Tokyo, Japan
Heart of the Wind Ensemble Series #4
Photographs: Noruyaki Kawamura

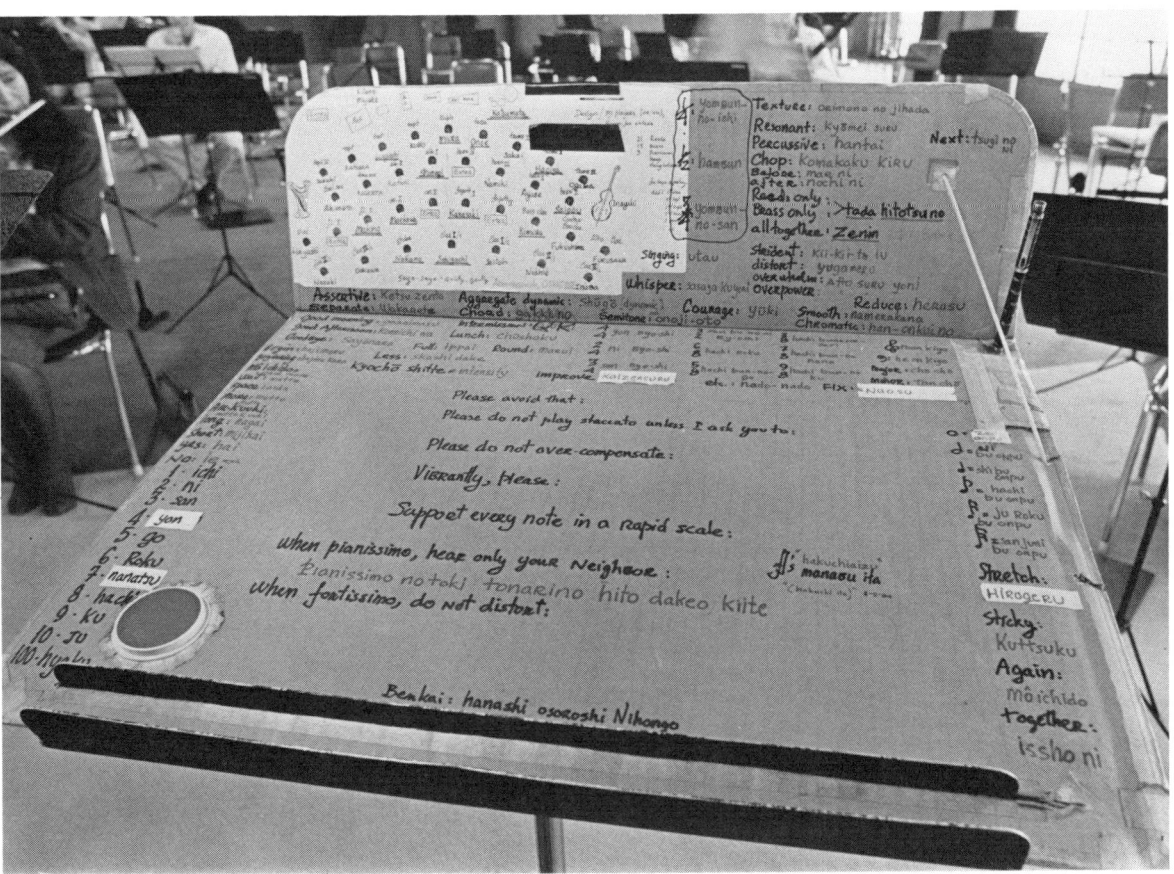

My treasured "idiot board" which got me through the first few weeks in 1984.
Shows placement, musician names and various terms in Japanese.
Photo courtesy of FF

| | |
|---|---|
| **ALBUM TITLE:** | **American March Forever** |
| **LABEL:** Firebird  **MONO** | **STEREO** K28C 405 |
| **GOLDEN IMPORTS  SRI** | **ALBUM REFERENCE NO.** 77 |
| **COVER ART:** Yoshio Shiraki | **LINER NOTES:** In Japanese |
| **ENGINEER:** Hatsuro Takanami | **TAPE TRANSFER:** Akira Makino |
| **RECORDING DATE:** September 28, 1984 | **PERSONNEL LIST:** |

### PROGRAM
\* = Premier recording

The Stars and Stripes Forever - John Philip Sousa, edited by Frederick Fennell
National Emblem - Edwin E. Bagley, edited by Frederick Fennell
The Fairest of the Fair - John Philip Sousa, edited by Frederick Fennell
Bugles and Drums - Edwin Franko Goldman
Our Director - Frederick E. Bigelow
Manhattan Beach - John Philip Sousa, edited by Frederick Fennell
On The Mall - Edwin Franko Goldman
Lights Out - Earl E. McCoy, arr. by A. Roth
King Cotton - John Philip Sousa, edited by Frederick Fennell
Barnum and Bailey's Favorite - Karl L. King
Semper Fidelis - John Philip Sousa, edited by Frederick Fennell
Washington Grays - Claudio S. Grafulla, re-arranged by G.H. Reeves, edited by Frederick Fennell
His Honor - Henry Fillmore, edited by Frederick Fennell
The U.S. Field Artillery - John Philip Sousa, arr. by Mayhew L. Lake, edited by Frederick Fennell

### NOTES

Released under other title "Greatest American Marches"

FF: I edited all of the titles, published or not! Distributed by KING RECORD CO, LTD. Japan, who also released the EWE Mercury's in Japan for Philips.

Recording date: 28-29 September 1984
Recording site: Iruma - Shi Shiminkaikan
Producer: Motohiko Takawa
Director: Katsuhiko Nishida
Assistant Engineer: Seiji Kaneko
Released on LP and cassette: 21 February 1985 [Cassette K28W-5045]
Released on compact disc: 5 April 1985 [CD K33Y-113]

Hokkaido – September 1985. A restful day walking in a white birch grove. Photo courtesy of Kosei Publishing

| | |
|---|---|
| **ALBUM TITLE:** **Contest Band Music Selections 1984** | |
| **LABEL:** CBS Sony      **MONO** | **STEREO**  25 AG 967 |
| **GOLDEN IMPORTS    SRI** | **ALBUM REFERENCE NO.**  78 |
| **COVER ART:**  Hisaji Kusunoki | **LINER NOTES:** |
| **ENGINEER:**  Kenichi Handa | **TAPE TRANSFER:** |
| **RECORDING DATE:** February 22, 1984 | **PERSONNEL LIST:** |

### PROGRAM
*= Premier recording*

Appalachian Overture for Band - James Barnes
Majestia - James Swearingen
Symphonic Sketches for Band - Elliot A. Del Borgo
Viva Musica [A Concert Overture for Winds] - Alfred Reed
Flourishes - W. Francis McBeth
Moorside Suite - Gustav Holst, arr. by Denis Wright
Fox River Festival - James Curnow

### NOTES

Recording date: 22 February 1984 [11:00 - 18:00]
Rehearsals: 20-21 February 1984 [10:30 - 15:30]
Recording site: Asaka Citizen Hall
Producer: Tomohiko Asaka
Issue date: 21 April 1984
Concert Master: Hitoshi Sekiguchi

| | |
|---|---|
| **ALBUM TITLE:** **Band Series 1984 - I** | |
| **LABEL:** King      **MONO** | **STEREO**  CNT 1049 |
| **GOLDEN IMPORTS    SRI** | **ALBUM REFERENCE NO.**  79 |
| **COVER ART:**  Makoto Hiraishi | **LINER NOTES:** |
| **ENGINEER:**  Hatsuro Takanami | **TAPE TRANSFER:** |
| **RECORDING DATE:** February 28, 1984 | **PERSONNEL LIST:** |

### PROGRAM
*= Premier recording*

Americans We - Henry Fillmore, edited by Frederick Fennell
Toccata - Girolamo Frescobaldi, arr. by Earl Slocum
Geschwindmarsch by Beethoven [Paraphrase from the "Symphonia Serena"] - Paul Hindemith, arr by Juan V. MasQuiles
Sarabande and Polka - Malcolm Arnold, arr. John P. Paynter
Chorale and Alleluia - Howard Hanson
Five Waltzes - Carl Maria von Weber, arr. Bram Wiggins
Cordoba - Isaac Albeniz
Holiday - Clare Grundman

### NOTES

Issued by Buffet Crampon in cassette version only.
Rehearsal dates: 24-25 February 1984 [10:30 - 15:30]
   25 February 1984 [16:30 - 20:30] and 27 February 1984 [10:30 - 15:30]
Recording dates: 28-29 February 1984 [11:00 - 18:00]
Recording site: Urayasu Culture Hall.  Recorded by King Record Co., LTD.
Concert Master:  Hitoshi Sekiguchi

**ALBUM TITLE: Band Series 1984 - II**

**LABEL:** King     **MONO**     **STEREO** CNT 1050

**GOLDEN IMPORTS** SRI     **ALBUM REFERENCE NO.** 80

**COVER ART:** Makoto Hiraishi     **LINER NOTES:** None

**ENGINEER:** Hatsuro Takanami     **TAPE TRANSFER:** Cassette only

**RECORDING DATE:** February 29, 1984     **PERSONNEL LIST:**

### PROGRAM
*\* = Premier recording*

Water Music Suite - George Frederick Handel, arr. by Hershey Kay
Night Vigil, Opus 66 - Martin Mailman
Military Escort March - Harold Bennett, edited by Frederick Fennell
Le Chant de L'arbe - Serge Lancen
Symphonic Dances III - Serge Rachmaninoff, arr. Masato Satoh

### NOTES

See entry 79 [Band Series 1984 - I] for rehearsal and recording dates. Both of these issues were done in the same rehearsals and recording session.
Recording site: Urayasu Culture Hall
Concert Master: Hitoshi Sekiguchi
Producer: Katsuhiko Nishida
Recorded by: King Record Co., LTD.
Issued by Buffet-Crampon in cassette version only.

West Coast Conducting Symposium, 1977. FF with Terry
Summa of Foothill College, California.
Photo courtesy of Monte LaBonte

**ALBUM TITLE:** <u>The Best European Marches</u>

**LABEL:** King    **MONO**    **STEREO** K28C 438 [LP]

**GOLDEN IMPORTS  SRI**    **ALBUM REFERENCE NO.** 81

**COVER ART:** Wazumi Sakaguchi    **LINER NOTES:**

**ENGINEER:** Hatsuro Takanami    **TAPE TRANSFER:**

**RECORDING DATE:** September 28, 1984    **PERSONNEL LIST:**

### PROGRAM
\* = Premier recording

Marche Lorraine - Louis Ganne
Father of Victory - Louis Ganne
Norwegian March "Valdres" - Johannes Hanssen, arr Glenn C. Bainum
Wien Bleibt Wien - Joseph Schrammel
With Sword and Lance - Hermann Starke
Colonel Bogey - Kenneth J. Alford
Under the Double Eagle - Josef F. Wagner
Florentiner March - Julius Fucik
Le Regiment de Sambre e Muse - J.F. Rauski
Amparito Roca - Jaime Texidor
Little English Girl - Davide Delle Cese
Old Comrades - Carl Teike

### NOTES

Recording dates: 28-29 September 1984
Recording times: 11:00 - 17:00 each day
Producer: Motohiko Takawa, Katsuhiki Nishida
Recording site: Iruma-shi-Shimin Kaikan
Concert Master: Hitoshi Sekiguchi
Photographer: Michio Mikami

Also released on compact disc K33Y 164
Issue date for both LP and CD: 21 October 1985


**ALBUM TITLE:** <u>A Miracle in Sound</u>

**LABEL:** Mercury    **MONO**    **STEREO** SRD - 3

**GOLDEN IMPORTS  SRI**    **ALBUM REFERENCE NO.** 82

**COVER ART:**    **LINER NOTES:**

**ENGINEER:**    **TAPE TRANSFER:**

**RECORDING DATE:**    **PERSONNEL LIST:**

### PROGRAM
\* = Premier recording

**Eastman Wind Ensemble**
  Lisbon Bay from Lincolnshire Posy - Percy A. Grainger - from SR 90173

### NOTES

A recoupling and sampler album.

| | | |
|---|---|---|
| **ALBUM TITLE:** | **Stars and Stripes Forever - Music of John Philip Sousa** | |
| **LABEL:** Mercury CD | **MONO** | **STEREO** 416147-2 |
| **GOLDEN IMPORTS   SRI** | | **ALBUM REFERENCE NO.** 83 |
| **COVER ART:** Paco North, photographer | | **LINER NOTES:** Eric Kisch |
| **ENGINEER:** | | **TAPE TRANSFER:** |
| **RECORDING DATE:** | | **PERSONNEL LIST:** |

**PROGRAM**
\* = Premier recording

**Marches of John Philip Sousa**

The Liberty Bell, The National Game, The Gridiron Club, The Glory of the Yankee Navy, Manhattan Beach, The Kansas Wildcats, Hands Across the Sea, Riders for the Flag, The High School Cadets, Sabre and Spurs, Bullets and Bayonets, The Picadore, Sound Off, The Invincible Eagle, The Rifle Regiment, The Pride of the Wolverines, Stars and Stripes Forever, King Cotton, The Washington Post, The Thunderer, U.S. Field Artillery and El Capitan

**NOTES**

See notes on album 101 of the same title.

22 of the 31 Sousa marches on 101 are included in this one disc set. Liner notes are slightly abbreviated from the 2 LP set. Photo of Sousa is replaced by a close-up of a much older Sousa. All other information regarding 101 applies to this release.

| | | |
|---|---|---|
| **ALBUM TITLE:** | **CBDNA 19th National Conference** | |
| **LABEL:** Crest | **MONO** | **STEREO** CBDNA 77-4 |
| **GOLDEN IMPORTS   SRI** | | **ALBUM REFERENCE NO.** 84 |
| **COVER ART:** | | **LINER NOTES:** |
| **ENGINEER:** | | **TAPE TRANSFER:** |
| **RECORDING DATE:** March 9, 1977 | | **PERSONNEL LIST:** |

**PROGRAM**
\* = Premier recording

Drei Lustige Marsche, Op. 44 [Three Merry Marches] - Ernst Krenek
Hill-Song No. 2 - Percy A. Grainger

**NOTES**

Donald Hunsberger conducts:
Music With Sculpture - Toshiro Mayazumi
Evostrata - Keith Foley
La Fiesta Mexicana - H. Owen Reed
... and the mountains rising nowhere - Joseph Schwantner

Recording dates: 9-11 March 1977
Recording site: University of Maryland
Group listed as Eastman Wind Ensemble

| | |
|---|---|
| **ALBUM TITLE:** | **The Cleveland Symphonic Winds** |

**LABEL:** Telarc CD   **MONO**    **STEREO** CD 80038

**GOLDEN IMPORTS  SRI**    **ALBUM REFERENCE NO.** 85

**COVER ART:** Ray Kirschensteiner    **LINER NOTES:** Frederick Fennell

**ENGINEER:** Jack Renner    **TAPE TRANSFER:**

**RECORDING DATE:**    **PERSONNEL LIST:**

**PROGRAM**
\* = Premier recording

First Suite in E-Flat, Op. 28, No. 1 - Gustav Holst
Second Suite in F, Op. 28, No. 2 - Gustav Holst
Fantasia in G Major - Johann Sebastian Bach, transcription R.F. Goldman/Robert Leist
Music for The Royal Fireworks - George Frederick Handel, arr. Anthony Baines & Charles Mackerras

**NOTES**

Recorded in Severance Hall, Cleveland
Recording dates: 4-5 April 1978
Producer: Robert Woods
Recorder: Soundstream Digital Tape Recorder - See album #53

No personnel listing.. See listing of personnel on album #53.
All selections previously released on Telarc Digital LP

---

**ALBUM TITLE:** **Stars and Stripes**

**LABEL:** Telarc CD   **MONO**    **STEREO** CD 80099

**GOLDEN IMPORTS  SRI**    **ALBUM REFERENCE NO.** 86

**COVER ART:** Ray Kirschensteiner    **LINER NOTES:** Frederick Fennell

**ENGINEER:** Jack Renner    **TAPE TRANSFER:**

**RECORDING DATE:**    **PERSONNEL LIST:** Not listed

**PROGRAM**
\* = Premier recording

Three Fanfares - Leo Arnaud
Commando March - Samuel Barber
Belgian Paratroopers - Pierre Leemans
Florentiner, Op. 214 - Julius Fucik
Barnum and Bailey's Favorite - Karl King
Anchors Aweigh - Charles Zimmerman & Alfred Miles
Radetzky March - Johann Strauss
Sea Songs - Ralph Vaughan Williams
The Stars and Stripes Forever - John Philip Sousa
English Folk Song Suite - Ralph Vaughan Williams
Lincolnshire Posy - Percy A. Grainger
Shepherd's Hey - Percy A. Grainger

**NOTES**

A re-issue Compact Disc of material from Telarc digital LP's 10038 and 10043. All recording specs are the same.
Recorded in Severance Hall, Cleveland, Ohio on 3 December 1978 and 18 November 1979.
Producer: Robert Woods
Editor: Elaine Martone

**ALBUM TITLE:** Telarc Sampler Volume 2

**LABEL:** Telarc CD     MONO     **STEREO** CD 80102

**GOLDEN IMPORTS** SRI     **ALBUM REFERENCE NO.** 87

**COVER ART:**     **LINER NOTES:**

**ENGINEER:**     **TAPE TRANSFER:**

**RECORDING DATE:**     **PERSONNEL LIST:**

**PROGRAM**
\* = Premier recording

Olympic Fanfare - Leo Arnaud

**NOTES**

Sampler selection of :57 seconds from issue #55 Telarc DG 10050.
All specs the same. Cover art not worth mentioning.

---

**ALBUM TITLE:** Telarc Sampler Volume 5

**LABEL:** Telarc CD     MONO     **STEREO** CD 80105

**GOLDEN IMPORTS** SRI     **ALBUM REFERENCE NO.** 88

**COVER ART:**     **LINER NOTES:**

**ENGINEER:**     **TAPE TRANSFER:**

**RECORDING DATE:**     **PERSONNEL LIST:**

**PROGRAM**
\* = Premier recording

Stars and Stripes Forever - John Philip Sousa

**NOTES**

Sampler selection of 3:35 from Telarc CD "Stars and Stripes Forever" 80099
All specs the same. Cover shows original cover of CD release.

| | | | |
|---|---|---|---|
| **ALBUM TITLE:** | **Frederick Fennell Conducts Victor Herbert** | | |
| **LABEL:** Mercury | **MONO** MG 20954 | **STEREO** SR 60954 | |
| **GOLDEN IMPORTS** SRI | | **ALBUM REFERENCE NO.** 90 | |
| **COVER ART:** | | **LINER NOTES:** Edward N. Waters/F. Fennell | |
| **ENGINEER:** | | **TAPE TRANSFER:** | |
| **RECORDING DATE:** | | **PERSONNEL LIST:** | |

## PROGRAM
\* = Premier recording

**All selections by Victor Herbert** [all arrangements by Richard Hayman]

Italian Street Song
The Irish Have A Great Day Tonight
A Kiss in the Dark
Romany Life
Thine Alone
Kiss Me Again
Streets of New York
Habanera
I'm Falling In Love With Someone
March of the Toys
Sweethearts
Ah, Sweet Mystery of Life

## NOTES

Re-issue of PPS 6007 - same selections - different arrangement of sides [see album # 49]

Different Mercury series 20000/60000 Definitely intended for a different type of listening audience than would purchase the "Audio" PPS series.

No personnel. Liner notes condensed from the original issue. No foldout cover as in the PPS series. The caricature of Victor Herbert has been reversed and reduced in size and placed next to the selection listing.

Picture of "Romantic Couple" on cover which is printed by Wayne Printing Corporation, 1964

| | |
|---|---|
| **ALBUM TITLE:** <u>American Music Spectacular</u> | |
| **LABEL:** Reader's Digest    MONO | **STEREO** RDA 236A |
| **GOLDEN IMPORTS    SRI** | **ALBUM REFERENCE NO.** 91 |
| **COVER ART:** | **LINER NOTES:** |
| **ENGINEER:** | **TAPE TRANSFER:** |
| **RECORDING DATE:** | **PERSONNEL LIST:** |

**PROGRAM**
\* = Premier recording

**Eastman Wind Ensemble [see notes]**

El Capitan - John Philip Sousa
The Washington Post - John Philip Sousa
American Patrol - Frank W. Meacham

**NOTES**

Group listed as "Frederic Fennell and the Eastman Symphonic Woodwind Ensemble"
Cover graphics of Golden Gate Bridge with fireworks

RR: One would think that an organization as large as Reader's Digest would do complete editing and double check all titles, spellings, references, etc.

FF: Amen!

Frederick Fennell in his study – Taiyoso, Tokyo, Japan – 1985
Photo courtesy of FF

| | | | |
|---|---|---|---|
| ALBUM TITLE: | **Life History of the United States -- The Sounds of History** | | |
| LABEL: | MONO | | STEREO |
| GOLDEN IMPORTS  SRI | | ALBUM REFERENCE NO. 92 | |
| COVER ART: | | LINER NOTES: | |
| ENGINEER: | | TAPE TRANSFER: | |
| RECORDING DATE: | | PERSONNEL LIST: | |

### PROGRAM
\* = Premier recording

**Eastman Wind Ensemble**

The White Cockade
Dixie
The Bonnie Blue Flag
Bugles and Drums
Fifes and Drums
Bugle Ensemble
Semper Fidelis
El Capitan
The Washington Post March

### NOTES

Issued in conjunction with the LIFE "History of the United States ". The recordings accompanied a twelve volume set of books. Original covers of the books were light tan to match the recordings. Second issue of books was a padded maroon. The recordings include famous speeches and representative music from the various eras, up through 1945.

Selections by the Eastman Wind Ensemble are included on:

**Volume 2**: "The Making of A Nation"
 The White Cockade [MG 50111]
**Volume 5**: "The Union Sundered"
 Dixie, The Bonnie Blue Flag [LPS 2-901]
**Volume 6**: "The Union Restored"
 Bugles and Drums, Fifes and Drums, Bugle Ensemble [LPS 2-901]
**Volume 7**: "The Age of Steel and Steam
 Semper Fidelis [MG 50080]
**Volume 8**: "Reaching For Empire"
 El Capitan, The Washington Post [MG 50080]

Produced by Time-Life, 1963-1964
Music Editor: Virgil Thomson

| ALBUM TITLE: | **Galaxy 30 - A Galaxy of Mercury Greats !** | |
|---|---|---|
| **LABEL:** Mercury | **MONO** MGD 2-13 | **STEREO** |
| **GOLDEN IMPORTS** SRI | | **ALBUM REFERENCE NO.** 93 |
| **COVER ART:** | | **LINER NOTES:** |
| **ENGINEER:** | | **TAPE TRANSFER:** |
| **RECORDING DATE:** | | **PERSONNEL LIST:** |

**PROGRAM**
\* = Premier recording

**Eastman Wind Ensemble**
Manhattan Beach - John Philip Sousa - from SR 90284

**NOTES**

A recoupling sampler album featuring 30 Mercury artists including Cugat, Patti Page, Dinah Washington, Sarah Vaughan, Quincy Jones, Byron Janis, Antal Dorati, Paul Paray, Howard Hanson and Frederick Fennell.

| ALBUM TITLE: | **The Civil War - Dealer Demonstration Record** | |
|---|---|---|
| **LABEL:** Mercury | **MONO** | **STEREO** LPSD - 1 |
| **GOLDEN IMPORTS** SRI | | **ALBUM REFERENCE NO.** 94 |
| **COVER ART:** see notes | | **LINER NOTES:** |
| **ENGINEER:** | | **TAPE TRANSFER:** |
| **RECORDING DATE:** | | **PERSONNEL LIST:** |

**PROGRAM**
\* = Premier recording

Selections from Volume I & II of Civil War 4-record set.

**NOTES**

This is a very unusual album. A **one-sided** Dealer Demonstration Record. It is marked DEALER DEMONSTRATION RECORD - NOT FOR SALE along the front and back cover. The photo from the Volume I issue is reproduced in black and white on the cover.

An unidentified narrator leads you through the various sounds and the making of this historic album. There are a couple of interviews and excerpts from the recording session with voice of Frederick Fennell discussing the process of the rehearsal and recording of album.

| ALBUM TITLE: | **Music to Live By** | | |
|---|---|---|---|
| **LABEL:** Mercury | **MONO** PJC - 1 | | **STEREO** |
| **GOLDEN IMPORTS**   **SRI** | | **ALBUM REFERENCE NO.** 95 | |
| **COVER ART:**   see notes | | **LINER NOTES:** | |
| **ENGINEER:** | | **TAPE TRANSFER:** | |
| **RECORDING DATE:** | | **PERSONNEL LIST:** | |

**PROGRAM**
\* = Premier recording

**Eastman Symphonic Wind Ensemble**
U.S. Field Artillery March  - John Philip Sousa - from MG 50105

**NOTES**

A recoupling and sampler album containing Mercury jazz, popular and classical selections. The classical side [B] is listed as Mercury Living Presence High Fidelity Showcase.

The cover photo is purely posed. A family, father in tie and suit, mother seated next to father, young boy in slacks, shirt and vest, daughter looking at deluxe Mercury release of "The Sleeping Beauty". List price of this demo disk is "$1.29 tax included".

| ALBUM TITLE: | **Promo Recording No. 1** | | |
|---|---|---|---|
| **LABEL:** Sam Fox | **MONO** | | **STEREO** 7-33-8 |
| **GOLDEN IMPORTS**   **SRI** | | **ALBUM REFERENCE NO.** 96 | |
| **COVER ART:** | | **LINER NOTES:** | |
| **ENGINEER:** Bobby Dukoff | | **TAPE TRANSFER:** | |
| **RECORDING DATE:** June 3, 1967 | | **PERSONNEL LIST:** | |

**PROGRAM**
\* = Premier recording

Invocation of Alberich from "Das Rheingold" - Richard Wagner, arr. Lucien Cailliet
Air Alsacien from "Scenes Alsaciennes" - Jules Massenet, arr. Frank Erickson
Symphonic Dance #3 - "Fiesta" - J. Clifton Williams

**NOTES**

The ubiquitous 7" stiff vinyl "promo" records from the publisher.
Group listed as University of Miami Wind Ensemble, Frederick Fennell, Conductor
Recording site: Criteria Studio, Miami, Florida
Recording date: 3 June 1967
Engineer: Bobby Dukoff
Produced by Alfred Reed

**ALBUM TITLE: Promo Recording No. 2**

**LABEL:** Sam Fox          **MONO**                    **STEREO** 7-33-9

**GOLDEN IMPORTS     SRI**                              **ALBUM REFERENCE NO.** 97

**COVER ART:**                                          **LINER NOTES:**

**ENGINEER:**                                           **TAPE TRANSFER:**

**RECORDING DATE:**                                     **PERSONNEL LIST:**

### PROGRAM
* = Premier recording

Symphonic Dance #2 "The Maskers" - J. Clifton Williams
Minnesota March - John Philip Sousa
The Kadiddlehopper March - Red Skelton, arr. Ron Roullier
Stornello - Giuseppi Verdi, arr. Frank Erickson

### NOTES

Another of those ubiquitous 7" stiff vinyl "promo" records
Group listed as University of Miami Wind Ensemble, Frederick Fennell, Conductor
Recording Site:
Recording Date:
Engineer:
Produced by Ralph Satz

**ALBUM TITLE: Promo Recording No. 3**

**LABEL:** Sam Fox          **MONO**                    **STEREO** 7-33-13

**GOLDEN IMPORTS     SRI**                              **ALBUM REFERENCE NO.** 97a

**COVER ART:**                                          **LINER NOTES:**

**ENGINEER:** Mack Emmerman                             **TAPE TRANSFER:**

**RECORDING DATE:** May 12, 1970                        **PERSONNEL LIST:**

### PROGRAM
* = Premier recording

In Dulci Jubilo - Alfred Reed
Trail Scenes - J. Clifton Williams
New Mexico March - John Philip Sousa

### NOTES

Another 7" "promo" records
Group listed as University of Miami Wind Ensemble, Frederick Fennell, Conductor
Recording Site: Criteria Studios, Miami Beach, Florida
Recording Date: 12 May 1970
Engineer: Mack Emmerman
Produced by Ralph Satz

| ALBUM TITLE: | **Wagner - Coates - Prokofiev** | | |
|---|---|---|---|
| LABEL: Japanese Philips | MONO | STEREO | 18PC - 111 |
| GOLDEN IMPORTS   SRI | | ALBUM REFERENCE NO. | 98 |
| COVER ART: | | LINER NOTES: | In Japanese |
| ENGINEER: | | TAPE TRANSFER: | |
| RECORDING DATE: | | PERSONNEL LIST: | |

### PROGRAM
\* = Premier recording

Elsa's Procession to the Cathedral - Richard Wagner
Overture to "Rienzi" - Richard Wagner
Prelude to Act III and Bridal Procession from "Lohengrin" - Richard Wagner
Faust Ballet Music - Charles Gounod
Knightsbridge March - Eric Coates
March, Op. 99 - Sergei Prokofiev

### NOTES

A recoupling of earlier recordings "Hands Across the Sea" [SR 90207], "Ballet For Band" [SR 90256] and "Wagner for Band" [SR 90276] See album listing #15, 19 and 21
Group listed as Eastman Wind Ensemble
Cover is close up of three brass instruments - bugle, euphonium and trombone.
Manufactured by Nippon Phonogram

| ALBUM TITLE: | **Grainger - Holst - Walton** | | |
|---|---|---|---|
| LABEL: Japanese Philips | MONO | STEREO | 18PC - 112 |
| GOLDEN IMPORTS   SRI | | ALBUM REFERENCE NO. | 99 |
| COVER ART: | | LINER NOTES: | In Japanese |
| ENGINEER: | | TAPE TRANSFER: | |
| RECORDING DATE: | | PERSONNEL LIST: | |

### PROGRAM
\* = Premier recording

Lincolnshire Posy - Percy A. Grainger
Hammersmith: Prelude and Scherzo, Op. 52 - Gustav Holst
Crown Imperial: A Coronation March - William Walton
Symphonic Songs For Band - Robert Russell Bennett
Fanfare and Allegro - J. Clifton Williams

### NOTES

Recoupling of earlier recordings. "Winds in Hi-Fi" [SR 90173];  "British Band Classics II" [SR 90197] and "American Masterpieces for Concert Band" [SR 90220].
Group listed as Eastman Wind Ensemble
Cover uses elements from the British Band Classics II release [SR 90197].
Bennett selection is listed as "Symphonic Song For Band".

**ALBUM TITLE:** <u>Reed - Persichetti - Bennett</u>

**LABEL:** Japanese Philips  **MONO**  **STEREO** 18PC - 113

**GOLDEN IMPORTS** SRI  **ALBUM REFERENCE NO.** 100

**COVER ART:**  **LINER NOTES:** In Japanese

**ENGINEER:**  **TAPE TRANSFER:**

**RECORDING DATE:**  **PERSONNEL LIST:**

### PROGRAM
\* = Premier recording

La Fiesta Mexicana - H. Owen Reed
Chorale and Alleluia - Howard Hanson
Suite of Old American Dances - Robert Russell Bennett
Divertimento for Band - Vincent Persichetti
Commando March - Samuel Barber

### NOTES

A recoupling of earlier recordings "La Fiesta Mexicana" [MG 50084]; "American Concert Band Masterpieces" [MG 50079].
Cover is an instrumental collage.
Front cover lists group as Eastman Wind Ensemble. Back cover lists Eastman Symphonic Wind Ensemble.
Recording dates as per back cover: 1953 [Side 2], 1954 [Side 1]
All liner notes in Japanese.

One of those special looks!
Photo by Kawamura – courtesy of Kosei Publishing Co.

| | |
|---|---|
| **ALBUM TITLE:** | **Stars and Stripes Forever** |
| **LABEL:** Mercury Import  **MONO** | **STEREO** |
| **GOLDEN IMPORTS   SRI** 2-77010 | **ALBUM REFERENCE NO.** 101 |
| **COVER ART:** Paco North, photographer | **LINER NOTES:** Eric Kisch |
| **ENGINEER:** C.R. Fine | **TAPE TRANSFER:** |
| **RECORDING DATE:** | **PERSONNEL LIST:** |

### PROGRAM
\* = Premier recording

**Music of John Philip Sousa**
Stars and Stripes Forever, Washington Post, The Thunderer, King Cotton, U.S. Field Artillery, El Capitan, Nobles of the Mystic Shrine, The Gallant Seventh, The Invincible Eagle, Riders for the Flag, The High School Cadets, Sabre and Spurs, Bullets and Bayonets, Our Flirtations, The Picadore, Sound Off, The Liberty Bell, Solid Men to the Front, Golden Jubilee, Ancient and Honorable Artillery Company, The Rifle Regiment, The Pride of the Wolverines, Sesqui-Centennial Exposition, The National Game, The Gridiron Club, The Glory of the Yankee Navy, Manhattan Beach, The Black Horse Troop, New Mexico, The Kansas Wildcats and Hands Across the Sea

### NOTES

Recoupling of earlier SRI Golden Imports "Marching Along" [SRI 75004], "Sound Off!" [SRI 75047] and "Sousa on Review" [SRI 75064]

A total of 31 marches by John Philip Sousa. Frederick Fennell and the Eastman Wind Ensemble recorded a total of 34 marches by John Philip Sousa. The following three have been omitted from this release: *Corcoran Cadets, The Daughters of Texas* and *Semper Fidelis*.

A fold-out album with a great photo of John Philip Sousa, courtesy of the Music Division, the New York Public Library, Lincoln Center.

This album was a great re-release for the United States Bicentennial.

The front and back cover photos are by Paco North representing "from sea to shining sea" with Old Glory waving over the shore.

As with all Golden Imports, record was made in Holland and sleeve states "Printed in the Netherlands".

A compact disc [shorter version with only 22 of these 31 titles] is also available. See album reference 83.

FF: C.R. Fine's great sound considerably compressed, too. [April 1991]

In Bob Fine's truck at the first session of the Eastman Wind Ensemble
Photo courtesy of William L. Decker

| ALBUM TITLE: | **Music of the Civil War** | | |
|---|---|---|---|
| LABEL: Mercury Import | **MONO** | **STEREO** | |
| GOLDEN IMPORTS   SRI  2 - 77011 | | ALBUM REFERENCE NO.  102 | |
| COVER ART:  Fred Holtz | | LINER NOTES:  David Hall | |
| ENGINEER: | | TAPE TRANSFER: | |
| RECORDING DATE: | | PERSONNEL LIST: | |

**PROGRAM**
\* = Premier recording

**MUSIC OF THE CIVIL WAR**

See music listings on album references 31 and 32.

**NOTES**

*Star Spangled Banner* in the original issue is listed as arranged by Claudio S. Grafulla, however David Hall states the arrangement is by "well-known bandmaster and instrument inventor, Allen Dodworth".   [David Hall's notes include the typo "intrument"]

FF:   The *Star Spangled Banner*, as on our Civil War recording, was played from the Ingalls Books [Port Royal Band Books], and the pen is the same as all of the Grafulla titles.  I say Grafulla.  [April 1991]

The music of the original release [LPS 2-901 and LPS 2-902] is basically intact.  The narration and gun firing has been omitted from this release.  On 11 December 1990, an almost complete compact disc release was made available through Mercury Living Presence Series [see album reference 160].

Front and back cover collage is keyed on inside

| ALBUM TITLE: | **Marching Along** | | |
|---|---|---|---|
| LABEL: Mercury Import | **MONO** | **STEREO** | |
| GOLDEN IMPORTS    SRI   75004 | | ALBUM REFERENCE NO.  103 | |
| COVER ART:   Kim Ford Studios | | LINER NOTES:  Frederick Fennell | |
| ENGINEER: | | TAPE TRANSFER: | |
| RECORDING DATE: | | PERSONNEL LIST: | |

**PROGRAM**
\* = Premier recording

**John Philip Sousa:**
   The U.S. Field Artillery, The Thunderer, Washington Post, King Cotton, El Capitan, The Stars and Stripes Forever

American Patrol - Frank W. Meacham
On The Mall - Edwin Franko Goldman
Lights Out - Earl E. McCoy
Barnum and Bailey's Favorite - Karl L. King
Colonel Bogey - Kenneth J. Alford
The Billboard - John N. Klohr

**NOTES**

A re-issue of Mercury SR 90105, MG 50113 and SR 90291.  It is strange that MG 50113 is listed, in that none of the material from that album was recorded in stereo.

Cover photo is another one of those "generic" marching bands, definitely taken later in the decade than the famous "A" band on the original release of "Marching Along"  [SR 90105], the first EWE release in Stereo.

**ALBUM TITLE:** <u>**Holst - Vaughan Williams - Grainger**</u>

**LABEL:** Mercury Import     MONO         STEREO

**GOLDEN IMPORTS**    SRI   75011        **ALBUM REFERENCE NO.** 104

**COVER ART:**                                             **LINER NOTES:** David Hall

**ENGINEER:**                                                 **TAPE TRANSFER:**

**RECORDING DATE:**                           **PERSONNEL LIST:**

### PROGRAM
\* = Premier recording

Folk Song Suite - Ralph Vaughan Williams
Suite No. 2 in F for Military Band, Op. 28b - Gustav Holst
Suite No. 1 in E-flat for Military Band, Op. 28a - Gustav Holst
Hill Song No. 2 - Percy A. Grainger
Toccata Marziale - Ralph Vaughan Williams

### NOTES

A re-issue of album #5 "British Band Classics" which is different from album #4. #5 included *Hill Song No. 2* by Grainger.
Liner notes [David Hall] are basically the same as those for album #4 and #5 with the added Grainger.
Cover photo of instruments in close-up view. See further information on album reference #4.
Golden Imports cassette MRI 75011.

Frederick Fennell with Monte LaBonte – West Coast Conducting Symposium –
1982. Photo by Roger E. Rickson

| | | |
|---|---|---|
| **ALBUM TITLE:** | **Music of Leroy Anderson** | |
| **LABEL:** Mercury Import | **MONO** | **STEREO** |
| **GOLDEN IMPORTS SRI** 75013 | | **ALBUM REFERENCE NO.** 105 |
| **COVER ART:** | | **LINER NOTES:** Eric Kisch |
| **ENGINEER:** | | **TAPE TRANSFER:** |
| **RECORDING DATE:** | | **PERSONNEL LIST:** |

## PROGRAM
\* = Premier recording

All selections by Leroy Anderson

Sandpaper Ballet
Forgotten Dreams
Serenata
Trumpeter's Lullaby
Penny Whistle Song
Sleigh Ride
Bugler's Holiday
The Irish Washerwoman
The Minstrel Boy
The Rakes of Mallow
The Wearing of the Green
The Last Rose of Summer
The Girl I Left Behind Me

## NOTES

Re-issue of Mercury SR 90009 with the same arrangement of selections. The Irish Suite is listed by movement on this issue, however the original only lists the movements in the liner notes by Alfred E. Simon. An excellent biography of Frederick Fennell, who's name is misspelled in the final paragraph of the liner notes.
Also issued on Golden Imports Cassette MRI 75013.

Cover art is a generic out-of-focus oboe
Group listed as Eastman-Rochester POPS Orchestra

A relaxing moment with a score at Cal-State, San Bernardino – January 1981
Photo by Roger E. Rickson

| | |
|---|---|
| **ALBUM TITLE:** | **British Band Classics** |

**LABEL:** Mercury Import    **MONO**            **STEREO**

**GOLDEN IMPORTS   SRI   75028**         **ALBUM REFERENCE NO.** 106

**COVER ART:**                            **LINER NOTES:** Frederick Fennell

**ENGINEER:**                             **TAPE TRANSFER:**

**RECORDING DATE:**                       **PERSONNEL LIST:**

## PROGRAM
\* = Premier recording

William Byrd Suite - Gordon Jacob
The Earle of Oxford's March
Pavana
Jhon Come Kisse Me Now
The Mayden's Song
Wolsey's Wilde
The Bells

Crown Imperial: A Coronation March - William Walton
Hammersmith: Prelude and Scherzo, Op. 52 - Gustav Holst

## NOTES

With this title, one might assume that this would be a re-issue of the same selections as SR 90038, but it is actually a re-issue of British Band Classics, Volume II, SR 90157.

This issue uses a cover similar to Volume II with the Life Guard's Helmet repositioned. The liner notes are taken freely from the original issue, but still listed as by Frederick Fennell, but we miss his great use of prose in his descriptions. Also issued on Golden Imports Cassette MRI 75028.

Group listed as Eastman Wind Ensemble

| | | | |
|---|---|---|---|
| **ALBUM TITLE:** | **Ruffles and Flourishes** | | |
| **LABEL:** Mercury Import | **MONO** | **STEREO** | |
| **GOLDEN IMPORTS   SRI** 75034 | | **ALBUM REFERENCE NO.** 107 | |
| **COVER ART:**   See notes | | **LINER NOTES:** Anonymous | |
| **ENGINEER:** | | **TAPE TRANSFER:** | |
| **RECORDING DATE:** | | **PERSONNEL LIST:** | |

## PROGRAM
\* = Premier recording

**Side 1:**
Music for Rendering Honors:  Ruffles and Flourishes; General's March; To the Colors; Funeral March
Sound Off; General Dooley and the Old Guard; The American Flag; The Cavaliers; Old Six-eight; I've Got Three Years to Do This In; Hens and Chickens; No Slum Today
Carry On; Swinging Down the Street
Sound Off; Holy Joe; Soapsuds Row; The Colonel's Daughter; The Prisoner, Rip Van Winkle; The Garrison Belle, General Burt

**Side 2:**
Bugle Calls of the U.S. Army; Ruffles and Flourishes; Assembly; Adjutant's Call; Church Call; Drill Call; General's Call; Mail Call; Mess Call; Retreat; Call to Quarters; Reveille; Tattoo; Taps
Carry On; Connecticut Half-time
Sound Off; You're in the Army Now; Spanish Guard Mount; The Red Hussars; A-Hunting We Will Go; Pay Day and Double Time; The President's March
The Star Spangled Banner

## NOTES

Selections are listed very differently from the original issue [see album #8]. No personnel listed as on the original and group listed as the Eastman Wind Ensemble, omitting 'members of' from the original. [See #8 for specific list of personnel - the only selection by the complete EWE is Star Spangled Banner].
Cover photo USMA Band at the Amphitheater, United States Military Academy. Courtesy of the Public Affairs Office, West Point, New York. [Original issue uses photo of the U.S. Marine Corps Drum and Bugle Corps, Washington, D.C.]. Timings of each section are listed on this issue.

Liner notes are given no credit. Interesting information which amplifies and extends the information provided by Frederick Fennell on the original.

Album is re-release of SR 90112. Golden Imports cassette MRI 75034

| | | |
|---|---|---|
| **ALBUM TITLE:** | _Sound Off - Marches By John Philip Sousa_ | |
| **LABEL:** Mercury Import | **MONO** | **STEREO** |
| **GOLDEN IMPORTS   SRI** 75047 | | **ALBUM REFERENCE NO.** 108 |
| **COVER ART:** See notes | | **LINER NOTES:** Frederick Fennell |
| **ENGINEER:** | | **TAPE TRANSFER:** |
| **RECORDING DATE:** | | **PERSONNEL LIST:** |

### PROGRAM
\* = Premier recording

All selections by John Philip Sousa:
Sound Off, Nobles of the Mystic Shrine, Sabre and Spurs, The Picadore, Our Flirtations, The High School Cadets, The Invincible Eagle, Bullets and Bayonets, The Liberty Bell, Riders for the Flag, Solid Men to the Front, The Gallant Seventh

### NOTES

Re-issue of SR 90264 [album also lists SR 90291, which was a reissue of previous].

Cover photo is of West Point Military Academy Drum and Bugle Corps, courtesy of same.

RR: It is interesting to note that the Golden Imports re-issue of "Ruffles and Flourishes" cover photo depicts the full Academy Band, but contains only music for trumpets and drums, when this album contains music for full ensemble and the cover photo is the Academy Drum and Bugle Corps.

Also available on Golden Imports cassette MRI 75047.

| | | |
|---|---|---|
| **ALBUM TITLE:** | _The Spirit of '76 - Music for Fifes and Drums_ | |
| **LABEL:** Mercury Import | **MONO** | **STEREO** |
| **GOLDEN IMPORTS   SRI** 75048 | | **ALBUM REFERENCE NO.** 109 |
| **COVER ART:** Russell Connor | | **LINER NOTES:** Frederick Fennell |
| **ENGINEER:** | | **TAPE TRANSFER:** |
| **RECORDING DATE:** | | **PERSONNEL LIST:** |

### PROGRAM
\* = Premier recording

**Side 1:**
Yankee Doodle; Sergeant O'Leary; The Belle of the Mohawk Vale
Fancy 6/8 (drum solo)
The Camp Duty of the U.S. Army:
The Three Camps; The Slow Scotch; The Austrian; Dawning of the Day; The Hessian; Dusky Night; The Prussian; The Dutch; The Quick Scotch; The Three Camps

**Side 2:**
Gary Owen; Dixie; Sentry Box; The Dinner Call; Wrecker's Daughter; Hell on the Wabash; Downfall of Paris (drum solo); Connecticut Half-time (drum solo)
Rally 'round the Flag; Bonnie Blue Flag; White Cockade

### NOTES

A re-issue of SR 90111 of the same title. Side and selection arrangement the same as original.

Cover art by Russell Connor is a more contemporary version of the Archibald M. Willard painting of "The Spirit of '76".

Group listed as Eastman Wind Ensemble with "members of" omitted.  Specific personnel as listed on the original is also omitted.  Golden Imports cassette MRI 75048

| | |
|---|---|
| **ALBUM TITLE:** <u>**March Time**</u> | |
| **LABEL:** Mercury Import    MONO | STEREO |
| **GOLDEN IMPORTS  SRI  75055** | **ALBUM REFERENCE NO.** 110 |
| **COVER ART:** Rudy Sutherland photo | **LINER NOTES:** Frederick Fennell |
| **ENGINEER:** | **TAPE TRANSFER:** |
| **RECORDING DATE:** | **PERSONNEL LIST:** |

### PROGRAM
\* = Premier recording

**Side 1:**
Bugles and Drums - Edwin Franko Goldman
Illinois March - Edwin Franko Goldman
Children's March - Edwin Franko Goldman
The Interlochen Bowl - Edwin Franko Goldman
Onward-Upward - Edwin Franko Goldman
Boy Scouts of America - Edwin Franko Goldman

**Side 2:**
Americans We - Henry Fillmore
Officer of the Day - Robert Browne Hall
March Grandioso - Roland Forrest Seitz
Second Regiment Connecticut National Guard March - David Wallis Reeves
The Mad Major - Kenneth John Alford
Guadalcanal March from "Victory at Sea" - Richard Rodgers, arr. E. Leidzen

### NOTES

Re-issue of SR 90170 of the same title. All selections the same. The liner notes duplicate exactly those by Frederick Fennell on the original issue, with no credit. Phonogram Classette Import 412 300-4 does not resemble the Golden Imports cassette productions, which basically mirror the LP releases.

Cover photo by Rudy Sutherland is another one of the "anonymous" bands standing in concert formation on the field. Group listed as Eastman Wind Ensemble.

At my first ABA in 1958 with Karl King and Henry Fillmore
Photo courtesy of FF

**ALBUM TITLE:** <u>**Hindemith - Schoenberg - Stravinsky**</u>

**LABEL:** Mercury Import       MONO        STEREO

**GOLDEN IMPORTS   SRI** 75057         **ALBUM REFERENCE NO.** 111

**COVER ART:** Russell Connor          **LINER NOTES:** Frederick Fennell

**ENGINEER:**                          **TAPE TRANSFER:**

**RECORDING DATE:**                    **PERSONNEL LIST:**

## PROGRAM
\* = Premier recording

**Side 1:**
Symphony in B-flat for Concert Band - Paul Hindemith

**Side 2:**
Theme and Variations, Op. 43a - Arnold Schoenberg
Symphonies of Wind Instruments - Igor Stravinsky

## NOTES

Re-issue of SR 90143 of the same title. Liner notes duplicate exactly those by Frederick Fennell, with no credit listed.

Cover painting by Russell Connor.
Group listed as Eastman Wind Ensemble.

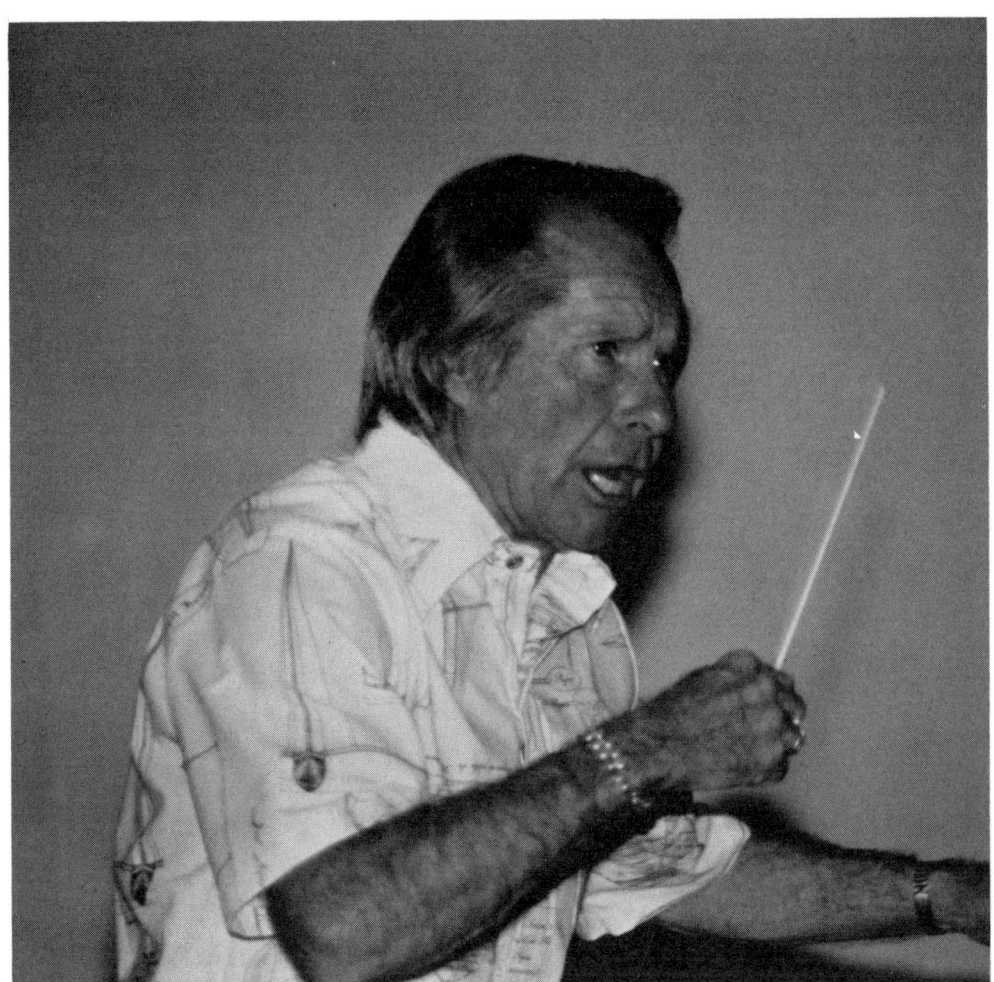

Cal-State San Bernardino –
January 1981
Photo by Roger E. Rickson

**ALBUM TITLE:** <u>**Sousa on Review**</u>

**LABEL:** Mercury Import  **MONO**  **STEREO**

**GOLDEN IMPORTS  SRI**  75064  **ALBUM REFERENCE NO.**  112

**COVER ART:**  See notes  **LINER NOTES:**  Frederick Fennell

**ENGINEER:**  **TAPE TRANSFER:**

**RECORDING DATE:**  **PERSONNEL LIST:**

## PROGRAM
* = Premier recording

**Side 1:**
The Rifle Regiment
The Pride of the Wolverines
Golden Jubilee
The Gridiron Club March
New Mexico March
Sesqui-Centennial Exposition March

**Side 2:**
The Black Horse Troop
Kansas Wildcats
Manhattan Beach
Ancient and Honorable Artillery Company
The National Game
The Glory of the Yankee Navy

## NOTES

A re-issue of SR 90284 of the same title. Same arrangement of selections and liner notes, minus one paragraph, duplicate those of the original issue, with proper credit. Golden Imports cassette MRI 75064.

Cover art is not given credit. A very distinctive cover with a rope-slung field drum in red, white and blue; a modern piccolo and a one-valved bugle. Much more imaginative and colorful than the original cover depicting a series of three-valved trumpets, as if on parade.

Group listed as Eastman Wind Ensemble

Maestro at session with TOKWO
Photo by Kawamura
courtesy of Kosei Publishing

**ALBUM TITLE:** <u>American Concert Band Masterpieces</u>

**LABEL:** Mercury Import   **MONO**   **STEREO**

**GOLDEN IMPORTS SRI** 75086   **ALBUM REFERENCE NO.** 113

**COVER ART:** See notes   **LINER NOTES:** David Hall

**ENGINEER:**   **TAPE TRANSFER:**

**RECORDING DATE:**   **PERSONNEL LIST:**

## PROGRAM
\* = Premier recording

**Side 1:**
Divertimento For Band - Vincent Persichetti
Ballad For Band - Morton Gould
George Washington Bridge - An Impression for Band - William Schuman

**Side 2:**
Suite of Old American Dances - Robert Russell Bennett
Tunbridge Fair - Intermezzo for Band - Walter Piston
Commando March - Samuel Barber

## NOTES

A re-issue of MG 50079 which was issued only in mono. Re-issue contains the statement: "electronically altered to simulate stereo". Liner notes are somewhat excerpted from the original issue, also by David Hall. Selections and side arrangement are the same as the original. Cover photo, courtesy of the Port Authority of New York and New Jersey, is of George Washington Bridge at sunset. Original issue [MG 50079] has photo of George Washington Bridge at dawn. See listing of MG 40006, which has yet a different cover illustration. Both original releases include "Symphonic" in group listing.
Golden Imports cassette MRI 75086

FF: This, of course, is the very first Eastman Wind Ensemble recording, re-issued almost thirty years after the original recording session.

Group listed as Eastman Wind Ensemble

Maestro at session with TOKWO
Photo by Kawamura
courtesy of Kosei Publishing

| | |
|---|---|
| **ALBUM TITLE:** | **Screamers: Circus Marches** |
| **LABEL:** Mercury Import  MONO | **STEREO** |
| **GOLDEN IMPORTS** SRI 75087 | **ALBUM REFERENCE NO.** 114 |
| **COVER ART:** See notes | **LINER NOTES:** Frederick Fennell |
| **ENGINEER:** | **TAPE TRANSFER:** |
| **RECORDING DATE:** | **PERSONNEL LIST:** |

### PROGRAM
\* = Premier recording

**Side 1:**
In Storm and Sunshine - John C. Heed
Whip and Spur - Thomas S. Allen
Invictus - Karl L. King
The Big Cage - Karl L. King
Bones Trombones - Henry Fillmore
Them Basses - Getty H. Huffine
The Circus Bee - Henry Fillmore
The Screamer - Frederick Jewell

**Side 2:**
Thunder and Blazes - Entry of the Gladiators - Julius Fucik
Robinson's Grand Entree - Karl L. King
Circus Days - Karl L. King
Bombasto - Orion R. Farrar
The Squealer - Will Huff
Rolling Thunder - Henry Fillmore
Bennett's Triumphal - John H. Ribble
Bravura - Charles E. Duble

### NOTES

A re-issue of SR 90314 of the same title. Original title also included "A Collection of Exciting Marches from the Circus Ring." Liner notes are slightly abbreviated from the original, omitting the two personal statements by Fennell regarding the playing and his final recording session with the Eastman Wind Ensemble. Selections and side order remain the same. [Bennett's Triumphal is misspelled on liner notes and title listing. "Bennet's Triumphal]. Golden Imports cassette MRI 75087

The great circus cover is not credited. The clown on the front is even using the famous "Frederick Fennell "bass drum beater.

Group listed as Eastman Wind Ensemble

Historic Mission Inn –
Riverside, California
April 1981
Photo by Roger E. Rickson

**ALBUM TITLE:** <u>Grainger - Rogers - Milhaud - Strauss</u>

**LABEL:** Mercury Import    **MONO**         **STEREO**

**GOLDEN IMPORTS  SRI**  75093    **ALBUM REFERENCE NO.** 115

**COVER ART:** Peter J. Clancy, Jr.    **LINER NOTES:** Frederick Fennell

**ENGINEER:**    **TAPE TRANSFER:**

**RECORDING DATE:**    **PERSONNEL LIST:**

### PROGRAM
\* = Premier recording

**Side 1:**
Lincolnshire Posy - Percy A. Grainger
Three Japanese Dances - Bernard Rogers

**Side 2:**
Suite Francaise - Darius Milhaud
Serenade in E-flat, Op. 7 - Richard Strauss

### NOTES

Re-issue of SR 90173 - "Winds in Hi-Fi". Same sequence of selections. The original liner notes are slightly abbreviated.
Golden Imports cassette MRI 75093
Cover painting - water color of woodwind and brass instruments in muted colors.

FF: This is the one you had to tell me had been selected as one of the 50 best recordings of the Centenary of the Phonograph.

Group listed as Eastman Wind Ensemble

---

**ALBUM TITLE:** <u>Gould - Persichetti - Williams - Khachaturian</u>

**LABEL:** Mercury Import    **MONO**         **STEREO**

**GOLDEN IMPORTS  SRI**  75094    **ALBUM REFERENCE NO.** 116

**COVER ART:** Army Photo    **LINER NOTES:** Frederick Fennell

**ENGINEER:**    **TAPE TRANSFER:**

**RECORDING DATE:**    **PERSONNEL LIST:**

### PROGRAM
\* = Premier recording

**Side 1:**
West Point Symphony - Morton Gould
Fanfare and Allegro - J. Clifton Williams

**Side 2:**
Symphony No. 6 for Band - Vincent Persichetti
Armenian Dances - Aram Khachaturian, arr. Ralph Satz

### NOTES

Re-issue of two previous albums. SR 90220 "American Masterpieces for Concert Band" and SR 90221 "Diverse Winds". See album listings 16 and 17. Liner notes are a combination from the two original issues to correspond to the above coupling.

Cover photo supplied by the U.S. Army is from the West Point grounds.
Group listed as Eastman Wind Ensemble.

| | |
|---|---|
| **ALBUM TITLE:** <u>**Wagner For Band**</u> | |
| **LABEL:** Mercury Import  MONO | STEREO |
| **GOLDEN IMPORTS SRI** 75096 | **ALBUM REFERENCE NO.** 117 |
| **COVER ART:** see notes | **LINER NOTES:** Frederick Fennell |
| **ENGINEER:** | **TAPE TRANSFER:** |
| **RECORDING DATE:** | **PERSONNEL LIST:** |

### PROGRAM
\* = Premier recording

**All music by Richard Wagner**

Prelude to Act III and Bridal Chorus from "Lohengrin" - arr. Frank Winterbottom
Entry of the Gods into Valhalla from "Das Rheingold" - arr. Dan Godfrey
Elsa's Procession to the Cathedral from "Lohengrin" - arr. Lucien Cailliet
Overture to "Rienzi" - arr. Victor Grabel
Good Friday Music from "Parsifal" - arr. Dan Godfrey

### NOTES

A re-issue of SR 90276. Golden Imports cassette MRI 75096

Same selections and side order are preserved in this re-issue.
Liner notes by Fennell are slightly abbreviated.

Cover is close up photo of trombone, tuba and bell of trumpet. No credit is given. Same cover as on album #98, Japanese 18PC - 111.

Group listed as Eastman Wind Ensemble

With Keating Johnson at
Cal-State San Bernardino –
January 1981
Photo courtesy of Monte LaBonte

**ALBUM TITLE:** <u>**Malaguena and Other Favorites**</u>

**LABEL:** Mercury Imports     MONO         STEREO

**GOLDEN IMPORTS**   SRI   75097      **ALBUM REFERENCE NO.** 118

**COVER ART:** see notes         **LINER NOTES:** Frederick Fennell

**ENGINEER:**         **TAPE TRANSFER:**

**RECORDING DATE:**         **PERSONNEL LIST:**

### PROGRAM
\* = Premier recording

Brazilian Sleigh Bells - Percy Faith
Andalucia - Ernesto Lecuona
Malaguena - Ernesto Lecuona
Intermezzo from "Goyescas" - Enrique Granados
Jamaican Rumba - Arthur Benjamin
Batuque - Oscar Fernandez
Amparito Roca - Jaime Texidor
Ritual Fire Dance from "El Amor Brujo" - Manuel de Falla
The Bullfighter's Prayer - Joaquin Turina
Brazilian Dance - Camargo Mozart Guarnieri

### NOTES

A re-issue of SR 90144.

Same selections and side order are preserved in this re-issue.
Liner notes are slightly abbreviated from the original issue.
Cover photo of flamenco dancers. No credit is given.

Group listed as Eastman-Rochester Pops Orchestra.

West Coast Conducting
Symposium, Saddleback
College – June 1982
Photo by Roger E. Rickson

| | |
|---|---|
| **ALBUM TITLE:** _Hands Across the Sea_ | |
| **LABEL:** Mercury Imports   **MONO** | **STEREO** |
| **GOLDEN IMPORTS  SRI  75099** | **ALBUM REFERENCE NO.** 119 |
| **COVER ART:** Sylvia Kaufman | **LINER NOTES:** Frederick Fennell |
| **ENGINEER:** | **TAPE TRANSFER:** |
| **RECORDING DATE:** | **PERSONNEL LIST:** |

## PROGRAM
*= Premier recording

Hands Across the Sea - John Philip Sousa  
Father of Victory - Gustave Luis Ganne  
The Golden Ear - Mariano San Miguel  
Old Comrades - Carl Teike  
March, Op. 99 - Serge Prokofiev  
Valdres March - Johannes Hanssen  
Inglesina - Davide Della Cese  
Knightsbridge March - Eric Coates  

## NOTES

Same selections and side order are preserved in this re-issue os SR 90207 of the same title. Liner notes are slightly abbreviated from the original issue.

Cover photo of the Tall Ships [a favorite of the conductor] is by Sylvia Kaufman.

Groups listed as Eastman Wind Ensemble.

West Coast Conducting Symposium, Saddleback College  
Photo by Roger E. Rickson

**ALBUM TITLE:** <u>Country Gardens and Other Favorites by Percy Grainger</u>

**LABEL:** Mercury Imports   **MONO**   **STEREO**

**GOLDEN IMPORTS   SRI** 75102   **ALBUM REFERENCE NO.** 120
**COVER ART:** Niki Ekstrom   **LINER NOTES:** Frederick Fennell
**ENGINEER:**   **TAPE TRANSFER:**
**RECORDING DATE:**   **PERSONNEL LIST:**

### PROGRAM
\* = Premier recording

**All music by Percy A. Grainger**

Country Gardens
Shepherd's Hey
Colonial Song
Children's March
Immovable Do
Mock Morris
Handel in the Strand
Irish Tune
Spoon River
My Robin is to the Greenwood Gone
Molly on the Shore

### NOTES

A re-issue of SR 90219.

Same selections and side order are preserved in this re-issue. Liner notes are faithfully reproduced from the original. Golden Imports cassette MRI 75102

Back cover includes a black and white, autographed photo of Percy Grainger. This photo is inscribed " To Oscar Spiresco with cordial greetings from Percy Grainger. March 1917." Photo taken by Aime Dupont, New York.

Cover photo by Niki Ekstrom of a flower-filled garden supplied by Old Westbury Gardens, Inc.
Group listed as Eastman-Rochester Pops Orchestra.

Community College Honor Band at Riverside Community College – April 1981
Photo by Roger E. Rickson

| | |
|---|---|
| **ALBUM TITLE:** | **Frederick Fennell conducts music by Eric Coates** |

**LABEL:** Mercury Imports  **MONO**  **STEREO**

**GOLDEN IMPORTS  SRI** 75109  **ALBUM REFERENCE NO.** 121

**COVER ART:** see notes  **LINER NOTES:** Stanley Green

**ENGINEER:**  **TAPE TRANSFER:**

**RECORDING DATE:**  **PERSONNEL LIST:**

### PROGRAM
\* = Premier recording

**All music by Eric Coates**

London Suite
"Four Ways" Suite
The Three Elizabeths

### NOTES

Same selections and side order are preserved in this re-issue of SR 90439 of the same title.
Liner notes are faithfully reproduced from the original, omitting the short biographical sketch of Frederick Fennell.

Front cover reproduces the original with the addition of a gold "Imported from Europe" seal.
Group listed as London Pops Orchestra.

With Monte LaBonte, Chairman, West Coast Conducting
Symposium, Saddleback College – June 1982
Photo by Roger E. Rickson

| | |
|---|---|
| **ALBUM TITLE:** Music of Cole Porter | |
| **LABEL:** Mercury Imports  **MONO** | **STEREO** |
| **GOLDEN IMPORTS  SRI** 75110 | **ALBUM REFERENCE NO.** 122 |
| **COVER ART:** see notes | **LINER NOTES:** Eric Kisch |
| **ENGINEER:** | **TAPE TRANSFER:** |
| **RECORDING DATE:** | **PERSONNEL LIST:** |

## PROGRAM
\* = Premier recording

All music by Cole Porter. Arrangements by Rayburn Wright.

Blow Gabriel Blow
So In Love
Ridin' High
In the Still of the Night
Begin the Beguine
Night and Day
My Heart Belongs to Daddy
Anything Goes
I've Got You Under My Skin
It's Delovely
You'd Be So Nice To Come Home To

## NOTES

A re-issue of PPS 6024.

This re-issue omits "It's All Right With Me." Remaining eleven selections are intact with same order.
All liner notes are new and very informative about the life of Cole Porter.

Cover illustration is pencil drawing by Mona Mark from a photo in COLE, edited by Robert Kimball. "Thanks to John F. Wharton, Trustee of Cole Porter Musical and Literary Property Trusts."

Group listed as Frederick Fennell and his Orchestra.

| | | | |
|---|---|---|---|
| **ALBUM TITLE:** | **Broadway Marches** | | |
| **LABEL:** Mercury Imports | **MONO** | **STEREO** | |
| **GOLDEN IMPORTS  SRI** 75115 | | **ALBUM REFERENCE NO.** 123 | |
| **COVER ART:** David Chalk | | **LINER NOTES:** Stanley Green | |
| **ENGINEER:** | | **TAPE TRANSFER:** | |
| **RECORDING DATE:** | | **PERSONNEL LIST:** | |

### PROGRAM
\* = Premier recording

All selections arranged by John Krance.

Strike Up the Band - George and Ira Gershwin
I Ain't Down Yet - Meredith Willson
There is Nothin' Like a Dame - Richard Rodgers and Oscar Hammerstein
Stouthearted Men - Sigmund Romberg and Oscar Hammerstein
Broadway Minstrel Medley - John Krance
Consider Yourself - Lionel Bart
There's No Business Like Show Business - Irving Berlin
The March of the Siamese Children - Richard Rodgers and Oscar Hammerstein
Seventy-Six Trombones - Meredith Willson
Give My Regards to Broadway - George M. Cohan
Wintergreen for President - George and Ira Gershwin
Get Me to the Church on Time - Frederick Loewe and Alan Jay Lerner

### NOTES

Same selections and side order are preserved in this re-issue of SR 90390 of the same title.
Liner notes are faithfully reproduced from the original with the following biographical sketch of the arranger. "John Krance's professional musical activities embrace every branch of music and all of the media. Many of his arrangements, transcriptions and compositions are published by several firms, and comprise works for concert band, wind ensemble and orchestra. A versatile musician of wide experience, Krance received his formal musical training at the Eastman School of Music, where his association with Frederick Fennell began in 1951 and continued when he played French horn in the Eastman Wind Ensemble, the celebrated wind-brass-percussion group founded by Fennell."

Cover photo is out-of-focus shot of neon lights, probably Broadway in New York.
Group listed as Fennell Symphonic Winds.

**ALBUM TITLE:** _Music of George Gershwin_

**LABEL:** Mercury Imports  **MONO**  **STEREO**

**GOLDEN IMPORTS SRI** 75127  **ALBUM REFERENCE NO.** 124

**COVER ART:** Mona Mark  **LINER NOTES:** Edward Jablonski/ F. Fennell

**ENGINEER:**  **TAPE TRANSFER:**

**RECORDING DATE:**  **PERSONNEL LIST:**

### PROGRAM
\* = Premier recording

All music by George Gershwin. Arrangements by Rayburn Wright, Fred Karlin and Dick Lieb.

I Got Rhythm
Love is Sweeping the Country
Love Walked In
'S Wonderful
Bidin' My Time
Oh, Lady Be Good
Fascinating Rhythm
Liza
Embraceable You
The Man I Love
Someone to Watch Over Me
But Not For Me

### NOTES

Same selections and side order are preserved in this re-issue of PPS 6006. Golden Imports cassette MRI 75127 Liner notes are slightly abbreviated from the original issue and no photo of Fennell is presented on the back cover.

Cover illustration by Mona Mark is provided with special thanks to the Gershwin Archive and Edward Jablonski. Group is listed as Frederick Fennell and his Orchestra.

Arranger Dick Lieb – 1993
Photo courtesy of Dick Lieb

Arranger Rayburn Wright, c. 1990
Photo courtesy of FF

| ALBUM TITLE: | **Music of Andrea and Giovanni Gabrieli** | | |
|---|---|---|---|
| **LABEL:** Mercury Imports | **MONO** | **STEREO** | |
| **GOLDEN IMPORTS   SRI** 75130 | | **ALBUM REFERENCE NO.** 125 | |
| **COVER ART:** see notes | | **LINER NOTES:** Jane Haber | |
| **ENGINEER:** | | **TAPE TRANSFER:** | |
| **RECORDING DATE:** | | **PERSONNEL LIST:** | |

**PROGRAM**
\* = Premier recording

Aria della Battaglia
Sonata octavi toni
Sonata pian e forte
Canzon duodecimi toni
Canzon noni toni
Canzon septimi toni
Canzon quarti toni

**NOTES**

A re-issue of SR 90245.

Same selections and side order are preserved on this re-issue.
Liner notes by Jane Haber add to the historical information presented by Egon Kenton on the original issue.

Cover illustration is photo of instruments from the collection of the Gemeentemuseum, The Hague.  Colour photo is by Van Heerde of Phonogram International.
Group is listed as the Eastman Wind Ensemble.  See album 18 for personnel list.

| ALBUM TITLE: | **Ballet For Band** | | |
|---|---|---|---|
| **LABEL:** Mercury Imports | **MONO** | **STEREO** | |
| **GOLDEN IMPORTS   SRI** 75138 | | **ALBUM REFERENCE NO.** 126 | |
| **COVER ART:** Michael Cardacino | | **LINER NOTES:** Frederick Fennell | |
| **ENGINEER:** | | **TAPE TRANSFER:** | |
| **RECORDING DATE:** | | **PERSONNEL LIST:** | |

**PROGRAM**
\* = Premier recording

Pineapple Poll Suite - Arthur Sullivan - Charles Mackerras - arr. W. J. Duthoit
La Boutique Fantasque - Gioacchino Rossini - arr. Dan Godfrey
Ballet Music from "Faust" - Charles Gounod - arr. William Winterbottom

**NOTES**

A re-issue of SR 90256.

Same selections and side order are preserved in this re-issue.  Liner notes are slightly abbreviated from the original issue.
Cover photo by Michael Cardacino of ballet slippers on a French Horn.
Group listed as Eastman Wind Ensemble.

| | | |
|---|---|---|
| **ALBUM TITLE:** | **Heart of the March** | |
| **LABEL:** Mercury | **MONO** | **STEREO** SR 2-9131 |
| **GOLDEN IMPORTS** SRI | | **ALBUM REFERENCE NO.** 127 |
| **COVER ART:** | | **LINER NOTES:** |
| **ENGINEER:** | | **TAPE TRANSFER:** |
| **RECORDING DATE:** | | **PERSONNEL LIST:** |

### PROGRAM
\* = Premier recording

**Eastman Wind Ensemble**
John Philip Sousa - Stars and Stripes Forever, El Capitan, Washington Post, King Cotton, The Picadore, Hands Across the Sea, The Thunderer, Our Flirtations

American Patrol - Frank W. Meacham
The Billboard - John N. Klohr
In Storm and Sunshine - John C. Heed
Circus Bee - Henry Fillmore
On the Mall - Edwin Franko Goldman
Second Regiment Connecticut National Guard - David W. Reeves
Old Comrades - Carl Teike
The Screamer - Fred Jewell
Thunder and Blazes - Entry of the Gladiators - Julius Fucik

**Eastman-Rochester POPS Orchestra**
March Militaire - Franz Schubert

### NOTES

A two LP re-issue of previously released material. Compiled and organized by Joseph Bott and Scott Mampe from the New York office of Mercury Records.
Inside cover shows sixteen Mercury releases by Frederick Fennell. There are no albums by Paul Paray illustrated even though there are three selections with the Detroit Symphony Orchestra. Front and back cover have great art work with wind and percussion instruments, civil war figures, the Spirit of '76 trio and marching musicians. No credit is given for the very nice cover.

| | | |
|---|---|---|
| **ALBUM TITLE:** | **Heart of the Ballet** | |
| **LABEL:** Mercury | **MONO** | **STEREO** SR 2-9127 |
| **GOLDEN IMPORTS** SRI | | **ALBUM REFERENCE NO.** 127a |
| **COVER ART:** | | **LINER NOTES:** Doris Parkes Petan |
| **ENGINEER:** | | **TAPE TRANSFER:** |
| **RECORDING DATE:** | | **PERSONNEL LIST:** |

### PROGRAM
\* = Premier recording

**Eastman-Rochester POPS Orchestra**
Russian Sailors Dance - Reinhold Gliere

### NOTES

A two LP re-issue of previously released material.
Inside cover differs from "Heart of the March" which displayed sixteen record covers of Fennell Mercury releases. There are no Fennell recordings pictured. Cover depicts dancers and a flock of white doves on skyblue background.

| | | | |
|---|---|---|---|
| **ALBUM TITLE:** | _Toccata and Fugue_ | | |
| **LABEL:** Kosei | **MONO** | **STEREO** | KOR/KOCD 8415/2815 |
| **GOLDEN IMPORTS SRI** | | **ALBUM REFERENCE NO.** 128 | |
| **COVER ART:** S. Katoh/M. Kajino | | **LINER NOTES:** In Japanese | |
| **ENGINEER:** S. Wakabayashi/J. Itoh | | **TAPE TRANSFER:** S. Wakabayashi | |
| **RECORDING DATE:** September 25, 1985 | | **PERSONNEL LIST:** | |

**PROGRAM**
\* = Premier recording

**Johann Sebastian Bach**

Toccata and Fugue in d minor - arr. by Genba Fujita, edited by Frederick Fennell
Come, Sweet Death - transcribed by Alfred Reed
Sheep May Safely Graze - transcribed by Alfred Reed
Fugue in g minor [Little Fugue] - transcribed by Takuzo Inagaki
Fantasia and Fugue in g minor - Wind orchestration by John Boyd
Jesu, Joy of Man's Desiring - transcribed by Alfred Reed
Forget Me Not, O Dearest Lord - transcribed by Alfred Reed
Fugue a la Gigue - arranged by Gustav Holst

**NOTES**

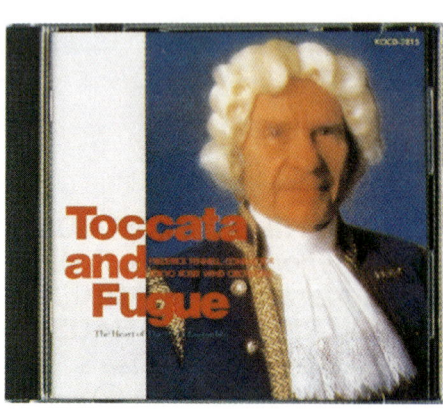

Subtitle: Heart of the Wind Ensemble Series #5

Recording dates: 25-26 September 1985
Recording site: Fumon Hall, Tokyo, Japan
Group listed as Tokyo Kosei Windorchestra
Cover photos: N. Kawamura

FF: I was asked if I would agree to the idea of dressing up for the cover photo of this recording. I said that I don't usually do things like that, but anything to make the record go would be fine with me. So, they drove me to NHK, the big main studios of Japanese radio and television. They brought out from the costume department the jacket of the court musician. It looked very fine and it fit me very well. We added the customary white jabot. And then they brought out a wig for me, and they put it on my head. Having never seen myself in a wig before, my immediate reaction was to laugh - which was the wrong thing to do. But, it was an obvious immediate reaction on my part, and there's nothing I could have done about that, except to apologize for offending them, if that is indeed what I had done. But I said obviously anybody would like the idea of this court musician, and maybe there's a wig back there someplace that will look real well and fit. We then left and went out and had the white wig made, so that it would fit me as well as it does and look as really natural as it does. Then I went way far back in my business of looking up to see where could I find someone in the blood line of Bach, who I might be representing. Someone, who, of course, would not be Johann Sebastian. In the process, I was trying to find the exact ... someone way back in the Bach family. I can't put my finger on it right now. This was not to be Johann Sebastian Fennell.

Issued both on LP and CD [see above numbers]. Sheep May <u>Safety</u> Graze appears on both issues.

| | |
|---|---|
| **ALBUM TITLE:** <u>An American in Paris</u> | |
| **LABEL:** Kosei     MONO | **STEREO**  KOR/KOCD 8416/2816 |
| **GOLDEN IMPORTS   SRI** | **ALBUM REFERENCE NO.** 129 |
| **COVER ART:**  S. Katoh/S. Shiki | **LINER NOTES:** In Japanese |
| **ENGINEER:**  S. Wakabayashi/J. Itoh | **TAPE TRANSFER:** S. Wakabayashi |
| **RECORDING DATE:** April 3, 1986 | **PERSONNEL LIST:** not listed |

### PROGRAM
\* = Premier recording

Broadway Curtain Time - arranged by John Krance
Blues For A Killed Kat - Jack End
Overture to Candide - Leonard Bernstein, arranged by Walter Beeler
Wedding Dance - Jacques Press, arranged by Herbert N. Johnston
An American in Paris - George Gershwin, arranged by Hiroshi Hoshina
The Wiz - Charlie Smalls, arranged by Bob Lowden

### NOTES

Subtitle: Heart of the Wind Ensemble Series # 6

Recording dates: 23-24 April 1986
Recording site: Fumon Hall, Tokyo, Japan
Group listed as Tokyo Kosei Windorchestra
Cover Photos: N. Kawamura

Both LP and CD contain same selections, but in different order.
LP 8416 contains "generic" English liner notes with bio on Fennell and history of TOKWO.

### TOKYO KOSEI WINDORCHESTRA
### BASIC PERSONNEL
### Frederick Fennell, Principal Conductor

**Piccolo & Flute**
Masazumi Makino
Yasuro Hayashi

**Oboe**
Hitoshi Wakui

**B-flat Clarinet**
Kiyosumi Ogura
Hitoshi Sekiguchi
Mitsuro Inaba
Kiichi Sato
Katsuo Okawa
Takeshi Nozaki

**E-flat Clarinet**
Masaru Nakano

**Alto Clarinet**
Kiyoshi Arai

**Bass Clarinet**
Makio Kimura

**Contrabass Clarinet**
Nobuo Fukushima

**Bassoon**
Mamoru Kanazaki
Atsushi Murakami

**Saxophone**
Nobuya Sugawa [Concertmaster]
Yasuo Akimoto
Yasuto Tanaka
Mamoru Nakata

**Trumpet**
Yoshikazu Kubo
Kazuo Hayashi
Shinzo Katsura
Taizo Okuyama

**Horn**
Hiroshi Uehara
Hiromi Hamiki
Masanori Saigo
Atsushi Kimura

**Trombone**
Katsumi Hagiya
Toshiaki Oguma
Ichiya Sakai

**Euphonium**
Toru Miura

**Tuba**
Shigeru Onoe
Sadayuki Ogura
[Associate Concertmaster]

**String Bass**
Takuro Inagaki

**Percussion**
Takafumi Miyake
Kenichi Kitano

**Kettledrums**
Itaru Katsumata

| | |
|---|---|
| **ALBUM TITLE:** | **Hands Across the Sea** |

**LABEL:** Kosei   **MONO**   **STEREO** KOR/KOCD 8417/2817

**GOLDEN IMPORTS   SRI**   **ALBUM REFERENCE NO.** 130

**COVER ART:** S. Katoh/S. Shiki   **LINER NOTES:** In Japanese

**ENGINEER:** S. Wakabayashi/J. Itoh   **TAPE TRANSFER:** S. Wakabayashi

**RECORDING DATE:** April 23, 1986   **PERSONNEL LIST:** Not listed

**PROGRAM**
\* = Premier recording

**All selections by John Philip Sousa**

Hands Across the Sea
The Liberty Bell
The Rifle Regiment
The Glory of the Yankee Navy
The Black Horse Troop
Daughters of Texas
The High School Cadets
The Thunderer March
The Free Lance March
Riders for the Flag
The Corcoran Cadets
El Capitan
The Washington Post
Bullets and Bayonets

**NOTES**

Subtitle: Heart of the Wind Ensemble Series #7

Recording dates: 23-24 April 1986
Recording site: Fumon Hall, Tokyo, Japan
Group listed as Tokyo Kosei Windorchestra
Cover photos: N. Kawamura

Both LP and CD contain the same selections in the same order.
The LP version contains a chronological listing of the 136 marches by John Philip Sousa [omitted in the CD release].

Cover photos, as on most, duplicate issues of LP and CD, are close-up pictures of Frederick Fennell. The CD will include only the cover photo and omit the back cover photo.

| | |
|---|---|
| **ALBUM TITLE:** Lincolnshire Posy | |
| **LABEL:** Kosei   MONO | **STEREO** KOR/KOCD 8418/2818 |
| **GOLDEN IMPORTS   SRI** | **ALBUM REFERENCE NO.** 131 |
| **COVER ART:** S. Katoh/S. Shiki | **LINER NOTES:** In Japanese |
| **ENGINEER:** S. Wakabayashi/K. Okawa | **TAPE TRANSFER:** S. Wakabayashi |
| **RECORDING DATE:** October 22, 1986 | **PERSONNEL LIST:** not listed |

### PROGRAM
\* = Premier recording

Lincolnshire Posy - Percy A. Grainger, edited by Frederick Fennell
Pineapple Poll Suite from the Ballet - Arthur Sullivan/Charles Mackerras, arranged by W. J. Duthoit
Armenian Dances Part II - Alfred Reed
Kaddish - Wm. Francis McBeth

### NOTES

Subtitle: Heart of the Wind Ensemble Series #8

Recording dates:  22-23 October 1986
Recording site:  Fumon Hall, Tokyo, Japan
Group listed as Tokyo Kosei Windorchestra
Cover photos: N. Kawamura

The LP version contains a Frederick Fennell signature and a picture of his baton and baton case which are omitted on the CD version.  Liner notes of both issues are in Japanese.  No "generic" English notes included with the LP.  The LP version also includes an ELF Enterprises sticker.  [ELF = Elizabeth Ludwig Fennell, who is the exclusive United States distributor of the TOKWO recordings].

Back of CD KOCD 2818 lists the title as "Lincolshire Posy".  Front is correct with the "n" in Lincolnshire.

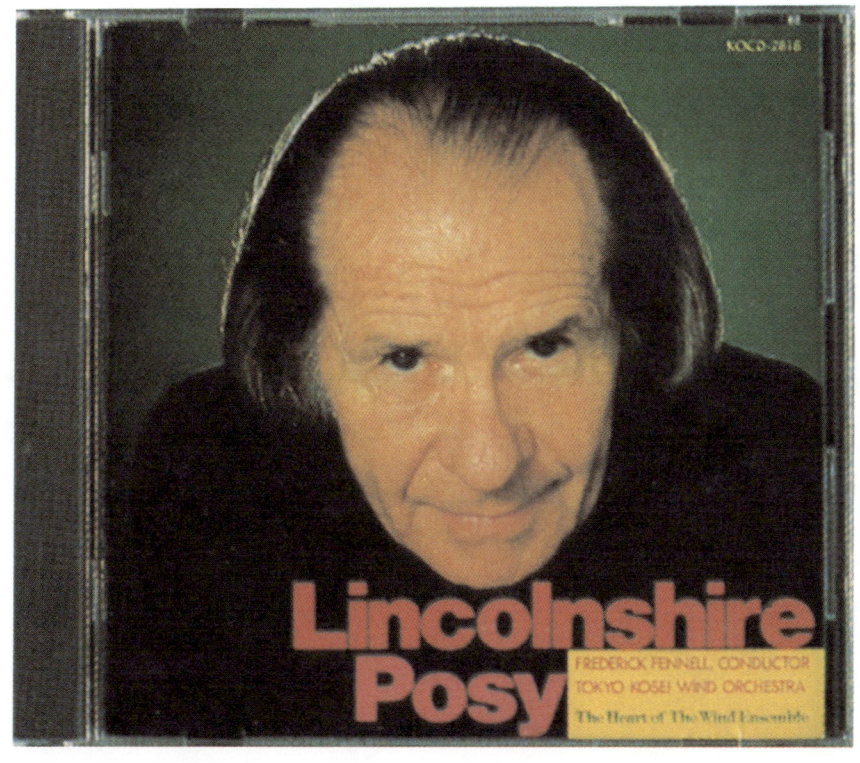

| ALBUM TITLE: | **Symphonic Songs for Band** | | |
|---|---|---|---|
| LABEL: Kosei | MONO | STEREO | KOR/KOCD 8781-82/3562 |
| GOLDEN IMPORTS SRI | | ALBUM REFERENCE NO. | 132 |
| COVER ART: S. Katoh | | LINER NOTES: | in Japanese |
| ENGINEER: S. Wakabayashi/J. Itoh | | TAPE TRANSFER: | S. Wakabayashi |
| RECORDING DATE: March 24, 1987 | | PERSONNEL LIST: | |

### PROGRAM
\* = Premier recording

Symphonic Songs for Band - Robert Russell Bennett
Country Band March - Charles Ives, arr. James Sinclair
Pastorale - J. Clifton Williams
Masquerade - Vincent Persichetti
Elegy For A Young American - Ronald LoPresti
George Washington Bridge - William Schuman
Ballad For Band - Morton Gould
An Outdoor Overture - Aaron Copland

### NOTES

Subtitle: American Band Classics by Frederick Fennell Series

Recording dates: 24-25 March 1987
Recording site: Fumon Hall, Tokyo, Japan
Group listed as Tokyo Kosei Windorchestra
Cover photo: Camera Tokyo Service

CD version has same selections in different arrangement. Both LP and CD begin with title selection.
Photo in both versions was taken in 1967.

FF: Photo below is of J. Clifton Williams, myself, Aaron Copland and William F. Lee [Dean, Miami School of Music]. Aaron came for a Festival of his music. He was Dorothy's and my house guest for three days; a very charming time. We met for the first time at Tanglewood in the summer of 1942. The photographer was on the staff of the University of Miami.

| | | | |
|---|---|---|---|
| ALBUM TITLE: | **English Folk Songs** | | |
| LABEL: Kosei | MONO | STEREO | KOR/KOCD 8783-84/ 3563 |
| GOLDEN IMPORTS   SRI | | ALBUM REFERENCE NO. | 133 |
| COVER ART:  M. Kajino | | LINER NOTES: | In Japanese |
| ENGINEER:  S. Wakabayashi/K. Oikawa | | TAPE TRANSFER: | S. Wakabayashi |
| RECORDING DATE: November 25, 1987 | | PERSONNEL LIST: | |

### PROGRAM
\* = Premier recording

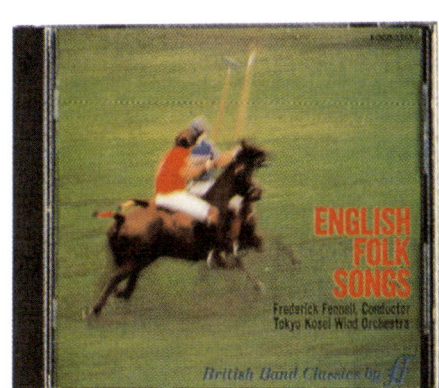

A Moorside Suite - Gustav Holst, arranged by Denis Wright
Three from Facade - William Walton, arranged by Robert O'Brien
William Byrd Suite - Gordon Jacob
Second Suite in F for Military Band, Op. 28b - Gustav Holst
Intermezzo from "An Original Suite" - Gordon Jacob
English Folk Song Suite - Ralph Vaughan Williams
Crown Imperial: A Coronation March - William Walton, arranged by W.J. Duthoit

### NOTES

Subtitle:   British Band Classics by FF

Recording dates:  25-26 November 1987
Recording site:  Fumon Hall, Tokyo, Japan
Group listed as Tokyo Kosei Windorchestra
Cover photo: Orion Press

LP and CD versions contain the same material in different line-up. As usual the back photo is omitted from the CD release. The last to be issued in the LP format. "What a Difference a Decade Makes"

At Riverside Community College for Music Association of California Community Colleges Honor Band – April 1981
Photo by Roger E. Rickson

| | |
|---|---|
| **ALBUM TITLE:** _Suite Francaise_ | |
| **LABEL:** Kosei        **MONO** | **STEREO**  KOCD 3101 |
| **GOLDEN IMPORTS    SRI** | **ALBUM REFERENCE NO.** 134 |
| **COVER ART:**   H. Hijikata | **LINER NOTES:**  In Japanese |
| **ENGINEER:**   J. Timperly/T. Leader | **TAPE TRANSFER:** |
| **RECORDING DATE:** July 13, 1989 | **PERSONNEL LIST:** |

## PROGRAM
\* = Premier recording

Suite Francaise - Darius Milhaud
William Tell Overture - Giocomo Rossini, arranged by T. Inagaki
Offrande A La Liberte [Lyrique] - F. J. Gossec, arranged by D. Dondeyne
Symphony For Band, Op. 69  [Symphony No. 6] - Vincent Persichetti
Three Dance Episodes from the Ballet "Spartacus" - Aram Khachaturian, arranged by Donald Hunsberger

## NOTES

Subtitle:  1989 European Concerts by FF

Recording dates:  13-14 July 1989
Recording site:  Angel Recording Studio, London, England
Group listed as Tokyo Kosei Windorchestra
Engineer:  John Pimperley
Editor:  Tom Leader
Cover photo of Eiffel Tower - no credit
Issued on CD format only.

FF:  Photos by Teruyoshi Shibata, producer of the recording for Kosei Publishing Co.
Back of CD insert lists the instrumentation for each selection.

FF:  Regarding the recording site;  Angel Studio must not be confused with the EMI Angel recording company.  This is a wonderful recording studio that is located in a part of London where the bus stop and the subway stop is called Angel.  It's on the British map of subways and other things as Angel stop.  You can see that in the Boohawkes books.  That's the important point to make; that it's not the EMI studio.  It's a private studio.  It is a big old brick church that was gutted and the exterior kept, but a fantastic new studio was constructed inside of that shell.  Never worked in a better one.

| | |
|---|---|
| **ALBUM TITLE:** **Romeo and Juliet** | |
| **LABEL:** Kosei   MONO | **STEREO** KOCD 3311 |
| **GOLDEN IMPORTS · SRI** | **ALBUM REFERENCE NO.** 135 |
| **COVER ART:** H. Hijikata | **LINER NOTES:** In Japanese |
| **ENGINEER:** S. Wakabayashi | **TAPE TRANSFER:** S. Wakabayashi |
| **RECORDING DATE:** November 28, 1986 | **PERSONNEL LIST:** |

### PROGRAM
\* = Premier recording

Music from the Ballet "Romeo and Juliet" - Sergei Prokofiev, arranged by Akira Yodo
Dances of Galanta - Zoltan Kodaly, arranged by R. Mark Rogers
Fountains of Rome - Ottorino Respighi, arranged by Lawrence Odom
West Point Symphony - Morton Gould

### NOTES

Subtitle: TOKWO Concert Series #1

Recording dates: Live sessions - #1 and #4 - 40th Regular concert 21 March 1987
   Live sessions - #2 and #3 - 39th Regular concert 28 November 1986
Recording site: Shinjuku Bunka Center, Tokyo
Group listed as Tokyo Kosei Windorchestra
Cover illustration: Y. Uemoto
Photos: Kyodo Photo Service, Ongaku No Tomosha Corporation

| | |
|---|---|
| **ALBUM TITLE:** **Premiere Rhapsodie** | |
| **LABEL:** Kosei   MONO | **STEREO** KOCD 3313 |
| **GOLDEN IMPORTS   SRI** | **ALBUM REFERENCE NO.** 136 |
| **COVER ART:** H. Hijikata/N. Ishiguro | **LINER NOTES:** In Japanese |
| **ENGINEER:** K. Oikawa/S. Wakabayashi | **TAPE TRANSFER:** S. Wakabayashi |
| **RECORDING DATE:** December 10, 1989 | **PERSONNEL LIST:** |

### PROGRAM
\* = Premier recording

The Magic Flute - Wolfgang Amadeus Mozart, arranged by Frank Winterbottom
Premiere Rhapsodie - Claude Debussy, arranged by T. Inagaki - Guy Dangain, soloist
Petite Suite - Claude Debussy, arranged by H. Kuwabara
Il Staccato - Charles Graffeuil, arranged by O. Coquelet
Rigoletto de Verdi - Luigi Bassi, arranged by Th. Dureau [Fantasie for Clarinet solo]
Suite Gayaneh - Aram Khachaturian, arranged by T. Inagaki

### NOTES

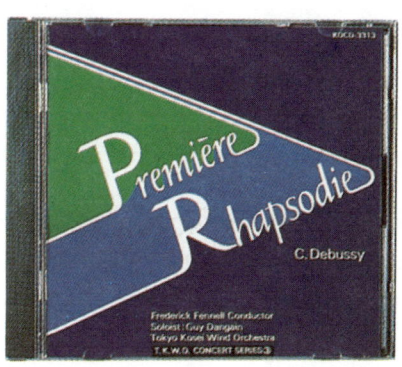

Subtitle: TOKWO Concert Series #3

Recording date: Nonaka Special Concert, 10 December 1989 [recorded LIVE]
Recording site: Maeda Hall, Tokyo, Japan
Group listed as Tokyo Kosei Windorchestra

Clarinet soloist: Guy Dangain for *Premiere Rhapsodie*, *Il Staccato* and *Rigoletto de Verdi*.

| | | | |
|---|---|---|---|
| **ALBUM TITLE:** | **Bacchus on Blue Ridge** | | |
| **LABEL:** Kosei | MONO | **STEREO** | KOCD 3564 |
| **GOLDEN IMPORTS** SRI | | **ALBUM REFERENCE NO.** 137 | |
| **COVER ART:** Aflo Foto Agency | | **LINER NOTES:** In Japanese | |
| **ENGINEER:** S.Wakabayashi/K. Oikawa | | **TAPE TRANSFER:** | |
| **RECORDING DATE:** December 6, 1988 | | **PERSONNEL LIST:** | |

### PROGRAM
\* = Premier recording

La Battaglia di Legnano Overture - Giuseppi Verdi, arranged by W. Kalischnig
Sinfonia "Il Fume" - Jurriaan Andriessen
Le Chant de l' Arbre - Serge Lancen
Svenska Folkvisor Och Dancer - A. Soderman/S. Gustafson
Bacchus on Blue Ridge - Joseph Horovitz

### NOTES

Subtitle: European Band Repertoire by FF

Recording dates: 6-7 December, 1988
Recording site: Parthenon Tama, Tokyo
Group listed as Tokyo Kosei Windorchestra
Recording Engineers: Shunsuke Wakabayashi and K. Oikawa
Jacket design: M. Kajino
Fennell is misspelled on back cover of CD. "La Battaglia" is also misspelled both in insert and on back cover. Correct on CD.
All liner notes are in Japanese. A great photo of Frederick Fennell from Orion Press, appears in the booklet. The same photo also appears on the LP "English Folk Songs" - KOR 8783-84.

FF: In correspondence dated 30 October 1989 - If you have picked up "Sinfonia Il Fume", that is made [last December] in our new recording place, Tama Parthenon, so named because in a massive development of a super Tokyo bedroom town, the Keio Railroad is developing Tama Center. The Parthenon, of course is at the top of it all. Great sound as you will hear.

FF: In the 1987 season it became obvious that a tour in Europe was in the making, and the enterprising publisher, Jan Molenaar of the Netherlands, offered the attractive repertory on this date as possible "bait," our repertory being heavily British and American. The Verdi Overture is early in his work and a strong score, typically his. I knew it <u>not at all</u>, and was happy to record it; so were the players. Andriessen's brilliant score was the test piece for the 1985 Kerkrade competition. I did not know this when I programmed it for Kerkrade 1989, but we made it with that performance. A first-rate contemporary piece. Lancen has a very happy style; his "Song of the Tree" carries it through a years' life cycle. The *Svenska* pieces are set for young groups and they are charming and very fresh. Joseph Horovitz has a great command, and he is at home in the whole world of music. *Bacchus* is a true adventure into the music one may imagine in/at/on -- or around the Beautiful Blue Ridge Mountains. Bacchus has his holiday in these charming essays in the American Style -- but, it is not jazz. The jacket photo etc., - not my bag. [August 1991]

| | | | |
|---|---|---|---|
| ALBUM TITLE: | **The Firebird and Pictures at an Exhibition** | | |
| LABEL: Kosei | MONO | STEREO | KOCD 3565 |
| GOLDEN IMPORTS  SRI | | ALBUM REFERENCE NO. | 138 |
| COVER ART:  M. Kajino | | LINER NOTES:  In Japanese | |
| ENGINEER:  S. Wakabayashi/K. Oikawa | | TAPE TRANSFER: | |
| RECORDING DATE: October 23, 1989 | | PERSONNEL LIST: | |

### PROGRAM
\* = Premier recording

The Firebird [1919] Suite from the Ballet - Igor Stravinsky - Transcribed by Randy Earles, ed. Frederick Fennell
Pictures at an Exhibition - Modest Petrovich Moussorgsky - Transcribed by Mark Hindsley

### NOTES

Subtitle:  Classics Arranged for Band

Recording dates:  23-24 October 1989
Recording site:  Parthenon Tama, Tokyo
Group listed as Tokyo Kosei Windorchestra
Recording Engineers:  Shunsuke Wakabayashi and K. Oikawa
Jacket design:  M. Kajino
Photo of electrical storm provided by Aflo Foto Agency.

All liner notes are in Japanese, except for instrumentation list on back cover.  Another great photo of Frederick Fennell on podium, complete with glasses, jeans and sneakers.  No credits given in English.

FF:  All Japan photos of me on KOR are by Kawamura.  The Tokyo Kosei Windorchestra players so strongly prefer to play only those transcriptions that are in the original key, that our librarian, Kiyohisa Suzuki transposed and re-copied Hindsley's parts.

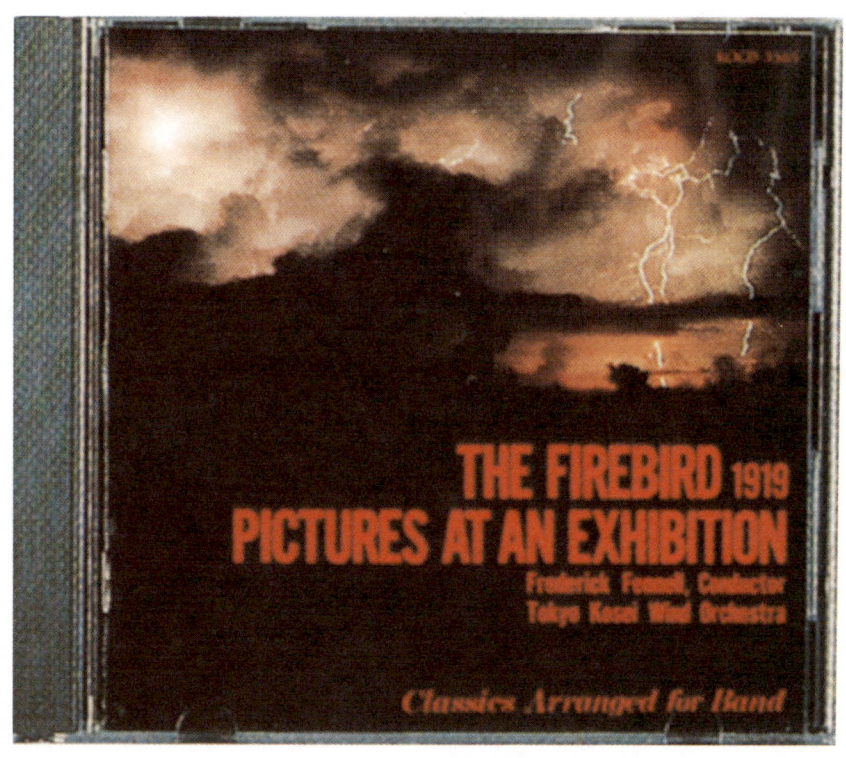

| | | |
|---|---|---|
| ALBUM TITLE: **Peer Gynt** | | |
| LABEL: Kosei | MONO | STEREO KOCD 3566 |
| GOLDEN IMPORTS SRI | | ALBUM REFERENCE NO. 139 |
| COVER ART: Masaaki Kajino | | LINER NOTES: In Japanese |
| ENGINEER: Kimio Oikawa | | TAPE TRANSFER: |
| RECORDING DATE: April 12, 1990 | | PERSONNEL LIST: |

**PROGRAM**
\* = Premier recording

Suite: The Comedians - Dmitri Kabalevsky, transcribed by Genba Fujita
Elegy - John Barnes Chance
Overture for Winds, Op. 24 - Felix Mendelssohn-Bartholdy, arranged & edited by John Boyd
Italian Polka - Sergei Rachmaninoff, arranged by Erik W.G. Leidzen, edited by Frederick Fennell
Vocalise, Op. 34, No. 14 - Sergei Rachmaninoff, arranged by Akira Yodo
Peer Gynt - Edvard Hagerup Grieg, arranged by Genba Fujita and Masaru Kawasaki
Molly on the Shore - Percy A. Grainger
Irish Tune from County Derry - Percy A. Grainger

**NOTES**

Subtitle: Concert Repertoire 1

Recording dates: 12-13 April 1990
Recording site: Niiza Shimin Kaikan
Group listed as Tokyo Kosei Windorchestra
Recording Engineers: Shunsuke Wakabayashi, Yumi Suzuki and Kimio Oikawa
Jacket design: Masaaki Kajino
Photograph: Aflo Foto/Kyoko Harada

All liner notes are in Japanese except for instrumentation list.
Black and white photo of Fennell in notes appeared as the cover of "Serenata", KOR 8413.

| | | | |
|---|---|---|---|
| **ALBUM TITLE:** | Mozart - Serenade No. 10 - Serenade No. 12 | | |
| **LABEL:** Kosei | **MONO** | **STEREO** | KOCD 3567 |
| **GOLDEN IMPORTS** | **SRI** | **ALBUM REFERENCE NO.** | 140 |
| **COVER ART:** | Sekai Bunka Photo | **LINER NOTES:** | Frederick Fennell |
| **ENGINEER:** | Kimio Oikawa | **TAPE TRANSFER:** | |
| **RECORDING DATE:** | October 30, 1990 | **PERSONNEL LIST:** | Included in folder |

### PROGRAM
\* = Premier recording

Serenade No. 10 in B-flat - Wolfgang Amadeus Mozart
Serenade No. 12 in C Minor - Wolfgang Amadeus Mozart

### NOTES

Subtitle: Great Wind Serenades by FF

Recording dates: 30-31 October 1990
Recording site: IMA Hall, Tokyo
Group listed as Tokyo Kosei Windorchestra
Recording Engineers: Shunsuke Wakabayashi, Yumi Suzuki and Kimio Oikawa
Jacket design: Masaaki Kajino
Photography: Noriyuki Kawamura
Cover photo: Sekai Bunka Photo

This is the first release to include liner notes in both Japanese and English. Notes are by Frederick Fennell. There is a short bio of Fennell and a short history of TOKWO.
Personnel and instrumentation for each Serenade are listed in the notes.
Pictures of the ensemble in both concert and recording session are included in the notes.

FF: IMA is a city that is being built by the controlling elected officials of the area and it is on the site of one of the American Army camps of the occupation in Japan. Those forty story high-rises for all of the bedroom community of Tokyo, so to speak, and they are building everything around it, including great halls, and this IMA Hall is a marvelous chamber music hall. And that is the first time we have used it, and I am sure we will be using it again. The seating is probably no more than five-hundred.

Performance score and parts were prepared by Frederick Fennell and published by Ludwig Music Publishing Co., Inc.

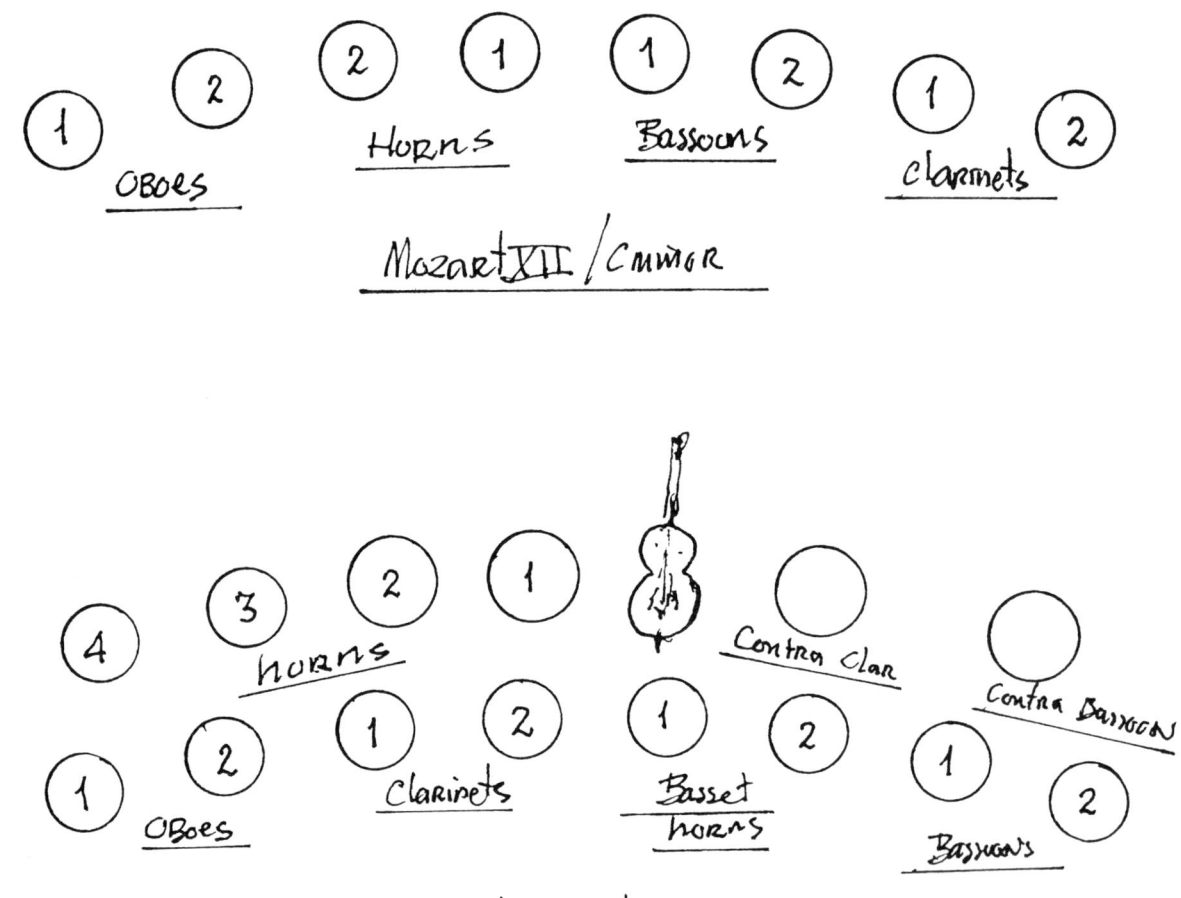

Mozart session, October 1990.
Photo by Noriyuki Kawamura,
courtesy of Kosei Publishing Co.

| | | | |
|---|---|---|---|
| **ALBUM TITLE:** | **Hungarian Rhapsody** | | |
| **LABEL:** Kosei | **MONO** | **STEREO** | KOCD 3568 |
| **GOLDEN IMPORTS** SRI | | **ALBUM REFERENCE NO.** | 141 |
| **COVER ART:** * see notes | | **LINER NOTES:** | |
| **ENGINEER:** Kimio Oikawa | | **TAPE TRANSFER:** | |
| **RECORDING DATE:** April 11, 1991 | | **PERSONNEL LIST:** | |

### PROGRAM
\* = Premier recording

Hungarian Rhapsody No. 2 - Franz Liszt, transcribed by Kazuto Miyazawa
Prayer and Dream Pantomime from "Hansel and Gretel" - Englebert Humperdinck, transcribed by Joseph E. Maddy
Ballet Music from the opera "Faust" - Charles Gounod, transcribed by Takuzo Inagaki
Voices of Spring, Waltz - Johann Strauss II, transcribed by Aubrey Winter and Alfred Hibbert
March Slav - Peter Ilyich Tschaikowsky, transcribed by Yoshihiro Kimura
Finlandia - Jean Sibelius, transcribed by Makio Kimura, edited by Frederick Fennell

### NOTES

Subtitle: Concert Repertoire No. 2

Recording dates: 11-12 April 1991
Recording site: Tama Parthenon Hall
Group listed as Tokyo Kosei Windorchestra
Cover design: Masaaki Kajino
Cover photo: Sekai Bunka Photo
Photography: Noriyuki Kawamura

FF: Arranger/Transcriber Makio Kimura plays Bass Clarinet in TOKWO.

TOKWO at WASBE 1989 Kerkrade, Holland. Photo Courtesy of Kosei Publishing Co.

| | | | |
|---|---|---|---|
| **ALBUM TITLE:** | _Piece of Mind - The Contemporary Mix_ | | |
| **LABEL:** Kosei | **MONO** | **STEREO** | KOCD 3569 |
| **GOLDEN IMPORTS** SRI | | **ALBUM REFERENCE NO.** 142 | |
| **COVER ART:** | | **LINER NOTES:** Frederick Fennell | |
| **ENGINEER:** Kimio Oikawa | | **TAPE TRANSFER:** | |
| **RECORDING DATE:** October 24, 1991 | | **PERSONNEL LIST:** | |

### PROGRAM
\* = Premier recording

Piece of Mind - Dana Wilson
\*Scenes - Verne Reynolds
\*Dance Suite - Joseph Horovitz
Sinfonia No. IV - Walter Sinclair Hartley
\*Stones in Time - Tomoki Kawade
\*Morning Alleluias for the Winter Solstice - Ron Nelson

### NOTES

Subtitle: Contemporary Mix

Recording dates: 24-25 October 1991
Recording site: The Parthenon, Tama City, Japan
Group listed as Tokyo Kosei Windorchestra
Recording Engineers: Shunsuke Wakabayashi, Yumi Suzuki and Kimio Oikawa
Photography: Noriyuki Kawamura
Cover photo: Sekai Bunka Photo

FF: In correspondence dated 10 October 1991 - Everyone worked very hard to bring the Reynolds and Hartley together -- and only on the 4th day. Hartley's piece is so transparent, no place to hide. At Eastman we called him Mr. Kleen, there being only the notes <u>needed</u>, no dirt. _Scenes_ is a 12 tone achievement of the highest order - a frantic piece. Hartley also writes in rows of 12 but the two pieces are very different. Walter has a dodecophonic lyricism that is very successful. And _Scenes_ is a very difficult piece rhythmically - 18 minutes of utter concentration, virtuosity the norm per bar. If we are lucky we can make a good recording, but it is tough. And I know it from two previous performances. The Strauss and Dvorak as balance on the program went lavishly.

FF: In correspondence dated 12 December 1991 - English notes are by Frederick Fennell. The release date will be 10 March 1992. All of these are first recordings for me; premier recordings for _Scenes, Dance Suite, Stones in Time_ and _Morning Alleluias_. The center-fold photo was taken during _Morning Alleluias_, a great shot, crystal clear, showing every player and the instrument, shot across stage from above right ... and ... all six composers are alive at the time of recording; it was the same with the first Eastman Wind Ensemble recording, too.

Between the Wilson, Nelson and Reynolds, we had to assemble the largest total group of players for any of my sessions, and as far back as May 1991, I had to assign players - extras, that is, so that I could use rehearsals [4] before the recording rehearsals [also 4] with the same players for Reynolds and Hartley, at the Casals Hall concert on 9 October 1991! The recording has the most difficult repertory yet, especially Reynolds, Kawade and Hartley; many high school groups at the All Japan Band Competition played _Stones in Time_ from memory! ... just to tell, again, where teaching, rehearsing, dedication, and performance are for Japanese youth.

| | | | |
|---|---|---|---|
| ALBUM TITLE: | **The Roman Trilogy - Pines, Fountains, Festivals** | | |
| LABEL: Kosei | MONO | STEREO | KOCD 3570 |
| GOLDEN IMPORTS   SRI | | ALBUM REFERENCE NO. | 143 |
| COVER ART: *see notes | | LINER NOTES: | Frederick Fennell |
| ENGINEER: Kimio Oikawa | | TAPE TRANSFER: | |
| RECORDING DATE: April 22, 1992 | | PERSONNEL LIST: | |

## PROGRAM
\* = Premier recording

The Pines of Rome, Symphonic Poem - Ottorino Respighi, transcribed by Eiji Suzuki
The Fountains of Rome, Symphonic Poem - Ottorino Respighi, transcribed by Yoshihiro Kimura
Roman Festivals, Symphonic Poem - Ottorino Respighi, transcribed by Yoshihiro Kimura

## NOTES

Subtitle: Classics arranged for Band

Recording dates: 22 -23 April 1992
Recording site: Tama Parthenon Hall
Group listed as Tokyo Kosei Windorchestra
Cover design: Masaake Kajino
Cover photo: Sekai Bunka Photo
Photography: Noriyuki Kawamura

FF: In correspondence dated 23 April 1992 from Tama-shi, Japan – It is a bright and very beautiful spring morning in Tama-shi where yesterday we put together *The Pines* and *The Fountains*. They always put me up in this hotel [Keio Plaza Hotel - Tama] so I can be fully rested and ready for the next day of recording, and on this one we will complete the Trilogy with *The Festivals*. For this we will have [as for *Fountains*], organ – the biggest Yamaha electric, and the off stage BANDA, too; plus for *Festivals*, the mandolin! – going all the way.

FF: In correspondence dated 26 May 1992 – We're off tomorrow on the last tour of this trip, 24 concerts in 12 days [that's how you keep the technique in shape] = 19 Toccatas and Fugues, etc. This the third tour and all cooking! The April sessions' fruit arrived the other day ... so much sound, Parthenon was having a time to handle it all. The end of *The Pines* is simply overpowering, and you never heard more notes than the reeds put out at the last four minutes of Festivals, plus a complete <u>melee</u> of sound, action, frenzy ... never heard anything like it. The quiet of *Fountains* at the end – WOW!. I do hope you will like it. The only other really big piece left to do is *Planets*. Maybe that's next, I don't know. ... Saw much of the bare Frederick Fennell Hall and it's finish is under way. Lots to do, and the donor is going to conduct *Finlandia* at the opening. It will be a very nice small hall for all the young people of Kofu who have no other place in which to present chamber music, solo material, etc. ... a great gift to his community. I still really can't believe it!

Recording of *Morning Alleluias* – October 1991. Photo by Kawamura courtesy of Kosei Publishing Co.

| | |
|---|---|
| **ALBUM TITLE:** | **Celebration - Contemporary Mix 2** |
| **LABEL:** Kosei   MONO | **STEREO** KOCD 3571 |
| **GOLDEN IMPORTS   SRI** | **ALBUM REFERENCE NO.** 144 |
| **COVER ART:** | **LINER NOTES:** Frederick Fennell |
| **ENGINEER:** Kimio Oikawa/S. Wakabayashi | **TAPE TRANSFER:** |
| **RECORDING DATE:** November 4, 1992 | **PERSONNEL LIST:** |

### PROGRAM
*\* = Premier recording*

Celebration - Philip Sparke
Sinfonietta - Ingolf Dahl
Fanfare on Motifs of Die Gurrelieder - Arnold Schoenberg
Variations on a Shaker Melody - Aaron Copland
Solemn Procession - George Perle
Fantasies on a Theme by Haydn - Norman Dello Joio

### NOTES

Subtitle: Contemporary Mix 2

Recording date: 4-5 November 1992
Recording site: Lilia Hall, Kawaguchi
Group listed as Tokyo Kosei Windorchestra
Cover design: Masaaki Kajino
Cover photo: Sekai Bunka Photo
Photography: Noriyuki Kawamura
Assistant Director: Yuni Suzuki
Engineer: Kimio Oikawa
Tape Editor: Kazuie Sugimoto [JVC]

"Let's hear that *again*!" Photo by Kawamura courtesy of Kosei Publishing Co.

| | |
|---|---|
| **ALBUM TITLE:** _Introduction_ | |
| **LABEL:** Kikushima Co, Ltd.  **MONO** | **STEREO** |
| **GOLDEN IMPORTS   SRI** | **ALBUM REFERENCE NO.** 145 |
| **COVER ART:** Hiroyyuki Gomi | **LINER NOTES:** In Japanese |
| **ENGINEER:** Yasuo Shimura | **TAPE TRANSFER:** |
| **RECORDING DATE:** July 17, 1992 | **PERSONNEL LIST:** |

## PROGRAM
\* = Premier recording

Voices of Spring - Johann Strauss II, transcribed by Aubrey Winter & Alfred Hibbert
The Sound of Music - Richard Rodgers, arr. Iwai
Festive Overture - Dmitri Shostakovich, arr. Donald Hunsberger [conducted by Hiroshi Genma]
Rifle Regiment - John Philip Sousa, ed. Frederick Fennell [conducted by Tokio Kikushima]
Bugler's Holiday - Leroy Anderson, arr. M. Edwards
Clarinet Candy - Leroy Anderson
National Emblem - Edwin E. Bagley, ed. Frederick Fennell
His Honor - Henry Fillmore, ed. Frederick Fennell

## NOTES

This is a private issue by Kikushima Co. Ltd., the builder and dedicator of the new Frederick Fennell Hall in Kofu, Japan. This is a recording made at the premier concert on 17 July 1992. The disc also contains part of a concert recorded by a youth group on 23 August 1992, conducted by Hiroshi Genma.
The cover photo is of the interior stage of Frederick Fennell Hall.

Recording date: 17 July 1992
Recording site: Frederick Fennell Hall, Kofu, Japan
Group listed as Tokyo Kosei Windorchestra
Engineer: Yasuo Shimura

RR: The following is printed in English in the CD insert ... "To Frederick Fennell with appreciation and respect.

Dear Sir,
It was our great pleasure to have an opportunity to meet you. When you visited our company for the first time, Frederick Fennell Hall had the concrete floor and the steel poles in place, but not the roof yet. You were walking with your wife, keeping away from rain puddles. We will never be able to forget when the sunshine appeared and you said "Oh, sunshine!", smiling with your eyes brightenning like a young boy, and reaching your hands up to the sky. We also can't forget your wife looking at you with a beautiful smile. We met just twice before but had thought about you a lot and admired your personality. You told us our work was similar, both of us creating beauty. What you told us at that time, the way you were impressed by a lot of things and your sensitive and curious manner encourage us and inspire us to brush up our own sensitivity. With us you always smiled and looked very gentle but once you were on stage you looked like a different person who really was big and powerful with a lot of confidence, as if you were sending us some sort of message. We were very much impressed with your professional attitude. We learned a lot from you and would like to say thank you very much. We hope you will take very good care of yourself and your wife and we are very much looking forward to seeing you again. Yours sincerely, Kikushima Co., Ltd.

# FREDERICK FENNELL HALL

## "How it all Began"
Delivered by Frederick Fennell
Premier Concert in Frederick Fennell Hall
Kofu, Japan

Dear Friend Tokio Kikushima:

This occasion grants a rare privilege, for you honor me in a most unique way. And, in honoring me and my name in this continuing manner, you also honor before me -- the name of my father.

Fred Fennell was a very talented man, born in a time before the art of music was studied in American schools. But what was denied him in opportunity, he did all that a mill-worker could do to provide for his son's education and musical experiences. This afternoon I remember him and his affectionate thoughtfulness. And I express my thanks to all of the Fennell family, to the many teachers and colleagues whose guidance, devotion, and performance brought me first, to The Eastman Wind Ensemble -- and now to The Tokyo Kosei Windorchestra.

Thank you, Tokio Kikushima for this beautiful room dedicated today to people, to music -- and to the beauty of all arts.

Welcome to Frederick Fennell Hall !

RR: This speech was delivered in Japanese by Frederick Fennell on 17 July 1992. He quoted this to me, in Japanese, on 6 February 1993.

Entrance to Frederick Fennell Hall in Kofu, Japan. Photos on left wall are of Fennell in rehearsal and performance with the Tokyo Kosei Windorchestra. Photo courtesy of Tokio Kikushima

| | | |
|---|---|---|
| ALBUM TITLE: | **Symphonies** | |
| LABEL: Kosei | MONO | STEREO KOCD 2711 |
| GOLDEN IMPORTS SRI | | ALBUM REFERENCE NO. 146 |
| COVER ART: | | LINER NOTES: Frederick Fennell |
| ENGINEER: S. Wakabayashi | | TAPE TRANSFER: |
| RECORDING DATE: April 21, 1993 | | PERSONNEL LIST: |

### PROGRAM
\* = Premier recording

Symphony No. 7 - Ludwig van Beethoven - trans. by Josef Triebensee
Symphony No. 39 in E-flat - First movement - Wolfgang Amadeus Mozart
Symphony No. 92 [Oxford] - Joseph Haydn - trans. by Josef Triebensee

### NOTES

Recording date: 21-22 April 1993
Recording site: IMA Hall, Tokyo
Jacket design: unavailable at press time
Photography: unavailable at press time
Cover photo: unavailable at press time

Personnel:
Oboe: Hitoshi Wakui, Masato Miyagawa
Clarinet: Hitoshi Sekiguchi, Kiyosumi Ogura [Haydn]
Bassoon: Mamoru Kanazaki
Horn: Hiroshi Uehara, Hiromi Namiki, Masanori Saigo, Atsushi Kimura
Contra-bassoon: I. Okouchi
String contrabass: Takuro Inagaki
Trumpet: Kazuo Hayashi

Another "special look from the Maestro." Photo by Kawamura courtesy of Kosei Publishing Co.

| | | |
|---|---|---|
| **ALBUM TITLE:** | **Music from Dragon Quest** | |
| **LABEL:** Telarc | **MONO** | **STEREO** PHCT-211 CD 80121 |
| **GOLDEN IMPORTS   SRI** | | **ALBUM REFERENCE NO.** 147 |
| **COVER ART:** ADMAX | | **LINER NOTES:** In Japanese |
| **ENGINEER:** Michael Bishop | | **TAPE TRANSFER:** |
| **RECORDING DATE:** May 7, 1993 | | **PERSONNEL LIST:** Listed in notes |

## PROGRAM
\* = Premier recording

Music from Dragon Quest by Koichi Sugiyama

Arrangement by J. Samuel Pilafian
Percussion editions by Richard Jensen

Overture
Chateau Ladutorm
Rondo
Minuet
Comrades : Intermezzo, A Lonely Soldier, Minx Princess March,
   Weapon Merchant Toruneco, Gypsy's Dance, Gypsy's Journey, Intermezzo
Wagon Wheels March
Cursed Towers – Frightening Dungeons
Dungeons – Tower – Phantom Ship
Balloon's Flight
Casino Rag
Violent Enemies
Noble Requiem – Saint
Satan
Heaven
Bridal Waltz
Into the Legend

## NOTES

Recording date: 6- 8 May 1993
Recording site: Music Hall, Cincinnati, Ohio
Producer: Elaine Martone
Executive Producer: Robert Woods
Technical Assistance: Scott Burgess
Supervising Editor: Erica Brenner
Assistant Editors: Scott Burgess, Tom Knab
Production Assistance: Erica Brenner
Cover Computer Graphics: ADMAX
Cover Illustration: Seiji Yamashita
Art Director: Yukimasa Kagi
Recorded in Telarc 20 bit digital and surround sound
Group listed as The Cincinnati Brass and Percussion
Dr. Frederick Fennell, Conducting

Personnel:
Philip Collins, principal trumpet and flugelhorn
Marie Speziale, assistant trumpet and flugelhorn
Steven Pride, trumpet and flugelhorn
Robin Graham, principal horn
Thomas Sherwood, assistant horn
Duane Dugger, assistant horn
Peter Norton, tenor and bass trombone
J. Samuel Pilafian, tuba
Richard Jensen, principal timpani and percussion
David Fishlock, timpani and percussion

Front and center – Elaine Martone, Frederick Fennell and Sam Pilafian.   Photos by Michael Bishop – Courtesy of Telarc International

| ALBUM TITLE: | **Civil War Favorites** | | |
|---|---|---|---|
| **LABEL:** Private | **MONO** | **STEREO** 8RB | |
| **GOLDEN IMPORTS** SRI | | **ALBUM REFERENCE NO.** 150 | |
| **COVER ART:** | | **LINER NOTES:** | |
| **ENGINEER:** | | **TAPE TRANSFER:** | |
| **RECORDING DATE:** | | **PERSONNEL LIST:** | |

**PROGRAM**
\* = Premier recording

Washington Grays - Claudio S. Grafulla
Other Civil War songs not conducted by Frederick Fennell

**NOTES**

Recording dates and sites not listed.
Group listed as: The 8th Regiment Band, Rome, Georgia
Production dedicated to Dr. Frederick Fennell.
Chief Musician: John Carruth

Disc available: P.O. Box 2593, Rome, Georgia 30164

| ALBUM TITLE: | **The Civil War - Its Music and Its Sounds** | | |
|---|---|---|---|
| **LABEL:** Mercury CD | **MONO** | **STEREO** 432 591-2 | |
| **GOLDEN IMPORTS** SRI | | **ALBUM REFERENCE NO.** 160 | |
| **COVER ART:** see notes | | **LINER NOTES:** Original | |
| **ENGINEER:** C.R. Fine | | **TAPE TRANSFER:** | |
| **RECORDING DATE:** | | **PERSONNEL LIST:** #9 | |

**PROGRAM**
\* = Premier recording

See albums No. 31 and 32.
Selections are almost complete as on the original release.

**NOTES**

Quote from CD notes: ... Due to maximum CD side length, *Cape May Polka*, *Rachel Waltzes*, the single track of *The Star Spangled Banner* [which is repeated at the end of Disc 2], and *Marching Through Georgia* from Volume II of the LP release, have regrettably been omitted.

Original liner notes have been preserved and a correction of the personnel listing, re-naming the E Flat Flat Tuba to the E Flat Tuba. A correction made thirty years after the first release of the 4 LP set. The 35mm logo, made famous with this initial release, is strangely missing from this re-release. The 35mm logo is seen on album 162, "Screamers and March Time".

This important CD release marks the first in a series of re-issues of the Eastman Wind Ensemble with its founder, Frederick Fennell.

Produced, musically supervised,and 3- to 2-channel conversion for Compact Disc by Wilma Cozart Fine
Musical Supervisor and Narration Script: Harold Lawrence
Chief Engineer and Technical Supervisor: C. Robert Fine
Associate Engineer: Robert Eberenz
Original album design: George Maas
Original album coordinator : Clair W. Van Ausdall
Mastering Engineer for Compact Disc: Dennis Drake
Booklet Coordinator for Compact Disc: Sedgwick Clark

| | | | |
|---|---|---|---|
| **ALBUM TITLE:** | **British and American Band Classics** | | |
| **LABEL:** Mercury CD | **MONO** | **STEREO** | 432 009-2 |
| **GOLDEN IMPORTS** SRI | | **ALBUM REFERENCE NO.** | 161 |
| **COVER ART:** see notes | | **LINER NOTES:** Frederick Fennell | |
| **ENGINEER:** C.R. Fine | | **TAPE TRANSFER:** | |
| **RECORDING DATE:** | | **PERSONNEL LIST:** | |

## PROGRAM
\* = Premier recording

Suite - "William Byrd" - Gordon Jacob
  The Earle of Oxford's March
  Pavana
  Jhon Come Kisse Me Now
  The Mayden's Song
  Wolsey's Wilde
  The Bells

Crown Imperial: A Coronation March - William Walton
Hammersmith: Prelude and Scherzo, Op. 52 - Gustav Holst
Symphonic Songs for Band - Robert Russell Bennett
Fanfare and Allegro - Clifton Williams

## NOTES

Re-issue of some of the finest recordings of wind literature ever produced.
Photo of Frederick Fennell by Mary Morris.

The original cover of British Band Classics II, is used for the CD cover as are Mercury Living Presence 35mm and other logos. The original liner notes are adapted from the original by Frederick Fennell. Additional notes are provided by Harold Lawrence, former Musical Supervisor for Mercury Living Presence.

Produced, musically supervised, and 3- to 2-channel conversion for Compact Disc by Wilma Cozart fine
Mastered for CD by Dennis Drake
Liner note editor: Sedgwick Clark
Only ORIGINAL MASTERS used for transfer to Compact Disc.
All works recorded in the Eastman Theatre in Rochester, N.Y. on 3 track half-inch tape.
Jacob, Walton and Holst were recorded 21 November 1958 using one 201 and two M56 Telefunken microphones.
Bennett and Williams were recorded 3 May 1959 using three Telefunken 201 microphones.
Recording Director: Wilma Cozart
Musical Supervisor: Harold Lawrence
Chief Engineer and Technical Supervisor: C. Robert Fine
Associate Engineer: Robert Eberenz

| | |
|---|---|
| **ALBUM TITLE:** | **Screamers and March Time** |
| **LABEL:** Mercury CD     **MONO** | **STEREO** 432 019-2 |
| **GOLDEN IMPORTS** SRI | **ALBUM REFERENCE NO.** 162 |
| **COVER ART:** see notes | **LINER NOTES:** Frederick Fennell |
| **ENGINEER:** C.R. Fine | **TAPE TRANSFER:** |
| **RECORDING DATE:** | **PERSONNEL LIST:** |

## PROGRAM
\* = Premier recording

In Storm and Sunshine - John C. Heed
Whip and Spur - Thomas S. Allen
Invictus - Karl L. King
The Big Cage - Karl L. King
Bones Trombones - Henry Fillmore
Them Basses - Getty H. Huffine
The Circus Bee - Henry Fillmore
The Screamer - Fred Jewell
Thunder and Blazes - Entry of the Gladiators - Julius Fucik
Robinson's Grand Entree - Karl L. King
Circus Days - Karl L. King
Bombasto - Orion R. Farrar
The Squealer - Will Huff
Rolling Thunder - Henry Fillmore
Bennett's Triumphal - John H. Ribble
Bravura - Charles E. Duble
Bugles and Drums - Edwin Franko Goldman
Illinois March - Edwin Franko Goldman
Children's March - Edwin Franko Goldman
The Interlochen Bowl - Edwin Franko Goldman
Onward-Upward - Edwin Franko Goldman
Boy Scouts of America - Edwin Franko Goldman
Americans We - Henry Fillmore
Officer of the Day - Robert Browne Hall
March "Grandioso" - Roland F. Seitz

## NOTES

A re-issue of the two original albums. It is nice to note that the full names of the composers along with dates are listed for each title. An omission that should not have been made on the original releases.

A likeness of the original Mercury 35mm logo appears on this Compact Disc release.
The selections from "Screamers" are the only titles recorded with the 35mm process. Only ORIGINAL MASTERS were used for transfer to Compact Disc.

RR: <u>Screamers</u> being the final recording of the Eastman Wind Ensemble with Frederick Fennell at the helm, the following statement from Harold Lawrence in correspondence dated 23 March 1983 is appropriate with this re-issue - "Frederick Fennell is one of America's most vital music makers who has made a very distinctive contribution to our culture. His achievements as founder and director of the Eastman Wind Ensemble are perhaps his greatest. Even in comparison with the latest digital super discs, these early Mercury recordings are as lively and exciting today as they were in the 50's and 60's when they were first released."

Produced, musically supervised, and 3- to 2-channel conversion for Compact Disc by Wilma Cozart Fine
Mastering Engineer for Compact Disc: Dennis Drake
Line Note Editor: Sedgwick Clark
Recording Director: Wilma Cozart
Musical Supervisor: Harold Lawrence
Chief Engineer and Technical Supervisor: C. Robert Fine
Associate Engineer: Robert Eberenz ["Screamers"]

158

| | | | |
|---|---|---|---|
| **ALBUM TITLE:** | **Fennell Conducts Grainger, Persichetti & Others** | | |
| **LABEL:** Mercury CD | **MONO** | **STEREO** 432 754-2 | |
| **GOLDEN IMPORTS   SRI** | | **ALBUM REFERENCE NO.** 163 | |
| **COVER ART:** see notes | | **LINER NOTES:** Frederick Fennell | |
| **ENGINEER:** C.R. Fine | | **TAPE TRANSFER:** | |
| **RECORDING DATE:** | | **PERSONNEL LIST:** | |

### PROGRAM
\* = Premier recording

Lincolnshire Posy - Percy A. Grainger - edited by Frederick Fennell
Hill Song No. 2 - Percy A. Grainger
Symphony for Band [Symphony No. 6] - Vincent Persichetti
Armenian Dances - Aram Khachaturian, arranged by Ralph Satz, edited by Frederick Fennell
Concerto for 23 Winds - Walter Hartley
Three Japanese Dances - Bernard Rogers

### NOTES

Third in the series of Living Presence compact discs from Mercury Records. Faithful reproduction of cover art and liner notes from the original issues SR 90173 [2 March 1958] and SR 90221 [4 May 1959].

Produced, musically supervised, and 3- to 2-channel conversion for Compact Disc by Wilma Cozart Fine
Mastering Engineer for compact disc:  Dennis Drake
Liner Note Editor:  Sedgwick Clark
Recording Director: Wilma Cozart
Musical Supervisor: Harold Lawrence
Chief Engineer and Technical Supervisor: C. Robert Fine
Associate Engineer: Robert Eberenz [Armenian Dances, Symphony, Hill Song, and Concerto for 23 Winds]

*"I'm ready. Let's Go!"*
Photo courtesy of
Kosei Publishing Co.

| **ALBUM TITLE:** | **Fennell conducts SOUSA - "Sound Off" & "Sousa on Review"** | | |
|---|---|---|---|
| **LABEL:** Mercury CD | **MONO** | **STEREO** | 434 300-2 |
| **GOLDEN IMPORTS   SRI** | | **ALBUM REFERENCE NO.** | 164 |
| **COVER ART:**   see notes | | **LINER NOTES:** | Frederick Fennell |
| **ENGINEER:** C. R. Fine | | **TAPE TRANSFER:** | |
| **RECORDING DATE:** | | **PERSONNEL LIST:** | |

### PROGRAM
\* = Premier recording

Sound Off
Nobles of the Mystic Shrine
Sabre and Spurs
The Picadore
Our Flirtation
The High School Cadets
The Invincible Eagle
Bullets and Bayonets
The Liberty Bell
Riders for the Flag
Solid Men to the Front !
The Gallant Seventh
The Rifle Regiment
The Pride of the Wolverines
Golden Jubilee
The Gridiron Club
New Mexico March
Sesqui-Centennial Exposition
The Black Horse Troop
The Kansas Wildcats
Manhattan Beach
Ancient and Honorable Artillery Company
The National Game
The Glory of the Yankee Navy

### NOTES

A re-issue of SR 90264 and SR 90284 with the Eastman Wind Ensemble.  Cover is from SR 90284.  My choice would have been "Sound OFF !" - SR 90264
Notes are by Frederick Fennell from the original issues and edited by Sedgwick Clark for the CD release.
All technical information is listed in booklet.

This issue contains 24 of the recorded 34 Sousa marches by the Eastman Wind Ensemble and Frederick Fennell.
Inside back cover shows four other EWE CD releases.  The back insert card lists [15] *Golden Jubilee* twice and omits [14] *Pride of the Wolverines*.   The booklet cover is correct, with all titles listed.

Produced, musically supervised, and 3- to 2-channel conversion for Compact Disc by Wilma Cozart Fine
Mastering Engineer for Compact Disc: Andrew Nicholas
Line Note Editor:  Sedgwick Clark
Recording Director: Wilma Cozart
Musical Supervisor: Harold Lawrence
Chief Engineer and Technical Supervisor: C. Robert Fine
Associate Engineer: Robert Eberenz

| | | | |
|---|---|---|---|
| **ALBUM TITLE:** | _Frederick Fennell conducts the music of Leroy Anderson_ | | |
| **LABEL:** Mercury CD | **MONO** | **STEREO** | 432 013-2 |
| **GOLDEN IMPORTS   SRI** | | **ALBUM REFERENCE NO.** | 165 |
| **COVER ART:** see notes | | **LINER NOTES:** see notes | |
| **ENGINEER:** C. R. Fine/Robert Eberenz | | **TAPE TRANSFER:** | |
| **RECORDING DATE:** | | **PERSONNEL LIST:** | |

## PROGRAM
\* = Premier recording

Belle of the Ball
Horse and Buggy
The Waltzing Cat
Blue Tango
Summer Skies
Song of the Bells
The Typewriter
The Syncopated Clock
The Girl in Satin
China Doll
Saraband
Fiddle-Faddle
Sleigh Ride
Serenata
Promenade
Chicken Reel
Phantom Regiment
Jazz Legato
Jazz Pizzicato
Plink Plank Plunk
The Bluebells of Scotland
The First Day of Spring
Song of Jupiter

## NOTES

A re-issue of selections from the three volumes of Leroy Anderson and Frederick Fennell. Volume I [SR 90009]; Volume II [SR 90043] and Volume III [SR 90400]. Cover is from Volume II.
Notes are from originals by Clair W. Van Ausdall, Alfred E. Simon and Stanley Green. Liner notes were edited for this release by Sedgwick Clark. Great photo of FF by Mary Morris.

Produced, musically supervised, and 3- to 2-channel conversion for Compact Disc by Wilma Cozart Fine
Mastering Engineer for Compact Disc: Andrew Nicholas
Line Note Editor: Sedgwick Clark
Recording Director: Wilma Cozart [1-14]; Harold Lawrence [15-23]
Musical Supervisor: Harold Lawrence [1-14]
Chief Engineer and Technical Supervisor: C. Robert Fine [1-14]; Robert Eberenz [15-23]

Page 15 of booklet lists this release as performed by the Eastman Wind Ensemble, which of course, is incorrect. Booklet lists this compilation 1992 - disc lists this compilation 1991
Groups listed as Eastman-Rochester POPS Orchestra and Orchestra conducted by Frederick Fennell.

**ALBUM TITLE:** <u>**Gould - West Point Symphony**</u>

**LABEL:** Mercury CD  MONO  STEREO 434 320-2

**GOLDEN IMPORTS  SRI**  **ALBUM REFERENCE NO.** 166

**COVER ART:** see notes  **LINER NOTES:** Frederick Fennell

**ENGINEER:** C.R. Fine/Robert Eberenz  **TAPE TRANSFER:**

**RECORDING DATE:** May 3, 1959  **PERSONNEL LIST:**

### PROGRAM
\* = Premier recording

West Point Symphony - Morton Gould
Symphony No. 4 - Alan Hovhaness [Clyde Roller, conducting]
Symphony No. 3 - Vittorio Giannini [Clyde Roller, conducting]

### NOTES

A re-issue of selections from SR 90220 conducted by Frederick Fennell.  Cover art is from the original issue of SR 90220. Fennell's liner notes from the original are duplicated in tact.

RR: I would like to have seen a coupling with the Hindemith and Stravinsky recordings, keeping the disc completely Fennell for the re-issue.  Hopefully these will surface in the future.

Produced, musically supervised, and 3- to 2-channel conversion for Compact Disc by Wilma Cozart Fine
Mastering Engineer for Compact Disc: Andrew Nicholas
Liner Note Editor: Sedgwick Clark
Recording Director: Wilma Cozart
Musical Supervisor: Harold Lawrence
Chief Engineer and Technical Supervisor: C. Robert Fine [Gould]; Robert Eberenz [Giannini and Hovhaness]
Associate Engineer: Robert Eberenz [Gould]

*The Maestro* in Great Sacred Hall.  Photo courtesy of Kosei Publishing Co.

| | | | |
|---|---|---|---|
| **ALBUM TITLE:** | **Ballet for Band - Wagner** | | |
| **LABEL:** Mercury CD | **MONO** | **STEREO** | 434 322-2 |
| **GOLDEN IMPORTS SRI** | | **ALBUM REFERENCE NO.** | 167 |
| **COVER ART:** see notes | | **LINER NOTES:** | Frederick Fennell |
| **ENGINEER:** C.R. Fine/Robert Eberenz | | **TAPE TRANSFER:** | |
| **RECORDING DATE:** October 23, 1959 | | **PERSONNEL LIST:** | |

### PROGRAM
\* = Premier recording

Pineapple Poll Suite - Arthur Sullivan – arr. W.J. Duthoit
La Boutique Fantasque - Rossini/Respighi – arr. Dan Godfrey
Ballet Music from Faust - Charles Gounod – arr. William Winterbottom
Prelude to Act III and Bridal Chorus from "Lohengrin" - Richard Wagner – arr. Frank Winterbottom
Elsa's Procession to the Cathedral from "Lohengrin" - Richard Wagner – arr. Lucien Cailliet
Entry of the Gods into Valhalla from "Das Rheingold" - Richard Wagner – arr. Dan Godfrey

### NOTES

A re-issue from SR 90256 [info omitted from CD credits] and SR 90276. All technical information is same as LP releases. Cover art is from SR 90256 and Fennell's liner notes are duplicated from the original releases. *Overture to Rienzi* and *Good Friday Music* from "Parsifal" are not included in this re-issue.

Produced, musically supervised, and 3- to 2-channel conversion for Compact Disc by Wilma Cozart Fine
Mastering Engineers for compact disc: Andrew Nicholas and Thomas Ruff
Liner note editor: Sedgwick Clark.
Recording Director: Wilma Cozart
Musical Supervisor: Harold Lawrence
Chief Engineer and Technical Supervisor: C. Robert Fine
Associate Engineer: Robert Eberenz

FF: correspondence dated 31 January 1993 ... Roger, I think my note in the box on the LP is one of the best I have written about the evolution of repertory from transcription to original music ... the Cinderella idea, might be included here.

"With this album of transcriptions from the musical literature of the ballet orchestra, the Eastman Wind Ensemble and I enjoy a momentary departure from our principal tasks and interests in this continuing series of recording for Mercury Records. The fifteen albums thus far released have been devoted exclusively to original music for winds, and this vital concentration will remain as our primary objective. In presenting the music on this disc we seek, first of all, to continue to offer a pleasant and faithful listening experience. Second, we recognize that to countless thousands of record listeners, pleasant listening is not predicated upon the "purity" of the musical letter -- that transcriptions fashioned with taste and charm, executed with skill and devotion, are a vital and accepted part of the musical scene. To those for whom these transcriptions from orchestral literature may recall nostalgic experiences as players or listeners, we add that we enjoyed them too.

This is all part of the exciting activity that has grown out of the formation and public acceptance of the Eastman Wind Ensemble through our stimulating and rewarding association with Mercury Records. In the brief span of eight years we have begun to see the emergence of the Wind Ensemble as an expression that will have earned its place in the conscience of the composer, without whom - be it clearly understood -- we cannot hope to achieve musical citizenship. Toward that end we have been obliged to borrow status from ensembles that are accepted. Consequently, the beautiful transcriptions which are the repertory of this disc, are a part of the heritage of all wind groups. In their borrowed existence of the past, they might be compared to Cinderella and her pumpkin pulled by mice, which all these years have awaited the incantation of the magic words and a waft of the wand of destiny. No longer must the wind band sit by the fire. Prince Charming, the composer, has come to save it from itself. At last the glass slipper fits."

| | | | |
|---|---|---|---|
| **ALBUM TITLE:** | *Frederick Fennell Conducts Cole Porter & George Gershwin* | | |
| **LABEL:** Mercury CD | **MONO** | **STEREO** | 434 327-2 |
| **GOLDEN IMPORTS   SRI** | | **ALBUM REFERENCE NO.** | 168 |
| **COVER ART:** Original Gershwin release | | **LINER NOTES:** Frederick Fennell | |
| **ENGINEER:** C. Robert Fine | | **TAPE TRANSFER:** | |
| **RECORDING DATE:** | | **PERSONNEL LIST:** Listed in notes | |

## PROGRAM
\* = Premier recording

Cole Porter:
  Blow, Gabriel, Blow; So In Love; It's All Right with Me; Ridin' High; In the Still of the Night; Begin the Beguine; Night and Day; My Heart Belongs to Daddy; Anything Goes; I've Got You under My Skin; It's De-lovely; You'd Be So Nice to Come Home to

George Gershwin:
  I Got Rhythm; Love Is Sweeping the Country; Love Walked In; 'S Wonderful; Bidin' My Time; Oh, Lady, Be Good; Fascinating Rhythm; Liza; Embraceable You; The Man I Love; Someone to Watch Over Me; But Not for Me

## NOTES

Frederick Fennell Remembers: " It would have been difficult in the late 1950s for an inquisitive musician to be unaware of the enormous amount of popular music constantly coming onto the listening scene. For treatment of those ballads, beyond what was possible for even the largest of the big bands, there were those magical and brilliant full orchestral settings that recall the names of Morton Gould and Andre Kostelanetz.

As the fifties were winding down, however, C. Robert Fine, engineer extraordinaire, who had "heard it all" by way of his mixing console, felt that a fresh re-statement of the great popular standards [which seemed to be coming through his console less and less often now] needed to be made; and those feelings were shared by Wilma Cozart, Harold Lawrence, and me. Although we were all deep into our Civil War project [Mercury Living Presence CD 432 591-2] when these showcase albums of the music of Gershwin and Porter entered our lives, this addition of another musical dimension, rather than confusing us, became a handy foil for our thoughts.

Up to this point, all of my recording activity had been in the University of Rochester's Eastman Theatre and the Eastman Wind Ensemble and Eastman-Rochester "Pops" Orchestra, using only the three microphones of Mercury's tried-and-true Living Presence technique. As Bob Fine had taught us, once the microphones had been hung and set, the control of the music was in the hands of the conductor and players. Like any concert preparation, that performance had been shaped during normal rehearsal, and the music to be recorded had been written originally for concert-hall presentation from a stage to an audience. It all worked.

Now came a new scene for me: music distributed throughout a score with signal direction totally in mind, separating sounds according to their arrangement by my old friend Rayburn Wright and his staff. Those sounds were picked up by a roomful of state-of-the-art microphones and delivered to an enormous multi-channel mixing board ... just a bit different from those three 201's hanging by clothesline from the flys of the Eastman Theatre! Fine's ballroom studio in the old Great Northern Hotel on West 57th Street in New York City also was a beautiful chamber -- great sound to begin with. He had learned its every resource, as he had in the symphonic-sized room at his Bayside studios on Long Island, [Queens is listed in booklet] where the Porter was recorded.

In our discussions of the music and the choice of titles, Ray's desire was that the arrangements include the complete, and less well known, introductions to the Gershwin tunes -- vital music [and lyrics] that set mood and reason for the magical wedding of all that followed. The introduction that Ray scored as a solo for harpist Janet Remington in "Oh, Lady, Be Good" is the perfect example of his plan to include the song in its entirety. In all my life as a listener [and set player], that song was played as an "up" tune. Here, Ray went back to the source of the music in the show, which was the lyricist's and the composer's intention.

I had only one long night to study and mark those first sessions' scores with a small box of hotel drugstore-bought Crayolas. I really didn't need more time; Ray had thought of everything. And he knew the "famous fifty" players so well that he wrote for them -- and in the case of the multiple-reed doublers, for their incredible skills on four or five instruments. Everything I needed to know in this first bath of commercial recording was there in the scores.

Greeting the players, I saw a few faces I'd seen behind Eastman music stands, and the rest were probably players I'd been hearing for years on countless other recordings. So far, not all that much was different for me.

Then, here it was; one more time the great deep breath, and appropriate downbeat, and I was launched among friends into the best of all commercial worlds, where rehearsal was a rare [and usually unnecessary] luxury. Call the tune, read it down, wait for the sound booth's microphone adjustments, talk with Ray on the phone for his reactions -- then, silence -- watch for the light to come on: "Take One, SPEED!" We're rolling. What a great and memorable music experience. Frederick Fennell, 1992.

RR: It is interesting to note the addition of **"The Studio Sessions"** to this release.
Cover is from the original issue of Gershwin.

Produced, musically supervised, and 3- to 2-channel conversion for Compact Disc by Wilma Cozart Fine
Mastering Engineer for Compact Disc: Andrew Nicholas
Liner Note Editor: Sedgwick Clark
Recording Director: Wilma Cozart
Musical Supervisor: Harold Lawrence
Mixing Engineer and Technical Supervisor: C. Robert Fine
Associate Engineer: Robert Eberenz

---

**ALBUM TITLE:** <u>**Frederick Fennell Conducts Grainger and Coates**</u>

**LABEL:** Mercury CD    **MONO**    **STEREO** 434 330-2

**GOLDEN IMPORTS   SRI**    **ALBUM REFERENCE NO.** 169

**COVER ART:** Original Grainger release    **LINER NOTES:** Frederick Fennell/Stanley Green

**ENGINEER:**    **TAPE TRANSFER:**

**RECORDING DATE:**    **PERSONNEL LIST:**

---

### PROGRAM
\* = Premier recording

Percy Aldridge Grainger
  Country Gardens, Shepherd's Hey, Colonial Song, Children's March, The Immovable Do, Mock Morris, Handel in the Strand, Irish Tune from County Derry, Spoon River, My Robin is to the Greenwood Gone, Molly on the Shore

Eric Coates
  The Three Elizabeths: Halcyon Days, Springtime in Angus, Youth of Britain

### NOTES

A re-issue [complete] of SR 90219 "Country Gardens" and part of SR 90439 "Frederick Fennell Conducts Music by Eric Coates"

Produced, musically supervised, and 3-to 2-channel conversion for Compact Disc by Wilma Cozart Fine
Mastering Engineer for Compact Disc: Andrew Nicholas
Liner Note Editor: Sedgwick Clark
Recording Director: Wilma Cozart [Grainger]; Harold Lawrence [Coates]
Musical Supervisor: Harold Lawrence [Grainger]
Chief Engineer and Technical Supervisor: C. Robert Fine [Grainger]; Robert Eberenz [Coates]
Associate Engineer: Robert Eberenz [Grainger]

| | |
|---|---|
| **ALBUM TITLE:** | **La Fiesta Mexicana** |

**LABEL:** Japan World     **MONO**           **STEREO** WL 8504

**GOLDEN IMPORTS  SRI**           **ALBUM REFERENCE NO.** 170

**COVER ART:** see notes           **LINER NOTES:** in Japanese

**ENGINEER:**           **TAPE TRANSFER:**

**RECORDING DATE:** October 31, 1984           **PERSONNEL LIST:**

### PROGRAM
\* = Premier recording

Akizora "Under Autumn Sky" March - Yoichi Ueoka
La Fiesta Mexicana - H. Owen Reed
His Honor - Henry Fillmore
L'Inglesina - Davide Delle Cese
First Suite in E-flat for Military Band, Op. 28a - Gustav Holst
Fantasia in G, BWV 572 - Johann Sebastian Bach, arranged Goldman/Leist

### NOTES

Cover art: Photo of Tokyo Kosei Windorchestra with insert of Frederick Fennell
Group listed as: Osaka Municipal Symphonic Band
Recording site: Festival Hall, Osaka, Japan
All selections conducted by Frederick Fennell

---

**ALBUM TITLE:** **The 21st Regular Concert**

**LABEL:** Japan World     **MONO**           **STEREO** WL 8602

**GOLDEN IMPORTS  SRI**           **ALBUM REFERENCE NO.** 171

**COVER ART:** see notes           **LINER NOTES:** in Japanese

**ENGINEER:**           **TAPE TRANSFER:**

**RECORDING DATE:** November 21, 1985           **PERSONNEL LIST:**

### PROGRAM
\* = Premier recording

Fantasia in G, BWV 572 - Johann Sebastian Bach, arranged Goldman/Leist
Elsa's Procession from "Lohengrin" - Richard Wagner, arranged by Lucien Cailliet
Cakewalk from "Suite of Old American Dances" - Robert Russell Bennett
Othello and Desdemona from "Othello" - Alfred Reed
Polka and Fugue from "Schwanda" - Jaromir Weinberger, arranged by G. C. Bainum
Intermezzo from "Original Suite" - Gordon Jacob
King Cotton - John Philip Sousa
Le Regiment de Sambre e Meuse - Josef F. Rauski
His Honor - Henry Fillmore

### NOTES

Cover art is large color photo of Frederick Fennell with his distinctive signature in silver at lower right of album cover.
Group listed as: Kinki University Band
Recording site: Festival Hall, Osaka, Japan
All selections conducted by Frederick Fennell

| | |
|---|---|
| **ALBUM TITLE:** **Music for Contest** | |
| **LABEL:** Nippon Columbia CD **MONO** | **STEREO** CD 32CG-1294 |
| **GOLDEN IMPORTS   SRI** | **ALBUM REFERENCE NO.** 172 |
| **COVER ART:**   see notes | **LINER NOTES:**  in Japanese |
| **ENGINEER:** | **TAPE TRANSFER:** |
| **RECORDING DATE:** October 15, 1986 | **PERSONNEL LIST:** |

### PROGRAM
\* = Premier recording

El Camino Real - Alfred Reed
A Little Concert Suite for Winds - Alfred Reed
Overture Jubiloso - Frank Erickson
Alvamar Overture - James Barnes
Carnival of Roses Overture - Joseph Olivadoti
Symphonic Poem "Only One Earth" - Takanobu Saitoh
Ballade I for Symphonic Band - Bin Kaneda
Catastrophe for Symphonic Band - Hiroshi Hoshina

### NOTES

Cover art is large photo of unassembled clarinet - no inside photos
Group listed as Tokyo Kosei Windorchestra
Recording dates:  15, 17 & 18 October 1986
Recording site:  Urayasu Citizen Hall, Tokyo, Japan
Producer:  Eiji Inoue, A & R Department 4, Nippon Columbia
Chief Engineer:  Norio Okada
Second Engineer:  Yasuo Kozaka
Assistant :  Genichi Kitami

| | |
|---|---|
| **ALBUM TITLE:** **Music for Contest II** | |
| **LABEL:** Nippon Columbia CD **MONO** | **STEREO**  CD 32GC-1295 |
| **GOLDEN IMPORTS   SRI** | **ALBUM REFERENCE NO.** 173 |
| **COVER ART:** | **LINER NOTES:**  in Japanese |
| **ENGINEER:**  see issue 172 | **TAPE TRANSFER:** |
| **RECORDING DATE:** October 18, 1986 | **PERSONNEL LIST:** |

### PROGRAM
\* = Premier recording

Festival Music for Band - R. Hirose
Song of the High Cascades - Alfred Reed
Centennial Suite - John Morrissey
Lamentation of Archangel Michael - Genba Fujita
Kaze-No-Kuni - M. Kitazume
Dai-Kagura - K. Koyama
Folklore for Band - Jim Andy Caudill
American Salute - Morton Gould, arranged by Philip Lang
This Glorious Silver World - N. Yamamoto

### NOTES

Technical data same as issue 172

| | |
|---|---|
| **ALBUM TITLE:** | **Concert Marches for Glory and Tragedy - Classical Music Gallery** |
| **LABEL:** Denon CD     **MONO** | **STEREO**  CD 32CO-2365 |
| **GOLDEN IMPORTS   SRI** | **ALBUM REFERENCE NO.**  174 |
| **COVER ART:**  see notes | **LINER NOTES:**  in Japanese |
| **ENGINEER:**  see notes | **TAPE TRANSFER:** |
| **RECORDING DATE:** February 29, 1988 | **PERSONNEL LIST:** |

## PROGRAM
\* = Premier recording

March from the opera "Aida" - Giuseppi Verdi, arranged by J.S. Seredy
Funeral March of a Marionette - Charles F. Gounod, arranged by Mayhew L. Lake
Wedding March from "A Midsummer Nights Dream" - Felix Mendelssohn, arranged by L.P. Laurendeau
Trauersinfonie - Richard Wagner, arranged by Eric Leidzen
March of the Little Leaden Soldiers - Gabriel Pierne, arranged Dan Godfrey
March to the Scaffold - Hector Berlioz , arranged by J.H. Foulds/Brown
Grand March from "Tannhauser" - Richard Wagner, arranged by John Hartmann
Pieces of Eight Concert March [based on themes from Beethoven Symphony No. 8] - Joseph Wilcox Jenkins/ Jerome Neff
March from "Love of the Three Oranges" - Sergei Prokofiev, arranged by W. J. Duthoit
Funeral March in Memory of Composer Rikaard Nordrak - Edvard Grieg, edited by Frederick Fennell
Pomp and Circumstance No. 1 - Edward Elgar

## NOTES

Cover art photo of a king on horseback, central niche in unidentified public building
Inside photo of Frederick Fennell and group photo of ensemble.
Recording dates:  29 February and 1 March 1988
Recording site:  Musashino Shiminbunkakaikan
Group listed as Tokyo Kosei Windorchestra
Mixer:  Kuro Iida
Recording director:  Eiji Inoue

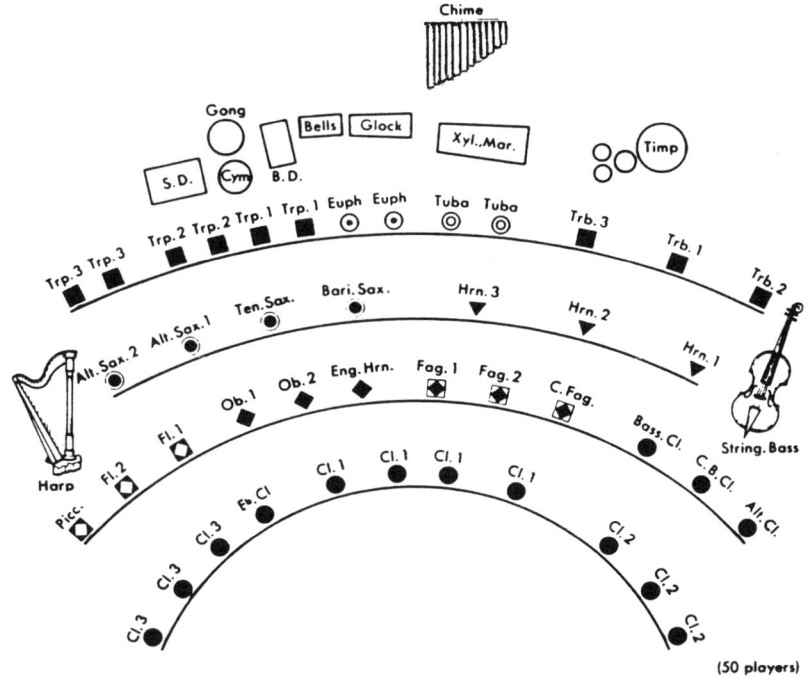

Frederick Fennell's set       Tokyo Kosei Wind Orchestra
3-24-25-'84                             KOR8411 Recording set.

| | | |
|---|---|---|
| **ALBUM TITLE:** | **Seagate Overture** | |
| **LABEL:** Nippon Columbia   **MONO** | | **STEREO**   CAY-899/CD 32 CG 3175 |
| **GOLDEN IMPORTS   SRI** | | **ALBUM REFERENCE NO.**   175 |
| **COVER ART:** | | **LINER NOTES:** |
| **ENGINEER:** Norio Okada | | **TAPE TRANSFER:** |
| **RECORDING DATE:** December 8, 1988 | | **PERSONNEL LIST:** |

## PROGRAM
* = Premier recording

Seagate Overture - James Swearingen
Incantation and Dance - John Barnes Chance
Appalachian Overture - James Barnes
A Song of the Sea - Rex Mitchell
Manatee Lyric Overture - Robert Sheldon
The Hounds of Spring - Alfred Reed
Overture in C - Charles Simon Catel, edited by Richard Franko Goldman and Roger Smith
Covington Square - James Swearingen

All first recordings by Frederick Fennell

## NOTES

Issued in cassette and CD formats - CD 32CG 3175

Recording dates:  8-10 December 1988
Group listed as:  Tokyo Kosei Windorchestra
Recording site: Urayasu Citizen Hall, Tokyo, Japan
Engineer: Norio Okada
Producer: Eiji Inoue

FF:  Just for your discography.  This recording in CD and cassette distributed in Japan only.

*The Maestro* in Great Sacred Hall. Photo courtesy of Kosei Publishing Co.

| | | | |
|---|---|---|---|
| ALBUM TITLE: | **Symphonic Movement** | | |
| LABEL: Nippon Columbia | MONO | STEREO | CAY-900/CD 32CG 3176 |
| GOLDEN IMPORTS  SRI | | ALBUM REFERENCE NO. | 176 |
| COVER ART: | | LINER NOTES: | |
| ENGINEER: Norio Okada | | TAPE TRANSFER: | |
| RECORDING DATE: December 8, 1988 | | PERSONNEL LIST: | |

## PROGRAM
\* = Premier recording

Symphonic Movement - Vaclav Nelhybel
*Invocation and Toccata - James Barnes
*Festive Overture, Op. 96 - Dmitri Shostakovich, transcribed by Donald Hunsberger
Elsa's Procession to the Cathedral from "Lohengrin" - Richard Wagner, transcribed by Lucien Cailliet
*Coppelia, Ballet Suite - Leo Delibes, transcribed by Soichi Konagaya
*Buckaroo Holiday from "Rodeo" - Aaron Copland, arranged by Soichi Konagaya
*Final Dance [Jota] from "The Three-Cornered Hat" - Manuel de Falla, transcribed by Bram Wiggins

\* First recording by Frederick Fennell

## NOTES

Issued in cassette and CD formats for distribution in Japan only.

Recording dates: 8-10 December 1988
Group listed as: Tokyo Kosei Windorchestra
Recording site: Urayasu Citizen Hall, Tokyo, Japan
Producer: Eiji Inoue
Engineer: Norio Okada

WASBE – Valencia, Spain – July 1993. Frank Byrne, John Bourgeois, Frederick Fennell, Joseph Horovitz, Donald Hunsberger and Elizabeth Ludwig Fennell. Photo courtesy of ELF

| | |
|---|---|
| **ALBUM TITLE:** <u>**Fennell Favorites !**</u> | |
| **LABEL:** Reference Recordings **MONO** | **STEREO** RR 43 |
| **GOLDEN IMPORTS   SRI** | **ALBUM REFERENCE NO.** 177 |
| **COVER ART:** Wayne Pope | **LINER NOTES:** Frederick Fennell |
| **ENGINEER:** Keith O. Johnson | **TAPE TRANSFER:** |
| **RECORDING DATE:** January 8, 1991 | **PERSONNEL LIST:** Not available |

### PROGRAM
\* = Premier recording

Passacaglia and Fugue in C minor - J.S. Bach, arr. Donald Hunsberger
Two Chorale Preludes - Johannes Brahms, arr. Ralph Guenther
  1. "A Lovely Rose is Blooming"   2. "O God, Thou Holy God"
Woodland Sketches - Edward MacDowell, transcribed by Frank Winterbottom
  1. To a Wild Rose  2. Will-O'-the-Wisp  3. At an Old Trysting Place  4. In Autumn  5. From an Indian Lodge
  6. To a Water Lily  7. From Uncle Remus  8. A Deserted Farm  9. By a Meadow Brook  10. Told at Sunset
Entry March of the Boyars - Johan Halvorsen, transcribed by Frederick Fennell
Rustic Wedding Symphony - Karl Goldmark - arr. H. Kappey
  1. Intermezzo   2. Scherzo
Love for Three Oranges - Serge Prokofiev, arr. W.J. Duthoit
  1. "Scherzo"  2. "March"

### NOTES

Recorded live with the Dallas Wind Symphony - 8 January 1991
Program on above date "was designed as an evening of music borrowed by the wind band [in a time-honored tradition] from three sources: music composed for piano, organ and orchestra." FF

Recording site: Morton H. Meyerson Symphony Center - Dallas, Texas
Engineer: Keith O. Johnson
Producer: J. Tamblyn Henderson, Jr.
Musical Consultant: Stan Ricker
CD Mastering: Paul Stubblebine/JTH - The Rocket Lab
Executive Producers: Marcia Martin/JTH
Graphic Design: Wayne Pope, Pope Graphic Arts Center
Photography: David Love

Production dedicated "to the fond memory of the late Howard Dunn, whose tireless, buoyant spirit inspired us all." Howard Dunn was the founding conductor of the Dallas Wind Symphony.

The third release on Reference Recordings of the Dallas Wind Symphony. Also issued in LP format.

Liner notes by Frederick Fennell. A number of "contact" 35mm color photos of Fennell in action with the Wind Symphony. The cover photo shows Fennell on stage with ensemble in front of the impressive pipe organ. The cover also reproduces the now familiar FF logo of Fennell. The selections are all first recordings for Frederick Fennell.

**ALBUM TITLE:** <u>Trittico</u>

**LABEL:** Reference Recordings **MONO**   **STEREO** RR 52

**GOLDEN IMPORTS  SRI**   **ALBUM REFERENCE NO.** 178

**COVER ART:** Wayne Pope   **LINER NOTES:** Frederick Fennell

**ENGINEER:** Keith O. Johnson   **TAPE TRANSFER:**

**RECORDING DATE:** June 17, 1992   **PERSONNEL LIST:** Listed in notes

### PROGRAM
\* = Premier recording

Trittico - Vaclav Nelhybel
Feast Day in Seville - Isaac Albeniz, arr. Lucien Cailliet
Variants on a Medieval Tune - Norman Dello Joio
Funeral March in Memory of Rikaard Nordrak - Edvard Grieg, transcribed by Jan Eriksen, ed. Frederick Fennell
Symphony No. 3 - Vittorio Giannini, ed. Frederick Fennell

### NOTES

Recorded with the Dallas Wind Symphony - 18-19 June 1992
Recording site: Morton H. Meyerson Symphony Center - Dallas, Texas
Engineer: Keith O. Johnson
Second engineer: Michael "Pflash" Pflaumer
Producer: J. Tamblyn Henderson, Jr.
CD Mastering: Paul Stubblebine/JTH - The Rocket Lab
Executive Producers: Marcia Martin/JTH
Graphic Design: Wayne Pope, Pope Graphic Arts Center
Photography: David Love
Issued on 2-LP set and compact disc.

**ALBUM TITLE:** <u>Reference Recordings HDCD Sampler</u>

**LABEL:** Reference Recordings **MONO**   **STEREO** RR -S3CD

**GOLDEN IMPORTS  SRI**   **ALBUM REFERENCE NO.** 179

**COVER ART:** see notes   **LINER NOTES:**

**ENGINEER:** Keith O. Johnson   **TAPE TRANSFER:**

**RECORDING DATE:** June 17, 1992   **PERSONNEL LIST:** Not available

### PROGRAM
\* = Premier recording

Trittico - [1st Movement] Allegro Maestoso - Vaclav Nelhybel
Festival Day in Seville - Isaac Albeniz, arr. Lucien Cailliet

### NOTES

Recorded with the Dallas Wind Symphony - 17-19 June 1992
Recording site: Morton H. Meyerson Symphony Center - Dallas, Texas
Engineer: Keith O. Johnson
Producer: J. Tamblyn Henderson, Jr.
CD Mastering: Paul Stubblebine/JTH - The Rocket Lab
Executive Producers: Marcia Martin/JTH
Design: Pope Graphic Arts Center
Issued in short supply on CD ONLY

HDCD = High Definition Compatible Digital

| | |
|---|---|
| **ALBUM TITLE:** | <u>**Dallas Wind Symphony and Organ – Pomp & Pipes**</u> |

**LABEL:** Reference Recordings **MONO**  **STEREO** RR–58

**GOLDEN IMPORTS** SRI  **ALBUM REFERENCE NO.** 180

**COVER ART:** Wayne Pope  **LINER NOTES:** Frederick Fennell

**ENGINEER:** Keith O. Johnson  **TAPE TRANSFER:**

**RECORDING DATE:** July 26, 1993  **PERSONNEL LIST:**

### PROGRAM
\* = Premier recording

Poeme Heroique, Op. 33 for Organ with Trumpets, Trombones and Drum - Marcel Dupre
Grand Chorus in Dialogue for Organ and Brass Choir - Eugene Gigout - arr. Michael Harp
The Power of Rome and the Christian Heart for Band and Pipe Organ - Percy A. Grainger
Praise the Lord with the Drums and Cymbals [alla Handel] for Organ, Brass Choir and Percussion - Sigfrid Karg-Elert
Pebble Beach Sojourn [1983] for Organ, Brass and Percussion - Ron Nelson
Alleluia! Laudamus Te for Winds, Percussion and Organ - Alfred Reed
Polka and Fugue from the opera "Schwanda, the Bagpiper" - Jaromir Weinberger - trans. and adapted by G.C. Bainum
Salvum Fac Populum Tuum, Op. 84 [Lord Protect Thy People] - Charles Marie Widor
The Vikings - Arthur Willis

Paul Riedo, Organ soloist on the Herman W. & Amelia H. Lay Family Concert Organ

### NOTES

Recorded with the Dallas Wind Symphony - 26-27 July 1993
Recording site: Morton H. Meyerson Symphony Center - Dallas, Texas
Engineer: Keith O. Johnson
Second engineer: Michael "Pflash" Pflaumer
Producer: J. Tamblyn Henderson, Jr.
CD Mastering: Paul Stubblebine/JTH - The Rocket Lab
Executive Producers: Marcia Martin/JTH
Graphic Design: Wayne Pope, Pope Graphic Arts Center
Photography: David Love
Issued on both 2-LP set and compact disc

For more information regarding other releases through Reference Recordings 800-336-8866.

FF: I appreciate the help provided during the recording of this literature by the very talented Jerry Junkin of the University of Texas at Austin.

# SECTION II

# COMPOSER INDEX

# COMPOSER INDEX

| COMPOSER | TITLE | ARRANGER | ALBUM NUMBER |
|---|---|---|---|
| | Come, Dearest, the Daylight is Gone | Leinbach, J. | 31,102,160 |
| | Easter Galop | Leinbach, J. | 31,102,160 |
| | Garry Owen | Fennell, F. | 7,32,102,160 |
| | Juanita | Leinbach, J. | 32,102,160 |
| | Lulu Quickstep | Leinbach, J. | 31,102,160 |
| | Old Kentucky, Kentucky | Grafulla, C.S. | 32,102,160 |
| | Old North State | Leinbach, J. | 31,102,160 |
| | St. Patrick's Day in the Morning | Grafulla, C.S. | 32,102,160 |
| | Waltz No. 19 | Leinbach, J. | 31,102,160 |
| Albeniz, Isaac | Cordoba | MasQuiles, J.V. | 79 |
| Albeniz, Isaac | Festival Day in Seville | Cailliet, L. | 178,179 |
| Alford, Harry L. | Glory of the Gridiron | | 6,9 |
| Alford, Kenneth J. | Colonel Bogey | | 6,28,103 |
| Alford, Kenneth J. | Mad Major, The | | 11,28,110,162 |
| Allen, Thomas S. | Whip and Spur | | 24,114,162 |
| Anderson, Leroy | Belle of the Ball | | 27,34,42,47,74,165 |
| Anderson, Leroy | Blue Tango | | 34,41,47,74,165 |
| Anderson, Leroy | Bluebells of Scotland, The | | 44,75,165 |
| Anderson, Leroy | Bugler's Holiday | Edwards, M. (74) | 29,33,74,105,145 |
| Anderson, Leroy | Chicken Reel | | 44,165 |
| Anderson, Leroy | China Doll | | 34,75,165 |
| Anderson, Leroy | Christmas Festival | | 29,44,74 |
| Anderson, Leroy | Clarinet Candy | | 74,145 |
| Anderson, Leroy | Fiddle-Faddle | | 34,41,165 |
| Anderson, Leroy | First Day of Spring | | 44,165 |
| Anderson, Leroy | Forgotten Dreams | | 33,75,105 |
| Anderson, Leroy | Girl I Left Behind Me, The | | 75,105 |
| Anderson, Leroy | Girl in Satin, The | | 34,75,165 |
| Anderson, Leroy | Golden Years, The | | 75 |
| Anderson, Leroy | Home Stretch | | 74 |
| Anderson, Leroy | Horse and Buggy | | 34,75,165 |
| Anderson, Leroy | Irish Suite | | 33 |

| COMPOSER | TITLE | ARRANGER | ALBUM NUMBER |
|---|---|---|---|
| Anderson, Leroy | Irish Washerwoman, The | | 75,105 |
| Anderson, Leroy | Jazz Legato | | 44,165 |
| Anderson, Leroy | Jazz Pizzicato | | 44,165 |
| Anderson, Leroy | Last Rose of Summer, The | | 42,105 |
| Anderson, Leroy | Minstrel Boy, The | | 75,105 |
| Anderson, Leroy | Penny Whistle Song | | 33,74,105 |
| Anderson, Leroy | Phantom Regiment | | 44,74,165 |
| Anderson, Leroy | Pirate Dance | | 44 |
| Anderson, Leroy | Plink, Plank, Plunk | | 44,165 |
| Anderson, Leroy | Promenade | Cacavas, J. (75) | 44,75,165 |
| Anderson, Leroy | Rakes of Mallow, The | | 75,105 |
| Anderson, Leroy | Sandpaper Ballet | | 26,33,75,105 |
| Anderson, Leroy | Sarabande | | 34,47,165 |
| Anderson, Leroy | Serenata | | 34,47,75,105,165 |
| Anderson, Leroy | Sleigh Ride | | 33,41,68,74,105,165 |
| Anderson, Leroy | Song of Jupiter | | 44,165 |
| Anderson, Leroy | Song of the Bells | | 34,74,165 |
| Anderson, Leroy | Suite of Carols | | 44 |
| Anderson, Leroy | Summer Skies | Werle, F. (74) | 34,42,74,165 |
| Anderson, Leroy | Syncopated Clock | Lang, P. (74) | 34,41,74,165 |
| Anderson, Leroy | Ticonderoga March, The | | 75 |
| Anderson, Leroy | Trumpeter's Lullaby | Lang, P. (74) | 33,61,74,105 |
| Anderson, Leroy | Typewriter, The | Werle, F. (74) | 26,34,74,165 |
| Anderson, Leroy | Waltzing Cat, The | Lang, P. (75) | 34,75,165 |
| Anderson, Leroy | Wearing of the Green, The | | 29,105 |
| Andriessen, J. | Sinfonia "Il Fume" | | 137 |
| Army Bugle Call | Adjutant's Call | | 8,107 |
| Army Bugle Call | Assembly | | 8,107 |
| Army Bugle Call | Call to Quarters | | 8,107 |
| Army Bugle Call | Church Call | | 8,107 |
| Army Bugle Call | Drill Call | | 8,107 |
| Army Bugle Call | General Call | | 8,107 |

| COMPOSER | TITLE | ARRANGER | ALBUM NUMBER |
|---|---|---|---|
| Army Bugle Call | Mail Call | | 8,107 |
| Army Bugle Call | Mess Call | | 8,107 |
| Army Bugle Call | Retreat | | 8,107 |
| Army Bugle Call | Reveille | | 8,107 |
| Army Bugle Call | Ruffles and Flourishes | | 8,107 |
| Army Bugle Call | Taps | | 8,107 |
| Army Bugle Call | Tattoo | | 8,107 |
| Army Camp Duty | Austrian, The | | 7,109 |
| Army Camp Duty | Dawning of the Day | | 7,109 |
| Army Camp Duty | Dusky Night | | 7,109 |
| Army Camp Duty | Dutch, The | | 7,109 |
| Army Camp Duty | Hessian, The | | 7,109 |
| Army Camp Duty | Prussian, The | | 7,109 |
| Army Camp Duty | Quick Scotch, The | | 7,109 |
| Army Camp Duty | Slow Scotch, The | | 7,109 |
| Army Camp Duty | Three Camps, The | | 7,109 |
| Arnaud, Leo | Olympic Fanfare | | 87 |
| Arnaud, Leo | Three Fanfares for Brass-Percussion | | 55,86 |
| Arnold, Malcolm | Sarabande and Polka | Paynter, J. | 79 |
| Bach, J.S. | Come, Sweet Death | Reed, A. | 128 |
| Bach, J.S. | Fantasia and Fugue in G minor | Boyd, J. | 128 |
| Bach, J.S. | Fantasia in G | Goldman/Leist | 53,85,170,171 |
| Bach, J.S. | Forget Me Not, O Dearest Lord | Reed, A. | 128 |
| Bach, J.S. | Fugue a la Gigue | Holst, G. | 128 |
| Bach, J.S. | Fugue in G minor | Inagaki, T. | 128 |
| Bach, J.S. | Jesu, Joy of Man's Desiring | Reed, A. | 128 |
| Bach, J.S. | Passacaglia and Fugue in C minor | Hunsberger, D. | 177 |
| Bach, J.S. | Sheep May Safely Graze | Reed, A. | 128 |
| Bach, J.S. | Toccata and Fugue in D minor | Fujita, G /Fennell, F. | 128 |
| Bagley, Edwin E. | National Emblem | Fennell, F. | 2,9,77,145 |
| Barber, Samuel | Commando March | | 1,54,86,100,113 |
| Barnes, James | Alvamar Overture | | 172 |

| COMPOSER | TITLE | ARRANGER | ALBUM NUMBER |
|---|---|---|---|
| Barnes, James | Appalachian Overture for Band | | 78,175 |
| Barnes, James | Invocation and Toccata | | 176 |
| Bart, Lionel | Consider Yourself | Krance, J. | 30,63 |
| Bassi, Luigi | Rigoletto de Verdi | Dureau, Th. | 136 |
| Beethoven, Ludwig van | Symphony No. 7 | Triebensee, Josef | 146 |
| Beethoven, Ludwig van | Turkish March | | 38,39 |
| Benedict, Sir Julius | Hunters Chorus "The Rose of Erin" | | 52 |
| Benjamin, Arthur | Cotillon Suite | | 46 |
| Benjamin, Arthur | Jamaican Rumba | | 35,40.118 |
| Bennett, Harold | Military Escort March | Fennell, F. | 80 |
| Bennett, Robert Russell | Cakewalk | | 171 |
| Bennett, Robert Russell | Celebration | | 29,69 |
| Bennett, Robert Russell | Spiritual | | 43 |
| Bennett, Robert Russell | Suite of Old American Dances | | 1,100,113 |
| Bennett, Robert Russell | Symphonic Songs for Band | | 16,17a,99,130,161 |
| Berlin, Irving | There's No Business Like Show Business | Krance, J. | 30,63,123 |
| Berlioz, Hector | March to the Scaffold | Foulds, J.H./Brown | 174 |
| Bernstein, Leonard | Danzon from "Fancy Free" | Krance, J. | 76 |
| Bernstein, Leonard | Overture to "Candide" | Beeler, W. | 129 |
| Bicknell, G. | You Naughty, Naughty Men | | 51 |
| Bigelow, Frederick E. | Our Director March | | 2,9,77 |
| Blackmar, A.E. | Goober Peas | | 32 |
| Bolzoni, Giovanni | Minuet | | 46,47 |
| Borodin, Alexander | Prince Igor March | | 38 |
| Bourgeois, Louis | Old Hundredth | | 31,102,160 |
| Brahms, Johannes | Two Chorale Preludes | Guenther/Fennell | 73,177 |
| Catel, Charles Simon | Overture in C | Goldman, R.F./Smith | 175 |
| Caudill, Jim Andy | Folklore for Band | | 173 |
| Cavez, Francesco | Tamboo | | Single 45 |
| Chance, John Barnes | Elegy | | 139 |
| Chance, John Barnes | Incantation and Dance | | 175 |
| Chance, John Barnes | Variations on a Korean Folk Song | | 72 |

179

| COMPOSER | TITLE | ARRANGER | ALBUM NUMBER |
|---|---|---|---|
| Coates, Eric | Four Ways Suite | | 45,121 |
| Coates, Eric | Knightsbridge March | | 15,98,119 |
| Coates, Eric | London Suite | | 45,121 |
| Coates, Eric | Three Elizabeths, The | | 45,121 |
| Cohan, George M. | Give My Regards to Broadway | Krance, J. | 30,47,63,123 |
| Copland, Aaron | An Outdoor Overture | | 132 |
| Copland, Aaron | Buckaroo Holiday from "Rodeo" | Konagaya, S. | 176 |
| Copland, Aaron | Variations on a Shaker Melody | | 144 |
| Cramatte, H.E. | Adjutant's Call Quickstep | | 51 |
| Cramatte, H.E. | Guard Mounting Quickstep | | 51 |
| Crammatti, H.E. | Review Quickstep | | 51 |
| Curnow, James | Fox River Festival | | 78 |
| Czibulka, Alphons | Love's Dream After the Ball | | 37,43 |
| Dahl, Ingolf | Sinfonietta | | 144 |
| de L'Isle, Claude J. R. | La Marseillaise | Grafulla, C.S. | 31,102,160 |
| Debussy, Claude | Claire de Lune | | 37,41,59 |
| Debussy, Claude | Petite Suite | Kuwabara, H. | 136 |
| Debussy, Claude | Premier Rhapsody | Inagaki, T. | 136 |
| Del Borgo, Elliot | Symphonic Sketches for Band | | 78 |
| Delibes, Leo | Coppelia, Ballet Suite | Konagaya, S. | 176 |
| Delle Cese, Davide | Inglesina | | 15,28,81,119,170 |
| Dello Joio, Norman | Fantasies on a Theme by Haydn | | 144 |
| Dello Joio, Norman | Variants on a Medieval Tune | | 178 |
| Dinicu, Gheorghe | Hora Staccato | | 37,41 |
| Duble, Charles E. | Bravura March | | 24,162 |
| Dupre, Marcel | Poeme Heroique, Op. 33 | | 180 |
| Elgar, Edward | Pomp and Circumstance No. 1 | | 174 |
| Emerson, L.O. | We Are Coming, Father Abra'am | Fennell, F. | 32,102,160 |
| Emmett, Daniel | Dixie | | 7,31,102,160 |
| End, Jack | Blues For A Killed Kat | Fennell, F. | 129 |
| Erickson, Frank | Overture Jubiloso | | 172 |
| Faith, Percy | Brazilian Sleigh Bells | | 26,35,118 |

| COMPOSER | TITLE | ARRANGER | ALBUM NUMBER |
|---|---|---|---|
| Falla, Manuel de | Final Dance from "The Three-Cornered Hat" | Wiggins, B | 176 |
| Falla, Manuel de | Ritual Fire Dance | | 35,118 |
| Farmer, Henry | Moonbeam Waltzes, The | Downing, D. | 52 |
| Farrar, Orion R. | Bombasto March | | 24,114,162 |
| Faust, Carl | Liebling's Polka | | 51 |
| Fernandez, Oscar | Batuque | | 35,118 |
| Fillmore, Henry | Americans We | Fennell, F. (79) | 11,79,162 |
| Fillmore, Henry | Bones Trombone | | 24,114,162 |
| Fillmore, Henry | Circus Bee, The | | 24,114,162,127 |
| Fillmore, Henry | His Honor | Fennell, F. (77) | 2,9,77,145,170,171 |
| Fillmore, Henry | Rolling Thunder | Fennell, F. | 24,162 |
| Fillmore, Henry | Free and Easy | Downing, D. | 52 |
| Forrest, Fanny | Ah, May the Red Rose Live Alway | | 52 |
| Foster, Stephen | Come Where My Love Lies Dreaming | | 32,102,160 |
| Foster, Stephen | Lulu's Gone | | 32,102,160 |
| Foster, Stephen | Old Memories | | 52 |
| Foster, Stephen | Why, No One To Love? | | 52 |
| Frescobaldi, Girolamo | Toccata | Slocum, E. | 79 |
| Fucik, Julius | Florentiner, Op. 214, The | Fennell, F. (72,81) | 54,72,81,86 |
| Fucik, Julius | Thunder and Blazes - Entry of the Gladiators | | 24,28,114,162,127 |
| Gabrieli, Andrea | Aria Della Battaglia | Ghedini | 18,65,125 |
| Gabrieli, Giovanni | Canzon Duodecimi Toni | | 18,125 |
| Gabrieli, Giovanni | Canzon Noni Toni | | 18,125 |
| Gabrieli, Giovanni | Canzon Quarti Toni | | 18,125 |
| Gabrieli, Giovanni | Canzon Septimi Toni | | 18,125 |
| Gabrieli, Giovanni | Sonata Octavi Toni | | 18,125 |
| Gabrieli, Giovanni | Sonata Pian e Forte | | 18,125 |
| Ganne, Louis | Father of Victory | | 15,81,119 |
| Ganne, Louis | Marche Lorraine | | 54,81 |
| German, Sir Edward | Henry VIII Dances | | 46 |
| Gershwin, George | An American in Paris | Hoshina, H. | 129 |
| Gershwin, George | Bidin' My Time | Wright, R. | 48,124,168 |

| COMPOSER | TITLE | ARRANGER | ALBUM NUMBER |
|---|---|---|---|
| Gershwin, George | But Not For Me | Lieb, R. | 48,124,168 |
| Gershwin, George | Embraceable You | Karlin, F. | 48,124,168 |
| Gershwin, George | Fascinating Rhythm | Karlin, F. | 48,124,168 |
| Gershwin, George | I Got Rhythm | Wright, R. | 43,48,124,168 |
| Gershwin, George | Liza | Wright, R. | 48,124,168 |
| Gershwin, George | Love is Sweeping the Country | Wright, R. | 48,124,168 |
| Gershwin, George | Love Walked In | Lieb, R. | 48,124,168 |
| Gershwin, George | Man I Love, The | Karlin, F. | 48,124,168 |
| Gershwin, George | Oh, Lady Be Good | Wright, R. | 48,124,168 |
| Gershwin, George | 'S Wonderful | Lieb, R. | 48,124,168 |
| Gershwin, George | Someone To Watch Over Me | Wright, R. | 48,124,168 |
| Gershwin, George | Strike Up The Band | Krance, J. | 30,63,124 |
| Gershwin, George | Wintergreen For President | Krance, J. | 30,63,124 |
| Giannini, Vittorio | Symphony No. 3 | | 178 |
| Gigout, Eugene | Grand Chorus in Dialogue for Organ and Brass Choir | ed. Fennell, F. | 180 |
| Gilmore, Patrick | When Johnny Comes Marching Home | | 32,102,160 |
| Gliere, Reinhold | Russian Sailor's Dance | | 37,127a |
| Goldman, Edwin Franko | Boy Scouts of America | | 11,110,162 |
| Goldman, Edwin Franko | Bugles and Drums | | 11,77,92,162 |
| Goldman, Edwin Franko | Cheerio | Lang, P. | 2 |
| Goldman, Edwin Franko | Children's March | Lang, P. | 11,110,162 |
| Goldman, Edwin Franko | Illinois March | Lang, P. | 11,110,162 |
| Goldman, Edwin Franko | Interlochen Bowl | | 11,110,162 |
| Goldman, Edwin Franko | On The Mall | Lake, M. | 6,9,42,77,103,127 |
| Goldman, Edwin Franko | Onward-Upward | | 11,28,110,162 |
| Goldmark, Karl | Rustic Wedding/Intermezzo/Scherzo | Kappey, H. | 177 |
| Goodwin, George H. | Door Latch Quickstep | | 52 |
| Gossec, F.J. | Offrande A La Liberte [Lyric] | Dondeyne, D. | 134 |
| Gould, Morton | American Salute | Lang, P. | 173 |
| Gould, Morton | Ballad for Band | | 1,113,132 |
| Gould, Morton | West Point Symphony | | 16,16a,116,135,166 |
| Gounod, Charles F. | Ballet Music from "Faust" | Inagaki, T. | 141 |

| COMPOSER | TITLE | ARRANGER | ALBUM NUMBER |
|---|---|---|---|
| Gounod, Charles F. | Ballet Music from "Faust" | Winterbottom, W. | 19,98,126,167 |
| Gounod, Charles F. | Funeral March of a Marionet | Lake, M. | 174 |
| Grabeu-Hoffman | Liebeshandel Duet | | 51 |
| Graffeuil, Charles | Il Staccato | Coquelet, O. | 136 |
| Grafulla, C.S. | Cape May Polka | | 32,102 |
| Grafulla, C.S. | Captain Finch's Quickstep | | 52 |
| Grafulla, C.S. | Captain Shepherd's Quickstep | | 52 |
| Grafulla, C.S. | Cavalry Quickstep | | 32,102,160 |
| Grafulla, C.S. | Freischutz Quickstep | | 31,102,160 |
| Grafulla, C.S. | Grafulla's 7th Regiment D.C. Quickstep | | 32,102,160 |
| Grafulla, C.S. | Nightingale Waltz | | 31,102,160 |
| Grafulla, C.S. | Parade | | 31,102,160 |
| Grafulla, C.S. | Port Royal Galop | | 31,102,160 |
| Grafulla, C.S. | Rachel Waltzes | | 32,102 |
| Grafulla, C.S. | Storm Galop | | 32,102,160 |
| Grafulla, C.S. | Washington Grays | Fennell, F. | 54,77 |
| Grainger, Percy A. | Children's March | | 25,26,36,120,169 |
| Grainger, Percy A. | Colonial Song | | 36,120,169 |
| Grainger, Percy A. | Country Gardens | | 36,41,120,169 |
| Grainger, Percy A. | Handel In The Strand | | 36,120,169 |
| Grainger, Percy A. | Hill Song No. 2 | | 5,17,84,104,163 |
| Grainger, Percy A. | Immovable Do, The | | 36,120,169 |
| Grainger, Percy A. | Irish Tune From County Derry | | 36,59,120,169 |
| Grainger, Percy A. | Irish Tune From County Derry [Winds] | | 139 |
| Grainger, Percy A. | Lincolnshire Posy | Fennell, F. (131) | 12,55,82,86,99,115,131,163 |
| Grainger, Percy A. | Mock Morris | | 36,43,120,169 |
| Grainger, Percy A. | Molly on the Shore | | 36,41,120,169 |
| Grainger, Percy A. | Molly on the Shore [Winds] | | 139 |
| Grainger, Percy A. | My Robin is to the Greenwood Gone | | 36,120,169 |
| Grainger, Percy A. | Power of Rome and the Christian Heart | | 180 |
| Grainger, Percy A. | Shepherd's Hey | | 36,43,55,86,120,169 |
| Grainger, Percy A. | Spoon River | | 36,120,169 |

| COMPOSER | TITLE | ARRANGER | ALBUM NUMBER |
|---|---|---|---|
| Granados, Enrique | Goyescas: Intermezzo | | 35,41,118 |
| Grieg, Edvard H. | Funeral March /Memory of Rikaard Nordrak | Fennell, F./Eriksen | 174,178 |
| Grieg, Edvard H. | Homage March - Sigurd Jorsalfar | | 38,39 |
| Grieg, Edvard H. | Peer Gynt - Suite No. 1 | Fujita, G./ Kawasake, M. | 139 |
| Grundman, Clare | Holiday | | 79 |
| Guarnleri, Camargo | Brazilian Dance | | 35,118 |
| Gungl, Joseph | Concordia March | | 51 |
| Gungl, Joseph | Farewell Waltzes | | 51 |
| Gungl, Joseph | Frederic March | | 51 |
| Hall, Robert B. | Officer of the Day | | 11,110,162 |
| Halvorsen, Johan | Entry March of the Boyars | Fennell, F. | 177 |
| Handel, G.F. | Music for the Royal Fireworks | Baines/Mackerras | 53,85 |
| Hanson, Howard | Chorale and Alleluia | | 3,79,100 |
| Hanson, Howard | March Carillon, Op. 19, No. 2 | Perry, R. | 2 |
| Hanssen, Johannes | Valdres March | | 15,81,119 |
| Hartley, Walter Sinclair | Concerto for 23 Winds | | 16a,17,163 |
| Hartley Walter Sinclair | Sinfonia No. IV | | 142 |
| Hauptmann, Moritz | Doppelquartett: Auf dem See | | 51 |
| Haydn, Joseph | Symphony No. 92 [Oxford] | Triebensee, Josef | 146 |
| Heed, John C. | In Storm and Sunshine | | 24,28,114,127,162 |
| Herbert, Victor | Ah, Sweet Mystery of Life | Hayman, R. | 49,90 |
| Herbert, Victor | Habanera | Hayman, R. | 49,90 |
| Herbert, Victor | I'm Falling In Love with Someone | Hayman, R. | 49,90 |
| Herbert, Victor | Irish Have a Great Day Tonight, The | Hayman, R. | 49,90 |
| Herbert, Victor | Italian Street Song | Hayman, R. | 49,90 |
| Herbert, Victor | Kiss in the Dark, A | Hayman, R. | 49,90 |
| Herbert, Victor | Kiss Me Again | Hayman, R. | 49,90 |
| Herbert, Victor | March of the Toys | Hayman, R. | 49,90 |
| Herbert, Victor | Romany Life | Hayman, R. | 49,90 |
| Herbert, Victor | Streets of New York | Hayman, R. | 43,49,60,90 |
| Herbert, Victor | Sweethearts | Hayman, R. | 49,90 |
| Herbert, Victor | Thine Alone | Hayman, R. | 49,90 |

| COMPOSER | TITLE | ARRANGER | ALBUM NUMBER |
|---|---|---|---|
| Herman, Strouse, Coleman | Broadway Curtain Time | Krance, J. | 129 |
| Hermann, Ralph | Prom Night | | 43 |
| Hindemith, Paul | Geschwindmarsch by Beethoven | Guiles, Mas | 79 |
| Hindemith, Paul | Symphony in B-flat for Concert Band | | 10,111 |
| Hirose, R. | Festival Music for Band | | 173 |
| Holst, Gustav | Hammersmith: Prelude and Scherzo | | 14,99,106,161 |
| Holst, Gustav | March from Suite in E-flat | | 62 |
| Holst, Gustav | Moorside Suite | Wright, D. [133] | 78,133 |
| Holst, Gustav | Suite No. 1 in E-flat for Military Band, Op. 28a | | 4,5,53,85,104,170 |
| Holst, Gustav | Suite No. 2 in F for Military Band, Op. 28b | | 4,5,53,85,104,133 |
| Horovitz, J. | Bacchus on Blue Ridge | | 137 |
| Horovitz, Joseph | Dance Suite | | 142 |
| Hoshina, Hiroshi | Catastrophe for Symphonic Band | | 172 |
| Huff, Will | Squealer, The | | 24,114,162 |
| Huffine, Getty H. | Them Basses | | 24,114,162 |
| Humperdinck, Engelbert | Prayer and Dream from "Hansel and Gretel" | Maddy, J. | 141 |
| Ives, Charles | Country Band March | Sinclair, J. | 132 |
| Jacob, Gordon | Intermezzo from "An Original Suite" | | 133,171 |
| Jacob, Gordon | Suite: William Byrd | | 14,106,133,161 |
| Jaeger, Edmund | Indiana Polka | Schatzman, | 52 |
| Jenkins, Joseph W. | Pieces of Eight | Neff, Jerome | 2,174 |
| Jewell, Fred | Screamer, The | | 24,114,127,162 |
| | Suite: The Comedians | Fujita, G. | 139 |
| Kabalevsky, Dmitri | | | |
| Kamioka, Yoichi | Akizora "Under Autumn Sky" March | | 170 |
| Kaneda, Bin | Ballade I for Symphonic Band | | 172 |
| Karg-Elert, Sigfrid | Praise the Lord with the Drums and Cymbals [alla Handel] | | 180 |
| Kawade, Tomoki | Stones in Time | | 142 |
| Khachaturian, Aram | Armenian Dance No. 2 | Satz, R. | 69 |
| Khachaturian, Aram | Armenian Dances | Satz, R. | 17,17a,163 |
| Khachaturian, Aram | Suite Gayaneh | Inagaki, T. | 136 |
| Khachaturian, Aram | Three Dance Episodes from "Spartacus" | Hunsberger, D. | 134 |
| King, Karl L. | Barnum and Bailey's Favorite | | 6,9,54,77,86,103 |

| COMPOSER | TITLE | ARRANGER | ALBUM NUMBER |
|---|---|---|---|
| King, Karl L. | Big Cage, The | | 24,114,162 |
| King, Karl L. | Circus Days | | 24,114,162 |
| King, Karl L. | Invictus | | 24,114,162 |
| King, Karl L. | Pride of the Illini | | 2,9 |
| King, Karl L. | Robinson's Grand Entree | | 24,114,162 |
| Kitazume, M. | Kaze-No-Kuni | | 173 |
| Kittredge, Walter | Tenting Tonight on the Old Camp Ground | Fennell, F. | 32 |
| Klohr, John N. | Billboard, The | | 6,9,103,127 |
| Knaeble, Simon | General Taylor Storming Monterey | | 52 |
| Kodaly, Zoltan | Dances of Galanta | Rogers, R.M. | 135 |
| Koyama, K. | Dai-Kagura | | 173 |
| Krance, John | Broadway Minstrel Medley | | 30,63,123 |
| Krenek, Ernst | Drei Lustige Marsche, Op. 44 "Three Merry Marches" | | 84 |
| Lancen, Serge | Le Chant de l'Arbe | | 80,137 |
| Lecuona, Ernesto | Andalucia | Gould, M. | 35,43,47,118 |
| Lecuona, Ernesto | Malaguena | Gould, M. | 35,43,118 |
| Leemans, Pierre | March of the Belgian Paratroopers | | 54,86 |
| Leinbach, Julius | Twenty-sixth Regiment Quickstep | | 32 |
| Lindblad, Adolf F. | Herdsman's Mountain Song, The | | 52 |
| Lindblad, Adolf F. | Upon a Summer's Day | | 52 |
| Liszt, Franz | Hungarian Rhapsody No. 2 | Miyazawa, K. | 141 |
| Liszt, Franz | Liebestraum | | 37,43 |
| Loewe, Frederick | Get Me to the Church on Time | Krance, J. | 30,47,63,123 |
| LoPresti, Ronald | Elegy For A Young American | | 132 |
| Ludwig, William F. | Fancy 6/8 | | 7,109 |
| Lysberg, Charles-Samuel | La Fontaine | | 52 |
| MacDowell, Edward | Woodland Sketches | Winterbottom, F. | 177 |
| Mailman, Martin | Night Vigil | | 80 |
| Massenet, Jules | Air Alsacien (Scenes Alsaciennes) | Erickson, F. | 96 |
| McBeth, W. Francis | Flourishes | | 78 |
| McBeth, W. Francis | Kaddish | | 131 |
| McCarthy, Harry | Bonnie Blue Flag | Fennell, F. | 7,31,92,109 |

185

| COMPOSER | TITLE | ARRANGER | ALBUM NUMBER |
|---|---|---|---|
| McCoy, Earl E. | Lights Out | Roth, A (77) | 6,77,103 |
| Meacham, Frank W. | American Patrol | | 6,66,91,103 |
| Mendelssohn, Felix | Overture for Winds, Op. 24 | Boyd, J. | 139 |
| Mendelssohn, Felix | Wedding March from "Midsummer Nights Dream" | Laurendeau, L.P. | 174 |
| Mennin, Peter | Canzona | | 3 |
| Milburn, Richard | Listen to the Mockingbird | Grafulla, C.S. | 31,102,160 |
| Milhaud, Darius | Provence | | 43 |
| Milhaud, Darius | Suite Francaise | | 12,115,134 |
| Miller & Beacham | Maryland, My Maryland | Leinbach, J. | 31,102,160 |
| Mitchell, Rex | Song of the High Seas, A | | 175 |
| Moore, J. Burns | Connecticut Half-time | | 7,8,109 |
| Morrissey, John | Centennial Suite | | 173 |
| Moussorgsky, Modest P. | Pictures at an Exhibition | Hindsley, M. | 138 |
| Mozart, Wolfgang A. | Magic Flute, The [Overture] | Winterbottom, F. | 136 |
| Mozart, Wolfgang A. | Serenade No. 10 in B-flat, K. 361 | Fennell, F. (140) | 13,58,140 |
| Mozart, Wolfgang A. | Serenade No. 12 in C Minor, K. 388 | Fennell, F. | 140 |
| Mozart, Wolfgang A. | Symphony No. 39 in E-Flat [First movement] | | 146 |
| Neff, Jerome | Pieces of Eight | Jenkins, J.W. | 2,174 |
| Nelhybel, Vaclav | Symphonic Movement | | 72,176 |
| Nelhybel, Vaclav | Trittico | | 178,179 |
| Nelson, Ron | Morning Alleluias For the Winter Solstice | | 142 |
| Nelson, Ron | Pebble Beach Sojourn for Organ, Brass and Percussion | | 180 |
| Noeren, J.M. | Slow March: Midnight | Schatzman, J. | 52 |
| Olivadoti, Joseph | Carnival of Roses Overture | | 172 |
| Ordway, J.P. | Twinkling Stars Quickstep | Grafulla, C.S. | 32 |
| Osser, Glenn | Beguine for Band | | 43 |
| Perle, George | Solemn Procession | | 144 |
| Persichetti, Vincent | Divertimento for Band | | 1,100 |
| Persichetti, Vincent | Masquerade | | 132 |
| Persichetti, Vincent | Psalm for Band | | 3 |
| Persichetti, Vincent | Symphony No. 6 for Band | | 17,17a,116,134,163 |
| Pierne, Gabriel | March of the Little Leaden Soldiers | Godfrey, D. | 174 |

| COMPOSER | TITLE | ARRANGER | ALBUM NUMBER |
|---|---|---|---|
| Piston, Walter | Tunbridge Fair | | 1,113 |
| Porter, Cole | Anything Goes | Wright, R. | 50,122,168 |
| Porter, Cole | Begin the Beguine | Wright, R. | 50,122,168 |
| Porter, Cole | Blow, Gabriel, Blow | Wright, R. | 43,50,122,168 |
| Porter, Cole | I've Got You Under My Skin | Wright, R. | 50,122,168 |
| Porter, Cole | In the Still of the Night | Wright, R. | 50,122,168 |
| Porter, Cole | It's Alright With Me | Wright, R. | 50,168 |
| Porter, Cole | It's Delovely | Wright, R. | 50,122,168 |
| Porter, Cole | My Heart Belongs to Daddy | Wright, R. | 26,50,65,122,168 |
| Porter, Cole | Night and Day | Wright, R. | 50,122,168 |
| Porter, Cole | Ridin' High | Wright, R. | 50,122,168 |
| Porter, Cole | So In Love | Wright, R. | 50,67,122,168 |
| Porter, Cole | You'd Be So Nice to Come Home to | Wright, R. | 50,122,168 |
| Press, Jacques | Wedding Dance | Johnston, H. | 72,129 |
| Prokofiev, Serge | Ballet Music from "Romeo and Juliet" | Yodo, A. | 135 |
| Prokofiev, Serge | Love for Three Oranges - March and Scherzo | Duthoit, W. J. | 177 |
| Prokofiev, Serge | March from "Love of the Three Oranges" | Duthoit, W.J. | 174 |
| Prokofiev, Serge | March, Op. 99 | | 15,98 |
| Puffhold, J. | Souvenir Polka | | 51 |
| Rachmaninoff, Sergei | Italian Polka | Leidzen, E. ed. F.F. | 139 |
| Rachmaninoff, Sergei | Prelude in G Minor | | 37 |
| Rachmaninoff, Sergei | Symphonic Dances III | Satoh, | 80 |
| Rachmaninoff, Sergei | Vocalise, Op. 34, No. 14 | Yodo, A. | 139 |
| Rauski, Josef F. | Le Regiment de Sambre e Meuse | Fennell, F. | 81,171 |
| Reed, Alfred | Alleluia! Laudamus Te for Winds, Percussion and Organ | | 180 |
| Reed, Alfred | Armenian Dances, Part II | | 131 |
| Reed, Alfred | El Camino Real | | 172 |
| Reed, Alfred | Hounds of Spring, The | | 175 |
| Reed, Alfred | In Dulci Jubilo | | 97a |
| Reed, Alfred | Little Concert Suite for Winds, A | | 172 |
| Reed, Alfred | Othello and Desdemona | | 171 |
| Reed, Alfred | Song of the High Cascades | | 173 |

| COMPOSER | TITLE | ARRANGER | ALBUM NUMBER |
|---|---|---|---|
| Reed, Alfred | Viva Musica (A Concert Overture for Winds) | | 78 |
| Reed, H. Owen | La Fiesta Mexicana | | 3,76,100,170 |
| Reeves, David W. | Second Regiment Connecticut N.G. March | | 11,28,110,127,162 |
| Respighi, Ottorino | Fountains of Rome | Odom, L. | 135 |
| Respighi, Ottorino | Fountains of Rome, Symphonic Poem | Kimura, Y. | 143 |
| Respighi, Ottorino | Pines of Rome, Symphonic Poem | Suzuki, E. | 143 |
| Respighi, Ottorino | Roman Festival, Symphonic Poem | Kimura, Y. | 143 |
| Reynolds, Verne | Scenes | | 142 |
| Ribble, John H. | Bennett's Triumphal | | 24,162 |
| Richardson, Norman | Beachcomber, The | | Unreleased |
| Rimsky-Korsakov, Nicholas | Dance of the Tumblers | | 46 |
| Rimsky-Korsakov, Nicholas | Procession of the Nobles | | 37 |
| Rodgers, Richard | Carousel Waltz | Walker, Mark | 46 |
| Rodgers, Richard | Guadalcanal March | Leidzen, E. | 11,110,162 |
| Rodgers, Richard | March of the Siamese Children, The | Krance, J. | 30,47,63,123 |
| Rodgers, Richard | Sound of Music, The | | 145 |
| Rodgers, Richard | There is Nothin' Like A Dame | Krance, J. | 30,63,123 |
| Rogers, Bernard | Japanese Sword Dance | | 69 |
| Rogers, Bernard | Three Japanese Dances | | 12,115,163 |
| Romberg, Sigmund | Stouthearted Men | Krance, J. | 30,63,123 |
| Root, George F. | Rally 'Round the Flag | Fennell, F. | 7,109 |
| Root, George F. | Tramp, Tramp, Tramp | Fennell, F. | 32 |
| Rossini, Gioacchino A. | La Boutique Fantasque | Godfrey, D. | 19,76,126,167 |
| Rossini, Gioacchino A. | Passo a sei (William Tell) | | 46 |
| Rossini, Gioacchino A. | William Tell Overture | Inagaki, T. | 134 |
| Rowlathem, J. | Palmyra Schottische | Grafulla, C.S. | 31,102,160 |
| Russell, Henry | Cheer Boys Cheer | Leinbach, J. | 31,102,160 |
| Sachse, J. | Concertino for E-flat Cornet | | 51 |
| Saitoh, Takanobu | Symphonic Poem "Only One Earth" | | 172 |
| San Miguel, Mariano | Golden Ear, The (La Oreja de Oro) | Fennell, F. | 15,25,119 |
| Sanderson, James | Hail to the Chief | | 31,102,160 |
| Schoenberg, Arnold | Fanfare on Motifs of Die Gurrelieder | | 144 |

| COMPOSER | TITLE | ARRANGER | ALBUM NUMBER |
|---|---|---|---|
| Schoenberg, Arnold | Theme and Variations, Op. 43a | | 10,73,111 |
| Schrammel, Joseph | Wien Bleibt Wien | | 81 |
| Schubert, Franz | Marche Militaire | | 38,41,127 |
| Schuman, William | George Washington Bridge | | 1,113,132 |
| Schumann, Robert | Familien-Gemalde Duet | | 51 |
| Schumann, Robert | Liebesgarten Duet | | 51 |
| Seitz, Roland F. | March Grandioso | | 11,162 |
| Seitz, Roland F. | University of Pennsylvania Band March | | 54 |
| Sheldon, Robert | Manatee Lyric Overture | | 175 |
| Shostakovich, Dmitri | Festive Overture, Op. 96 | Hunsberger, D. | 145,176 |
| Shostakovich, Dmitri | Polka from "The Golden Age" | | 37 |
| Sibelius, Jean | Alla Marcia (Karelia Suite) | | 38 |
| Sibelius, Jean | Finlandia | | 37 |
| Sibelius, Jean | Finlandia | Kimura, M. | 141 |
| Skelton, Red | Kadiddlehopper March | Roullier, R, | 97 |
| Smalls, Charlie | Wiz, The | Lowden, B. | 129 |
| Smith, John Stafford | Star Spangled Banner, The | Fennell, F. (Ab) | 8,66,107 |
| Smith, John Stafford | Star Spangled Banner, The | Grafulla, C.S. | 32 |
| Soderman, A. | Svenska Folkvisor Och Dancer | Gustafson, S. | 137 |
| Sousa, John Philip | Ancient and Honorable Artillery | Fennell, F. (130) | 22,57,101,112,164 |
| Sousa, John Philip | Black Horse Troop, The | Fennell, F. (130) | 2,22,23,57,130,101,112,164 |
| Sousa, John Philip | Bullets and Bayonets | Fennell, F. (130) | 20,23,130,101,108,164 |
| Sousa, John Philip | Corcoran Cadets | Fennell, F. (130) | 2,130 |
| Sousa, John Philip | Daughters of Texas | Fennell, F. (130) | 2,130 |
| Sousa, John Philip | El Capitan | Fennell, F. (130) | 6,23,57,83,92,130,101,103,127 |
| Sousa, John Philip | Fairest of the Fair, The | Fennell, F. (77) | 77 |
| Sousa, John Philip | Free Lance March, The | | 130 |
| Sousa, John Philip | Gallant Seventh, The | Fennell, F. (51) | 20,51,101,108,164 |
| Sousa, John Philip | Glory of the Yankee Navy | Fennell, F. (130) | 22,57,83,130,101,112,164 |
| Sousa, John Philip | Golden Jubilee | | 22,27,57,61,101,112,164 |
| Sousa, John Philip | Gridiron Club | | 22,57,83,101,112,164 |
| Sousa, John Philip | Hands Across the Sea | Fennell, F. (130) | 2,15,23,57,83,130,101,127 |

| COMPOSER | TITLE | ARRANGER | ALBUM NUMBER |
|---|---|---|---|
| Sousa, John Philip | High School Cadets | | 20,57,83,101,108,164 |
| Sousa, John Philip | Invincible Eagle, The | | 20,57,101,108,164 |
| Sousa, John Philip | Kansas Wildcats | | 22,23,83,101,112,164 |
| Sousa, John Philip | King Cotton | Fennell, F. (77) | 6,23,57,77,83,92,101,103,127,171 |
| Sousa, John Philip | Liberty Bell, The | | 20,23,83,130,101,108,164 |
| Sousa, John Philip | Manhattan Beach | Fennell, F. (77) | 2,9,22,23,57,77,83,93,101,112,164 |
| Sousa, John Philip | Minnesota March | Fennell, F. | 97 |
| Sousa, John Philip | National Game | | 22,28,57,83,101,112,164 |
| Sousa, John Philip | New Mexico March | Fennell, F. | 22,26,57,97a,101,112,164 |
| Sousa, John Philip | Nobles of the Mystic Shrine | Fennell, F. | 20,26,57,101,108,164 |
| Sousa, John Philip | Our Flirtations | | 20,57,101,108,127,164 |
| Sousa, John Philip | Picadore, The | | 20,28,57,83,101,108,127,164 |
| Sousa, John Philip | Pride of the Wolverines, The | Fennell, F. | 22,57,83,101,112,164 |
| Sousa, John Philip | Riders For the Flag | Fennell, F. (130) | 20,23,57,83,101,108,130,164 |
| Sousa, John Philip | Rifle Regiment | Fennell, F. (130) | 2,22,57,83,101,112,130,145,164 |
| Sousa, John Philip | Sabre and Spurs | Fennell, F. | 20,23,57,83,101,108,164 |
| Sousa, John Philip | Semper Fidelis | Fennell, F. (77) | 2,9,77,92 |
| Sousa, John Philip | Sesqui-Centennial Exposition | | 22,28,57,101,112,164 |
| Sousa, John Philip | Solid Men to the Front | | 20,28,101,108,164 |
| Sousa, John Philip | Sound Off! | | 20,57,83,101,108,164 |
| Sousa, John Philip | Stars and Stripes Forever, The | Fennell, F. (77) | 6,9,54,57,66,77,83,86,88,101,103,127 |
| Sousa, John Philip | Thunderer, The | | 6,57,83,101,103,127,130 |
| Sousa, John Philip | U.S. Field Artillery March | Lake/Fennell (77) | 6,9,23,57,77,95,101,103 |
| Sousa, John Philip | Washington Post, The | Fennell, F. (130) | 6,23,57,83,91,92,101,103,130 |
| Sparke, Philip | Celebration | | 144 |
| Starke, Hermann | With Sword and Lance | | 81 |
| Steffe, William | Battle Hymn of the Republic, The | | 32,66 |
| Strauss, | Amor March | | 51 |
| Strauss II, Johann | Voices of Spring - Waltz | Winter & Hibbert | 141,145 |
| Strauss, Johann | Radetzky March | | 54,86 |
| Strauss, Richard | Allerseelen | Davis/Fennell | 73 |
| Strauss, Richard | Serenade in E-flat, Op. 7 | | 12,115 |

| COMPOSER | TITLE | ARRANGER | ALBUM NUMBER |
|---|---|---|---|
| Stravinsky, Igor | Symphonies of Wind Instruments | | 10,111 |
| Stravinsky, Igor | The Firebird [1919] Suite from the Ballet | Earles, R./F. Fennell | 138 |
| Street, William G. | Swinging Down the Street | | 8,107 |
| Sugiyama, Koichi | Music from Dragon Quest | Pilafian, S. | 147 |
| Sullivan, Arthur | Finale - Pineapple Poll | Mackerras/Duthoit | 43 |
| Sullivan, Arthur | Pineapple Poll Suite | Mackerras/Duthoit | 19,126,167 |
| Swearingen, James | Covington Square | | 175 |
| Swearingen, James | Majestia | | 78 |
| Swearingen, James | Seagate Overture | | 175 |
| Telke, Carl | Old Comrades | | 15,28,81,119,127 |
| Texidor, Jaime | Amparito Roca | | 35,47,81,118 |
| Thomson, Virgil | A Solemn Music | | 3 |
| Toyama, Yuzo | Rhapsodie for Wind Orchestra | Fujita, G. | 76 |
| Traditional | A-hunting We Will Go | | 8,107 |
| Traditional | American Flag, The | | 8,107 |
| Traditional | Appomattox Bugle, The | | 32,102,160 |
| Traditional | Camp and Field Duty Calls | | 32,102,160 |
| Traditional | Cavaliers, The | | 8,107 |
| Traditional | Cavalry Bugle Signals | | 31,102,160 |
| Traditional | Colonel's Daughter, The | | 8,107 |
| Traditional | Double Time | | 8,107 |
| Traditional | Drum Calls [Improvised by Fennell] | | 32,102,160 |
| Traditional | Field Music of Union and Confederate Troops | | 31,102,160 |
| Traditional | Field Music of Union and Confederate Troops | | 32,102,160 |
| Traditional | Funeral March | | 8,107 |
| Traditional | Garrison Belle, The | | 8,107 |
| Traditional | General Burt | | 8,107 |
| Traditional | General Dooley | | 8,107 |
| Traditional | General's March | | 8,107 |
| Traditional | Hens and Chickens | | 8,107 |
| Traditional | Holy Joe | | 8,107 |
| Traditional | I've Got Three Years To Do This In | | 8,107 |

| COMPOSER | TITLE | ARRANGER | ALBUM NUMBER |
|---|---|---|---|
| Traditional | Marches and Inspection Pieces | | 8,107 |
| Traditional | No Slum Today | | 8,107 |
| Traditional | Old Guard, The | | 8,107 |
| Traditional | Old Six-eight | | 8,107 |
| Traditional | Pay Day | | 8,107 |
| Traditional | President's March, The | | 8,107 |
| Traditional | Prisoner, The | | 8,107 |
| Traditional | Red Hussars, The | | 8,107 |
| Traditional | Rip van Winkle | | 8,107 |
| Traditional | Scots Wha Hae | Wallace | 32 |
| Traditional | Soapsuds Row | | 8,107 |
| Traditional | Spanish Guard Mount | | 8,107 |
| Traditional | To The Color | | 8,107 |
| Traditional | Yankee Doodle | | 7,66,109 |
| Traditional | You're In The Army Now | | 8,107 |
| Traditional Fifes and Drums | Belle of the Mohawk Vale, The | Fennell, F. | 7,109 |
| Traditional Fifes and Drums | Breakfast Call "Peas Upon a Trencher" | | 7,109 |
| Traditional Fifes and Drums | Dinner Call "Roast Beef" | | 7,109 |
| Traditional Fifes and Drums | Downfall of Paris | | 7,109 |
| Traditional Fifes and Drums | Hell on the Wabash | | 7,109 |
| Traditional Fifes and Drums | Sentry Box | Fennell, F. | 7,109 |
| Traditional Fifes and Drums | Sergeant O'Leary | Fennell, F. | 7,109 |
| Traditional Fifes and Drums | White Cockade | Fennell, F. | 7,92,109 |
| Traditional Fifes and Drums | Wrecker's Daughter Quickstep | | 7,109 |
| Tschaikowsky, Peter I. | March Slav | Kimura, Y. | 141 |
| Tull, Fisher | Concerto No. 2 for Trumpet and Orchestra | | 71 |
| Turina, Joaquin | Bullfighter's Prayer | | 35,118 |
| Verdi, Giuseppe | La Battaglia di Legnano Overture | Kalischnig, W. | 137 |
| Verdi, Giuseppe | March from "Aida" | Seredy, J.S. | 174 |
| Verdi, Giuseppe | Stornello | Erickson, F. | 97 |
| Verdi, Giuseppe | Un Ballo in Maschera Quickstep | Grafulla, C.S. | 32,102,160 |
| Vizzutti, Allen/Tyzik, Jeff | Concerto for Trumpet and Orchestra | | 71 |

| COMPOSER | TITLE | ARRANGER | ALBUM NUMBER |
|---|---|---|---|
| Wagner, J. F. | Under the Double Eagle | | 81 |
| Wagner, Joseph | Festive Fanfare, A | | 64 |
| Wagner, Richard | Elsa's Procession to the Cathedral | Cailliet, L. | 21,73,98,117,167,171,176 |
| Wagner, Richard | Entry of the Gods into Valhalla | Godfrey, D. | 21,117,167 |
| Wagner, Richard | Good Friday Music (Parsifal) | Godfrey, D. | 21,117 |
| Wagner, Richard | Invocation of Alberich (Das Rheingold) | Cailliet, L. | 96 |
| Wagner, Richard | Overture to Rienzi | Grabel, V. | 21,98,117 |
| Wagner, Richard | Prelude to Act III - Bridal Chorus (Lohengrin) | Winterbottom, F. | 21,98,117,167 |
| Wagner, Richard | Tannhauser March | | 38 |
| Wagner, Richard | Trauersinfonie | Leidzen, E. | 174 |
| Walton, William | Crown Imperial: A Coronation March | Duthoit, W.J. | 14,25,70,99,106,133,161 |
| Walton, William | Orb and Sceptre | | 38 |
| Walton, William | Three from "Facade" | O'Brien, R. | 133 |
| Weber, Carl Maria von | Five Waltzes | Wiggins, B. | 79 |
| Weinberger, Jaromir | Polka and Fugue from "Schwanda" | | 37,41,171 |
| Weinberger, Jaromir | Polka and Fugue from "Schwanda" [Winds] | Bainum, G.C. | 180 |
| White, Charles T. | Carry Me Back (To Old Virginny's Shore) | Leinbach, J. | 32 |
| Widor, Charles Marie | Salvum Fac Populum Tuum, Op. 84 | | 180 |
| Wilder, Alec | An Entertainment 1 | | 56 |
| Wilder, Alec | Concerto for Euphonium and Wind Orchestra | | 56 |
| Wilder, Alec | Concerto No. 2 for Trumpet and Flugelhorn | | 56 |
| Williams, J. Clifton | Fanfare and Allegro | Fennell, F. (16,73) | 16,17a,73,99,116,161 |
| Williams, J. Clifton | Pastorale | | 132 |
| Williams, J. Clifton | Symphonic Dance #2 - The Maskers | | 97 |
| Williams, J. Clifton | Symphonic Dance #3 - Fiesta | | 96 |
| Williams, J. Clifton | Symphonic Suite | | 72 |
| Williams, J. Clifton | Trail Scenes | | 97a |
| Williams, Ralph Vaughan | English Folksong Suite | | 4,5,55,86,104,133 |
| Williams, Ralph Vaughan | Sea Songs | | 54,86 |
| Williams, Ralph Vaughan | Toccata Marziale | | 4,5,55,73,104 |
| Willis, Authur | Vikings, The | | 180 |
| Willson, Meredith | I Ain't Down Yet | Krance, J. | 30,47,63,123 |

| COMPOSER | TITLE | ARRANGER | ALBUM NUMBER |
|---|---|---|---|
| Willson, Meredith | Seventy-six Trombones | Krance, J. | 30,47,63,123 |
| Wilson, Dana | Piece of Mind | | 142 |
| Work, Henry C. | Marching Through Georgia | | 32 |
| Work, Julian | Autumn Walk | Fennell, F. | 16,16a |
| Yamamoto, N. | This Glorious Silver World | | 173 |
| Zimmerman, Charles A. | Anchors Aweigh | Miles, Alfred H. (lyrics) | 54,86 |

# SECTION III

# TITLE INDEX

# TITLE INDEX

| COMPOSER | TITLE | ARRANGER | ALBUM NUMBER |
|---|---|---|---|
| Thomson, Virgil | A Solemn Music | | 3 |
| Traditional | A-hunting We Will Go | | 8,107 |
| Army Bugle Call | Adjutant's Call | | 8,107 |
| Cramatte, H.E. | Adjutant's Call Quickstep | | 51 |
| Foster, Stephen | Ah, May the Red Rose Live Alway | | 52 |
| Herbert, Victor | Ah, Sweet Mystery of Life | Hayman, R. | 49,90 |
| Massenet, Jules | Air Alsacien (Scenes Alsaciennes) | Erickson, F. | 96 |
| Kamioka, Yoichi | Akizora "Under Autumn Sky" March | | 170 |
| Sibelius, Jean | Alla Marcia (Karelia Suite) | | 38 |
| Reed, Alfred | Alleluia! Laudamus Te for Winds, Percussion and Organ | | 180 |
| Strauss, Richard | Allerseelen | Davis/Fennell | 73 |
| Barnes, James | Alvamar Overture | | 172 |
| Traditional | American Flag, The | | 8,107 |
| Meacham, Frank W. | American Patrol | | 6,66,91,103 |
| Gould, Morton | American Salute | Lang, P. | 173 |
| Fillmore, Henry | Americans We | Fennell, F. (79) | 11,79,162 |
| Strauss, | Amor March | | 51 |
| Texidor, Jaime | Amparito Roca | | 35,47,81,118 |
| Gershwin, George | An American in Paris | Hoshina, H. | 129 |
| Wilder, Alec | An Entertainment 1 | | 56 |
| Copland, Aaron | An Outdoor Overture | | 132 |
| Zimmerman, Charles A. | Anchors Aweigh | Miles, Alfred H. (lyrics) | 54,86 |
| Sousa, John Philip | Ancient and Honorable Artillery | | 22,57,101,112,164 |
| Lecuona, Ernesto | Andalucia | Gould, M. | 35,43,47,118 |
| Porter, Cole | Anything Goes | Wright, R. | 50,122,168 |
| Barnes, James | Appalachian Overture for Band | | 78,175 |
| Traditional | Appomattox Bugle, The | | 32,102,160 |
| Gabrieli, Andrea | Aria Della Battaglia | Ghedini | 18,65,125 |
| Khachaturian, Aram | Armenian Dance No. 2 | Satz, R. | 69 |
| Khachaturian, Aram | Armenian Dances | Satz, R. | 17,17a,163 |
| Reed, Alfred | Armenian Dances, Part II | | 131 |
| Army Bugle Call | Assembly | | 8,107 |

| COMPOSER | TITLE | ARRANGER | ALBUM NUMBER |
|---|---|---|---|
| Army Camp Duty | Austrian, The | | 7,109 |
| Work, Julian | Autumn Walk | Fennell, F. | 16,16a |
| Horovitz, J. | Bacchus on Blue Ridge | | 137 |
| Gould, Morton | Ballad for Band | | 1,113,132 |
| Kaneda, Bin | Ballade I for Symphonic Band | | 172 |
| Gounod, Charles F. | Ballet Music from "Faust" | Winterbottom, W. | 19,98,126,167 |
| Gounod, Charles F. | Ballet Music from "Faust" | Inagaki, T. | 141 |
| Prokofiev, Serge | Ballet Music from "Romeo and Juliet" | Yodo, A. | 135 |
| King, Karl L. | Barnum and Bailey's Favorite | | 6,9,54,77,86,103 |
| Steffe, William | Battle Hymn of the Republic, The | | 32,66 |
| Fernandez, Oscar | Batuque | | 35,118 |
| Richardson, Norman | Beachcomber, The | | Unreleased |
| Porter, Cole | Begin the Beguine | Wright, R. | 50,122,168 |
| Osser, Glenn | Beguine for Band | | 43 |
| Anderson, Leroy | Belle of the Ball | | 27,34,42,47,74,165 |
| Traditional Fifes and Drums | Belle of the Mohawk Vale, The | Fennell, F. | 7,109 |
| Ribble, John H. | Bennett's Triumphal | | 24,162 |
| Gershwin, George | Bidin' My Time | Wright, R. | 48,124,168 |
| King, Karl L. | Big Cage, The | | 24,114,162 |
| Klohr, John N. | Billboard, The | | 6,9,103,127 |
| Sousa, John Philip | Black Horse Troop, The | Fennell, F. (130) | 2,22,23,57,130,101,112,164 |
| Porter, Cole | Blow, Gabriel, Blow | Wright, R. | 43,50,122,168 |
| Anderson, Leroy | Blue Tango | | 34,41,47,74,165 |
| Anderson, Leroy | Bluebells of Scotland, The | | 44,75,165 |
| End, Jack | Blues For A Killed Kat | Fennell, F. | 129 |
| Farrar, Orion R. | Bombasto March | | 24,114,162 |
| Fillmore, Henry | Bones Trombone | | 24,114,162 |
| McCarthy, Harry | Bonnie Blue Flag | Fennell, F. | 7,31,92,109 |
| Goldman, Edwin Franko | Boy Scouts of America | | 11,110,162 |
| Duble, Charles E. | Bravura March | | 24,162 |
| Guarnieri, Camargo | Brazilian Dance | | 35,118 |
| Faith, Percy | Brazilian Sleigh Bells | | 26,35,118 |

| COMPOSER | TITLE | ARRANGER | ALBUM NUMBER |
|---|---|---|---|
| Traditional Fifes and Drums | Breakfast Call "Peas Upon a Trencher" | | 7,109 |
| Herman, Strouse, Coleman | Broadway Curtain Time | Krance, J. | 129 |
| Krance, John | Broadway Minstrel Medley | | 30,63,123 |
| Copland, Aaron | Buckaroo Holiday from "Rodeo" | Konagaya, S. | 176 |
| Anderson, Leroy | Bugler's Holiday | Edwards, M. (74) | 29,33,74,105,145 |
| Goldman, Edwin Franko | Bugles and Drums | | 11,77,92,162 |
| Sousa, John Philip | Bullets and Bayonets | Fennell, F. (130) | 20,23,130,101,108,164 |
| Turina, Joaquin | Bullfighter's Prayer | | 35,118 |
| Gershwin, George | But Not For Me | Lieb, R. | 48,124,168 |
| Bennett, Robert Russell | Cakewalk | | 171 |
| Army Bugle Call | Call to Quarters | | 8,107 |
| Traditional | Camp and Field Duty Calls | | 32,102,160 |
| Gabrieli, Giovanni | Canzon Duodecimi Toni | | 18,125 |
| Gabrieli, Giovanni | Canzon Noni Toni | | 18,125 |
| Gabrieli, Giovanni | Canzon Quarti Toni | | 18,125 |
| Gabrieli, Giovanni | Canzon Septimi Toni | | 18,125 |
| Olivadoti, Joseph | Canzona | | 172 |
| Mennin, Peter | Canzona | | 3 |
| Grafulla, C.S. | Cape May Polka | | 32,102 |
| Grafulla, C.S. | Captain Finch's Quickstep | | 52 |
| Grafulla, C.S. | Captain Shepherd's Quickstep | | 52 |
| Olivadoti, Joseph | Carnival of Roses Overture | | 172 |
| Rodgers, Richard | Carousel Waltz | Walker, Mark | 46 |
| White, Charles T. | Carry Me Back (To Old Virginny's Shore) | Leinbach, J. | 32 |
| Hoshina, Hiroshi | Catastrophe for Symphonic Band | | 172 |
| Traditional | Cavaliers, The | | 8,107 |
| Traditional | Cavalry Bugle Signals | | 31,102,160 |
| Grafulla, C.S. | Cavalry Quickstep | | 32,102,160 |
| Bennett, Robert Russell | Celebration | | 29,69 |
| Sparke, Philip | Celebration | | 144 |
| Morrissey, John | Centennial Suite | | 173 |
| Russell, Henry | Cheer Boys Cheer | Leinbach, J. | 31,102,160 |
| Goldman, Edwin Franko | Cheerio | Lang, P. | 2 |

199

| COMPOSER | TITLE | ARRANGER | ALBUM NUMBER |
|---|---|---|---|
| Anderson, Leroy | Chicken Reel | | 44,165 |
| Goldman, Edwin Franko | Children's March | Lang, P. | 11,110,162 |
| Grainger, Percy A. | Children's March | | 25,26,36,120,169 |
| Anderson, Leroy | China Doll | | 34,75,165 |
| Hanson, Howard | Chorale and Alleluia | | 3,79,100 |
| Anderson, Leroy | Christmas Festival | | 29,44,74 |
| Army Bugle Call | Church Call | | 8,107 |
| Fillmore, Henry | Circus Bee, The | | 24,114,162,127 |
| King, Karl L. | Circus Days | | 24,114,162 |
| Debussy, Claude | Claire de Lune | | 37,41,59 |
| Anderson, Leroy | Clarinet Candy | | 74,145 |
| Alford, Kenneth J. | Colonel Bogey | | 6,28,103 |
| Traditional | Colonel's Daughter, The | | 8,107 |
| Grainger, Percy A. | Colonial Song | | 36,120,169 |
| Bach, J.S. | Come, Dearest, the Daylight is Gone | Leinbach, J. | 31,102,160 |
| Foster, Stephen | Come, Sweet Death | Reed, A. | 128 |
| Barber, Samuel | Come Where My Love Lies Dreaming | | 32,102,160 |
| Sachse, J. | Commando March | | 1,54,86,100,113 |
| Hartley, Walter Sinclair | Concertino for E-flat Cornet | | 51 |
| Wilder, Alec | Concerto for 23 Winds | | 16a,17,163 |
| Vizzutti, Allen/Tyzik, Jeff | Concerto for Euphonium and Wind Orchestra | | 56 |
| Wilder, Alec | Concerto for Trumpet and Orchestra | | 71 |
| Tull, Fisher | Concerto No. 2 for Trumpet and Flugelhorn | | 56 |
| Gungl, Joseph | Concerto No. 2 for Trumpet and Orchestra | | 71 |
| Moore, J. Burns | Concordia March | | 51 |
| Bart, Lionel | Connecticut Half-time | Krance, J. | 7,8,109 |
| Delibes, Leo | Consider Yourself | Konagaya, S. | 30,63 |
| Sousa, John Philip | Coppelia, Ballet Suite | Fennell, F. (130) | 176 |
| Albeniz, Isaac | Corcoran Cadets | MasQuiles, J.V. | 2,130 |
| Benjamin, Arthur | Cordoba | | 79 |
| Ives, Charles | Cotillon Suite | | 46 |
| | Country Band March | Sinclair, J. | 132 |

| COMPOSER | TITLE | ARRANGER | ALBUM NUMBER |
|---|---|---|---|
| Grainger, Percy A. | Country Gardens | | 36,41,120,169 |
| Swearingen, James | Covington Square | | 175 |
| Walton, William | Crown Imperial: A Coronation March | Duthoit, W.J. | 14,25,70,99,106,133,161 |
| Koyama, K. | Dai-Kagura | | 173 |
| Rimsky-Korsakov, Nicholas | Dance of the Tumblers | | 46 |
| Horovitz, Joseph | Dance Suite | | 142 |
| Kodaly, Zoltan | Dances of Galanta | Rogers, R.M. | 135 |
| Bernstein, Leonard | Danzon from "Fancy Free" | Krance, J. | 76 |
| Sousa, John Philip | Daughters of Texas | Fennell, F. (130) | 2,130 |
| Army Camp Duty | Dawning of the Day | | 7,109 |
| Traditional Fifes and Drums | Dinner Call "Roast Beef" | | 7,109 |
| Persichetti, Vincent | Divertimento for Band | | 1,100 |
| Emmett, Daniel | Dixie | | 7,31,102,160 |
| Goodwin, George H. | Door Latch Quickstep | | 52 |
| Hauptmann, Moritz | Doppelquartett: Auf dem See | | 51 |
| Traditional | Double Time | | 8,107 |
| Traditional Fifes and Drums | Downfall of Paris | | 7,109 |
| Krenek, Ernst | Drei Lustige Marsche, Op. 44 "Three Merry Marches" | | 84 |
| Army Bugle Call | Drill Call | | 8,107 |
| Traditional | Drum Calls [Improvised by Fennell] | | 32,102,160 |
| Army Camp Duty | Dusky Night | | 7,109 |
| Army Camp Duty | Dutch, The | | 7,109 |
| | Easter Galop | Leinbach, J. | 31,102,160 |
| Reed, Alfred | El Camino Real | | 172 |
| Sousa, John Philip | El Capitan | Fennell, F. (130) | 6,23,57,83,92,130,101,103,127 |
| Chance, John Barnes | Elegy | | 139 |
| LoPresti, Ronald | Elegy For A Young American | | 132 |
| Wagner, Richard | Elsa's Procession to the Cathedral | Cailliet, L. | 21,73,98,117,167,171,176 |
| Gershwin, George | Embraceable You | Karlin, F. | 48,124,168 |
| Williams, Ralph Vaughan | English Folksong Suite | | 4,5,55,86,104,133 |
| Halvorsen, Johan | Entry March of the Boyars | Fennell, F. | 177 |
| Wagner, Richard | Entry of the Gods into Valhalla | Godfrey, D. | 21,117,167 |

201

| COMPOSER | TITLE | ARRANGER | ALBUM NUMBER |
|---|---|---|---|
| Sousa, John Philip | Fairest of the Fair, The | Fennell, F. (77) | 77 |
| Schumann, Robert | Familien-Gemalde Duet | | 51 |
| Ludwig, William F. | Fancy 6/8 | | 7,109 |
| Williams, J. Clifton | Fanfare and Allegro | Fennell, F. (16,73) | 16,17a,73,99,116,161 |
| Schoenberg, Arnold | Fanfare on Motifs of Die Gurrelieder | Boyd, J. | 144 |
| Bach, J.S. | Fantasia and Fugue in G minor | Goldman/Leist | 128 |
| Bach, J.S. | Fantasia in G | | 53,85,170,171 |
| Dello Joio, Norman | Fantasies on a Theme by Haydn | | 144 |
| Gungl, Joseph | Farewell Waltzes | | 51 |
| Gershwin, George | Fascinating Rhythm | Karlin, F. | 48,124,168 |
| Ganne, Louis | Father of Victory | | 15,81,119 |
| Albeniz, Isaac | Festival Day in Seville | Cailliet, L. | 178,179 |
| Hirose, R. | Festival Music for Band | | 173 |
| Wagner, Joseph | Festive Fanfare, A | | 64 |
| Shostakovich, Dmitri | Festive Overture, Op. 96 | Hunsberger, D. | 145,176 |
| Anderson, Leroy | Fiddle-Faddle | | 34,41,165 |
| Traditional | Field Music of Union and Confederate Troops | | 31,102,160 |
| Traditional | Field Music of Union and Confederate Troops | | 32,102,160 |
| Falla, Manuel de | Final Dance from "The Three-Cornered Hat" | Wiggins, B | 176 |
| Sullivan, Arthur | Finale - Pineapple Poll | Mackerras/Duthoit | 43 |
| Sibelius, Jean | Finlandia | | 37 |
| Sibelius, Jean | Finlandia | Kimura, M. | 141 |
| Anderson, Leroy | First Day of Spring | | 44,165 |
| Weber, Carl Maria von | Five Waltzes | Wiggins, B. | 79 |
| Fucik, Julius | Florentiner, Op. 214, The | Fennell, F. (72,81) | 54,72,81,86 |
| McBeth, W. Francis | Flourishes | | 78 |
| Caudill, Jim Andy | Folklore for Band | | 173 |
| Bach, J.S. | Forget Me Not, O Dearest Lord | Reed, A. | 128 |
| Anderson, Leroy | Forgotten Dreams | | 33,75,105 |
| Respighi, Ottorino | Fountains of Rome | Odom, L. | 135 |
| Respighi, Ottorino | Fountains of Rome, Symphonic Poem | Kimura, Y. | 143 |
| Coates, Eric | Four Ways Suite | | 45,121 |

| COMPOSER | TITLE | ARRANGER | ALBUM NUMBER |
|---|---|---|---|
| Curnow, James | Fox River Festival | | 78 |
| Gungl, Joseph | Frederic March | | 51 |
| Forrest, Fanny | Free and Easy | | 52 |
| Sousa, John Philip | Free Lance March, The | Downing, D. | 130 |
| Grafulla, C.S. | Freischutz Quickstep | | 31,102,160 |
| Bach, J.S. | Fugue a la Gigue | Holst, G. | 128 |
| Bach, J.S. | Fugue in G minor | Inagaki, T. | 128 |
| Traditional | Funeral March | | 8,107 |
| Grieg, Edward H. | Funeral March / Memory of Rikaard Nordrak | Fennell, F./Eriksen | 174,178 |
| Gounod, Charles F. | Funeral March of a Marionet | Lake, M. | 174 |
| Sousa, John Philip | Gallant Seventh, The | Fennell, F. (51) | 20,51,101,108,164 |
| Traditional | Garrison Belle, The | | 8,107 |
| | Garry Owen | Fennell, F. | 7,32,102,160 |
| Traditional | General Burt | | 8,107 |
| Army Bugle Call | General Call | | 8,107 |
| Traditional | General Dooley | | 8,107 |
| Knaeble, Simon | General Taylor Storming Monterey | | 52 |
| Traditional | General's March | | 8,107 |
| Schuman, William | George Washington Bridge | | 1,113,132 |
| Hindemith, Paul | Geschwindmarsch by Beethoven | Quiles, Mas | 79 |
| Loewe, Frederick | Get Me to the Church on Time | Krance, J. | 30,47,63,123 |
| Anderson, Leroy | Girl I Left Behind Me, The | | 75,105 |
| Anderson, Leroy | Girl in Satin, The | | 34,75,165 |
| Cohan, George M. | Give My Regards to Broadway | Krance, J. | 30,47,63,123 |
| Alford, Harry L. | Glory of the Gridiron | | 6,9 |
| Sousa, John Philip | Glory of the Yankee Navy | Fennell, F. (130) | 22,57,83,130,101,112,164 |
| San Miguel, Mariano | Golden Ear, The (La Oreja de Oro) | | 15,25,119 |
| Sousa, John Philip | Golden Jubilee | Fennell, F. | 22,27,57,61,101,112,164 |
| Anderson, Leroy | Golden Years, The | | 75 |
| Blackmar, A.E. | Goober Peas | | 32 |
| Wagner, Richard | Good Friday Music (Parsifal) | Godfrey, D. | 21,117 |
| Granados, Enrique | Goyescas: Intermezzo | | 35,41,118 |

| COMPOSER | TITLE | ARRANGER | ALBUM NUMBER |
|---|---|---|---|
| Grafulla, C.S. | Grafulla's 7th Regiment D.C. Quickstep | | 32,102,160 |
| Gigout, Eugene | Grand Chorus in Dialogue for Organ and Brass Choir | | 180 |
| Sousa, John Philip | Gridiron Club | | 22,57,83,101,112,164 |
| Rodgers, Richard | Guadalcanal March | Leidzen, E. | 11,110,162 |
| Cramatte, H.E. | Guard Mounting Quickstep | | 51 |
| Herbert, Victor | Habanera | Hayman, R. | 49,90 |
| Sanderson, James | Hail to the Chief | | 31,102,160 |
| Holst, Gustav | Hammersmith: Prelude and Scherzo | | 14,99,106,161 |
| Grainger, Percy A. | Handel In The Strand | | 36,120,169 |
| Sousa, John Philip | Hands Across the Sea | Fennell, F. (130) | 2,15,23,57,83,130,101,127 |
| Traditional Fifes and Drums | Hell on the Wabash | | 7,109 |
| German, Sir Edward | Henry VIII Dances | | 46 |
| Traditional | Hens and Chickens | | 8,107 |
| Lindblad, Adolf F. | Herdsman's Mountain Song, The | | 52 |
| Army Camp Duty | Hessian, The | | 7,109 |
| Sousa, John Philip | High School Cadets | | 20,57,83,101,108,164 |
| Grainger, Percy A. | Hill Song No. 2 | | 5,17,84,104,163 |
| Fillmore, Henry | His Honor | Fennell, F. (77) | 2,9,77,145,170,171 |
| Grundman, Clare | Holiday | | 79 |
| Traditional | Holy Joe | | 8,107 |
| Grieg, Edvard H. | Homage March - Sigurd Jorsalfar | | 38,39 |
| Anderson, Leroy | Home Stretch | | 74 |
| Dinicu, Gheorghe | Hora Staccato | | 37,41 |
| Anderson, Leroy | Horse and Buggy | | 34,75,165 |
| Reed, Alfred | Hounds of Spring, The | | 175 |
| Liszt, Franz | Hungarian Rhapsody No. 2 | Miyazawa, K. | 141 |
| Benedict, Sir Julius | Hunters Chorus "The Rose of Erin" | | 52 |
| Willson, Meredith | I Ain't Down Yet | Krance, J. | 30,47,63,123 |
| Gershwin, George | I Got Rhythm | Wright, R. | 43,48,124,168 |
| Herbert, Victor | I'm Falling In Love with Someone | Hayman, R. | 49,90 |
| Traditional | I've Got Three Years To Do This In | | 8,107 |
| Porter, Cole | I've Got You Under My Skin | Wright, R. | 50,122,168 |

| COMPOSER | TITLE | ARRANGER | ALBUM NUMBER |
|---|---|---|---|
| Graffeull, Charles | Il Staccato | Coquelet, O. | 136 |
| Goldman, Edwin Franko | Illinois March | Lang, P. | 11,110,162 |
| Grainger, Percy A. | Immovable Do, The | | 36,120,169 |
| Reed, Alfred | In Dulci Jubilo | | 97a |
| Heed, John C. | In Storm and Sunshine | | 24,28,114,127,162 |
| Porter, Cole | In the Still of the Night | Wright, R. | 50,122,168 |
| Chance, John Barnes | Incantation and Dance | | 175 |
| Jaeger, Edmund | Indiana Polka | Schatzman, | 52 |
| Delle Cese, Davide | Inglesina | | 15,28,81,119,170 |
| Goldman, Edwin Franko | Interlochen Bowl | | 11,110,162 |
| Jacob, Gordon | Intermezzo from "An Original Suite" | | 133,171 |
| King, Karl L. | Invictus | | 24,114,162 |
| Sousa, John Phillip | Invincible Eagle, The | | 20,57,101,108,164 |
| Barnes, James | Invocation and Toccata | | 176 |
| Wagner, Richard | Invocation of Alberich (Das Rheingold) | Cailliet, L. | 96 |
| Herbert, Victor | Irish Have a Great Day Tonight, The | Hayman, R. | 49,90 |
| Anderson, Leroy | Irish Suite | | 33 |
| Grainger, Percy A. | Irish Tune From County Derry | | 36,59,120,169 |
| Grainger, Percy A. | Irish Tune From County Derry [Winds] | | 139 |
| Anderson, Leroy | Irish Washerwoman, The | | 75,105 |
| Porter, Cole | It's Alright With Me | Wright, R. | 50,168 |
| Porter, Cole | It's Delovely | Wright, R. | 50,122,168 |
| Rachmaninoff, Sergei | Italian Polka | Leidzen, E. ed. F.F. | 139 |
| Herbert, Victor | Italian Street Song | Hayman, R. | 49,90 |
| Benjamin, Arthur | Jamaican Rumba | | 35,40,118 |
| Rogers, Bernard | Japanese Sword Dance | | 69 |
| Anderson, Leroy | Jazz Legato | | 44,165 |
| Anderson, Leroy | Jazz Pizzicato | | 44,165 |
| Bach, J.S. | Jesu, Joy of Man's Desiring | Reed, A. | 128 |
| | Juanita | Leinbach, J. | 32,102,160 |
| McBeth, W. Francis | Kaddish | | 131 |
| Skelton, Red | Kadiddlehopper March | Roullier, R, | 97 |

| COMPOSER | TITLE | ARRANGER | ALBUM NUMBER |
|---|---|---|---|
| Sousa, John Philip | Kansas Wildcats | | 22,23,83,101,112,164 |
| Kitazume, M. | Kaze-No-Kuni | | 173 |
| Sousa, John Philip | King Cotton | Fennell, F. (77) | 6,23,57,77,83,92,101,103,127,171 |
| Herbert, Victor | Kiss in the Dark, A | Hayman, R. | 49,90 |
| Herbert, Victor | Kiss Me Again | Hayman, R. | 49,90 |
| Coates, Eric | Knightsbridge March | | 15,98,119 |
| Verdi, Giuseppe | La Battaglia di Legnano Overture | Kalischnig, W. | 137 |
| Rossini, Gioacchino A. | La Boutique Fantasque | Godfrey, D. | 19,76,126,167 |
| Reed, H. Owen | La Fiesta Mexicana | | 3,76,100,170 |
| Lysberg, Charles-Samuel | La Fontaine | | 52 |
| de L'Isle, Claude J. R. | La Marseillaise | Grafulla, C.S. | 31,102,160 |
| Anderson, Leroy | Last Rose of Summer, The | | 42,105 |
| Lancen, Serge | Le Chant de l'Arbe | | 80,137 |
| Rauskl, Josef F. | Le Regiment de Sambre e Meuse | Fennell, F. | 81,171 |
| Sousa, John Philip | Liberty Bell, The | | 20,23,83,130,101,108,164 |
| Schumann, Robert | Liebesgarten Duet | | 51 |
| Grabeu-Hoffman | Liebeshandel Duet | | 51 |
| Liszt, Franz | Liebestraum | | 37,43 |
| Faust, Carl | Liebling's Polka | | 51 |
| McCoy, Earl E. | Lights Out | Roth, A. (77) | 6,77,103 |
| Grainger, Percy A. | Lincolnshire Posy | Fennell, F. (131) | 12,55,82,86,99,115,131,163 |
| Milburn, Richard | Listen to the Mockingbird | Grafulla, C.S. | 31,102,160 |
| Reed, Alfred | Little Concert Suite for Winds, A | | 172 |
| Gershwin, George | Liza | Wright, R. | 48,124,168 |
| Coates, Eric | London Suite | | 45,121 |
| Prokofiev, Serge | Love for Three Oranges - March and Scherzo | Duthoit, W. J. | 177 |
| Gershwin, George | Love is Sweeping the Country | Wright, R. | 48,124,168 |
| Gershwin, George | Love Walked In | Lieb, R. | 48,124,168 |
| Czibulka, Alphons | Love's Dream After the Ball | | 37,43 |
| Foster, Stephen | Lulu Quickstep | Leinbach, J. | 31,102,160 |
| | Lulu's Gone | | 32,102,160 |
| Alford, Kenneth J. | Mad Major, The | | 11,28,110,162 |

| COMPOSER | TITLE | ARRANGER | ALBUM NUMBER |
|---|---|---|---|
| Mozart, Wolfgang A. | Magic Flute, The [Overture] | Winterbottom, F. | 136 |
| Army Bugle Call | Mail Call | | 8,107 |
| Swearingen, James | Majestia | | 78 |
| Lecuona, Ernesto | Malagueña | Gould, M. | 35,43,118 |
| Gershwin, George | Man I Love, The | Karlin, F. | 48,124,168 |
| Sheldon, Robert | Manatee Lyric Overture | | 175 |
| Sousa, John Philip | Manhattan Beach | Fennell, F. (77) | 2,9,22,23,57,77,83,93,101,112,164 |
| Hanson, Howard | March Carillon, Op. 19, No. 2 | Perry, R. | 2 |
| Verdi, Giuseppe | March from "Aïda" | Seredy, J.S. | 174 |
| Prokofiev, Serge | March from "Love of the Three Oranges" | Duthoit, W.J. | 174 |
| Holst, Gustav | March from Suite in E-flat | | 62 |
| Seitz, Roland F. | March Grandioso | | 11,162 |
| Leemans, Pierre | March of the Belgian Paratroopers | | 54,86 |
| Pierne, Gabriel | March of the Little Leaden Soldiers | Godfrey, D. | 174 |
| Rodgers, Richard | March of the Siamese Children, The | Krance, J. | 30,47,63,123 |
| Herbert, Victor | March of the Toys | Hayman, R. | 49,90 |
| Prokofiev, Serge | March, Op. 99 | | 15,98 |
| Tschaikowsky, Peter I. | March Slav | Kimura, Y. | 141 |
| Berlioz, Hector | March to the Scaffold | Foulds, J.H./Brown | 174 |
| Ganne, Louis | Marche Lorraine | | 54,81 |
| Schubert, Franz | Marche Militaire | | 38,41,127 |
| Traditional | Marches and Inspection Pieces | | 8,107 |
| Work, Henry C. | Marching Through Georgia | | 32 |
| Miller & Beacham | Maryland, My Maryland | Leinbach, J. | 31,102,160 |
| Persichetti, Vincent | Masquerade | | 132 |
| Army Bugle Call | Mess Call | | 8,107 |
| Bennett, Harold | Military Escort March | Fennell, F. | 80 |
| Sousa, John Philip | Minnesota March | Fennell, F. | 97 |
| Anderson, Leroy | Minstrel Boy, The | | 75,105 |
| Bolzoni, Giovanni | Minuet | | 46,47 |
| Grainger, Percy A. | Mock Morris | | 36,43,120,169 |
| Grainger, Percy A. | Molly on the Shore | | 36,41,120,169 |

| COMPOSER | TITLE | ARRANGER | ALBUM NUMBER |
|---|---|---|---|
| Grainger, Percy A. | Molly on the Shore [Winds] | | 139 |
| Farmer, Henry | Moonbeam Waltzes, The | Downing, D. | 52 |
| Holst, Gustav | Moorside Suite | Wright, D. [133] | 78,133 |
| Nelson, Ron | Morning Alleluias For the Winter Solstice | | 142 |
| Handel, G.F. | Music for the Royal Fireworks | Baines/Mackerras | 53,85 |
| Porter, Cole | My Heart Belongs to Daddy | Wright, R. | 26,50,65,122,168 |
| Grainger, Percy A. | My Robin is to the Greenwood Gone | | 36,120,169 |
| Bagley, Edwin E. | National Emblem | Fennell, F. | 2,9,77,145 |
| Sousa, John Philip | National Game | | 22,28,57,83,101,112,164 |
| Sousa, John Philip | New Mexico March | Fennell, F. | 22,26,57,97a,101,112,164 |
| Porter, Cole | Night and Day | Wright, R. | 50,122,168 |
| Mailman, Martin | Night Vigil | | 80 |
| Grafulla, C.S. | Nightingale Waltz | | 31,102,160 |
| Traditional | No Slum Today | | 8,107 |
| Sousa, John Philip | Nobles of the Mystic Shrine | Fennell, F. | 20,26,57,101,108,164 |
| Hall, Robert B. | Officer of the Day | | 11,110,162 |
| Gossec, F.J. | Offrande A La Liberte [Lyric] | Dondeyne, D. | 134 |
| Gershwin, George | Oh, Lady Be Good | Wright, R. | 48,124,168 |
| Telke, Carl | Old Comrades | | 15,28,81,119,127 |
| Traditional | Old Guard, The | | 8,107 |
| Bourgeois, Louis | Old Hundredth | | 31,102,160 |
| | Old Kentucky, Kentucky | Grafulla, C.S. | 32,102,160 |
| Foster, Stephen | Old Memories | | 52 |
| | Old North State | Leinbach, J. | 31,102,160 |
| Traditional | Old Six-eight | | 8,107 |
| Arnaud, Leo | Olympic Fanfare | | 87 |
| Goldman, Edwin Franko | On The Mall | Lake, M. | 6,9,42,77,103,127 |
| Goldman, Edwin Franko | Onward-Upward | | 11,28,110,162 |
| Walton, William | Orb and Sceptre | | 38 |
| Reed, Alfred | Othello and Desdemona | | 171 |
| Bigelow, Frederick E. | Our Director March | | 2,9,77 |
| Sousa, John Philip | Our Flirtations | | 20,57,101,108,127,164 |

| COMPOSER | TITLE | ARRANGER | ALBUM NUMBER |
|---|---|---|---|
| Mendelssohn, Felix | Overture for Winds, Op. 24 | Boyd, J. | 139 |
| Catel, Charles Simon | Overture in C | Goldman, R.F./Smith | 175 |
| Erickson, Frank | Overture Jubiloso | | 172 |
| Bernstein, Leonard | Overture to "Candide" | Beeler, W. | 129 |
| Wagner, Richard | Overture to Rienzi | Grabel, V. | 21,98,117 |
| Rowlathem, J. | Palmyra Schottische | | 31,102,160 |
| Grafulla, C.S. | Parade | Grafulla, C.S. | 31,102,160 |
| Bach, J.S. | Passacaglia and Fugue in Cminor | Hunsberger, D. | 177 |
| Rossini, Gioacchino A. | Passo a sei (William Tell) | | 46 |
| Williams, J. Clifton | Pastorale | | 132 |
| Traditional | Pay Day | | 8,107 |
| Nelson, Ron | Pebble Beach Sojourn for Organ, Brass and Percussion | | 180 |
| Grieg, Edvard H. | Peer Gynt - Suite No. 1 | Fujita, G. / Kawasake, M. | 139 |
| Anderson, Leroy | Penny Whistle Song | | 33,74,105 |
| Debussy, Claude | Petite Suite | | 136 |
| Anderson, Leroy | Phantom Regiment | Kuwabara, H. | 44,74,165 |
| Sousa, John Philip | Picadore, The | | 20,28,57,83,101,108,127,164 |
| Moussorgsky, Modest P. | Pictures at an Exhibition | Hindsley, M. | 138 |
| Wilson, Dana | Piece of Mind | | 142 |
| Jenkins, Joseph W. | Pieces of Eight | Neff, Jerome | 2,174 |
| Neff, Jerome | Pieces of Eight | Jenkins, J.W. | 2,174 |
| Sullivan, Arthur | Pineapple Poll Suite | Mackerras/Duthoit | 19,126,167 |
| Respighi, Ottorino | Pines of Rome, Symphonic Poem | Suzuki, E. | 143 |
| Anderson, Leroy | Pirate Dance | | 44 |
| Anderson, Leroy | Plink, Plank, Plunk | | 44,165 |
| Dupre, Marcel | Poeme Heroique, Op. 33 | | 180 |
| Weinberger, Jaromir | Polka and Fugue from "Schwanda" | Bainum, G.C. | 37,41,171 |
| Weinberger, Jaromir | Polka and Fugue from "Schwanda" [Winds] | | 180 |
| Shostakovich, Dmitri | Polka from "The Golden Age" | | 37 |
| Elgar, Edward | Pomp and Circumstance No. 1 | | 174 |
| Grafulla, C.S. | Port Royal Galop | | 31,102,160 |
| Grainger, Percy A. | Power of Rome and the Christian Heart | | 180 |

| COMPOSER | TITLE | ARRANGER | ALBUM NUMBER |
|---|---|---|---|
| Karg-Elert, Sigfrid | Praise the Lord with the Drums and Cymbals [alla Handel] | | 180 |
| Humperdinck, Engelbert | Prayer and Dream from "Hansel and Gretel" | Maddy, J. | 141 |
| Rachmaninoff, Sergei | Prelude in G Minor | | 37 |
| Wagner, Richard | Prelude to Act III - Bridal Chorus (Lohengrin) | Winterbottom, F. | 21,98,117,167 |
| Debussy, Claude | Premier Rhapsody | Inagaki, T. | 136 |
| Traditional | President's March, The | | 8,107 |
| King, Karl L. | Pride of the Illini | | 2,9 |
| Sousa, John Philip | Pride of the Wolverines, The | Fennell, F. | 22,57,83,101,112,164 |
| Borodin, Alexander | Prince Igor March | | 38 |
| Traditional | Prisoner, The | | 8,107 |
| Rimsky-Korsakov, Nicholas | Procession of the Nobles | | 37 |
| Hermann, Ralph | Prom Night | | 43 |
| Anderson, Leroy | Promenade | Cacavas, J. (75) | 44,75,165 |
| Milhaud, Darius | Provence | | 43 |
| Army Camp Duty | Prussian, The | | 7,109 |
| Persichetti, Vincent | Psalm for Band | | 3 |
| Army Camp Duty | Quick Scotch, The | | 7,109 |
| Grafulla, C.S. | Rachel Waltzes | | 32,102 |
| Strauss, Johann | Radetzky March | | 54,86 |
| Anderson, Leroy | Rakes of Mallow, The | | 75,105 |
| Root, George F. | Rally 'Round the Flag | Fennell, F. | 7,109 |
| Traditional | Red Hussars, The | | 8,107 |
| Army Bugle Call | Retreat | | 8,107 |
| Army Bugle Call | Reveille | | 8,107 |
| Crammatti, H.E. | Review Quickstep | | 51 |
| Toyama, Yuzo | Rhapsodie for Wind Orchestra | Fujita, G. | 76 |
| Sousa, John Philip | Riders For the Flag | Fennell, F. (130) | 20,23,57,83,101,108,130,164 |
| Porter, Cole | Ridin' High | Wright, R. | 50,122,168 |
| Sousa, John Philip | Rifle Regiment | Fennell, F. (130) | 2,22,57,83,101,112,130,145,164 |
| Bassi, Luigi | Rigoletto de Verdi | Dureau, Th. | 136 |
| Traditional | Rip van Winkle | | 8,107 |
| Falla, Manuel de | Ritual Fire Dance | | 35,118 |

| COMPOSER | TITLE | ARRANGER | ALBUM NUMBER |
|---|---|---|---|
| King, Karl L. | Robinson's Grand Entree | | 24,114,162 |
| Fillmore, Henry | Rolling Thunder | | 24,162 |
| Respighi, Ottorino | Roman Festival, Symphonic Poem | Fennell, F. | 143 |
| Herbert, Victor | Romany Life | Kimura, Y. | 49,90 |
| Army Bugle Call | Ruffles and Flourishes | Hayman, R. | 8,107 |
| Gliere, Reinhold | Russian Sailor's Dance | | 37,127a |
| Goldmark, Karl | Rustic Wedding/Intermezzo/Scherzo | Kappey, H. | 177 |
| Gershwin, George | 'S Wonderful | Lieb, R. | 48,124,168 |
| Sousa, John Philip | Sabre and Spurs | Fennell, F. | 20,23,57,83,101,108,164 |
| Widor, Charles Marie | Salvum Fac Populum Tuum, Op. 84 | | 180 |
| Anderson, Leroy | Sandpaper Ballet | | 26,33,75,105 |
| Anderson, Leroy | Sarabande | | 34,47,165 |
| Arnold, Malcolm | Sarabande and Polka | Paynter, J. | 79 |
| Reynolds, Verne | Scenes | | 142 |
| Traditional | Scots Wha Hae | Wallace | 32 |
| Jewell, Fred | Screamer, The | | 24,114,127,162 |
| Williams, Ralph Vaughan | Sea Songs | | 54,86 |
| Swearingen, James | Seagate Overture | | 175 |
| Reeves, David W. | Second Regiment Connecticut N.G. March | | 11,28,110,127,162 |
| Sousa, John Philip | Semper Fidelis | Fennell, F. (77) | 2,9,77,92 |
| Traditional Fifes and Drums | Sentry Box | Fennell, F. | 7,109 |
| Strauss, Richard | Serenade in E-flat, Op. 7 | | 12,115 |
| Mozart, Wolfgang A. | Serenade No. 10 in B-flat, K. 361 | Fennell, F. (140) | 13,58,140 |
| Mozart, Wolfgang A. | Serenade No. 12 in C Minor, K. 388 | Fennell, F. | 140 |
| Anderson, Leroy | Serenata | | 34,47,75,105,165 |
| Traditional Fifes and Drums | Sergeant O'Leary | Fennell, F. | 7,109 |
| Sousa, John Philip | Sesqui-Centennial Exposition | | 22,28,57,101,112,164 |
| Willson, Meredith | Seventy-six Trombones | Krance, J. | 30,47,63,123 |
| Bach, J.S. | Sheep May Safely Graze | Reed, A. | 128 |
| Grainger, Percy A. | Shepherd's Hey | | 36,43,55,86,120,169 |
| Andriessen, J. | Sinfonia "Il Fume" | | 137 |
| Hartley Walter Sinclair | Sinfonia No. IV | | 142 |

| COMPOSER | TITLE | ARRANGER | ALBUM NUMBER |
|---|---|---|---|
| Dahl, Ingolf | Sinfonietta | | 144 |
| Anderson, Leroy | Sleigh Ride | | 33,41,68,74,105,165 |
| Noeren, J.M. | Slow March: Midnight | Schatzman, J. | 52 |
| Army Camp Duty | Slow Scotch, The | | 7,109 |
| Porter, Cole | So In Love | Wright, R. | 50,67,122,168 |
| Traditional | Soapsuds Row | | 8,107 |
| Perle, George | Solemn Procession | | 144 |
| Sousa, John Philip | Solid Men to the Front | | 20,28,101,108,164 |
| Gershwin, George | Someone To Watch Over Me | Wright, R. | 48,124,168 |
| Gabrieli, Giovanni | Sonata Octavi Toni | | 18,125 |
| Gabrieli, Giovanni | Sonata Pian e Forte | | 18,125 |
| Anderson, Leroy | Song of Jupiter | | 44,165 |
| Anderson, Leroy | Song of the Bells | | 34,74,165 |
| Reed, Alfred | Song of the High Cascades | | 173 |
| Mitchell, Rex | Song of the High Seas, A | | 175 |
| Rodgers, Richard | Sound of Music, The | | 145 |
| Sousa, John Philip | Sound Off! | | 20,57,83,101,108,164 |
| Puffhold, J. | Souvenir Polka | | 51 |
| Traditional | Spanish Guard Mount | | 8,107 |
| Bennett, Robert Russell | Spiritual | | 43 |
| Grainger, Percy A. | Spoon River | | 36,120,169 |
| Huff, Will | Squealer, The | | 24,114,162 |
| | St. Patrick's Day in the Morning | | 32,102,160 |
| Smith, John Stafford | Star Spangled Banner, The | Grafulla, C.S. | 8,66,107 |
| Smith, John Stafford | Star Spangled Banner, The | Fennell, F. (Ab) | 32 |
| Sousa, John Philip | Stars and Stripes Forever, The | Grafulla, C.S. | 6,9,54,57,66,77,83,86,88,101,103,127 |
| Kawade, Tomoki | Stones in Time | Fennell, F. (77) | 142 |
| Grafulla, C.S. | Storm Galop | | 32,102,160 |
| Verdi, Giuseppe | Stornello | Erickson, F. | 97 |
| Romberg, Sigmund | Stouthearted Men | Krance, J. | 30,63,123 |
| Herbert, Victor | Streets of New York | Hayman, R. | 43,49,60,90 |
| Gershwin, George | Strike Up The Band | Krance, J. | 30,63,124 |

| COMPOSER | TITLE | ARRANGER | ALBUM NUMBER |
|---|---|---|---|
| Milhaud, Darius | Suite Francaise | | 12,115,134 |
| Khachaturian, Aram | Suite Gayaneh | Inagaki, T. | 136 |
| Holst, Gustav | Suite No. 1 in E-flat for Military Band, Op. 28a | | 4,5,53,85,104,170 |
| Holst, Gustav | Suite No. 2 in F for Military Band, Op. 28b | | 4,5,53,85,104,133 |
| Anderson, Leroy | Suite of Carols | | 44 |
| Bennett, Robert Russell | Suite of Old American Dances | | 1,100,113 |
| Kabalevsky, Dmitri | Suite: The Comedians | Fujita, G. | 139 |
| Jacob, Gordon | Suite: William Byrd | | 14,106,133,161 |
| Anderson, Leroy | Summer Skies | Werle, F. (74) | 34,42,74,165 |
| Soderman, A. | Svenska Folkvisor Och Dancer | Gustafson, S. | 137 |
| Herbert, Victor | Sweethearts | Hayman, R. | 49,90 |
| Street, William G. | Swinging Down the Street | | 8,107 |
| Williams, J. Clifton | Symphonic Dance #2 - The Maskers | | 97 |
| Williams, J. Clifton | Symphonic Dance #3 - Fiesta | | 96 |
| Rachmaninoff, Sergei | Symphonic Dances III | Satoh, | 80 |
| Nelhybel, Vaclav | Symphonic Movement | | 72,176 |
| Saitoh, Takanobu | Symphonic Poem "Only One Earth" | | 172 |
| Del Borgo, Elliot | Symphonic Sketches for Band | | 78 |
| Bennett, Robert Russell | Symphonic Songs for Band | | 16,17a,99,130,161 |
| Williams, J. Clifton | Symphonic Suite | | 72 |
| Stravinsky, Igor | Symphonies of Wind Instruments | | 10,111 |
| Hindemith, Paul | Symphony in B-flat for Concert Band | | 10,111 |
| Giannini, Vittorio | Symphony No. 3 | | 178 |
| Mozart, Wolfgang A. | Symphony No. 39 in E-Flat [First movement] | ed. Fennell, F. | 146 |
| Persichetti, Vincent | Symphony No. 6 for Band | | 17,17a,116,134,163 |
| Beethoven, Ludwig van | Symphony No. 7 | Triebensee, Josef | 146 |
| Haydn, Joseph | Symphony No. 92 [Oxford] | Triebensee, Josef | 146 |
| Anderson, Leroy | Syncopated Clock | Lang, P. (74) | 34,41,74,165 |
| Cavez, Francesco | Tamboo | | Single 45 |
| Wagner, Richard | Tannhauser March | | 38 |
| Army Bugle Call | Taps | | 8,107 |
| Army Bugle Call | Tattoo | | 8,107 |

| COMPOSER | TITLE | ARRANGER | ALBUM NUMBER |
|---|---|---|---|
| Kittredge, Walter | Tenting Tonight on the Old Camp Ground | Fennell, F. | 32 |
| Stravinsky, Igor | The Firebird [1919] Suite from the Ballet | Earles, R./F. Fennell | 138 |
| Huffine, Getty H. | Them Basses | | 24,114,162 |
| Schoenberg, Arnold | Theme and Variations, Op. 43a | | 10,73,111 |
| Rodgers, Richard | There is Nothin' Like A Dame | Krance, J. | 30,63,123 |
| Berlin, Irving | There's No Business Like Show Business | Krance, J. | 30,63,123 |
| Herbert, Victor | Thine Alone | Hayman, R. | 49,90 |
| Yamamoto, N. | This Glorious Silver World | | 173 |
| Army Camp Duty | Three Camps, The | | 7,109 |
| Khachaturian, Aram | Three Dance Episodes from "Spartacus" | Hunsberger, D. | 134 |
| Coates, Eric | Three Elizabeths, The | | 45,121 |
| Arnaud, Leo | Three Fanfares for Brass-Percussion | | 55,86 |
| Walton, William | Three from "Facade" | O'Brien, R. | 133 |
| Rogers, Bernard | Three Japanese Dances | | 12,115,163 |
| Fucik, Julius | Thunder and Blazes - Entry of the Gladiators | | 24,28,114,162,127 |
| Sousa, John Philip | Thunderer, The | | 6,57,83,101,103,127,130 |
| Anderson, Leroy | Ticonderoga March, The | | 75 |
| Traditional | To The Color | | 8,107 |
| Frescobaldi, Girolamo | Toccata | Slocum, E. | 79 |
| Bach, J.S. | Toccata and Fugue in D minor | Fujita, G./Fennell, F. | 128 |
| Williams, Ralph Vaughan | Toccata Marziale | | 4,5,55,73,104 |
| Williams, J. Clifton | Trail Scenes | | 97a |
| Root, George F. | Tramp, Tramp, Tramp | Fennell, F. | 32 |
| Wagner, Richard | Trauersinfonie | Leidzen, E. | 174 |
| Nelhybel, Vaclav | Trittico | | 178,179 |
| Anderson, Leroy | Trumpeter's Lullaby | Lang, P. (74) | 33,61,74,105 |
| Piston, Walter | Tunbridge Fair | | 1,113 |
| Beethoven, Ludwig van | Turkish March | | 38,39 |
| Leinbach, Julius | Twenty-sixth Regiment Quickstep | | 32 |
| Ordway, J.P. | Twinkling Stars Quickstep | Grafulla, C.S. | 32 |
| Brahms, Johannes | Two Chorale Preludes | Guenther/Fennell | 73,177 |
| Anderson, Leroy | Typewriter, The | Werle, F. (74) | 26,34,74,165 |

| COMPOSER | TITLE | ARRANGER | ALBUM NUMBER |
|---|---|---|---|
| Sousa, John Philip | U.S. Field Artillery March | Lake/Fennell (77) | 6,9,23,57,77,95,101,103 |
| Verdi, Giuseppe | Un Ballo in Maschera Quickstep | Grafulla, C.S. | 32,102,160 |
| Wagner, J. F. | Under the Double Eagle | | 81 |
| Seitz, Roland F. | University of Pennsylvania Band March | | 54 |
| Lindblad, Adolf F. | Upon a Summer's Day | | 52 |
| Hanssen, Johannes | Valdres March | | 15,81,119 |
| Dello Joio, Norman | Variants on a Medieval Tune | | 178 |
| Chance, John Barnes | Variations on a Korean Folk Song | | 72 |
| Copland, Aaron | Variations on a Shaker Melody | | 144 |
| Willis, Authur | Vikings, The | | 180 |
| Reed, Alfred | Viva Musica (A Concert Overture for Winds) | | 78 |
| Rachmaninoff, Sergei | Vocalise, Op. 34, No. 14 | Yodo, A. | 139 |
| Strauss II, Johann | Voices of Spring - Waltz | Winter & Hibbert | 141,145 |
| | Waltz No. 19 | Leinbach, J. | 31,102,160 |
| Anderson, Leroy | Waltzing Cat, The | Lang, P. (75) | 34,75,165 |
| Grafulla, C.S. | Washington Grays | | 54,77 |
| Sousa, John Philip | Washington Post, The | Fennell, F. | 6,23,57,83,91,92,101,103,130 |
| Emerson, L.O. | We Are Coming, Father Abra'am | Fennell, F. (130) | 32,102,160 |
| Anderson, Leroy | Wearing of the Green, The | | 29,105 |
| Press, Jacques | Wedding Dance | Johnston, H. | 72,129 |
| Mendelssohn, Felix | Wedding March from "Midsummer Nights Dream" | Laurendeau, L.P. | 174 |
| Gould, Morton | West Point Symphony | | 16,16a,116,135,166 |
| Gilmore, Patrick | When Johnny Comes Marching Home | | 32,102,160 |
| Allen, Thomas S. | Whip and Spur | | 24,114,162 |
| Traditional Fifes and Drums | White Cockade | Fennell, F. | 7,92,109 |
| Foster, Stephen | Why, No One To Love? | | 52 |
| Schrammel, Joseph | Wien Bleibt Wien | | 81 |
| Rossini, Gioacchino A. | William Tell Overture | Inagaki, T. | 134 |
| Gershwin, George | Wintergreen For President | Krance, J. | 30,63,124 |
| Starke, Hermann | With Sword and Lance | | 81 |
| Smalls, Charlie | Wiz, The | Lowden, B. | 129 |
| MacDowell, Edward | Woodland Sketches | Winterbottom, F. | 177 |

215

| COMPOSER | TITLE | ARRANGER | ALBUM NUMBER |
|---|---|---|---|
| Traditional Fifes and Drums | Wrecker's Daughter Quickstep | | 7,109 |
| Traditional | Yankee Doodle | | 7,66,109 |
| Bicknell, G. | You Naughty, Naughty Men | | 51 |
| Porter, Cole | You'd Be So Nice to Come Home to | Wright, R. | 50,122,168 |
| Traditional | You're In The Army Now | | 8,107 |

# SECTION IV

**EASTMAN WIND ENSEMBLE PERSONNEL and SELECTED PROGRAMS 1952-1962**

**FREDERICK FENNELL Conductor**

# NATIONAL MUSIC CAMP
## Interlochen, Michigan

## "How it all Began"
Variations On The Interlochen Theme ...
From T. P. Giddings
21 July 1940

RR:  The following is taken from <u>The Scherzo</u>, National Music Camp, Interlochen, Michigan.

"What has struck my fancy since the beginning of camp?" repeated T. P. over his round-table-on-the-square Wednesday morning. "Well, to tell you that I'll have to tell you a story. I once had a little 'Hinglish 'ousemaid' who said she'd make my sister a ' 'andkercher' -- a beautiful one -- if I'd buy her some Valenciennes lace. So I went to a clerk I knew at Marshall Field, and said, 'I want some lace for a handkerchief.'

"He laid on the counter two bolts of lace in the same pattern. 'This,' he said, 'is machine-made lace at 35 cents a yard. And this,' pointing to the other, 'is hand-made at $3.50.'

" 'What's the difference?' I asked him. 'Look,' he explained. 'In the machine-made lace every little opening is exactly like every other little opening, because a machine can't make them any other way. But in the real lace, every little opening is just a shade different from every other. That's why the real lace is more soft -- and the reason it will make your sister the most beautiful handkerchief in the world.'

"A few weeks later Paderewski -- and I usually am bored by pianists -- made me see that the same laws apply to real musicianship as to real lace. If music is to be really fine -- if it is to hold our attention and demand our best efforts -- it must have the same infinite variety as the web of real lace. Only when he masters this law and can communicate it to those with whom he works, is a musician a real master.

"I think **FREDERICK FENNELL** has discovered this law, and the law of humility with it. And that's why I'm impressed more than anything else to date by his musicianship, and feel sure of his making a fine conductor in the years to come."

[Thaddeus P. Giddings was co-founder of Interlochen with Joseph Maddy]

**The
UNIVERSITY of ROCHESTER
CONCERT BAND
FREDERICK FENNEL, DIRECTOR
PHILLIP MANGOLD, PIANO SOLOIST**

**STRONG AUDITORIUM**
Friday Evening
January 18, 1935

---

| | |
|---|---:|
| Semper Fidelis - March | *Sousa* |
| "Rienzi Overture" | *Wagner* |
| Serenade Roccoco | *Meyer-Helmund* |
| The Clock and the Dresden Figures<br>    For Piano and Band - Phillip Mangold, Soloist | *Ketelby* |

INTERMISSION

| | |
|---|---:|
| Scherzo from "The Rustic Wedding" Symphony | *Goldmark* |
| Cockney Suite<br>    1st Movement, A State Procession<br>    2nd Movement, The Cockney Lover<br>    3rd Movement, Elegy<br>    4th Movement, The Palais de Danse | *Ketelby* |
| The Spirit of Youth - March<br>    This march was written in the composer's third summer at the National Music Camp, Interlochen, Michigan.  It is dedicated to Amos G. Wesler. | *Fennell* |

---

STAFF

| | |
|---|---:|
| Manager | James McBride |
| Librarian | Herbert Harp |
| Publicity Manager | Kenneth Miller |
| Board of Control Representatives | Mr. Donald R. Gilchrist |
| | Dr. Delos W. Canfield |

RR: Please note the misspelling of Fennell, which appeared on the program.  The cover also displays the University of Rochester Seal.  Program notes are included with each selection.

## EASTMAN SCHOOL OF MUSIC

Instrumental Ensemble Department

PERSONNEL FOR **WIND ENSEMBLE**

Effective 20 September 1952  Place of Rehearsal Kilbourn Hall

Time 3:10 - Thursday - 5:20  Date of Performance —

_[signature]_ Conductor

### FLUTES
- 66 Maclean, Donna
- 66 Shanley, Gretel
- 66 Bryan, Keith
  (fl. & Picc.)

### OBOE
- 66 Alexander, James
- ✓ Dufford, Catherine
- 66 Groth, Earl
  (3rd & Eng. Horn)

### BASSOONS
- 66 Phillips, Ronald
- 66 Grimes, Theodore
- 66 ~~Pugsley, Roger~~ ? John Bridges
  (3rd and Contra)

### Eb Clarinet
- 66 Fischer, Joseph

### ALTO SAXOPHONES
- ✓ Hartman, William
- 66 Silberstein, Robert

### HORNS
- 66 Bloomer, Barbara
- 10 Carpenter, Clyde (asst. 1st)
- 66 McCann, Zora
- ✓ Banks, Gay
- 66 Siverson, Peter

### Bb CLARINETS
- 66 Solo--Jones, George
- ✓ Macleod, Charles
- 64 Di Felice, Rudolph
- 66 Mandros, James
- ✓ Goodman, Barbara
- 66 Wheeler, Raymond
- 12 Johnston, Darrell
- ✓ Atkins, Richard

### TENOR SAXOPHONES
- ✓ Lo Presti, Ronald

### BARITONE SAXOPHONE
- ✓ Coley, Donald

### CORNETS
- 66 Lockwood, William
- 140 Patrylak, Daniel
- 66 Brower, William

### TRUMPETS
- 97 Hohstadt, Thomas
- 108 Fricano, Samuel

### ALTO CLARINET
- 770 Gaver, William

### BARITONES
- 78 Miller, Thomas
- 66 Hunsberger, Donald

### BASS CLARINET
- 130 Tomasick, Paul

### Trombones
- 66 Norden, Robert
- 66 Slezak, Lester
- 66 Fink, Reginald

### TUBAS
- 66 Butler, Bruce
- ✓ Zale, Donald

### HARP
- 66 Burke, Lauralee

### KETTLE DRUM
- 66 MATArrese, Antony

### PERCUSSION
- 66 Wendrich, Kenneth
- 66 Leonard, Stanley

### STRING BASS
- 66 Courtney, Neil

**ASSIGNMENT AND SEATING IS SUBJECT TO CHANGE.**

The first rehearsal call-sheet for the new Eastman Wind Ensemble, September 20, 1952 – 3:10 - 5:20 PM. [Numbers at left of names indicate each player's local union affiliation].

# EASTMAN SYMPHONIC WIND ENSEMBLE
## Frederick Fennell, Conductor
## 1952 - 1953
### #1

FLUTE
Maclean, Donna
Bryan, Keith
Shanley, Gretel [Piccolo] *

E-FLAT CLARINET
MacLeod, Charles

B-FLAT CLARINET
Jones, George *
Mandros, James
Kessler, Barbara
Fisher, Joseph
Weiss, Mitchell
Scharbo, Joseph
Johnston, Darrell [Sem II]
Atkins, Richard
Hartman, William

ALTO CLARINET
Gaver, William *

BASS CLARINET
Tomasick, Paul

OBOE
Alexander, James
Dufford, Catherine *
Groth, Earl [English Horn]

BASSOON
Phillips, Ronald
Grimes, Theodore
Bridges, John [Contra]

SAXOPHONE
Defelice, Rudolph [Alto]
Silberstein, Robert [Alto]
Brenner, Fred [Tenor]
Coley, Donald [Baritone]

HORN
Bloomer, Barbara
Carpenter, Clyde [Assistant]
McCann, Zora
Banks, Gay
Norem, Richard

CORNET
Lockwood, William *
Patrylak, Daniel
Brower, William

TRUMPET
Hohstadt, Thomas
Fricano, Samuel

BARITONE
Miller, Thomas
Hunsberger, Donald *

TROMBONE
Norden, Robert
Slezak, Lester *
Fink, Reginald *

TUBA
Butler, Bruce *
Zale, Donald

STRING BASS
Courtney, Neil

HARP
Campbell, Lauralee

PIANO
Van Ausdall, Clair W. *

PERCUSSION
Wendrich, Kenneth
Leonard, Stanley *
Matarrese, Anthony [Kettledrums]
Beck, John *

* Back for 25th Anniversary - 7-8 October 1977

---

**PREMIER SEASON ACTIVITIES**

First rehearsal - 20 September 1952
NBC Coast-to-Coast Broadcasts
23 February, 23 March, 1953
6 NYSSMA/RRN* Broadcasts
Debut Concert - 8 February 1953

Debut Recording - 14 May 1953
*New York State School Music Association
Rural Radio Network

# KILBOURN HALL

# EASTMAN WIND ENSEMBLE

FREDERICK FENNELL, *Conducting*

## DEBUT CONCERT

EASTMAN SCHOOL OF MUSIC
Of The University of Rochester
Sunday, February 8, 1953
4:00 P. M.

---

## Program

Serenade No. 10 in B flat major, K. 361      WOLFGANG AMADEUS MOZART

    Largo - Allegro molto
    Menuetto
    Adagio
    Menuetto: Allegretto
    Romanze: Adagio - Allegretto - Adagio
    Theme with variations: Andante
    Rondo: Allegro molto

### INTERMISSION

Nonet for Brass      WALLINGFORD RIEGGER
    First Rochester Performance

Symphony in B flat [1951]      PAUL HINDEMITH

    Moderately fast, with vigor
    Andantino grazioso
    Fugue: Rather broad

RR: This statement appeared in the Debut Program of the Eastman Wind Ensemble

The Eastman School of Music welcomes you to the premiere performance of the Eastman Wind Ensemble. In this, its first public concert, it will present three works written for wind instruments. This ensemble has been brought into existence to serve the cause of music through the presentation of original music for those instruments which are played by an embouchure.

The development of wind playing has been one of America's greatest contributions to the art of musical performance, and in establishing this group we have arrived at a point where, by the process of elimination of multiple doubling of the players, we hope to present the vast bulk of music written for these instruments in what we believe to be a proper balance of players. Our concerts will be played in proportions similar to this afternoon's program - one-third music for reeds, one-third music for brasses, and one-third music for the complete instrumentation listed elsewhere in this program. The Eastman School Symphony Band which has presented its outstanding concerts of music for band during the past eighteen years will continue to perform that literature which America has always loved to hear played by a fine band.

We welcome you today to the first of what we hope will be a significant series of music events which will provide pleasure and stimulation for the people of Rochester for many years to come.

*frederick fennell,*
Conductor

At Riverside Community College – April 1981
Photo by Roger E. Rickson

## PREMIER SEASON - 1952 - 1953

### NBC Coast - to - Coast Broadcast
### February 23, 1953
### PROGRAM #1

| | |
|---|---|
| Toccata Marziale | Ralph Vaughan Williams |
| Ballad | Morton Gould |
| Divertimento for Band | Vincent Persichetti |
| George Washington Bridge | William Schuman |
| Corcoran Cadets | John Philip Sousa |

### NBC Coast - to - Coast Broadcast
### March 23, 1953
### PROGRAM #2

| | |
|---|---|
| Youth Triumphant Overture | Henry Hadley |
| A Solemn Music | Virgil Thomson |
| Suite of Old American Dances | Robert Russell Bennett |
| Finale from "Symphony for Band" | Roy Harris |

## NYSSMA CONCERTS - RURAL RADIO NETWORK

### Number 1 - Monday, January 5, 1953

| | |
|---|---|
| March and Chorus from "Judas Maccabaeus" | George Frederick Handel |
| | arr. Richard Franko Goldman |
| Chorale - "Jesu, Who in Sorrow Dying" | Johann Sebastian Bach |
| | arr. Mayhew Lake |
| American Folk Rhapsody | Clare Grundman |
| Polka and Fugue from "Schwanda, the Bagpiper" | Jaromir Weinberger |
| | arr. Glenn Cliffe Bainum |

### Number 2 - Monday, January 12, 1953

| | |
|---|---|
| Chorale Melody "Come Sweet Death" | Johann Sebastian Bach |
| | arr. Erik Leidzen |
| Little Norwegian Suite | Erik Hanson |
| | arr. T. Conway Brown |
| Prayer from "Hansel and Gretel" | Engelbert Humperdinck |
| Ballad for Band | Morton Gould |

### Number 3 - Monday, January 26, 1953

| | |
|---|---|
| Two Moods Overture | Clare Grundman |
| South American Holiday | Dante Fiorillo |
| Sleepytime | Paul Yoder |
| Euryanthe Overture | Carl Maria von Weber |
| | arr. Dan Godfrey |

### Number 4 - Monday, February 2, 1953

| | |
|---|---|
| If Thou Be Near | Johann Sebastian Bach |
| | arr. R. L. Moehlmann |
| Dance of the Blessed Spirits from the Opera "Orpheus" | Christoph Willibald von Gluck |
| | arr. Eric DeLamarter |
| Ase's Death from Peer Gynt Suite No. 1 | Edward Grieg |
| | arr. G. E. Holmes |
| Suite No. 1 in E-flat | Gustav Holst |

### Number 5 - Monday, February 9, 1953

| | |
|---|---|
| Adoramus te and Sanctus | Giovanni Pierluigi daPalestrina |
| | arr. Russell Harvey |
| Three Street Corner Sketches | George Frederick McKay |
| Spiritual | Owen Reed |
| Rhapsodie: Espana | Emmanuel Chabrier |
| | arr. V. Safranek |

### Number 6 - Monday, February 16, 1953

| | |
|---|---|
| Prelude and Fugue in G minor | Johann Sebastian Bach |
| | arr. L. Cailliet |
| Lonely Landscape | Robert McBride |
| Shoontree | Henry Cowell |
| Andante, from Symphony No. 1, "Nordic" | Howard Hanson |
| | arr. Joseph E. Maddy |
| Provence from "Suite Francaise" | Darius Milhaud |

## SEASON TWO - 1953 - 1954
## NYSSMA CONCERTS - RURAL RADIO NETWORK

### Number 1 - Monday, January 4, 1954

| | |
|---|---|
| Youth Triumphant Overture | Henry Hadley |
| Chorale "Thou Prince of Life, O Christ, O Lord" | Johann Sebastian Bach |
| | arr. Mayhew Lake |
| Prayer and Dream Pantomime from "Hansel and Gretel" | Englebert Humperdinck |
| | arr. Joseph Maddy |
| Blue Tail Fly | Clare Grundman |

### Number 2 - Monday, January 11, 1954

| | |
|---|---|
| Sheep May Safely Graze | Johann Sebastian Bach |
| Procession of the Nobles from "Mlada" | Nicholas Rimsky-Korsakoff |
| | arr. Erik Leidzen |
| Thendara Overture | Maurice Whitney |
| Excerpt from "Death and Transfiguration" | Richard Strauss |
| | arr. A. A. Harding |

### Number 3 - Monday - January 25, 1954

| | |
|---|---|
| Overture to Goethe's Drama "Egmont" | Ludwig van Beethoven |
| | arr. Frank Winterbottom |
| Agnus Dei | Georges Bizet |
| Trauersinfonie | Richard Wagner |
| | arr. Erik Leidzen |
| Commando March | Samuel Barber |

### Number 4 - Monday, February 1, 1954

| | |
|---|---|
| Chorale and Fugue in G minor | Johann Sebastian Bach |
| Irish Tune from County Derry | Percy Aldridge Grainger |
| Legend of the Glass Mountain | Nino Rota |
| | arr. Dawson |
| Sequoia | Homer LaGassey |

### Number 5 - Monday, February 8, 1954

| | |
|---|---|
| From the Delta | William Grant Still |
| Suite from "The Gods Go A-Begging" | George Frederick Handel |
| | arr. Sir Thomas Beecham |
| English Folk Song Suite | Ralph Vaughan Williams |

### Number 6 - Monday, February 15, 1954

| | |
|---|---|
| Fugue in F Major | Johann Sebastian Bach |
| March Carillon | Howard Hanson |
| | arr. Erik Leidzen |
| Entry of the Gods into Valhalla from "Das Rhinegold" | Richard Wagner |
| | arr. Dan Godfrey |
| Glory of the Gridiron | Harry L. Alford |
| Pieces of Eight | Joseph Wilcox Jenkins/Jerome Neff |

**EASTMAN SYMPHONIC WIND ENSEMBLE**

**FREDERICK FENNELL, CONDUCTOR**

**KILBOURN HALL**

Eastman School of Music
of the University of Rochester
Sunday, November 1, 1953
4:00 PM

First Concert
Season 1953-1954

Program

| | |
|---|---|
| Motet: Tui Sunt Coeli for Eight Voice Double Brass Choir | Orlando De Lasso [1532-1594] |
| Suite No. 2 for Brass Instruments<br>Turmmusick - 1685<br>    Courante - Intrada - Bal - Sarabande - Gigue | Johann Pezel [1639-1694] |
| Music for King Charles II<br>    Pavan - Almand - Ayre | Matthew Locke [1630-1677] |
| Sacrae Symphoniae [1597]<br>    Sonata pian e forte<br>    Canzon Noni Toni a. 12 | Giovanni Gabrieli [1557-1612] |

INTERMISSION

| | |
|---|---|
| Symphonie for Wind Instruments<br>    Allegro con brio<br>    Andantino, sehr gemachlich<br>    Menuet: Etwas lebhaft<br>    Introduction and Allegro<br>        (First performance in America) | Richard Strauss [1864-1949] |

The trombone choir which performs the chorales preceding the concert is
from the class of Emory B. Remington

# EASTMAN SCHOOL OF MUSIC
*Of The University of Rochester*

Presents its
Fifth Annual Festival of Marches

Played by
THE EASTMAN SYMPHONIC WIND ENSEMBLE
FREDERICK FENNELL, *Conductor*

## KILBOURN HALL

Thursday, November 19, 1953
At 8:15 o'clock

---

Program

| | |
|---|---|
| Cheerio | EDWIN FRANKO GOLDMAN |
| Our Director | F. E. BIGELOW |
| His Honor | HENRY FILLMORE |
| March Carillon | HOWARD HANSON |
| Glory of the Gridiron | HARRY L. ALFORD |
| Pieces of Eight | JOSEPH WILCOX JENKINS and JEROME NEFF |
| Pride of the Illini | KARL L. KING |
| National Emblem | E. E. BAGLEY |

INTERMISSION

Eight Marches by John Philip Sousa (1856-1932)
    Rifle Regiment
    Corcoran Cadets
    Daughters of Texas
    Fairest of the Fair
    Black Horse Troop
    Hands Across the Sea
    Manhattan Beach
    Semper Fidelis

# EASTMAN SYMPHONIC WIND ENSEMBLE
Frederick Fennell, Conductor
1953 - 1954
#2

**FLUTE**
Shanley, Gretel
Geis, Donna
Gilbert, David [Piccolo]

**B-FLAT CLARINET**
Jones, George
Mandros, James
Kessler, Barbara
Sparks, Daniel
Scharbo, Joseph
Fisher, Joseph
Pizzarello, Theodore

**E-FLAT CLARINET**
Weiss, Mitchell

**ALTO CLARINET**
Gaver, William

**BASS CLARINET**
Tomasick, Paul

**CONTRABASS CLARINET**
Corey, Gerald

**SAXOPHONE**
Coley, Donald [Alto]
Marge, George [Alto]
Brenner, Fred [Tenor]
Carey, Jack [Baritone]

**OBOE**
Dufford, Catherine
Groth, Earl
Wilson, Dean [English Horn]

**BASSOON**
Phillips, Ronald
Grimes, Theodore
Corey, Gerald [Contrabassoon]

**HORN**
Haynes, JoAnn
Bloomer, Barbara
Helfrich, David
Benjamin, Barry
Krance, John

**CORNET**
Patrylak, Daniel
Hohstadt, Thomas
Sapiro, Maurice

**TRUMPET**
Fricano, Samuel
Ricksecker, Barbara

**BARITONE**
Miller, Thomas
Bockman, Guy

**TROMBONE**
Hunsberger, Donald
Slezak, Lester
Miller, Donald

**TUBA**
Zale, Donald
Zale, Robert

**STRING BASS**
Courtney, Neil

**HARP**
Kreig, Lois

**PIANO - CELESTE**
VanAusdall, Clair W.

**KETTLEDRUMS**
Leonard, Stanley

**PERCUSSION**
Beck, John
Dotson, James
Peters, Gordon
Peters, Mitchell

---

**ACTIVITIES**
First Concert - 1 November 1953
6 NYSSMA/RRN Broadcasts
Album - Marches
Album - La Fiesta Mexicana
Single - Tamboo

# EASTMAN SYMPHONIC WIND ENSEMBLE
Frederick Fennell, Conductor
1954 - 1955
#3

FLUTE
Gilbert, David
Hamilton, Michael
Gruskin, Shelly [Piccolo]

OBOE
Dufford, Catherine
Stolper, Daniel
Kummer, Keith [English Horn]

B-FLAT CLARINET
MacLeod, Charles
Tomasick, Paul
Coley, Donald
Stevens, Noel
Trojan, Dorothy
Coccagnia, Louis
Marge, George
Sparks, Daniel

E-FLAT CLARINET
Sumrall, John

E-FLAT ALTO CLARINET
Slattery, Thomas

B-FLAT BASS CLARINET
Freeman, Paul

B-FLAT CONTRABASS CLARINET
Puluse, Donald

SAXOPHONE
Carey, Jack [Alto]
Regni, Albert [Alto]
Dransite, Robert [Tenor]
Peterson, Thomas [Baritone]

BASSOON
Corey, Gerald
Kalman, Robert
Hall, Richard

HORN
Elworthy, Robert
Reed, Jack
Krance, John
Benjamin, Barry
Schultz, Kenneth

TRUMPET
Hohstadt, Thomas
Fricano, Samuel
Ricksecker, Barbara
Sapiro, Maurice
Sapiro, Erwin
Johnson, David

TROMBONE
Poindexter, Porter
Premru, Raymond
Miller, Donald

EUPHONIUM
Gray, Robert
Bockman, Guy

TUBA
Zale, Donald
Zale, Robert

STRING BASS
Angell, Lawrence

KETTLEDRUM
Frazeur, Theodore

PERCUSSION
Beck, John
Dotson, James
Peters, Gordon
Peters, Mitchell

HARP
Ewing, Rachel

---

### ACTIVITIES

Chicago Tour - CBDNA - December, 1954
[see following page for program]
Album - British Band Classics

**EASTMAN SYMPHONIC WIND ENSEMBLE**
**FREDERICK FENNELL, CONDUCTOR**

## ORCHESTRA HALL
Chicago, Illinois
Friday, December 17, 1954

Program

| | |
|---|---|
| Toccata Marziale | Ralph Vaughan Williams |
| First Suite in E Flat | Gustav Holst |
|     Chaconne | |
|     Intermezzo | |
|     March | |
| | |
| Divertimento | Vincent Persichetti |
|     Prologue | |
|     Song | |
|     Dance | |
|     Burlesque | |
|     Soliloquy | |
|     March | |
| | |
| La Fiesta Mexicana | H. Owen Reed |
|   A Mexican Folk-Song Symphony | |
|     Prelude and Aztec Dance | |
|     Mass | |
|     Carnival | |

INTERMISSION

| | |
|---|---|
| Suite of Old American Dances | Robert Russell Bennett |
|     Cake Walk | |
|     Schottische | |
|     Western One-Step | |
|     Wallflower Waltz | |
|     Rag | |
| | |
| Ballad | Morton Gould |
| | |
| Chorale and Alleluia | Howard Hanson |
| | |
| Three Marches | |
|     Cheerio | Edwin Franko Goldman |
|     Corcoran Cadets | John Philip Sousa |
|     Pieces of Eight | Joseph Jenkins and Jerome Neff |

In cooperation with G. Leblanc Company
and in association with George A. Kuyper

# EASTMAN SYMPHONIC WIND ENSEMBLE
Frederick Fennell, Conductor
1955 - 1956
#4

FLUTE
Gilbert, David
Eklund, Barbara
Gruskin, Shelly [Piccolo]

OBOE
Zepp, Martha
Stolper, Daniel
Denault, Florence [English Horn]

BASSOON
Corey, Gerald
Kalman, Robert
Hall, Richard [Contrabassoon]

SAXOPHONE
Stevens, Noel [Alto]
Regni, Albert [Alto]
Dransite, Robert [Tenor]
Hodkinson, Sydney [Baritone]

CLARINET
Peterson, Thomas [E-flat]
MacLeod, Charles
Carlucci, Joseph
Seath, Robert
Gauldin, Robert
Marge, George
Coccagnia, Louis
Colvin, Muriel
Spencert, Mary Anne
Slattery, Thomas [Alto]
Freeman, Paul [Bass]
Glenn, Sam [Contrabass]

HORN
Benjamin, Barry
Basta, James [Assistant]
Bouck, Aubrey
Comfort, Waldo
Konzer, Eleanor

CORNET
Hohstadt, Thomas
Still, Ruth [Assistant]
Johnson, David
Ricksecker, Barbara

TRUMPET
Alvarez, Manuel
Austin, James

TROMBONE
Poindexter, Porter
Premru, Raymond
Shroyer, George

EUPHONIUM
Inglefield, Kenley
Kramer, Rodger

TUBA
Zale, Robert
Bishop, Ronald

STRING BASS
Twaddell, Elizabeth

HARP
Litz, Lanalee

KETTLEDRUMS
Frazeur, Theodore

PERCUSSION
Peters, Gordon
Dotson, James
Peters, Mitchell
Tanner, Peter
Wendrich, Kenneth

---

### ACTIVITIES

Album - Marching Along
Album - The Spirit of '76
Album - Ruffles and Flourishes

# EASTMAN SYMPHONIC WIND ENSEMBLE
## Frederick Fennell, Conductor
## 1956 - 1957
## #5

FLUTE
Gilbert, David
Eklund, Barbara
Bruner, Elizabeth [Piccolo]

OBOE
Stolper, Daniel
Brooks, Vivian
Rubenstein, Bernard [English Horn]

BASSOON
Brown, Alan
Hall, Richard
Wiliams, Glen [Contrabassoon]

SAXOPHONE
Glenn, Samuel [Alto]
Coleman, Robert [Alto]
Regni, Albert [Tenor]
Hodkinson, Sydney [Baritone]

CLARINET
Peterson, Thomas [E-Flat]
Gauldin, Robert
Carlucci, Joseph
Weiss, Mitchell
Krusenstjerna, Charles
Legbandt, Rolf
Colvin, Muriel
Steinhagen, Jerry
Zoro, Eugene
Cherry, Paul [Alto]
Long, Ralph [Bass]
Sidorfsky, Frank [Contrabass]

HORN
Benjamin, Barry
Bouck, Aubrey
Schultz, Kenneth
Comfort, Waldo
Bommelje, William

CORNET
Austin, James
Schmaus, Donald
Toback, Stephen
Smith, Gary

TRUMPET
Alvarez, Manuel
Baker, Rodger

TROMBONE
Poindexter, Porter
Halt, Frederick
Clark, Jonathan

EUPHONIUM
Inglefield, Kenley
Briggs, Kenton

TUBA
Bobo, Roger
Schaffer, Charles

STRING BASS
Russell, Armand

HARP
Litz, Lanalee

KETTLEDRUMS
Tanner, Peter

PERCUSSION
Peters, Mitchell
Dotson, James
Peters, Gordon
Burnet, Jane

### ACTIVITES

Album - Hindemith/Schoenberg/Stravinsky
Single titles:
Prom Night - Ralph Hermann
Beguine for Band - Glenn Osser

# EASTMAN SYMPHONIC WIND ENSEMBLE
Frederick Fennell, Conductor
1957 - 1958
#6

FLUTE
Gilbert, David
Dickinson, Joanne
Bruner, Elizabeth

OBOE
Stolper, Daniel
Rubenstein, Bernard
Harrod, William

BASSOON
Brown, Alan
Campbell, Richard
Williams, Glenn

SAXOPHONE
Glenn, Sam [Alto - 1st Semester]
Loven, Larry [Alto - 2nd Semester]
Stevens, Noel [Soprano on Lincolnshire Posy]
Coleman, Robert [Alto]
Regni, Albert [Tenor]
Hodkinson, Sydney [Baritone]

CLARINET
Hadcock, Peter [E-Flat]
Gauldin, Robert
Ludewig, Elsa
Legbandt, Rolf
Zoro, Eugene
Webster, Richard
Steinhagen, Jerry
Combs, Larry
Vitous, Winston
Slattery, Thomas [Alto]
Long, Ralph [Bass]
Badalato, James [Contrabass]

HORN
Bouck, Aubrey
Schweikert, Norman
Seiffert, Stephen
Sweigart, Esther
Schultz, Kenneth

CORNET
Austin, James
Hood, Boyde
Montgomery, Ralph
Schmaus, Donald

TRUMPET
Alvarez, Manuel
Sherman, Roger

TROMBONE
Osborn, George
Halt, Frederick
Clark, Jonathan

EUPHONIUM
McNeil, Harold
Briggs, Kenton

TUBA
Bobo, Roger
Kearney, William

STRING BASS
Mann, Marie

HARP
Winey, Marjorie

KETTLEDRUMS
Tanner, Peter

PERCUSSION
Peters, Mitchell
Burnet, Jane
Emery, Vivian
Thome, Joel
Galm, John

## ACTIVITIES

Album - March Time
Album - Winds in Hi-Fi
Album - Mozart Serenade No. 10
Single titles:
A Christmas Festival - Leroy Anderson
The Beachcomber - Norman Richardson

# EASTMAN SYMPHONIC WIND ENSEMBLE
## Frederick Fennell, Conductor
## 1958 - 1959
## #7

FLUTE
Gilbert, David [1st Semester]
Carey, Gerald [2nd Semester]
Dickinson, Joanne
Tousey, Joanna [Piccolo]

OBOE
Gordon, Alice
Flesher, Sandra
Stacy, Thomas [English Horn]

BASSOON
Brown, Alan
Read, Vernon
Degen, Bruce [Contrabassoon]

CLARINET
Haddock, Peter [E-Flat]
Ludewig, Elsa
Legbandt, Rolf
Webster, Richard
Zoro, Eugene
Combs, Larry
Badolato, James
Bay, Charles
Persson, Roland
Levine, Jonathan [Alto]
Kohut, Daniel [Bass]
Mauro, John [Contrabass]

SAXOPHONE
Coleman, Robert [Alto]
Panhorst, Donald [Alto]
Browne, Philip [Tenor]
Corman, Ned [Baritone]

HORN
Schweikert, Norman
Seiffert, Stephen
Covert, John
Sheldon, Robert
Ladrach, Carol

CORNET
Austin, James
Koplin, Joel [Assistant]
Montgomery, Ralph
Sherman, Roger

TRUMPET
Shull, Paul
Landis, John

TROMBONE
Osborn, George
Fetter, David [Assistant]
Gillespie, Robert
Richey, David

EUPHONIUM
Hunsberger, Donald
Briggs, Kenton

TUBAS
Bobo, Roger
Kearney, William

KETTLEDRUMS
Tanner, Peter

PERCUSSION
Thome, Joel
Emery, Vivian
Galm, John
Barnett, Ronald
Kain, Dennis
Fickett, Norman

HARP
Winey, Marjorie

STRING BASS
Mann, Marie

CELESTE - PIANO
Spillman, Robert

ORGAN
Toth, Andrea

---

### ACTIVITIES

Album - Hands Across the Sea
Album - British Band Classics, Vol. II
Album - American Masterpieces for Concert Band
Troy Music Hall Concert
Renssaeler Polytechnic Institute

## EASTMAN SYMPHONIC WIND ENSEMBLE
### FREDERICK FENNELL, CONDUCTOR

## TROY MUSIC HALL
Renssaeler Polytechnic Institute
April 12, 1959

Program

| | |
|---|---|
| Toccata Marziale | Ralph Vaughan Williams |
| Suite in B-flat, Op 4 | Richard Strauss |
| Suite: William Byrd | Gordon Jacob |

INTERMISSION

| | |
|---|---|
| Serenade No. 10 in B-flat, K. 361 [excerpt] | Wolfgang Amadeus Mozart |
| Concerto for 23 Winds | Walter S. Hartley |
| Symphonic Songs for Band | Robert Russell Bennett |
| Three Symphonic Marches | |
|     Inglesina | Davide Delle Cese |
|     Valdres March | Johannes Hanssen |
|     March, Op. 99 | Sergei Prokofiev |

# EASTMAN WIND ENSEMBLE
Frederick Fennell, Conductor
1959 - 1960
#8

**FLUTE**
Carey, Gerald
Tousey, Joanna
Rosenblum, Susan [3rd and Piccolo]

**OBOE**
Gordon, Alice
Flesher, Sandra
Stacy, Thomas [English Horn]

**CLARINET**
Hadcock, Peter [E-Flat]
Ludewig, Elsa
Combs, Larry
Badolato, James
Zoro, Eugene
Maxey, Lawrence
Bay, Charles
Persson, Roland
Levine, Jonathan [Alto]
Kohut, Daniel [Bass]
Mauro, John [Contrabass]

**BASSOON**
Brown, Alan
Beadle, David
Horick, Robert

**SAXOPHONE**
Benscriscutto, Frank [Alto]
Murley, Kenneth [Alto]
Ward, David [Tenor]
Corman, Ned [Baritone - 1st Semester]
Tettamanti, Eugene [Baritone - 2nd Sem.]

**HORN**
Schweikert, Norman
Allison, Bette [Assistant]
Covert, John
Sheldon, Robert
Seiffert, Stephen

**CORNET**
Thyhsen, John
Koplin, Joseph
Montgomery, Ralph
MacKinnon, Albert
Cavanagh, George
Landis, John

**TROMBONE**
Fetter, David
Anderson, Early [Assistant]
Gillespie, Robert
Richey, David

**EUPHONIUM**
Campbell, Larry
Hanson, Byron

**TUBA**
Bobo, Roger
Kearney, William

**KETTLEDRUMS**
Kain, Dennis

**PERCUSSION**
Thome, Joel
Galm, John
Barnett, Ronald
Fickett, Norman
McMillan, Thomas

**STRING BASS**
Mann, Marie

**HARP**
Winey, Marjorie [1st Semester]
Barlow, Robert [2nd Semester]

---

**ACTIVITIES**

Album - Sound Off!
Album - Ballet for Band
Album - Wagner for Band
MENC - Atlantic City, New Jersey

**EASTMAN WIND ENSEMBLE**
**FREDERICK FENNELL, CONDUCTOR**

## Music Educators National Conference
Atlantic City, New Jersey
Sunday, March 20, 1960

Program

| | |
|---|---|
| Symphony in B-flat | Paul Hindemith |
| Serenade No 10 in B-flat, K. 361<br>    Romanza<br>    Theme and Variations<br>    Rondo | Wolfgang Amadeus Mozart |
| Lincolnshire Posy<br>    Lisbon<br>    Horkstow Grange<br>    Rufford Park Poachers<br>    The Brisk Young Sailor<br>    Lord Melbourne<br>    The Lost Lady Found | Percy Aldridge Grainger |

INTERMISSION

| | |
|---|---|
| Suite No. 1 in E-flat, Op. 28<br>    Chaconne<br>    Intermezzo<br>    March | Gustav Holst |
| Symphonies of Wind Instruments | Igor Stravinsky |
| Chorale and Alleluia | Howard Hanson |
| Three Marches<br>    March, Op. 99<br>    Inglesina<br>    National Emblem | <br>Sergei Prokofiev<br>Davide Della Cese<br>Edwin E. Bagley |

# EASTMAN WIND ENSEMBLE
## Frederick Fennell, Conductor
## 1960 - 1961
## #9

FLUTE
Tousey, Joanna
Levitin, Susan
Wilson, Doris [3rd and Piccolo]

OBOE
Flesher, Sandra
Parkes, Johnathan
Edlefsen, Blaine [3rd and English Horn]

CLARINET
Lang, Mary Jane [E-Flat]
Ludewig, Elsa
Bay, Charles
Combs, Larry
Smith, Jerry
Miyamura, Henry
Levine, Jonathan
Johnston, Daniel
Mader, Robert
Smith, Michael [Alto]
Sandidge, Daniel [Bass]
Anderson, William [Contrabass]

BASSOON
Campbell, Richard
Zimmerman, Robert
Horick, Robert [3rd and Contrabassoon]

SAXOPHONE
Hemke, Fred [Alto]
Welker, Gerald [Alto]
Ward, David [Tenor]
Tettamanti, Eugene [Baritone]
Jacobsen, Frank [Bass]

HORN
Schweikert, Norman
VanSickle, Linda
Miller, Janet
Sheldon, Robert
Spencer, Herbert

CORNET
Hood, Boyde
Hall, John [Assistant]
MacKinnon, Albert
Landis, John

TRUMPET
Bell, Glen
Greenhoe, David

TROMBONE
Gillespie, Robert
Kelleher, Stephen [Assistant]
Anderson, Early
Phillips, Peter

EUPHONIUM
Campbell, Larry
Hanson, Byron

TUBA
Bobo, Roger
Brown, Paul

KETTLEDRUMS
Kain, Dennis

PERCUSSION
Thome, Joel
Galm, John
Webster, Peter
Fickett, Norman
Preiss, James

STRING BASS
Zimmerman, Robert

HARP
Barlow, Robert

PIANO
Kirkpatrick, Gary

ORGAN
Labounsky, Anne

---

**ACTIVITIES**

Album - The Civil War I & II
Album - Gabrieli
Album - Sousa on Review
Cutler Concerts Inaugurated
Television - Mozart to Mambo

# EASTMAN SCHOOL OF MUSIC
## University of Rochester

## EASTMAN WIND ENSEMBLE
### FREDERICK FENNELL, CONDUCTOR

## CONCERTS AT CUTLER SERIES
### Sunday 30 October 1960

Program One
Cutler Union 3:00 PM

Soloist: RONALD LEONARD, Cellist

Serenade No. 12 in C Minor, K. 388 [1782] — Wolfgang Amadeus Mozart [1756-1791]

   Allegro
   Andante
   Minuetto in canone
   Allegro

Serenade, Op. 7 [1881] — Richard Strauss [1864-1949]

Introduction and Fugue for Cello and Symphonic Winds [1960] — Wallingford Riegger [1885- ]

Ronald Leonard, Cellist

- INTERMISSION -

Serenade for Thirteen Winds [1958] — Verne Reynolds [1926 - ]

   Overture
   Adagio
   Scherzo
   Recitativi

Chamber Symphony, Op. 2 for Fourteen Wind Instruments [1954] — Easley Blackwood [1933 - ]

   Sonata
   Romanza
   Toccata

**EASTMAN SCHOOL OF MUSIC**
University of Rochester

**EASTMAN WIND ENSEMBLE**
**FREDERICK FENNELL, CONDUCTOR**

**CONCERTS AT CUTLER SERIES**
Sunday 8 January 1961

Program Two
Cutler Union 3:00 PM

Serenade No. 11 in E-Flat, K. 375 [1781] — Wolfgang Amadeus Mozart [1756-1791]

    Allegro Maestoso
    Minuetto
    Adagio
    Minuetto
    Allegro

Intrada, Fugue and Postlude for Brass Ensemble [1959] — Wayne Barlow [1912 - ]

Suite in B-Flat, Op. 4 [1884] — Richard Strauss [1864-1949]

    Allegretto
    Romanze: Andante
    Gavotte: Allegro
    Introduction and Fugue

**EASTMAN SCHOOL OF MUSIC**
University of Rochester

**EASTMAN WIND ENSEMBLE**
**FREDERICK FENNELL, CONDUCTOR**

**CONCERTS AT CUTLER SERIES**
**Sunday 19 February 1961**

Program Three
Cutler Union 3:00 PM

Soloist: ROGER BOBO, Tuba

Suite Concertante for Tuba [1958]     Armand Russell
[1932 -   ]

    Capriccio
    Ballade
    Scherzo
    Burlesca

            Mr. Bobo

Serenade in D Minor, Op. 44 [1878]     Antonin Dvorak
[1841-1904]

    Moderato quasi Marcia
    Menuetto
    Andante con moto
    Finale: Allegro molto

**EASTMAN SCHOOL OF MUSIC**
University of Rochester

**EASTMAN WIND ENSEMBLE**
**FREDERICK FENNELL, CONDUCTOR**

**CONCERTS AT CUTLER SERIES**
Sunday 5 March 1961

Program Four
Cutler Union 3:00 PM

Soloist: RONALD LEONARD, Cellist
Narrator: CALVIN CULLEN

| | |
|---|---:|
| Integrales [1926] for small orchestra of winds and percussion | Edgar Varese [1885 - ] |
| The Musicians of Bremen [1957] | Bernard Rogers [1893 - ] |

Fairy tale after Grimm for narrator and thirteen players
Mr. Cullen, Narrator

| | |
|---|---:|
| Concerto for Cello and Wind Instruments [1925] | Jacques Ibert [1890 - ] |

Pastorale
Romance
Gigue

Mr. Leonard, Soloist

## EASTMAN WIND ENSEMBLE
### FREDERICK FENNELL, CONDUCTOR

## MOZART TO MAMBO
Television Broadcast
Recorded: 30 November 1960
Broadcast: 1 December 1960
Announcer: Don Lyon
Producer: Jack End

### Program

| | |
|---|---|
| Old Comrades | Carl Tieke |
| The Beachcomber | Norman Richardson |
| Four Old American Dances | Robert Russell Bennett |
| Serenade in B-flat, No. 10, K. 361<br>    Theme and Variations | Wolfgang Amadeus Mozart |
| Pineapple Poll<br>    Opening Number<br>    Jasper's Dance<br>    Poll's Dance<br>    Finale | Arthur Sullivan/C. Mackerras |
| Nobles of the Mystic Shrine | John Philip Sousa |
| Lincolnshire Posy<br>    Lisbon<br>    Brisk Young Sailor<br>    Lost Lady Found | Percy Aldridge Grainger |
| Tamboo | Francesco Cavez |
| Three Japanese Dances<br>    Dance with Swords | Bernard Rogers |

Closing Credits
Jasper's Dance from Pineapple Poll

# EASTMAN WIND ENSEMBLE
## Frederick Fennell, Conductor
## 1961 - 1962
## #10

**FLUTE**
Swanson, Philip
Levitin, Susan
Boldt, Ann Marie [Piccolo]

**OBOE**
Parkes, Jonathan
Sauser, Sharon
Turner, Joe [English Horn]

**CLARINET**
Cheskiewicz, Michael [E-Flat]
Loomis, Ralph
Sandidge, Daniel
Lang, Mary Jane
Mader, Robert
Johnston, Daniel
Abramson, Armand
Wohlmacher, William
Anderson, William
Macone, Philip [Alto]
Burlinghame, Marshall [Alto]
Thimmig, Leslie [Bass]
Williams, Lawrence [Contrabass]

**SAXOPHONE**
Hemke, Fred [Alto]
Welker, Gerald [Alto]
Ward, David [Tenor]
Tettamante, Eugene [Baritone]
Jacobsen, Frank [Bass]

**BASSOON**
Campbell, Richard
Kolker, Philip
Gibson, Gerald [Contrabassoon]

**HORN**
Sheldon, Richard
Bianchi, Jeff
VanSickle, Linda
Miller, Janet
Spencer, Herbert

**CORNET**
Hood, Boyde
Hall, John [Assistant]
Jones, Richard
Landis, John

**TRUMPET**
Greenhoe, David
Schaffer, Richard

**TROMBONE**
Anderson, Early
Martin, Perry [Assistant]
DeChario, Tony
Kline, Peter

**EUPHONIUM**
Campbell, Larry
Hanson, Byron

**TUBA**
Perantoni, Daniel
McEnulty, Joseph

**STRING BASS**
Zimmerman, Robert

**HARP**
Barlow, Robert

**KETTLEDRUMS**
Fickett, Norman

**PERCUSSION**
Gilbert, Donald
Cocuzzi, Frank
Preiss, James
Wyre, John

**ORGAN**
Toth, Andrea
Labounsky, Anne

**PIANO - CELESTE**
Kirkpatrick, Gary

---

**ACTIVITIES**

Concert - Orchard Park, New York
Concert - Albany, New York
Concert - Carnegie Hall, New York
Album - Circus Screamers !

**EASTMAN WIND ENSEMBLE**
**FREDERICK FENNELL, CONDUCTOR**

**CARNEGIE HALL**
New York, New York
November 17, 1961

Program

Toccata Marziale — Ralph Vaughan Williams

Suite: William Byrd — Gordon Jacob
    The Earle of Oxford's March
    Pavana
    Jhon come Kisse me now
    The Mayden's Song
    Wolsey's Wilde
    The Bells

Lincolnshire Posy — Percy Aldridge Grainger
    Lisbon
    Horkstow Grange
    Rufford Park Poachers
    The brisk Young Sailor
    Lord Melbourne
    The Lost Lady Found

Pineapple Poll — Arthur Sullivan/Charles Mackerras
    Opening Number
    Jasper's Dance
    Poll's Dance
    Finale

INTERMISSION

Symphonies of Wind Instruments — Igor Stravinsky

Theme and Variations, Op. 43 — Arnold Schoenberg

Symphony No. 6 for Band — Vincent Persichetti

Three Marches
    National Emblem — Edwin E. Bagley
    Valdres — Johannes Hanssen
    Black Horse Troop — John Philip Sousa

**EASTMAN WIND ENSEMBLE**
**FREDERICK FENNELL, CONDUCTOR**

**ORCHARD PARK CIVIC MUSIC ASSOCIATION**
Orchard Park, New York
November 5, 1961

**"A PROGRAM OF SERENADES"**

Program

Serenade in E-flat, No. 11, K. 375                Wolfgang Amadeus Mozart

INTERMISSION

Serenade in D minor, Op. 44                       Antonin Dvorak

Suite in B-Flat, Op. 4                            Richard Strauss

Frederick Fennell in rehearsal 1953
Photo courtesy of Edward Pettengill

**EASTMAN WIND ENSEMBLE**
FREDERICK FENNELL, CONDUCTOR

**TENTH SEASON - SIXTH CONCERT**
University of Rochester
Annex Rehearsal Room
Wednesday, May 2, 1962
1:00 PM

**SIXTY YEARS OF CIRCUS HIPPODROME MUSIC**
**1895 - 1955**

Program

| | |
|---|---|
| The Screamer [1921] | Fred Jewell |
| The Big Cage [1934] | Karl L. King |
| Rolling Thunder [1916] | Henry Fillmore |
| The Squealer [1912] | Will Huff |
| Bombasto [1895] | Orion R. Farrar |
| Them Basses [1924] | Getty H. Huffine |
| In Storm and Sunshine [1905] | John C. Heed |
| Whip and Spur [1902] | Thomas S. Allen |
| The Circus Bee [1908] | Henry Fillmore |
| Invictus [1921] | Karl L. King |
| Bravura [1918] | Charles E. Duble |
| Circus Days [1954] | Karl L. King |
| Bennett's Triumphal [1925] | John H. Ribble |
| Robinson's Grand Entree [1911] | Karl L. King |
| Bones Trombone [1922] | Henry Fillmore |
| Thunder and Blazes - Entry of the Gladiators [1936] | Julius Fucik |

[RR: The final concert with Frederick Fennell as founder and conductor. The recording session followed four days later in the Eastman Theatre.]

# SECTION V

# NUMERICAL ALBUM INDEX

# NUMERICAL ALBUM LISTING

| | | | |
|---|---|---|---|
| 1 | American Concert Band Masterpieces | Mercury | MG 40006/MG 50079 |
| 2 | Marches by Sousa and Others | Mercury | MG 40007/MG 50080 |
| 2a | Marches - John Philip Sousa | Philips (Japanese) | PC - 1628 |
| 3 | La Fiesta Mexicana | Mercury | MG 40011/MG 50084 |
| 4 | British Band Classics | Mercury | MG 40015/MG 50088 |
| 5 | British Band Classics | Mercury | MG 50388/SR 90388 |
| 6 | Marching Along | Mercury | MG 50105/SR 90105 |
| 7 | The Spirit of '76 | Mercury | MG 50111/SR 90111 |
| 8 | Ruffles and Flourishes | Mercury | MG 50112/SR 90112 |
| 9 | Marches for Twirling | Mercury | MG 50113 Mono Only |
| 10 | Hindemith-Schoenberg-Stravinsky | Mercury | MG 50143/SR 90143 |
| 11 | March Time | Mercury | MG 50170/SR 90170 |
| 12 | Winds in Hi-Fi | Mercury | MG 50173/SR 90173 |
| 13 | Mozart Serenade No. 10, K. 361 | Mercury | MG 50176/SR 90176 |
| 14 | British Band Classics, Vol. II | Mercury | MG 50197/SR 90197 |
| 15 | Hands Across the Sea | Mercury | MG 50207/SR 90207 |
| 16 | American Masterpieces for Concert Band | Mercury | MG 50220/SR 90220 |
| 16a | American Masterpieces for Concert Band | Philips (Japanese) | PC 1634 |
| 17 | Diverse Winds | Mercury | MG 50221/SR 90221 |
| 17a | Diverse Winds | Philips (Japanese) | PC 1603 |
| 18 | Music of Andrea and Giovanni Gabrieli | Mercury | MG 50245/SR 90245 |
| 19 | Ballet For Band | Mercury | MG 50256/SR 90256 |
| 20 | Sound Off! | Mercury | MG 50264/SR 90264 |
| 21 | Wagner For Band | Mercury | MG 50276/SR 90276 |
| 22 | Sousa On Review | Mercury | MG 50284/SR 90284 |
| 23 | Curtain Up! Sousa Favorites | Mercury | MG 50291/SR 90291 |
| 24 | Screamers! | Mercury | MG 50314/SR 90314 |
| 25 | Curtain Up! More March Favorites | Mercury | MG 50325/SR 90325 |
| 26 | Curtain Up! Plunk, Tinkle & Ting-a-Ling | Mercury | MG 50338/SR 90338 |
| 27 | Curtain Up! Gala Favorites | Mercury | MG 50339/SR 90339 |
| 28 | Curtain Up! Bravos in Brass | Mercury | MG 50360/SR 90360 |
| 29 | Curtain Up! Holidays Around the World | Mercury | MG 50361/SR 90361 |
| 30 | Broadway Marches | Mercury | MG 50390/SR 90390 |
| 31 | The Civil War, Vol. I | Mercury | LPS 2-501/2-901 |
| 32 | The Civil War, Vol. II | Mercury | LPS 2-502/2-902 |
| 33 | Music of Leroy Anderson, Vol. I | Mercury | MG 50130/SR 90009 |
| 34 | Music of Leroy Anderson, Vol. II | Mercury | MG 50043/SR 90043 |
| 35 | Hi-Fi A la Espanola | Mercury | MG 50144/SR 90144 |
| 36 | Country Gardens & Other Grainger Favorites | Mercury | MG 50219/SR 90219 |
| 37 | "POP" Overs | Mercury | MG 50222/SR 90222 |
| 38 | Marches for Orchestra | Mercury | MG 50271/SR 90271 |
| 39 | Curtain Up! Orchestral March Favorites | Mercury | MG 50292/SR 90292 |
| 40 | Curtain Up! Symphonic Dance Favorites | Mercury | MG 50293/SR 90293 |
| 41 | Curtain Up! Fennell Favorites | Mercury | MG 50294/SR 90294 |
| 42 | Curtain Up! Musical Almanac | Mercury | MG 50337/SR 90337 |
| 43 | Curtain Up! Fennell and the "POPS" | Mercury | MG 50340/SR 90340 |
| 43a | Great Music by Russian Composers | Mercury | MG 50346/SR 90346 |
| 43b | Khachaturian - Dorati/Fennell | Philips | LP627-187 - MC 7311-187 |
| 44 | Music of Leroy Anderson, Vol. III | Mercury | MG 50400/SR 90400 |
| 45 | Frederick Fennell Conducts Music of Eric Coates | Mercury | MG 50439/SR 90439 |
| 46 | Frederick Fennell Conducts Carousel Waltz | Mercury | MG 50440/SR 90440 |
| 47 | Fennell Spectacular: Musical Moods of Frederick Fennell | Mercury | MG 50510/SR 90510 |
| 48 | Frederick Fennell Conducts Gershwin | Mercury | PPS 2006/PPS 6006 |
| 49 | Frederick Fennell Conducts Victor Herbert | Mercury | PPS 2007/PPS 6007 |

| # | Title | Label | Catalog |
|---|---|---|---|
| 50 | Frederick Fennell Conducts Cole Porter | Mercury | PPS 2024/PPS 6024 |
| 51 | American Brass Band Journal Revisited | Sine Qua Non | SAS 2017 |
| 52 | Our Musical Past - Volume I [LP and CD] | Library of Congress | OMP 101-102 |
| 52a | Our Musical Past - Volume 2 [CD] | Library of Congress | OMP-103 CD |
| 53 | The Cleveland Symphonic Winds | Telarc | DG 10038 |
| 54 | Macho Marches - Cleveland Symphonic Winds | Telarc | DG 10043 |
| 54a | Marches - Cleveland Symphonic Winds | Telarc | DG 10043 (re-issue) |
| 55 | The Cleveland Symphonic Winds | Telarc | DG 10050 |
| 56 | The Compositions of Alec Wilder | Golden Crest | ATH 5070 |
| 57 | John Philip Sousa on Parade | Longines Symphonette | Boxed Edition |
| 57a | John Philip Sousa on Parade - demonstration disc | Longines Symphonette | 7" floppy disc |
| 58 | Great Music of the Classical Era | Mercury | MG 50412/SR 90412 |
| 59 | Music for Musing | Mercury | SR 2-9132 |
| 60 | Galaxy-Perfect Presence Sound Series | Mercury | PPSD 3-12 |
| 61 | Living Presence Galaxy | Mercury | SRD 10 |
| 62 | Living Presence High Fidelity Sampler | Mercury | OLD 6 |
| 63 | Broadway's Greatest Marches | Longines Symphonette | |
| 64 | Joseph Wagner Works for Concert Band | Orion | ORS 73118 |
| 65 | Perfect Presence Sound | Mercury | SRD 15 |
| 66 | Remember America | Mercury-Wing | SRW 18113 |
| 67 | Perfect Presence Sound | Mercury | PPSD 4-12 |
| 68 | Mercury Stereo Sampler, Vol. I | Mercury | SRD 1 |
| 69 | Bose Salutes the Sound of Mercury | Mercury Special Products | MB 1001 |
| 70 | Royal Pageant | Philips (England) | 6570-763 |
| 71 | Doc Severinsen Plays Modern Trumpet Concertos | Firstline | FDLP 5002 |
| 72 | Conducts the Tokyo Kosei Wind Orchestra | KOR/KOCD | 8103/3503 |
| 73 | Fanfare and Allegro | KOR/KOCD | 8411/2811 |
| 74 | Belle of the Ball | KOR/KOCD | 8412/2812 |
| 75 | Serenata | KOR/KOCD | 8413/2813 |
| 76 | La Fiesta Mexicana | KOR/KOCD | 8414/2814 |
| 77 | American March Forever | Firebird | K23C-405 |
| 78 | Contest Band Music '81 | Sony | 25AG 967 |
| 79 | Contest Band Series '84-I | King (Cassette) | CNT 1048 |
| 80 | Contest Band Series '84-II | King (Cassette) | CNT 1050 |
| 81 | Best European Marches, The | King (Cassette) | K28C-438 |
| 81a | Best European Marches, The | King CD | K33Y-164 |
| 82 | A Miracle in Sound (Sampler) | Mercury | SRD - 3 |
| 83 | Stars and Stripes Forever | Mercury CD | 416147-2 |
| 84 | CBDNA 19th National Conference | Crest | CBDNA 77-4 |
| 85 | Holst-Handel-Bach - Cleveland Symphonic Winds | Telarc CD | 80038 |
| 86 | Stars and Stripes - Cleveland Symphonic Winds | Telarc CD | 80099 |
| 87 | Sampler Vol. II | Telarc CD | 80102 |
| 88 | Sampler Vol. V | Telarc CD | 89105 |
| 90 | Frederick Fennell Conducts Victor Herbert | Mercury | MG 20954/SR 60954 |
| 91 | American Music Spectacular | Reader's Digest | RDA 236A |
| 92 | Sounds of History | Time-Life Records | Vols. 2,5,6,7,8 |
| 93 | Galaxy Sampler | Mercury | MGD 2-13 |
| 94 | The Civil War (Dealer Demo) | Mercury (One side) | LPSD - 1 |
| 95 | Music to Live By (Sampler) | Mercury | PJC 1 |
| 96 | Sam Fox Promo Record #1 | Sam Fox Music | 7-33-8 |
| 97 | Sam Fox Promo Record #2 | Sam Fox Music | 7-33-9 |
| 97a | Sam Fox Promo Record #3 | Sam Fox Music | 7-33-13 |
| 98 | Wagner - Coates - Prokofiev | Philips (Japanese) | 18PC - 111 |
| 99 | Grainger - Holst - Walton | Philips (Japanese) | 18PC - 112 |
| 100 | Reed - Persichetti | Philips (Japanese) | 18PC - 113 |
| 101 | Stars and Stripes Forever | Golden Imports | 2-77010 |

| | | | |
|---|---|---|---|
| 102 | The Civil War | Golden Imports | 2-77011 |
| 103 | Marching Along | Golden Imports | SRI 75004 / MRI 75004 |
| 104 | British Band Classics | Golden Imports | SRI 75011 / MRI 75011 |
| 105 | Music of Leroy Anderson | Golden Imports | SRI 75013 / MRI 75013 |
| 106 | British Band Classic, Vol. II | Golden Imports | SRI 75028 / MRI 75028 |
| 107 | Ruffles and Flourishes | Golden Imports | SRI 75034 / MRI 75034 |
| 108 | Sound Off! | Golden Imports | SRI 75047 / MRI 75047 |
| 109 | Spirit of '76 | Golden Imports | SRI 75048 / MRI 75048 |
| 110 | March Time | Golden Imports | SRI 75055 |
| 111 | Hindemith Symphony for Band | Golden Imports | SRI 75057 |
| 112 | Sousa on Review | Golden Imports | SRI 75064 / MRI 75064 |
| 113 | American Concert Band Masterpieces | Golden Imports | SRI 75086 / MRI 75086 |
| 114 | Screamers! Circus Marches | Golden Imports | SRI 75087 / MRI 75087 |
| 115 | Lincolnshire Posy | Golden Imports | SRI 75093 / MRI 75093 |
| 116 | West Point Symphony | Golden Imports | SRI 75094 |
| 117 | Wagner for Band | Golden Imports | SRI 75096 / MRI 75096 |
| 118 | Malaguena (Hi-Fi Ala Espanola) | Golden Imports | SRI 95097 |
| 119 | Hands Across the Sea | Golden Imports | SRI 75099 |
| 120 | Country Gardens | Golden Imports | SRI 75102 / MRI 75102 |
| 121 | Music of Eric Coates | Golden Imports | SRI 75109 |
| 122 | Music of Cole Porter | Golden Imports | SRI 75110 |
| 123 | Broadway Marches | Golden Imports | SRI 75115 |
| 124 | Music of George Gershwin | Golden Imports | SRI 75127 / MRI 75127 |
| 125 | Music of Gabrieli | Golden Imports | SRI 75130 |
| 126 | Ballet for Band | Golden Imports | SRI 75138 |
| 127 | Heart of the March | Mercury | SR 2-9131 |
| 127a | Heart of the Ballet | Mercury | SR 2-9127 |
| 128 | Toccata and Fugue | KOR/KOCD | 8415/2815 |
| 129 | An American in Paris | KOR/KOCD | 8416/2816 |
| 130 | Hands Across the Sea | KOR/KOCD | 8417/2817 |
| 131 | Lincolnshire Posy | KOR/KOCD | 8418/2818 |
| 132 | Symphonic Songs for Band | KOR/KOCD | 8781-82/3562 |
| 133 | English Folk Songs | KOR/KOCD | 8783-84/3563 |
| 134 | Suite Francaise | KOCD | 3101 |
| 135 | Romeo and Juliet | KOCD | 3311 |
| 136 | Premiere Rhapsodie | KOCD | 3313 |
| 137 | Bacchus on Blue Ridge | KOCD | 3564 |
| 138 | The Firebird/Pictures at an Exhibition | KOCD | 3565 |
| 139 | Peer Gynt - Concert Repertoire #1 | KOCD | 3566 |
| 140 | Mozart Serenades 10 and 12 | KOCD | 3567 |
| 141 | Hungarian Rhapsody | KOCD | 3568 |
| 142 | Piece of Mind | KOCD | 3569 |
| 143 | Roman Trilogy | KOCD | 3570 |
| 144 | Celebration - Contemporary Mix No. 2 | KOCD | 3571 |
| 145 | Introduction | Private issue | |
| 146 | Symphonies | KOCD | 2711 |
| 147 | Dragon Quest | Telarc | PHCT - 211 |
| 150 | Civil War Favorites | Private | 8 RB |
| 160 | The Civil War | Mercury CD | 432591-2 |
| 161 | British and American Band Classics | Mercury CD | 432009-2 |
| 162 | Screamers - March Time | Mercury CD | 432019-2 |
| 163 | Music of Grainger, Persichetti and Others | Mercury CD | 432754-2 |
| 164 | FENNELL conducts SOUSA ! | Mercury CD | 434300-2 |
| 165 | Frederick Fennell conducts the music of Leroy Anderson | Mercury CD | 432013-2 |
| 166 | West Point Symphony - Giannini & Hovhaness | Mercury CD | 434320-2 |
| 167 | Ballet for Band - Wagner for Band | Mercury CD | 434322-2 |

| | | | |
|---|---|---|---|
| 168 | Frederick Fennell Conducts Cole Porter & George Gershwin | Mercury CD | 434327-2 |
| 169 | Frederick Fennell Conducts Percy Grainger/Eric Coates | Mercury CD | 434330-2 |
| 170 | La Fiesta Mexicana | Japan World | WL 8504 |
| 171 | The 21st Regular Concert | Japan World | WL 8602 |
| 172 | Music for Contest | Nippon Columbia | CD 32 CG 1294 |
| 173 | Music for Contest II | Nippon Columbia | CD 32 CG 1295 |
| 174 | Concert Marches for Glory and Tragedy | Denon | CD 32 CO 2365 |
| 175 | Seagate Overture | Nippon Columbia | CAY-899/32 CG 3175 |
| 176 | Symphonic Movement | Nippon Columbia | CAY-900/32 CG 3176 |
| 177 | Fennell Favorites - Live with Dallas Wind Symphony [LP & CD] | Reference Recordings | RR - 43 |
| 178 | Trittico - With the Dallas Wind Symphony [LP & CD] | Reference Recordings | RR - 52 |
| 179 | Reference Recording HDCD Sampler | Reference Recordings | RR - S3CD |
| 180 | Dallas Wind Symphony with Pipe Organ - POMP & PIPES | Reference Recordings | RR - 58 |

# SECTION VI

# FENNELL NARRATIVE

Recorded by
Frederick Fennell
Siesta Key, Florida
February and July 1993

## FAMILY and CAMP ZEKE

## "How it all Began"
Taped narrative - Siesta Key, Florida
February 4-7, 1993

I was born 2 July 1914 into a rather different kind of family, and like us all, I had to have lived quite a few years before I began to put together and even, in many ways, to understand where I was growing up, or even how. My father Fred had married one of the daughters of Rhoda and William Putnam of a rather large family. Four boys and three girls. My mother Julia, was the middle daughter of the three.

The area I knew as home, was one which came into the family in payment for their participation in the American Revolution, when the State of Connecticut didn't have money to pay those who were in this militia, and who had survived the Revolution. So a reserve of land, which belonged to the State of Connecticut, on a western surveyors line, turned out to be called the Western Land Reserve of the State of Connecticut. It became known as Cleveland, Ohio. That's why the University there is called the Western Reserve University. A large parcel of farm land was cleared and farmed by mother's forbearers. When I came into the scene, it had already begun to be surrounded by the rest of Cleveland, which grew rather quickly to the Southeast. This is why we happened to be living at 11722 Miles Avenue, between 116th and 119th streets, on the south side of the Avenue.

The old farm area - the outbuildings of the farm- had been surviving and the house in which all of the Putnam children were born, was standing and in very good shape. Then next to it was a large house built by the senior son of Rhoda and William Putnam, Charles Ransom Putnam.

Early in his life, Charlie had become a very successful member of the Operations Staff of the American Steel and Wire Company of Cleveland. Having some definite clout in that company, he was sent to Waukegan, Illinois, during the First World War to oversee wire production there.

One day he and his wife were being driven in a car in that region, when they were struck by an inter-urban train. His wife was killed instantly, and he was severely damaged on his left side, particularly his left leg and left knee.

He had built for her, and for the family they were to raise, a rather commodious and attractive house on this property which faced Miles Avenue. This was a large, and at that time, a very empty house when my father had come into the sad part of his life. His very wonderful wife, Julia Putnam Fennell, died somewhat suddenly in the flu and diptheria epidemic that swept through the United States in 1914 and 1915. Julia died about six months after I was born. They had before that, my sister Marjorie, who was five years older than I. My father was here without anyone to take care of his two children. He had long been a part of the Putnam family and, as was the custom, married my mother's younger sister, Kathryn. She raised the both of us along with father. The Fennell family was invited by Uncle Charlie to move in with him in the big empty house. This is where I first have any consciousness about anything, this big house on Miles Avenue.

I began to become aware, when I was about five, of the existence of what was the remnants of a farm. There was at this time, a horse in his stall, a huge coop of chickens producing marvelous eggs; a turkey; some ducks, and a huge garden. Around the first house, as was the tradition, were many fruit trees and berry bushes, so the wife didn't have to go very far to find what she needed to make pies, jellies and jams. And of course, a small garden near by for the things needed to fill the table for a large number of people. Kathryn cooked, ironed, washed and sewed for my father and sister, Uncle Charlie, Uncle Will, herself. She also cooked dinners for an endless parade of guests and family members. She ran that house most magnificently. I don't know how she did it, but she did it joyfully. The men were men ... they didn't give her the support I felt she should have had, except for my father.

I became aware that there was also an establishment there which I came to know as Camp

Zeke. A club which was the hobby of Uncle Charlie. He also made it a hobby for his brothers and cousins. All together there were twelve of them, which made up a reconstituted kind of Civil War platoon. He created this camp to better study American History as a club. The tents and everything were acquired and everything built around this.

The camp took its name from an eagle he had found, as a young boy, that had fallen out of a nest in a tree a far distance in the woods from the house. He raised the eagle in captivity and named him "Zeke". When Zeke died, he was duly stuffed and mounted on a peg, and became the Zion of the camp.

Camp Zeke was a meeting place for the men of the family and their families from Memorial Day, when we started to put it together, through the great day of the Fourth of July. Camp meetings ended on Labor Day, that early Monday in September.

The Camp was totally mobile. It was stored up in a barn on the second floor. The tents, poles, stakes, and the floor boards, and everything that went with it, all stored away in the winter in the old barn where they used to put the hay in the days of farming. It was a fun thing to put it together and it was a fun place to be. Of course, for me, the best thing was the Fife and Drum Corps. My father was a fifer, and obviously a rather good one. I remember him never having forgotten a tune. Never making mistakes. He had a fife with a kind of special mouthpiece so he did not have to keep up an embouchure. He knew what to do with all of the tunes he played, and I think I got my musical talent from him. He also had a great concept of music and he had a singing voice that was very acceptable. I also remember seeing him play the guitar for dancing. He played with silk gloves on his left and right hands because of his very tender skin. He didn't have the calluses that come with constant practice, so he had to have something to take the place of that. He was a natural player. I really got it from him.

The other side of me, whatever that is, I got from Julia. She must have been quite a lady. My Uncle Maurice was the one who was the most talkative, and when I asked him, he was the one that told me the most about his sister Julia, my mother.

The Camp always had this big day, the Fourth of July. The Fife and Drum Corps always played several serenades during the day. These tunes were from the Revolution and the Civil War. I was attracted to this screeching and shrieking and thundering ensemble. One day, when I was five years old, Kathryn said that I broke away from her and ran into the center of the circle. The Fife and Drum Corps always played in a circle where everyone could see each other. I have not forgotten the wonderful sound of running into that circle with all that shrieking and drumming going on. The drum, of course, became my instrument.

Father later hung a drum around my neck and told me to play along with the rest of the men. I guess I was a natural player. I never had any problems doing it, or remembering it. If I might have missed anything, I was ready to get a sharp knock across the knuckles from one of the men who knew what to do, mainly my Uncle Maurice. In Camp Zeke, my interest in history was kindled. I didn't know what I was learning or reading about, except it was told to me as being something very important and very great. It was the history of our country and the family had always been involved in it.

The Putnam's actually came here from Holland in 1640. My father's family, the Fennell's, came from England. The name Fennell was derived in some way from Fingal, of the cave in the Hebrides, made so famous by Felix Mendelssohn. Fingal finally came around to Fennell, what we use today. The Putnam name came from Puttenham and Penn, and finally, in the United States, they adopted the name of Putnam.

The Putnam family became very interested in the beginnings of this country. There was a Brevet General on Washington's staff, Israel Putnam, who was a famous Indian fighter. He was an elderly man when he was appointed by Washington as a Brevet General. There were other Putnam privates in the war, who most of us used as our entry into the Son's of the American Revolution, which was a big part of Camp Zeke, because they were S.A.R.

History was something that was taught at these Camp meetings and lived in the family constantly. Uncle Charles had the largest private collection of replicas of every flag carried by all units in the American Revolution. It was a unique collection of flags. I remember as a boy, in my scout uniform, I would go everywhere he lectured about these flags and their significance in American History. I would hold the flag while he talked about it. I had a good dose of it from the very beginning of my life, I'm very happy to say. It affected me in a variety of ways that were to come later when I became involved in the business of recording.

The photo on the first page is my father Fred and me at Camp Zeke, Fourth of July, 1921. "Doing What Comes Naturally". I had a natural hand position, even at this early age. In the background is the Pavilion Tent showing one of Uncle Charlie's collection of American Revolution flag replicas.

The second photo is the Pavilion tent of Camp Zeke taken in July of 1919. The floor of this Pavilion tent was tongue and groove boards that were screwed down to underneath basic stringers and taken up every year. The process of putting that together and making it absolutely plumb and correct, was always one of those interesting achievements. It took the better part of the day to get that floor done. It was the largest of the four major tents and the most difficult floor to assemble. That's me standing in front of the tent, my sister Marjorie is seated on my left.

Above is a typical summertime weekend parade of the Society of the Sons of the American Revolution. This is the Spirit of '76 Unit. This was for a dedication of a monument in the town of Burton, Ohio. We dedicated a lot of monuments. If we didn't dedicate them, we re-dedicated them. Photo was taken by Kathryn about 1926.

This was the Sesquicentennial year of the United States. The town was all sharpened up for that. Uncle Charlie had the words to the *Star Spangled Banner*, *America*, the Pledge of Allegiance and the Declaration of Independence printed for this all-day occasion. It was a big day. We had everyone in the family and lots of invited guests. There were cases and cases of Coca-Cola, tubs of ice cream, watermelon – the whole thing. Of course it started at sun-up with the bugle, gun and cannon, and the neighborhood went crazy.

Camp Zeke, Fourth of July 1920. My father Fred is the fifer on the right. The barn in the background is where all of the 'gear' was stored. Also in this photo you see Uncle Will, cousins Tom Whittaker and Ike Waldeck and Uncle Ben Putnam.

This is 1933 at Interlochen. I am performing at the "blanket" into which people would drop their contributions at the end of the concert in the Interlochen Bowl.

The "Family Spirit of '76" at the Fennell home on Miles Avenue in Cleveland, 1932. Photo is by Mr. Strong of the Sons of the American Revolution.
Frederick, Uncle Maurice Putnam [drum] and Uncle Will Putnam [fife]. Doll house in background was built for mother Kathryn by Fred, who also provided many of the furnishings.

Main tent at Camp Zeke, circa 1926. Flags on the flagpoles, campfire bucket, wash basins and towels and equipment for camp life. Flags are stored in the boxes and trunks visible on the tent floor. Small Jackass canon in front of tent is collapsible and could be mounted on the back of a mule and carried to a higher location. The men slept in the Main Tent during the summer.

## EDUCATION and INTERLOCHEN

## "How it all Began"
Taped narrative - Siesta Key, Florida
February 4-7, 1993

Elementary music was available to me in Miles Elementary School, which was located one block from where we lived; across 119th Street. My grandfather, William Putnam, had been a teacher in schools as well as a farmer. He was a teacher in a beautiful red brick school house which was across from Miles Avenue, and a little bit farther East by 1000 feet. It was a charming brick building and I can remember two things from my days there. Sitting up on the desks and being taught to sing "*Row, Row, Row Your Boat*". We had to sit on the desks so we could make rowing motions as we sang. The other thing I remember is the first time I was given a bottle of milk and with the straw, I tasted the cream. It was a very vivid taste that I can remember to this day.

The later part of Miles Elementary, there was an orchestra, as it was called. It was conducted by a lady named, Kennerson. She conducted for us and we played out of the *Fox Orchestra Folio* and the *Bennett Band Book*. It was a conglomerate orchestra. All instruments were in this group. It was really an orchestra-band. Two girls playing piano [four hands], mellophones, cornets, trumpets, a few violins and a cello. We could make something happen because those books were written that way. Most important for me, out of all of that, I was invited, being a drummer, to provide the cadence sound to a girl pianist, down on the first floor of the school building, which was very resonant. Every morning we played to change the classes. We played *Our Director* until I knew it inside out and back. I tried to get a few other things started, but she never wanted to learn anything new. I enjoyed this very much, probably because I was in front of the public. That was my first public exposure for anyone other than my family.

From there I went to a large and very beautiful high school which was built in 1924. Many of the high schools in Cleveland were named after American presidents, and this one was for John Adams.

There, when I arrived, was in swing, a full blown music program. The supervisor of music in the public schools of Cleveland, was a man by the name of Russell V. Morgan, a very marvelous musician; wonderful pianist and organist. Obviously a tremendous administrator had put together a system for the Cleveland schools, that I think has never been surpassed by any secondary institution. We had the best that was possible for young people to have in this part of their secondary education. John Adams High School had a separate conductor for chorus and one for band and orchestra.

In addition to these men, there was, for the chorus, a full-time professional accompanist, John Elliot. John Roberts was the conductor of the chorus. Amos Wesler conducted the band and the orchestra. Mr. Elliot, in addition to being the official accompanist for everything happening in school, he had a class every morning at 11 o'clock, which introduced me, over the period of four years, to the mysteries of harmonic practice known as theory and harmony. In addition to this, there was also a class in orchestration and formal analysis. I learned enough theory from John in these classes, that I could have passed off my Fall semester at the Eastman School, which I am glad I did not do, because I really wanted to learn it the Eastman way.

John was the one who got me to thinking seriously about the possibility of being a conductor. When I casually mentioned that to him one day, he very positively put me down the road of the things I would need to know, if that was ever going to happen to me. I am very grateful to John for everything he set out for me to face. He introduced me to the Metropolitan Opera and I was with him on the stage at the big public hall in Cleveland, every year for three years. He took me to great restaurants and introduced me to dining. He taught me to not cloister for myself the experiences and knowledge that I had gathered, but to share it with other people, and to do with them and for them, what he enjoyed doing for and with me. He, in addition to all these other manners, was organist in the Methodist Church in Lakewood. He had constant music services there and I played in all of them using the John Adams High School kettledrums, which my faithful father hauled all over Northern Ohio for me.

In my first year at John Adams High School, the orchestra won the Ohio State Contest with *Die Meistersinger Overture* and the chosen piece was *Dance Macabre* by Camille Saint-Saens. For this the school had to buy a xylophone and somehow I was elected to play it. That was the beginning of my keyboard experiences. We went from there to Lincoln, Nebraska for the final National Contest where we placed third in the United States. It was a vital experience. A learning experience, as well as a personal experience one simply does not forget.

Drum Major uniform of John Adams High School. Fall, 1932. Photo by Kathryn Fennell.

The band in the high school was not as good as the orchestra in the days I was there. It later became equally so. The orchestra was the principal ensemble and we played about everything you could think of. Mr. Wesler's purpose was to have us play as much music as possible, so we did a great deal of reading, rather than just honing and polishing two or three pieces a year for some great public performance or competition. So, I had it pretty well spelled out for me in high school.

There was also a very interesting and unusual assistant principal. His name was Dwight Lott. He was a born showman and he produced more things in that high school than I can ever imagine that anyone could do. We needed money first to travel to Lincoln, Nebraska. I think that's what whetted his appetite and got him started. We put on all kinds of things; tag days, evening concerts, and countless shows to raise money for that trip, because schools did not come up with funds for things like that.

Every year after that we would produce at least two shows that he would dream up. He always insisted that every kind of performing student would be involved, and, of course, these would be accompanied by the band, the orchestra, and even our early dance band. All of this provided for us an introduction to the commercial side of music, which had always interested me as much as the classical side.

I was totally involved with everything happening in Cleveland. I played in about every one of the numerous and wonderful Polish and Bohemian halls and on Broadway, across from the mills. I loved going to play with the polka band because there was no music - you just had to listen to the band and play what they played. I learned a great deal about many styles going this way, which I later could put together with printed music.

In addition to that, I played in every kind of band, including one that was sponsored by the Postal Telegraph, a competitive company to Western Union. I played bass drum. We had uniforms of the Postal Telegraph Delivery Boy – fancy shaped pants with leather puttee's and a kind of overseas cap. It was a really sharp and snappy uniform, and I think that's what dragged half of us into participating.

At home I can remember something very important. Both Uncle Charles and Uncle Will had excellent phonographs. Uncle Charles had the Plus Ultra Victrola, the big one, and operatic arias and music for chorus and organ selections were always playing. Uncle Will had a beautiful Columbia Gramophone with the large silver horn and played a variety of recordings of symphonic music by Prince's Orchestra and Band. It was Prince's Orchestra that I remember hearing for the first time, *The William Tell Overture*. I have never forgotten the sound of that record and whatever that piece began to mean to me and millions more.

I remember the *Black Horse Troop March* played by the Sousa Band as it was recorded after my father and I had been to the concert in Cleveland where the first performance of it was played for the Black Horse Troop A, of the Cavalry, which was both a political, social and military organization.

At that concert, when it was time for the *Black Horse Troop* to be played for the first time, the horses came out on stage and stood behind the band. After that, when I went to another band concert and there weren't any horses on the stage, I thought there's something wrong with this concert. There's something missing!

There were things like that that were a part of shaping what I was listening to and doing. Although, no serious thought about it at all. At this point I had been given a teacher who worked with me about drums, but I really didn't learn very much from him. I only started to learn when I had to. I learned about the subtleties of reading and all the rest of that when I suddenly found myself in John Adams High School playing in a really first-class orchestra. Things began to come together very fast.

Summer 1936. San Diego Symphony at Ford Bowl in Balboa Park. "My first and only professional engagement as a kettle drummer".

I was very fond of the kettledrums and I inherited that position in high school in my second of the four years I was there, when Robert Golambos, who would become one of the great neurologists of the United States, graduated and went on to Harvard. I became the kettle drummer for both the band and the orchestra. That was my favorite of all the percussion instruments.

One Sunday afternoon, in my little house where I had a place to study, practice and read, I had the radio going and quite by chance on came a broadcast from the National Music Camp at Interlochen, Michigan. At that time it was the National High School Orchestra and Band Camp.

I listened to the announcer describing this place located amidst pine woods, in between two lakes. The student campers lived in their own cottages – divided into boys and girls cottages. All they did all day and all week, was play music.

Father Fred Fennell sitting in the Grove reading the morning paper. 1931, my first year at Interlochen.

I said to myself, I just have to get to that place, no matter how or what I would have to do. Although such an idea sounded so preposterous to me. The Putnam family on Miles Avenue was a very tight ensemble and they didn't like anybody going away to do almost anything. Here I am thinking, if I could swing it, I would be away from Camp Zeke and the family on the Fourth of July! Impossible thought! But, having heard that orchestra and having imagined what that camp must be like, I was dedicated to get there somehow.

Fortunately, one morning Amos Wesler came by the tent in which I was living in the Camp Zeke area, to say to me, "They are short of percussion players. Would you like to go? There is some sort of scholarship available." My father had to come up with some money, and he had to get me there. It was like it was a dream.

Father took a week of summer vacation time and mother Kathryn got things together. Kathryn and I went shopping and we bought a foot locker and all the stuff you had to have to go to a camp like that. The uniform was furnished, so there wasn't any problem about that, just a lot of sweat socks and summer type shoes, and lots of underwear and wool sweaters. Dad started out and drove me from Cleveland to Interlochen.

We were inching our way to Interlochen through and across farmers' fields. There was, not yet, any big through road in Michigan. At a grueling thirty-five miles an hour, it took us two and one-half days. I had seen a copy of a booklet called The Overture, the 1931 season of the camp. By the time we got there, I knew the camp inside-out. I knew what the buildings looked like; what the paths were like and what the Bowl was like. We finally arrived and my father helped me take the stuff to the cabin. I started to live a whole new life.

I can honestly say that from the day I arrived at Interlochen, I haven't *really* been home to Cleveland. Interlochen was everything I wanted in the world. It was everything my world was about.

This place was crawling with incredible players. I met percussion players there who were so dazzling. Men like Reinhardt Elster, who would later become the harpist of the Metropolitan Opera. A genius musician and a great percussionist in his days there. Jack Bryden, the same. A wonderful percussionist, from whom I learned an enormous amount that first summer at camp; those eight weeks, practicing my wrists out, trying to get everything as clean and as solid as I could possibly get it, and expanding everything about being a player.

I was never without a pair of sticks under my belt and a piece of red rubber inner tube in my pocket, so I could practice anywhere and not loose a second of time. It was good for me. I think I was a natural player, so it was this concentration of time to put me together the way I really had to be.

Bill Ludwig and me in 1932. Photo by Mrs. Rhadames Angelucci, wife of the first oboe player. She gave this to me on March 18, 1962
as I went to conduct the Civil War Concert
with the Minneapolis Symphony.

I started thinking, even as the first week of camp was coming to a close, how could I possibly get back here next summer?

I worked very hard to see if I couldn't do that. Fortunately in 1932, there was a large meeting in Cleveland, the last one of the Music Supervisors National Conference. For it, Dr. Maddy and T.P. Giddings assembled their last National High School Orchestra. They founded Interlochen in 1928.

My nineteenth birthday at Interlochen in 1933. Birthday cake, white shirt, sweater and Interlochen pins were gifts from my cabin mates.

Meeting with these gentlemen, who knew I wanted to return to camp, and they appreciated what I did, they found another scholarship for me, and I went back on a full scholarship that summer.

That summer I concentrated on being a Drum Major, because I knew our high school was going to get new uniforms the following Fall. I practiced and learned the art of the Drum Major in lots of very interesting ways. I've written some things about that [RR:. See Marches for Twirling – MG 50113]. I was admitted to Mark Hindsley's graduate class in field tactics/maneuvers and Drum Majoring. That set me up for what I needed to do that Fall at John Adams High School. Who said I was too short to be a Drum Major?

One of the biggest things of my life happened to me in the summer of 1932. I met Bill Ludwig, the son of William F. Ludwig, the founder of the great Ludwig Drum Company. Bill Ludwig and I really hit it off from the first day. He told me, many years later, that he came there considering he was the greatest drummer in the world, and when he met me, he said he had to go back to square one – which he didn't, but that's what he said.

Interlochen, 1940. Conducting the National High School Band. Being short, I made this podium, which raised me up. I used the same seating here as I used for the Eastman Symphony Band.
Courtesy of Interlochen Center for the Arts.

We then began to play together all of the time. We practiced anything we could get our hands on. We would get violin parts out of the library; pieces that we'd never seen before that were enormously difficult and do sight reading battles. We played together constantly. Not only playing, but canoeing, eating together, going to town for hair cuts, and all the things you do at camp. There fashioned at camp that summer of 1932, a life-long friendship with the great Bill Ludwig.

So I went back to John Adams High School and put together a thing for all the people of the band to read and learn. The 'Old Brown Gray Wren" John Adams High School Band suddenly was a dazzler. With our new uniforms, snappy marching and precise maneuvers. I was there in front of it with my spinning silver baton, which I enjoyed doing very much. I always had that leadership thing sticking in me – I liked being up in front.

Football season was over and the last thing we did was the charity football game, on an enormously – bone-chilling last November day at the Cleveland Stadium. All the bands from Cleveland performed for a game between the public and Catholic schools of Cleveland. After that was over, I figured I would put the baton away. I wouldn't need it anymore because I was out of high school. I was wrong. I was going to need it again.

The next summer at Interlochen my concentration was on doing something in composition.

William Skeat was the teacher in composition and had been at the Camp almost from the beginning. He put us through a great camp situation. We had to write a different project each two weeks. This meant four projects in the eight weeks. The first project I did was two different chorales; one in triple time and one in duple time. The second assignment was to write a typical military march. The third was something light and entertaining. The fourth was to write a vocal accompaniment, which I only had a chance to get as far as the sketch, which has since disappeared.

The conductor of the high school band was Albert Austin Harding, the Director of Bands at the University of Illinois. He was the real father of school bands in America. He and I got along very well because he was, in his lifetime, a real "march nut". He sort of sensed that I loved playing under him because he had a series of little signals he would give for accents on the bass drum and cymbals, or for something special from the snare drums in the typical marches we all knew. He never played them the way anybody else played them. He was interesting and imaginative. I enjoyed that about him very much.

He had offered me a scholarship to come to the University of Illinois to get my education and to be a member of the famous Illinois Concert Band.

At this point I was trying to get myself into the Eastman School of Music and I had been working on Howard Hanson for the two previous summers.

I had an application in there, which had not been acted upon as late as when Dr. Hanson came for his annual conducting that summer in 1933.

Harding had heard that I had written a march in class and he asked me about it. I showed him the score and he said "That looks pretty good. Why don't you copy out a set of parts and we'll run it through with the band at some rehearsal".

I furiously started copying out parts. A young lady, with whom I had a wonderful and enormous infatuation, helped me copy parts. She was one the piccolo players in the band. Barbara Booe. She was from Indiana and her mother was the hostess at the Interlochen Bowl Hotel. If I had not had that kind of help, we would not have had a chance to run through the tune. As it happened, Dr. Harding said, "Why don't you do this? You know what this is about". So, this was my debut in a rehearsal with them.

That summer the camp had its eighth week at the Century of Progress Exposition, 1933. We played two concerts a day at the Hall of States. We had the run of the Fair and it was my first time to be that way in Chicago. A long love affair with Chicago had begun. Of course, Chicago was Bill Ludwig's town. This was a combination that was impossible to beat. Between Elkhart and Chicago - that was LUDWIG.

At the invitation of Albert Austin Harding, I made my debut conducting my march, *The Spirit of Youth* with National High School Band for the final Sunday afternoon concert at the World's Fair.

Barbara Booe, seated in the front row of the band, took a photograph of me making my debut as a conductor. I treasure this photo. Everything is wrong about that pose for me to begin this march, except the look on my face. Over the years I have tried to correct the rest of it. I hope I don't loose the look on my face.

This would be the end of Interlochen. The bittersweet began to come into life, when you knew that this would be the last time that you would be a camper.

To meet all those great kids. To play all that great music every week. To beat your buddy's to the lake in the morning, and no matter how cold it was, to dive in before they threw you in. That's the wonderful thing of it. To canoe on the beautiful flat lake. To watch the sun go down.

I was trying to get into the Eastman School of Music. My high school grades were good enough, although they were more than a little bit warped by my total immersion in the music program. I most likely could have had straight A's if I'd done nothing else but. There were so many other things that fascinated me. I guess I got by.

I mentioned that Ludwig and I had come to this great understanding of about how to solve the problem of who's going to play kettledrums and who would be principal percussion for the week. We were just going to draw lots. That was going to be the way that it was going to fall. Someone else rigged up the lots and we drew.

For Howard Hanson's week - Bill drew. I made my personal appeal to him - "Bill, how about swapping with me? I gotta play for Hanson. This is his *Romantic Symphony* and I just gotta impress him". Reluctantly, Bill gave me his week.

I was also thinking about going to M.I.T. to become an architect or whatever. That may be what would have been done. But, I got a telegram one afternoon offering me a scholarship to the Eastman School of Music, which, thanks to Bill Ludwig, it was possible for me to do.

I asked my father and mother Kathryn for a one-way ticket to Rochester and $20.00. That's what they gave me.

But it didn't stop there with Kathryn, of course. There was that weekly laundry box [one of those black fiber cases that always contained my dirty laundry]. It always came back. Beautifully laundered and folded with great love. But more than that – cookies. Home-made ginger cookies, a package or two of Phillip Morris cigarettes and some Hershey bars.

It was those cookies that the guys in the Fraternity House were laying for.

So, in addition to my one-way ticket and the $20.00, they did all they could to see that I got through school. But I needed money pretty desperately, because although it was by no means a 'richboys' school, it was a school that had everything going for it.

It was the end of the depression, 1933, and it was an expense to live anywhere in those days.

Monday afternoon off at Interlochen. The bass I caught at the Point in August of 1957.

# EASTMAN SCHOOL OF MUSIC

## "How it all Began"
Taped narrative - Siesta Key, Florida
February 4-7, 1993

I remember getting off the train in Rochester, where I had never been, with thirteen of my friends from Cleveland. All of them were products of the great Cleveland Schools instrumental and vocal program. Everybody from that Cleveland arrival became somebody at the Eastman School

I settled into what was going to be a really tough school. Again, as at Interlochen, there were some wonderful players. I learned a great deal from them and from a wonderful teacher, William Street.

I wanted to attend Eastman because, at this time, I wanted to make it in both theory and percussion. At that time, the Eastman School was the only school of music in the United States offering a baccalaureate with a major in percussion and the possibility to graduate with a performance certificate, as well as the degree in your major instrument.

I thought that I had arrived at a wonderful place and that I had better find out what this new University was all about. I walked out one day to the River Campus. It was a very new campus.

I went to see the Director of Athletics because I wanted to see if I could audition to be the drum major of the marching band. I had a few strikes against me at that time. I was as short as I am now - five-foot-two and one-half inches. In my stocking feet. That's a little short to be a drum major! I knew that if I was going to be one, I had to be very, very good to make up for the six to seven inches that weren't there - and never would be there.

I located the Director of Athletics of the University of Rochester, Dr. Edwin Fauver, in the beautiful new building, The Palestra. Dr. Fauver was also the teacher for the Eastman School of Music's most hilarious course - "Hygiene". I asked if I could talk with the person in charge of the marching band. "We don't have a band - as far as I can remember, we've never had a marching band", he told me.

"I can get one for you, Dr. Fauver", I said. There was this silence and a look of incredulity on his face as he kind of chuckled and said, "You?". "Yes. I can get one for you. There are a lot of guys down at the Eastman School. I can put a band together for you without any problem". Well, he had to check on me, to see if I really was an Eastman freshman. He called and found out that yes, I was a student, and thus far my record was OK.

I told Dr. Fauver that we needed some kind of uniform and he responded by asking his secretary what might be in the inventory that we could use. They had a lot of white duck pants left over from something and dark blue sweaters that were used for various athletic events and a lot of crazy yellow freshman hats. That was the color of the University of Rochester. Dandelion yellow.

These things were right in line. He said he would produce the uniforms if I could produce the troops. So, I went down to the school and we started going through the YMCA [where a lot of us lived on a temporary basis] and through the practice rooms to line up guys to join up with the band.

I had the good fortune to have made a good friendship with Gordon Pulis, one of Emory Remington's star trombone pupils. [He would become one of the great trombone players in the United States]. Gordon, as a senior, had a lot of clout, and I just had to mention his name and along with the fifteen to twenty friends from Interlochen, who would try anything with me, it was a cinch. We produced a pretty good size band for the first rehearsal.

The pants, sweaters and hats all came from someplace and I don't know how, but everything fit. I had found out what the Alma Mater was, and scratched out something very quickly. After two weeks, I thought the guys looked like some kind of marching group.

**My Turn at Bat** - at the Chief's [Emory Remington] Trombone Picnic in Ellison Park. May 1962. Photo by Peter Kline.

It was a beautiful sunny day in the Fall in Rochester and the guys all showed up in the taxi cabs I had rented for the occasion to get them there and then back to the school. [I had borrowed money from the bank where I had a small account]. We kind of clicked on the drums on our way out to the stadiums left side about fifteen minutes before the kick-off. As we wheeled from there on to the center track, everybody was ready. It was a big roll-off – my favorite march – *National Emblem.*

I guess we were about halfway down the cinder track, which was a lousy business for trombone slides – in any kind of wind – that cinder track was 'death' on the slides – the people in the stands suddenly became aware of what they were hearing and seeing. They rose to greet us. We marched around the track and down the field. I threw the baton over the goal post and, very fortunately, caught it on the other side. My career as a conductor in Rochester had begun.

I did the marching band for ten more seasons, gradually convincing people that we needed some real uniforms and the like. We finally reduced the group to a forty-eight piece unit of only brass, saxophones, piccolos and drums. No clarinets or flutes. Only the stuff that would really blow out the sound. That was a very interesting experience. I learned a great deal from all of that.

I did seventy-seven shows – all the formations – and what music I didn't arrange, Fred Woolston did, or we used what could be purchased at that time. I imagine that if I were to walk down Main Street today, there would be someone who would come up to me and say, regardless of the wonderful things that have happened to me in my life since then, "Oh, I remember you when you led the band at the football games".

There was, of course, something else going on at the Eastman School of Music. Tough classes. Wonderful concerts. Wonderful rehearsals with a great orchestra in a remarkable institution. Not only remarkable buildings and plant, but an institution that was filled with very talented people.

After the last football game of the first season with the marching band - some of the guys came up to me ... "Hey, don't you think we can get together and play somewhere that's warmer than this?"

"You guys want to have some kind of concert band? Let's try it. We got away with this, maybe we can get away with the other one".

We got permission to use lower Strong [as it was called], a small stage in the lower part of Strong Auditorium. The University didn't have a budget for things like this, but the Student Board of Control always had a little something to play with. They gave us the money to use the hall for a Tuesday evening rehearsal. The guys walked out there in the snow ... I remember that very vividly.

I bummed music from everywhere I could. Finally, in 1935, after the football season, we had our debut concert as the University of Rochester Symphony Band.

I remember one thing about that concert. In addition to trying to put it all together; taking the program to the printer; writing all the notes; taking care of all the details with the University; the ushers and all the rest of that. We were about to begin the first concert and I asked one of the guys to run out and ask the head usher if Dr. Hanson had arrived. I knew when I said that, I knew I had made the biggest of all possible goofs. I'd forgotten to send him a complimentary ticket.

Well, I didn't dare let it bother me during the concert, but when it was over, I was really kind of scared. Having worked this hard, all of us, to make this happen, to have goofed it up by not sending the Number One guy a complimentary ticket.

Dr. Hanson came back stage to see me after the concert and he was wonderfully enthusiastic. He said, "Now, this is all very well and good, but we have to have this down at the school. This shouldn't be out here at the River Campus it should be down at the Eastman School. Go see Miss Vayo first thing in the morning and tell her I told you to check about a date when you can play this same concert at Kilbourn Hall".

We did play that same concert at Kilbourn Hall. I think it was about a month later. We kind of blew the dust off the rafters in that place. That was the beginning of my conducting at the Eastman School.

Forty years later, after the evening of the first concert at Strong Auditorium, I sent Dr. Hanson a check for $1.50, which would have been what he paid to get in to hear me make my debut. He never cashed it! The

First recording session, 1953. Checking pitch with the StroboConn.

Symphony Band became a steady part of Eastman concert life. It was on the schedule. It was early afternoon on Tuesday and Friday. The Friday was there because we needed that to be right close to the rehearsal which would follow for the Marching Band. We would rehearse the Marching Band music in the first hour. The guys all got into the taxi cabs and dashed out to the football field for rehearsal, racing against the setting sun, trying to get the show put together before it got so dark you couldn't see the music or the field.

Dorothy and me on the platform at New York Central, March 18, 1948. We are waiting for the train to take the Eastman Little Symphony to St. Lawrence University and Potsdam Normal, as it was called in those days. This is a cold March and she has her little fur jacket and hat.

School had all the good things that anybody could want. Shortly after I was there I met Dorothy Codner. I courted her in the Eastman Dormitory. I drove her everywhere in the car I had acquired to take care of the Marching Band business. It was a very interesting and wonderful courtship. Genuine and legitimate, for which we are both very grateful.

We were 'pinned' in March of 1934. Dorothy was a year ahead of me and graduated in 1936. She worked at home, teaching and so forth, for a year until we were married in June of 1937, after I had graduated.

We [the band] had gone all this distance and I had done what I could do to keep the band going and alive. In the Fall of 1937, I saw an announcement on the board. A competition - The International Prize in Conducting, sponsored by the National Education Association. My colleague in school, Victor Alessandro, had won this fellowship upon graduation. Victor was a talented young man, but he had done almost nothing at school. I had done something and I thought, maybe, I could get it. I filled out the slip, the registration and the request for consideration. Dr. Hanson and Jose Iturbi [Conductor of the Rochester Philharmonic at that time] agreed to be my sponsors.

I dropped the completed forms in the mail and I remember saying to myself "Oh, what the heck. Here goes nothing".

I heard nothing for a long time, but then I was informed that I had been granted a fellowship for a summer study at the Salzburg Mozarteum. I asked how this all happened and was informed they had sent an audition team to Rochester to watch me in dress rehearsal in the darkened Eastman Theatre.

It's always a very good idea to be very careful what you do and what you say. Someone just might be watching and listening. And obviously, they were. They also attended the concert that evening. That's how I wound up in Salzburg in 1938

That was the first year Dorothy and I were married and, being a financial genius, she saved everything possible out of my $500 fellowship for conducting the band. Charles Hutchinson, member of the Board of Managers of the Eastman School had helped send Victor to Salzburg, and he likewise wanted to send me. He provided money for my transportation which was across and back on two German boats, the Europa and the Bremen.

This fellowship to Salzburg was awarded me on the 10th of February, 1938. It was the third of March that Adolph Hitler marched into Austria. I didn't want to be involved with the Nazi thing at all. I sent in my resignation for the fellowship.

Dorothy and I made plans to go to Iowa for the summer and we had stored what few possessions we had with friends. While in Iowa I got a telephone call from Dr. Hanson's office telling me that the State Department insisted that I fulfill the obligation and that I had better get moving because I was due there on the ninth of July.

There we were in Iowa, in this wonderful pastoral atmosphere and I suddenly found myself on the deck of the wonderful German boat, the Europa.

On my way, I quickly grabbed what scores I could and planned to purchase the rest after I arrived in Salzburg. I also tried to cram as much German as I could on the boat. There began my summertime at the Mozarteum.

There were eleven of us in that special class. Many of them were from European countries and it was an interesting relationship between us. We were to be under the general auspices of Wilhelm Furtwangler, who was the head of the Salzburg Festival that summer, Toscanini having given it up because he didn't agree with the Nazi regime, of course. Furtwangler was the principal conductor and on opening night he presented *Die Meistersinger*. I sat in the front row, about three seats to his right, but it was well into the first act before I could see what he was doing. He had a most different conducting style – all over the place, but they sure played for him. He only came to class twice. All the general day-to-day business was taken care of by Herbert Albert. He was General Music Director in Stuttgart and a very wonderful teacher. He was one of those five-by-five German guys with no neck and a large head that sat directly on his shoulders, and he knew exactly what he was doing. He was a wonderful teacher.

The class and I all got along very well. I was stumbling my way through German and they were doing likewise with English. I was invited to conduct the *Scherzo and Finale* from *The New World Symphony* on the final concert, because I was a conductor from the New World. After that, I planned to stay on because the Mozart Orchestra of Salzburg had invited me to do the winter season.

One night while at my score desk at the opera house, a man I had a nodding acquaintance with, came by and introduced himself and produced identification of the State Department. He told me there was a train leaving the next night and that I was to be on it.

"What's up?", I asked. He said things were very unsettled. I had been consumed with my work and was not aware of the goings on in the political world. Dr. Hanson had asked the State Department to order me out.

I was quickly scuttling around and putting things in bags and getting ready to go the next night. I had done the concert two nights before, so I said good-bye to my friends.

I got on the train and what could have been the beginning of the war was obvious to me then. All night long troop trains were going on both tracks in our direction - to Czechoslovakia. In the early morning sun, I got off and went to Paris where I spent a few days and then on to London for a few more days. I caught the last sailing of the Bremen from Southampton. That fall I was back in Rochester to pick up with school.

I think most important, along with my exposure to things in Salzburg, was my chance to hear so many wonderful performances by the Vienna Philharmonic and the marvelously produced operas. I got a different look at life, although it was not always pleasant for me. The Nazi influence was quickly underway.

I bought a large stack of music by Mendelssohn for five cents. I visited museums and other sites in Munich. One afternoon I found myself on a streetcar going back to Bahnhof Square where everybody was assembling to hear Rudolph Hess speak. I heard him speak and he was, in a way, like Hitler,

Concert prior to Carnegie Hall trip. Daniel Johnston, Norman Fickett, Peter Hadcock, Joanna Tousey, Fred Hemke and John Landis

a very convincing speaker. I also got trapped in the torchlight parades in Nuremberg ... a bad scene.

When I arrived back in the United States, a wonderful thing had happened. I had gone up one gang-plank and down another in Bremerhofen. I went up one gang-plank in Southampton and down another gang plank in New York City. Four gang planks. I HAD BEEN TO EUROPE. NOW, I COULD CONDUCT.

It was absolutely true. Shortly after school began that fall, Vance Beach, the President of Phi Mu Alpha and one of my best friends, invited me to become the conductor of the Phi Mu Alpha Little Symphony. This was a chance for me to plan, program, rehearse and conduct. So, in addition to the band, there was now the Little Symphony.

This put a different twist on my life as a conductor. It was very important for me in every possible way, especially my immersion in the repertory of Haydn, Mozart, Scarlatti, early Beethoven, Schubert and contemporary chamber material, of which there was an enormous amount.

At this point I was in study for a Master's Degree in the Pedagogy of Theory with Allen McHose. My subject for the dissertation was agreed as <u>The Orchestral Development of the Kettle Drum from Purcell through Beethoven</u>. That was a marvelous topic because to fulfill it, I had to go through, in

"Here come the Reeds" [Indian file] in hats they made themselves. Any resemblance to a marching band was to be avoided. Prior to "Screamers" concert
Photo courtesy of Louis Ouzer.

Sibley Music Library, every score that was there, every piece of music to see where the kettle drum might have been used before Purcell. I did see a work, which at that time seemed very important, but which now is a spurious huge Mass by a man named Bennavoli, for the dedication of the Salzburg Cathedral in 1628. We know now it was not written by him, but by somebody else. Here was this piece for a large number of kettle drums in Salzburg. That trekked me off to other things. I went through Purcell, Haydn, Mozart, Beethoven — these were the scores where the kettle drum was really put together with the ensemble, because the symphony, which had arrived at its point of great acceptance in Mannheim, was the glory of Mozart, Haydn, and early Beethoven. The previous attempts by the Mannheim composers were very important. So this was my subject. The wonderful thing about that was my journey through every piece of Johann Sebastian Bach, the complete Gesellschaft, dealing with instrumental music. What a "bath of music". I wasn't turning pages quickly. I was jotting titles, pieces of music, getting ready to put down the basic stuff for a dissertation, but remembering music I wanted to play. By the time you've gone through every Haydn symphony and every Mozart symphony, you discover what damn little you know.

I haven't mentioned yet, or written about, the idea of thrusting myself into a leadership position in these earliest days at the Eastman School with the U of R's Marching Band. At the beginning I was "a drummer" – just a few notches above being a drum major. But a great percussionist and superb gentleman like our teacher, William G. Street, was an artist of the highest calibre. He instilled in all his pupils the basic belief that we were musicians, that we could play with anybody. Narrow-minded people sometimes classified us with clowns and jugglers, but with Bill Street that began to disappear – we became musicians. He was a wonderful teacher in all of the ways. And so in displaying myself on the football field in a white sweater with a fancy R on it, white flannels, white shoes and a big shiny baton, I could have been just about as far down on the musical and artistic totem-pole as you can get. That's possibly how it could have been in a lot of schools, but that's not how it was at Eastman.

Even the concertmaster of the Rochester Philharmonic, Alexander Leventon, a most intelligent artist, caught me back stage at the Eastman Theatre one morning before a game and saluted me as "The Admiral of The Azerbaijan Navy". The University had bought us all attractive Marching Band uniforms. Mine was white, trimmed in the University color of Dandelion Yellow; wife Dorothy called it my "... ice cream man's outfit". A quick look at our atlas told me that Leventon – an escapee from the Soviet Union – was really saying: "That's a good looking uniform" – for Azerbaijan is landlocked! He later told me that it was how well you do <u>what</u> you do that is really important and neither he nor any of my Eastman colleagues put me down for what I was doing with the Marching Band. My last game was on 6 November 1943.

When I returned to School in September 1945, after my work for the U.S.O., I made it a part of that to be relieved of the Marching Band which then passed through various hands and then out of existence in the tough sixties.

I barely had what most people would consider the minimum qualifications for being a conductor: a) I wasn't a pianist. It seemed I had no interest in becoming a pianist. (physically I could barely reach an octave, if I stretched my hand as far as I could stretch it. b) I didn't play a violin c) I wasn't a great chamber music player, and d) I wasn't a recognized [or un-recognized] composer. I didn't have those earmarks of what it took to be a conductor. I didn't measure up. It didn't bother enough people to have it make any difference. Certainly, it didn't bother Howard Hanson or my teacher, Bill Street, who knew early on that I was going to move from being a percussionist to a conductor – if I could make it. Fellow faculty members like Warren Fox, Harold Gleason and distinguished members of the Voice and Opera faculty were solid supporters. I guess, again, it was like Leventon said, "You either do it well, you're good at it, or your NOT".

And then the other side of it was the students. When we started to move the Symphony Band into the School, I was conducting weekly rehearsals with members of the Eastman student body, some of whom were graduate students and I was an undergraduate sophomore. Eastman was a seniority school in those days. That was the way Dr. Hanson saw it. He always thought in terms of the orchestra as the senior group. He later revised that.

Here I was, an undergraduate, planning a seasons' study and work, and posting a series of concerts, which I then, on the rehearsal time of School, would rehearse. The flak that would come up from this, I must say, I never heard. I don't think I was shielded by anything. I just went to rehearsal, maybe if anything, over-prepared.

I learned rather quickly, that one way to avoid difficulties was to keep everybody so busy, there was no time for them; rehearsals planned so that you didn't spend twenty minutes rehearsing four flutes while ninety other people sat there; knowing how to use the time; how to make it productive; how to make it creative; how to make it musical; and how to make it as "un-bandy" as I could make it, because there were all these things that people thought about how terrible were the bands they had played in [the conductor did or didn't do that] – I tried to avoid all of that and remove it from anything we did. I wanted to make this a most efficient band – make it the most musical experience possible that I could offer the people who were playing for me.

I must confess – I think it worked. I won't say that our concerts were all that great, or that my interpretations [or my knowledge of all the pieces], were that infinite, by any means, but it somehow was progressively better. The interest of the people was progressively so. I do not recall at any time a pogrom against me. Dr. Hanson never said anything and he backed me all the way. I don't recall that there was a business of a self-appointed committee going to the Director saying, "What's he doing up there?". I just didn't have time for politics. I didn't have time for favorites, as I think everybody knows.

After the War was a difficult time for many people. The difficult time for me as the conductor of the Eastman School Symphony Band was that there were people coming back for the completion of an under-graduate degree, or the beginning as a graduate. Men who had been excellent players when they were at school before the War, and who had found a slot in any number of the military bands that there were for three and four years had known only what was delivered to them.

Sometimes, I presume, it was not always of the most desirable calibre. They came back to School, as well as those who had been in the trenches or in the cockpits or on decks for that period of time, and who fortunately had survived.

These people were mature beyond the few years that they had spent away. They were making decisions very quickly and these decisions were for their future. They came back on the G.I. Bill, which was a wonderfully generous program for students returning to school. The G.I. Bill was paying their tuition so they didn't have to worry about what anybody would say about whether their performance was equal, or not, to their scholarship [or even to their graduate fellowship].

They were financially independent. One of the best under-graduate flute players said to me: "You know I'm back here now, and you're OK. You know what you're doing. I've had it for three years now, and I don't need it anymore. I don't care what you're offering. I don't want to play in this band anymore".

He wasn't the only one. He expressed it straight off. Now, what do you do as an administrator when the catalog says what the catalog says, and the instrumental department's administration and its clear statement from the reed, brass and percussion faculty, is that this is how it will be; you will participate.

Well, we were talking to a different student in a different time. This was 1946 - not 1937. So it had to be dealt with in a different way. All those matters were a part of a very careful discussion with all the faculty members. Of course, this all let me know *for sure*, what I was already prepared for and what surely was going to happen.

I began to be concerned very much about the big band. I'd had reservations for a great many years, but I never developed them. But now I was facing the fact that there were people coming back to our School who just plain didn't want to play in that group, and were extremely outspoken to tell me why. And most of what they were saying agreed with what I believed in the first place. How to handle this?

I had meetings with the faculty to tell them what I had experienced and what I thought was happening. Counseling with them for their suggestions as to what we should do were projects that I suggested, and that we did institute. In addition to the band and the orchestra, their operation would include, at the same time the Orchestra met, the orchestra ensemble classes [reeds, brass and percussion] for the study of symphonic literature -- the reed, brass and percussion parts, minus the strings.

Sometimes I would conduct, sometimes graduate assistants or my colleague, Paul White would conduct. There was always someone in acceptable authority musically there to do this. That helped some, but it never got rid of the idea of 'who needs that big old symphony band?'

The symphony band had now begun to stir from its slumber as far as the composer was concerned. Outstanding pieces of music were beginning to come across the desk, and to deal with them, you had to have great players. As a matter of fact, you needed the best players you could find.

Many of these pieces introduced a new wave of thought about the band, and of course, that was very highly desired. I tried many, many things, some of which worked and some didn't.

One time, at the height of despair over the subject of the symphony musician and the band, I proposed, at a meeting of the faculty, that we should abandon the band and that we should go to highly advanced rehearsal periods of time in the orchestral literature from the reed, brass and percussion point of view. Forget about playing concerts and just strictly work on repertory and repertorial disciplines and styles. The faculty didn't like that idea at all.

I was only able to rescue from that very serious faculty meeting, their promise that I could have one hour in the day from 1:10 to 2:00 PM when I could start to have some special rehearsals for reed, brass and percussion music, that wasn't necessarily on everybody's program. They granted me this hour, and it was not difficult for them to grant, because it was ten minutes after one. Everybody was still pretty much hung up on the idea that lunch began at noon and anything happening right after lunch was pretty .. YUK .. the time of day when things came to a point of definite repose.

I got the time and I used it for one year rehearsing combinations of players with pieces I had not seen since I went through my business with the kettle drum dissertation. It was called the Kilbourn Hall Wind/Brass Program and gave us the opportunity to put together a program that was a little different than we'd had at the School before.

I tried to involve every reed, brass and percussion performer in the School. We began with the music of Matthew Locke and the early Dutch composers. We went through the gradual development of wind literature .. Mozart *Serenade in B-flat*, Strauss *Serenade in E-flat*, the Gabrieli brass music, and on the final concert were the *Symphonies of Wind Instruments* of Stravinsky.

Eastman Theatre 1943 - stage show produced by General Motors, Rochester Products Division. Two shows a day for three days. Orchestra included Irving Nathanson, Paul White and Henry Freeman, father of Robert Freeman, current Director of the Eastman School of Music.

This was a program designed to say ... "Well, here it is people. Why don't we do something about it?" I simply advertised the program as what it was, and in advance of that, I had printed a small essay of why I felt we were doing it.

I opened the doors of Kilbourn Hall at 8 O'clock that evening, and at a quarter to twelve, the concert was just coming to a conclusion. The audience was still there.

It was the first time in Rochester, that *Symphonies of Wind Instruments* of Igor Stravinsky had been played. This is 1950-51. It didn't fit the Symphony Band premise. There were other reasons we hadn't done it before - it was a rental item and I had no "budget" – I usually had to go and beg for the money to do it. But I got the money for this concert.

Everybody who participated in the program, musicians and audience alike, were the happiest that it had happened. This was a great success, and I had hoped that in the following year we might have another one of these concerts in February, one of the doldrum months in Rochester with the winter being all the way into it. I, however, was denied the opportunity to have another one of those concerts, when on the advice of my dentist, I was sent to a dental surgeon for the removal of one of the lower and third molars.

The dental surgeon discovered that the first one to take out on the lower right side, was very deeply impacted. He needed sixteen injections of Novocain to keep me from going up the wall, while he was using every kind of chisel he could to remove that thing from my jaw.

Sixty days later my family doctor discovered that I had hepatitis. Sixty days to the day from my operation. The dentist of this operation, unbeknownst to him, was a carrier of this virus.

I was off conducting for the weekend at Hempstead High School. The outstanding young violinist at Eastman, Ray Gniewek, was a former student at Hempstead High School and went back with me to play the Tschaikowsky *Violin Concerto* with his high school orchestra. Dorothy was away on tour with the Rochester Philharmonic.

Dorothy and I both returned on Monday morning and she said to me, "You don't look very well, and on top of that your eyeballs are yellow." So, I prepared a urine sample which I dropped off on my way to rehearsal for an evening concert of the Eastman School Orchestra. I just put the name Fennell on the bottle.

The doctor didn't get to his laboratory work until the end of the day and he was shocked when he saw the results. He thought it was Dorothy, not me. I guess hepatitis is more deadly with the female gender. He rushed out to the house to tell her that

Frederick Fennell at Interlochen, August 1992.
Photo courtesy of David Speckman

it was very serious. She told him it was my sample, not hers and that I was at the Theatre conducting a concert. Charlie, the doctor said, "It's not possible. He just can't be doing this. He's a very sick man and I gotta get him out of there."

I'm ready to go back out on stage for the second half of the concert and in comes Dr. Charlie saying "Come on, you're finished here and you've gotta come with me to the hospital." Of course, I said "No way! I don't know what you're talking about, but conductors don't walk out on concerts. You just don't do that!" I convinced him to stick around while I enjoyed conducting two great pieces – *En saga* by Sibelius and *Till Eulenspiegel* by Strauss.

After the concert I came out and said, "What's this, Charlie?" On the trip to the hospital he told me that he was a senior officer in a fleet of Navy Hospital ships in the South Pacific during the war. "One thing we were more cautious about than the enemy, was what you have – hepatitis", he said.

I could only work on their diet, which was to flush the system with water and consume about a pound of sugar candy a day. That's what is was. It was a very careful diet to rid the body of this virus which was taking up housekeeping in my liver.

I was instructed to be as quiet as I could be all of the time. I lay in this hospital bed just staring up at the ceiling – days on end. During that period, I thought I should do some constructive dreaming, so I thought about this whole business of the band from beginning to some sort of end. In the process of thought, I worked my way down to the small group which represented the wind section of the great Rochester Civic Orchestra. All the teachers of the School were the first chair players there. When that group played, just the wind section, the reed and brass section of that orchestra sound just marvelous. Just wonderful.

Years before, in Interlochen, after coming away from the first concert of the summer with the

National High School Band and walking through the woods to the boys camp with Sidney Mear, I asked him what he thought of being the principal cornet player in the fine large band like this one,

Photo courtesy of Monte LaBonte.

and with a fine conductor like Dr. Harding? After awhile, he said, "You know, Harding was OK, certainly" .... [a moment later] ..."one thing I didn't like about it was, that anytime I put my horn down, I could hear ten other guys playing my part". This stuck with me, and while I was doing this business in the hospital bed, I said, "Well, let's cut it back to the absolute bone".

That turned out to be the instrumentation of the Eastman Wind Ensemble, which would allow it to play the distinguished music that had already been written, like the Hindemith *Symphony in B-flat* and pieces by Morton Gould, William Schuman, Gustav Holst, Ralph Vaughan Williams -to name a few off the top of my head. Then I thought, maybe we should make some recordings, 'cause there's nothing around like this. Well - a lot of dreaming there.

One day, when Dorothy came to visit me in the hospital, I asked her to follow up on a suggestion from Oscar Zimmerman, my bass teacher friend, who said I should write all of this down before it slipped away. She brought me the paper and I scratched it down. Dr. Hanson came to see me one day, very concerned about me, and after a very pleasant visit, he was about to leave when he said, "Is there anything I can do for you?" I said, "Well, since you asked, Dr. Hanson, yes, there is something you can do for me. I have an idea for a wind group for School that I really hope we might be able to try".

I gave him the papers I had worked out, and he stood there with his overcoat on, and looking at them, he removed his overcoat and kept reading. When he reached for the "inevitable cigar" and started to make those little conducting motions with the cigar, I sort of knew I had him. After reading the papers, all he said was "Well, now all you have to do is get out of this hospital bed. And when you do, we'll do this".

I imagine that was as much a great prod for recovery as anything could possibly be. So, I then got into more details about it. When they let me out of the hospital, I went home for more rest there. Dorothy took such wonderful care of me

When I could get up and go about and back to School [this is early April, 1952], I had a performance to do of *Facade* by William Walton, which I had also been studying while I was in the hospital, learning Edith Sitwell's poetry so I could speak it in tempo with the music.

I had to amplify ideas that I had about this wind group, so I put together a letter which I then mailed to 450 composers around the world, telling them that we were going to do this, and that we had no money for commissions, but if the performance with love and affection and great competence was of any interest to them, we were ready to play anything that they would send. I also requested a list of any music they may have already written for any reed, brass combination. The response was rather immediate. The first reply I received was from Percy Grainger. The next was from Vincent Persichetti; then Vaughan Williams and the Czech composer, Alois Haba. A large number of responses came back, I'm happy to say.

Armed with this amount of enthusiasm for something that didn't even exist, I submitted articles to a couple of important music magazines, one of which published the article announcing our beginning.

Monte LaBonte, Saddleback College.
Photo courtesy of Monte LaBonte.

Later, I was in Philadelphia at a meeting of the Music Educator's National Conference. I went to meet David Hall of Mercury Records who had worked with Dr. Hanson. He sold him on the idea of not giving up his American Festival series of recordings of music by American composers which had not been a success for Columbia and Victor, with whom he had previously made recordings.

The result of that meeting was that Eastman School signed a contract with Mercury Records for the production of music performed by the Eastman-Rochester Orchestra. Hall said he was very interested in that, but he and Mercury wanted the whole school; wanted Faculty Chamber Music and the chorus, and he wanted band music. He even told them at that time, he wanted the Holst Suites.

Photo by Ron Johnson in Kilbourn Hall at the 25th Anniversary concert in 1977. "A favorite picture for what it means to me". Courtesy of Ron Johnson.

At that Philadelphia meeting we sat in the Horn and Hardart Restaurant across from the Bellevue Stratford one afternoon. It was a kind of cataclysmic meeting. David Hall had forgotten more about recordings and recorded music than anybody I imagine ever, and what has not been, and should have been at that time and up to that moment.

We really hit it off, and he told me this was really going to have to happen. The Wind Ensemble was going to have to do this. I said, "We're not even born yet, April 1952." That afternoon we talked about and wrote down what became the basic repertory of the Eastman Wind Ensemble on Mercury Records. So ... back to Rochester, and back to work, having planted as many seeds as I felt I could.

The summer of 1952 began with the creation of the Eastman Chamber Orchestra to augment the summer program of the teachers on the faculty, and to institute a series of five concerts, followed by a sixth week of music to be read, which was written by the composers present in the summer. In other words, an extension into the summer program of what Dr. Hanson had been doing for many years in the winter program. This was a great impetus for that.

This gave me an opportunity to work very closely with people who had everything to do with the development of a program of professional work, like the Eastman Chamber Orchestra, which I conducted for the next ten years. It was one of the great ensembles of Rochester's history. There again was a chance to play all of that great chamber orchestra literature that I had done with great happiness with the Eastman Little Symphony.

The Eastman Wind Ensemble was, I guess, maybe four months old before Dr. Hanson brought up the subject of recording. I had carried around for a long time in my wallet, only one program I would want to record. One day he did call me in; he had been to concerts by the Wind Ensemble and everybody was very happy with what we were doing. We also did a series of broadcasts for the Rural Radio Network of the Dairymen's League and the New York State School Music Association. We read and rehearsed "cold" for that FM Network, selected music from their Manual of Music Recommended for their Spring Competition Festivals. That was one of the interesting things with which to begin.

Dr. Hanson said, "What would you like to record? I'll give you $2.000 for a session". He figured out that's what it would cost for forty-five musicians. I whipped out my little piece of paper and told him what I wanted to record. And there followed the silence I had learned to respect from him. After which he said, "Well, you know Fred, you won't sell ten of these". With that I said, "Dr. Hanson, that's not my plan in making this recording that you invited us to do. This, I think, has to be the statement of where music for the wind band by American composers of original music for the wind band stands in May of 1953. This is where it is".

There was another silence, after which his utterance was classic. "Well," he said, "You know, we can always give them to the alumni". Classic Hanson. Fortunately we didn't have to give them to the alumni. We sold several re-issues, and introduced the Eastman Wind Ensemble to the world, and obliged a basic re-consideration of the wind band as a medium for serious music making.

This offered a great opportunity for the composer to enter an area where they had seemingly not spent very much time. The Eastman Wind Ensemble was founded in the Fall of 1952, and played its first rehearsal on the 20th of September. Everybody who was chosen to play, and I chose them, knew from the beginning that we had something special. I had, of course, chosen the very best students in the School and I think that was the first time that a group had been chosen only for the highest quality of players. It set everyone on their ear. That was the beginning, I'm happy to say.

In addition to our series of broadcasts for the

New York State School Music Association, we did two broadcasts for the National Broadcasting Company series that Dr. Hanson had once again promoted. That was the introduction of the group to the United States before the first record was released on October 19, 1953.

This was a different group, a different way to do things. People frequently asked me what made the group different. What was special about it, and I could only say it was their attitude. Their attitude about each other; the music they were playing; their attitude about playing at all in that kind of situation. Attitude – the one word I would always choose to describe as to what made the Eastman Wind Ensemble at the beginning and what sustains it today.

The Wind Ensemble was put on the schedule to

piccolo was the next point of consideration. That's where we had the auditions. That was a tremendously important chair, and still is, of course, in this or in any wind group.

The Mercury challenge was going from there, once we had made the first record. "What are we going to do for the next one?" Of course, everyone thought we were going to start with an album of marches. While I'm most likely one of the nuttiest "march nuts" in the world, I would not choose to begin with that. I began with what we recorded because I never expected to make more than one record. And if I was going to only make one, it was going to be that one. But for the next one, I said, "OK, if marches are what you want, we'll be very glad to put one together". We put one together that was, unbelievably recorded in a two-hour session,

Eastman Wind Ensemble 1952-53. Photo courtesy of Louis Ouzer

rehearse four times a week for fifty minutes at a time. I don't think we could have rehearsed longer than that, because we worked at such a wonderful fever pitch of intensity, that when it got to be two o'clock, everybody *knew* that it *was* two o'clock, and that was that.

In the choice of players over the ten years, we had to have three auditions. Otherwise, I chose all the players from my knowledge of them even before they came to School. The three auditions were as follows; two were for piccolo and one was for bass trombone. There were so many good bass trombone players in that School; Mr. Remington had brought them there and Joe Mariano's flute class was loaded. The flute thing was never much of a problem either, because there were so many good ones and people honored the one I chose. But the

plus one-half hour overtime. That's exactly 100-minutes of music for sixteen marches. That cuts the retake time down to about the least.

That was a ploy which was a little different. We hit them with what they thought was going to be the first album with the second one. Then, for the third one, we went more deeply into the symphonic side of what we were doing. Finally, by the time we were finished and ready to end the monaural era and join the great stereo revolt going on, we had pretty well exhausted the idea that we thought would be the kind of repertory we would record. That included the album titled La Fiesta Mexicana. The title selection by H. Owen Reed; the piece by Virgil Thomson, *A Solemn Music*; *Psalm* by Vincent Persichetti, and Peter Mennin's *Canzona*.

We didn't expect to make this recording at that time. Dr. Hanson's mother had very recently died, and a very wonderfully close family that was, and he had scheduled for that session time, his *Cherubic Hymn*, dedicated to her, and he didn't feel he could quite do that. Mercury could not come to Rochester for less than six marketable sides, or the trip with Robert Fine's truck and all of the other expense of recording would have been prohibitive.

Technical moment for the first recording session.
Photo courtesy of William L. Decker.

So, we were able to fill in for Dr. Hanson on that occasion. He did four sides and we did two. That gave us the La Fiesta Mexicana album which was a big talking point all the way throughout the profession. That didn't hurt us a bit. We finished all of these very important monaural sessions with the fourth of these recordings, which was the first volume of British Band Classics. The two Holst *Suites*, *Toccata Marziale*, The *English Folk Song Suite* by Vaughan Williams. This turned out to be one of the most important records that we could make.

I imagine, and some have told me that this is so; that this recording was an embarrassment to the British establishment. Why hadn't they done it? Well, I couldn't worry about what they had or hadn't done. I was only very much involved in what I needed to do, and to record those pieces and that's something we simply had to do. We didn't have any choice and I didn't want to have any choice. I loved the pieces and I felt that people needed to know them, and they did not know them. It was a very important recording in every way for us. It then set up the next point, because at the end of this one, we went into the stereo era.

Next came the Marching Along album, which borrowed its title from John Philip Sousa's Autobiography, and this one contained only twelve marches. These were twelve outstanding ones and again did so much to acquaint the world with this very unique and very extraordinary group.

The working out of all kinds of things for a recorded repertory was something I had spent a lot of time thinking about and planning for. We were able to practice, and I won't go into point by point title, the necessity of the man who always ran that very nice, tightly run, small little family-owned grocery store. He loved to have bananas in his store to sell to the people who liked bananas, but he was very aware of their fragility; that they didn't last very long, and they had a tendency to rot on him if not sold. So he had to counter that with something else. He had to have an item of fruit that would pretty well survive for a long period of time, encased within its own very solid skin. That was the orange. There came of course, years before this, the wonderful expression, "We survive by the fact that our business is oranges and bananas". You have to have the bananas for the people who want them, but you have to have the oranges in order to stay in business.

Well, that was us! Our oranges were the albums of marches that we made, and they always poured the money back into the revolving fund. Therefore, we had money there with which to make an album of music by Vincent Persichetti, Percy Grainger, Bernard Rogers, Richard Strauss, Walter Hartley – we had the money in the kitty to record these "bananas". I didn't have to ask Dr. Hanson for it, because I knew it was there.

So that let us go on to do all sorts of things like Hindemith, Schoenberg, Stravinsky, and then follow that with March Time, and then we would do something like Persichetti's *Symphony No. 6* and other works of this kind. We would then counter with something like Sound Off, an album of Sousa marches. One thing kept bouncing back and forth from the other. We kept the record buyer in an interested disarray as to what we were going to put out next. They found us there suddenly with a really classic and remarkably successful album of *Serenade No. 10 in B-flat, Gran Partita* by Mozart. That's how we worked.

Saddleback Conducting Symposium.
Photo courtesy of John Maltester.

Then at the time of the Centennial of the Civil War, I had been planning to do something about that for a long time. It wound up as an enormous project between Mercury's Special Products Division and the University of Rochester. With a grant from the University for the preparation of this material, I set out to make what became The Civil War - Its Music and Its Sounds.

This was marketed in two volumes with eight sides. The eighth side was the discussion of weapons and their sound and the like. That was another one of those block-busters that did things and then broke barriers that people didn't know about. As a matter of fact, looking at a photograph of the Reconstituted Third New Hampshire Band, our Union Army Band during the Civil War, that is the band whose music we used. A stage full of wonderful brass players, playing on great brass instruments, some of them over one-hundred years old. Some of these instruments hadn't been played for the same amount of time. Here we were with a brass band and we were actually doing this at a very interesting and critical time in the development of things in the wind-band world.

Gettysburg, 29 October 1960. Civil War recording of firing of cannon, hand and shoulder pieces. I'm holding the sponge for a twelve pound parrot rifle canon of the Second New Jersey Light Artillery.
Photo courtesy of William L. Decker

I had been the President of the College Band Directors National Association, the really very important group of its kind among the conductors and leaders. They were having their bi-ennial national meeting in Chicago, and one of the very big topics they were discussing [in my absence], was "The Brass Band". That was rather typical of what the Eastman Wind Ensemble stands for: as they were there discussing it, we were in Rochester recording it – from the very music books of the Civil War, on the authentic full range of instruments, complete from the E-flat Soprano to the E-flat Bombard Bass – one of those very interesting observations.

In rounding everything out, we included the recording of the music of the Gabrieli's, the uncle and nephew - the genii of Venice, which we recorded, not in the Eastman Theatre, but in Christ Church, across East Avenue, where there was this spacious area of hard surfaces and a certain kind of decay that fit that music marvelously well. We had enormous plans to keep going on doing all sorts of things. I had proposed to Wilma Cozart Fine, in a long list of things many years before, that we should do an album of Circus marches, and it just happened that this May of 1962 was going to be the Circus time.

This was an unusual year at School, because we had received, in June of 1961, an invitation from the State Department to make a three month tour of Europe, the Mid-East, Poland and Russia with the Eastman Philharmonia.

Dr. Hanson had created the Philharmonia after the Wind Ensemble, and this orchestra reversed his process of the past. He went for that like I had gone for with the Wind Ensemble, with only the best players in the school, no matter who they were or what there age or student seniority was. This became a really first-class orchestra. We then departed, after a long bit of preparation, for Spain. This was the day after Thanksgiving, 1961. We were gone until the twenty-sixth of February, 1962, during which time we travelled to sixteen countries.

While I was gone, Donald Hunsberger [my assistant, who was then in graduate school and was the assistant conductor of the Eastman Wind Ensemble] assumed that responsibility. Of course, I had with me all the best reed, brass and percussion players in the School, so he had to make up another ensemble, which he did. It was a very successful group and he did it very well.

We finished the 1962 season with the album of exciting music from the circus, <u>Screamers</u>.

"Off We Go" ... LAX to Tokyo, January 1985.
Photo by Roger E. Rickson

It was Palm Sunday and Dorothy and I had just signed the papers for a new home that she had found while I was on tour in Europe. It was located in the Allen's Creek area of Rochester on a nice little stream of water and a very nice neighborhood. That afternoon I had a telephone call from John Meyers, who identified himself as President of the Minneapolis Symphony Orchestra, and did I have some time to talk with him. I said, "Yes, I had time to talk to him".

I had been in Minneapolis in March, after we

West Coast Conducting Symposium at Saddleback College. Photo courtesy of John F. Maltester

came back from tour, to do a concert of music of the Civil War with the Minneapolis Symphony, celebrating that and the Sioux uprising in Minnesota. Both were celebrated the same year.

Meyers said, "I have just come from a meeting with ten other presidents of major orchestras in the United States, and we've been discussing our future. I'm a business man and it's a very successful business, but we all know that if we don't diversify, we will certainly not survive. This was the subject of the symphony orchestra at these meetings with these men. I'm calling you because I think you can help us in the survival of the Minneapolis Symphony. Would you be interested in joining us in a hired position as a conductor? We have things you could do and we are sure, since we record for the same company, that we can continue the recording program for you and for us".

I said, "Well, gee, my wife and I just signed the contract on a new house here on a pretty stream", to which John Meyers said, "We've got a lot of water in Minnesota".

I didn't know what to do about this, but before my yea or nay, the simplest thing to do was to get on a plane and go there and talk with them. Which I did.

With Stanislaw Skrowaczewski, then the Music Director of the Orchestra, John Meyers and members of the board, and members of the committee of the Orchestra, we discussed this whole subject very thoroughly. I was then offered a contract as Associate Music Director of the Minneapolis Symphony Orchestra.

Well, I carried it home and then Dorothy and I had to sit down and talk it over. I also had to talk with the acting official of the University of Rochester who was a Provost. We didn't have a president at that time for they were searching for one.

I asked these people, and there were more than one at this conference, "can you, by any chance, give me some idea how far I might be able to go at the Eastman School of Music? I've been in Rochester for thirty years and I've been a full-time member of the faculty since my Master's Degree in 1939, and an adjunct member of the faculty since 1937, and an active student conductor since I arrived. What's my future here?"

The Provost said, "You don't have one".

"You mean I've gone as far as I can go here?" I asked. "Yes", he replied.

That meant that eliminated me from any consideration for any possibility as being the next Director of the School or in any other executive position. I had really gone a big distance at the Eastman School and here was a great challenge awaiting me.

I went to talk with Dr. Hanson about it right away. He didn't make any move to push me one way or the other, until our final meeting, which was about the fourth one. At that time Dr. Hanson said, "I want to lay blank pieces of paper in front of you and you fill them in".

"That's really not it, Dr. Hanson. That's not why I'm going to go to Minneapolis. I know this side of life very well, but I don't know what's on the other side of the mountain. I've never really seen it. I don't know if I can sell out a series of professional concerts or if I am only a conductor for a scattered audience of two hundred people in the Eastman Theatre that seats three thousand. Where do I fit? I need to know". That was my statement to him.

And this, I thought, was my opportunity to discover it [the other side] with a distinguished orchestra in a distinguished position. One of the other things I thought about was that a lot of people did not believe that the Eastman Wind Ensemble will survive my going. I didn't believe that.

I thought to myself – they'll find out that it will not only survive my going, but it will continue to thrive and reach into new dimensions. The Eastman Wind Ensemble will continue to grow. They will continue to be an effective music ensemble for those in the world who are interested in this.

Thereupon, Dr. Hanson and I shook hands and it would soon be good-bye to the Eastman School for me.

All of this was just four days before we played our concert for the <u>Screamers</u> album.

John Maltester, author and Frederick Fennell.
Courtesy of John Maltester.

While this is all going on; while we are rehearsing all of this, the kids don't know that I'm leaving. I never told them until I made the announcement two days after the recording session, which was preceded by a gala concert.

I casually suggested we have a circus. Next thing I know the kids have got it all organized with peanuts and popcorn; sawdust, uniforms and clowns and the whole school is jumping to come and hear that concert played in the annex rehearsal room. Now, of course, the recording is a marvelous one. That was the end of my tenure as Director of the Eastman Wind Ensemble — from September 1952 to May 1962.

I took me most of the summer to pack what I had acquired for thirty years upstairs in my studio and get it ready to go to Minneapolis for the beginning of another life. After these really remarkable years, I just figure that I went to school at Eastman for thirty years.

Fred at Miles Elementary School 1993

Fred at John Adams High School 1993

Miles Elementary School 1993

John Adams High School 1993. All photos by Roger Rickson

# MINNEAPOLIS and BEYOND

## "How it all Began"
Taped narrative - Siesta Key, Florida
February 4-7, 1993

The Minneapolis Symphony was a joyous collection of first-class musicians, marvelous orchestral players, people whose ensemble pedagogy and performance achievements over the years, had come from really first-class conductors, the most recent being Dimitri Mitropoulos and Antal Dorati. It was a remarkable association and a wonderful community of people. They enjoyed each other at home and on tour – and they always produced.

Upon Dorati's departure, the management engaged Stanislaw Skrowaczewski as Music Director. When I began to work with the Orchestra and to listen to his rehearsal, his personality didn't seem to be to be in sync with the Orchestra. He did many things well, but I didn't feel an exchange of warmth there, which I soon began to discover, was also something that included me. What I was and whatever it was that I came there to do, did not seem to mean, in the end, what we all thought it was supposed to be. I was on my own at the end of our two-year contract.

I was "at liberty" and sent letters to a few places – with no response – and no surprise. A few things came along and as soon as our daughter Cathy's school was out for the summer, we went to our home at Interlochen, Michigan that I had built in 1959. There I enjoyed the silence of the woods and the beauty of the lake in which we all found the pleasure of swimming and on which I pursued the only hobby I've ever had — sailing any kind of boat, sail it and fussing with it to make it and me better at what we do together. It was a wonderful summer and I was as free as the birds that were my only alarm clock.

Back at our Hermitage Hills home in Minnetonka, Minnesota, Cathy came to breakfast one morning and told us that she had a vivid and beautiful dream in which we were going to move someplace where there was a lot of water. That afternoon I had a phone call from Dr. William F. Lee, Dean of the School of Music at the University of Miami in Coral Gables, Florida. He said that he was in his second year there and that the conductorship of the Orchestra would be available in the following fall — was I interested? Coral Gables – Miami, lots of water there! After a winter of conductorial barnstorming, we moved into a brand new Florida house, complete with swimming pool on the 25th of April 1965. Cathy's dream had,

Boating on Chippewa Lake, Ohio – circa 1905
My father Fred; behind is first wife Julia Putnam – my mother holding parasol. When Julia died in 1915, father married her sister Kathryn, the other lady in the boat. Photo courtesy of FF.

indeed, come true.

At the University it was my goal to develop the student orchestra that Miami did not have; the University of Miami Symphony Orchestra was, from the beginning of the University in 1925, the orchestra of the area, made up of professionals, amateurs, and some students, conducted by professionals from the faculty. By the October of my invitation, the University's deficit for a season of professional concerts was $100,000, and it was decided to terminate their sponsorship. Then came the Greater Miami Philharmonic, the area's new group. Tending to my work at the University, I helped the Dean in his search for the excellent faculty he was assembling, started a wind ensemble, and became a Resident Conductor of the Miami Philharmonic, now defunct.

The search for the right deep-water sailboat

found me refurbishing, completely, a 24' fiberglass sloop that could take me anywhere in the Keys; all spare time for six months went to that. All was very pleasant, well ordered when — and suddenly, everything in my personal life began to suffer the combination of turmoil and euphoria that accompanies falling in love.

Dorothy and I had been married and happily for thirty-two years. Without her love, encouragement, solid criticism and steadfast belief — beginning in our student years, in my potential as a conductor, I might never have put it all together. We sacrificed so many things to simply stay afloat in the earliest years. The birth of our wonderful daughter, Cathy, ten years into our marriage had so brightened our life.

Lynne and me off on a cruise in my ketch "Ching ∬OOM II" — the great joy in my life.
Photo courtesy of FF.

But in spite of my consideration of all of this, I was hopelessly in love with Lynne Doherty, a young graduate student assistant who played french horn. The painful thought for Dorothy of separation and divorce was concluded and Lynne and I were married in February of 1970. She was twenty-three years old. I took her everywhere I went. There were many happy times, and she became a first-class sailor. My years took their toll and our marriage ended eleven years later; there was no issue.

During the Miami years three other prudent undertakings made the years there productive and contributive: the decision to try to teach conducting, the beginning of the writing of the Study/Performance Essays of Basic Band Literature, and the return to professional recording.

My first pupil was Doc Severinsen who called one day to say that Johnny Carson was going to make him leader of the NBC Tonight Show Orchestra and that he could handle the usual big-band stuff and the production cues "... but what do I do when Maria Callas is on with one of those tricky Puccini arias?" He had a date in Atlanta on a Thursday night, so he came to stay with Dorothy and me for the week-end. First off, I got him in the pool to relate the physical intensity of moving hands and arms in conducting through 48" of water to the supported breath by which he plays the trumpet so magnificently. This was the way to convince him of the horizontal movement by which he and that great band could stay with Ms. Callas' beautiful legato vocal production.

I reminded him, when he asked about it, that he needn't fear one of her long-held fermatas; all he had to do about that was — like so much conducting — remember what he had to do as a player. In this case, the ample breath could be replaced by his very slow motion UPWARD, and that would match any dramatic fermata sung by anybody. We worked at a few more basic physicals in the pool and out; he still calls me "teach".

A few weeks later the American Band Masters Association was in Miami for the annual convention and we invited Associate Member-friends, Nels Vogel, Sandy Sandberg and composer Clifton Williams for a cook-out. Between swims I told them about my recent experience with Doc. At the end of my passes to the shallows, Nels Vogel leaned down to say – "When do we start our conducting clinic?" That was the beginning of what brought Roger Rickson and me together.

So many things get done at the [now] International Mid-West Clinic in Chicago each December. There's where Lynne committed me to writing for Kenneth L. Neidig, then Editor of The Instrumentalist. I wasn't in on it at all until Ken and I sat for details of what became one of my most important undertakings scheduled, open-end.

One afternoon a call came from Jack Renner and Robert Woods in Cleveland inquiring if I might be interested in making a recording with the winds of the Cleveland Orchestra? Meaning no offense, I asked if this wasn't a pair of my Texas band-director-friends putting me on, which of course, they weren't. They told me all about their recording philosophy, so compatible with my own. I knew of their very successful LP Direct from Cleveland with Lorin Maazel, and this was to be my way, too. We settled repertory and no sooner than we had hung up I began to edge myself in the direction of Telarc Records.

Taking the scores and parts down from their so-silent slots, they began to live again — Holst, Bach, Handel! In the midst of checking everything, Renner called asking if I had read anything about digital possibilities in recording? Yes, I had — and mind-jinggling, too! "Well', said Jack, "that's the way we've decided to go". Back to the old copy of Audio. I knew that my part in all of this was on the signal side of what I was about to see, and, of course, there wasn't much to see. Hearing, however, was to be very different.

The descriptive adjective, great, flows a little too easily — but not where any thought of The Cleveland Orchestra is beheld. They knew their job. I knew mine. There was a read-through – then a take and a listen. There was neither time nor need for rehearsal. For any performance except rentals, the parts are always mine, every measure numbered like the score, the parts carefully edited [and corrected] to gain time and provide the performance I have studied to produce. The recording materials even arrive in my own folders. All the players have to do is open the folder and play what is called for.

Interlochen 1993 – FF receiving award.
Photo courtesy of ELF.

This produced, from the Severance Hall stage, what went to Jack Renner's microphones and on from there to him and to Dr. Tom Stockham's Soundstream digital recorder to produce the first symphonic digitally recorded LP. Renner and Woods displayed, from the beginning of all of this, a simple and positive no-nonsense idea of making records. They knew from the start how to tell their tale. Everybody who had anything to do with the production, the promotion, and distribution of this first digital LP was invited to the sessions to hear it as it went down.

After it was done, we all hit out for a near-by Italian restaurant. At the mop-up, everybody said their piece. When it came to me I could not miss the opportunity to say that — as the first magnetic recordings were made by the frontal-signal brass instruments [rather than Brahms' favorite violas]. So too, would be the arrival of the digital era by winds as great as any in the world!

We did a few more sessions for Telarc which are still in the catalogs, and since life and art are unpredictable, there is always the possibility of more.

It was year two of my separation from the University, having passed that magic year sixty-five, when I received a letter of invitation for a guest appearance with the Tokyo Kosei Windorchestra. Alfred Reed, who had just returned from their performance of his Symphony – The Lotus Sutra, urged me to accept.

The visit was memorable. Magnificent playing, hot spirit, incredible personal and ensemble discipline, warm and appreciative communication in the rehearsal where technique took the place of language. After the concert and recording, I returned home, not expecting ever to return to Japan.

Two months later I received a mounted photo taken at one concert, signed by the principal players, across the top of which in bold English was a phrase I was to learn as standard with many Japanese: SEE YOU AGAIN!

Before the Tokyo visit the early weeks of July 1981 were spent as guest conductor of the Vienna Festival of orchestras and choruses, and prior to my return to Tokyo as Principal Conductor, I spent the fall semester at Michigan State University. At its conclusion I began to re-organize my life to accept the invitation to become Principal Conductor, their first, of the Tokyo Kosei Windorchestra, arriving in Tokyo 14 January 1984.

In the middle of that first year the calendar identified me as at the age of seventy; the ensuing party began on 2 July at 2:00 PM and ended at 11:00. I'm still trying to bring the gifts home, ten years later.

The Tokyo Kosei Windorchestra is totally sponsored by the lay Buddhist Association, Rissho Kosei-Kai, organized for mutual exchange among people of the Buddhist faith for the perfecting of personality through the Lotus Sutra.

The Windorchestra is the re-organization [1960] of a previously sponsored large symphonic band.

Thirty-six players are contracted annually by the sponsor beyond which the management of the Orchestra is in the hands of the former members while the members operate the Orchestra's function in a totally democratic fashion, electing the Concertmasters and the ten members of the Performance Committee. They invited me to become their first Principal Conductor.

Elizabeth W. Ludwig, the President of Ludwig Music Publishing Co., Inc., and I had known each other since my last year in high school when, as a cellist, she was coming into the All-City Orchestra I was about to leave. We met occasionally at conferences and conventions of mutual interest. By the Spring of 1986, I had been a bachelor for five years and she a widow for about the same time. We were married in March 1986 and our first "love", a year later, was the full score edition of Percy Grainger's masterpiece, *Lincolnshire Posy*. Elizabeth has begun a series of editions, in my name, of masterworks for wind instruments. Our marriage and my continual commitment to the Tokyo Kosei Windorchestra, together with our interest in the Eastman School of Music of the University of Rochester, and to The Interlochen Center for the Arts — and Elizabeth's independent publishing company, add to a busy and productive alliance.

We enjoy each other very much and we're about the same age, of course, I'm about two years older than she and she takes wonderful care of me, I hasten to say. We are not together as much as both would like, but we meet in airports and we join up, we go places and we have a wonderful time together. So it was a wonderful idea for me to do and for her to do. I am very grateful for this opportunity, for this really very happy marriage with Elizabeth.

---

## ffennell ffoto gallery

Camp Frederick in Wickliffe, Ohio. A beautiful home in the suburbs of Cleveland where FF and ELF may relax or work. The home is surrounded by three and one-half acres of silent woods.

Severence Hall, Cleveland, Ohio – 1993
Photo by Roger Rickson

The peaceful woods surrounding Camp Frederick in
Wickliffe, Ohio – 1993
Photo by Roger Rickson

A favorite of FF, the Eagle announces the
entrance to Camp Frederick
Photo by Roger Rickson

Daughter Cathy with husband Lloyd Martensen.
1991 – courtesy of ELF.

Elizabeth and me taken August 11, 1991 in the Green Room at Kresge Auditorium
at Interlochen. Dedicated as the **Frederick Fennell Green Room**, a gift from
my wife, Elizabeth. I am wearing the Interlochen Medal of Honor exactly
sixty years after my first year at Interlochen
Photo courtesy of Kenneth Neidig

FF relaxing in Hawaii – June 1993
Photo courtesy ELF

ELF in Hawaii – June 1993
Photo courtesy ELF

ELF and FF in apartment in Japan
Photo courtesy ELF

FF and ELF at Interlochen – July 1993
Photo courtesy ELF

INTERLOCHEN
Alumni Organization presents the Third Annual
1993 Distinguished Alumnus Award to
Dr. Frederick Fennell
Photo courtesy ELF

Velencia, Spain. WASBE 1993
Pierre Kuijpers, Conductor, Royal Military Band of Holland; Col. John Bourgeois, Conductor, "The President's Own"; FF and William V. Johnson, Cal-Poly, San Luis Obispo
Photo courtesy ELF

Frederick Fennell with author Roger Rickson
Saddleback College – 1982
Photo courtesy Roger Rickson

FF concluding a rehearsal of ENCORES of the TOKWO 1985
Tour to Okinawa. "KIITE" - translation – "LISTEN"
Photo courtesy of Kosei Publishing Co.

FF working at desk in 'social room' of apartment 402.
Tayioso – Tokyo, 1986. Photo courtesy of Kosei Publishing Co.

FF in stocking feet sorting scores prior to TOKWO 1985 tour to Okinawa  Photo courtesy of Kosei Publishing Co.

Elizabeth and I had just visited the site and the beginnings of **Frederick Fennell Hall** in Kofu, Japan.  Tokio Kikushima [patron and builder] took us on a tour through some of the beautiful canyon country adjacent to Kofu.  We stopped for a bit of rest and something to drink, and here Kikushima and I share our first "Campai", a Japanese toast which means "empty the glass".
Photo courtesy of Tokio Kikushima

Ching ƒƒOOM – "That says it all".
Original drawing by FF presented to EWErs
and guests aboard his ketch.
Courtesy of FF

The Maestro in jet black 1954 MG – TF, in Siesta Key, Florida – 1991
"There's more to come"
Photo by Roger Rickson

# SECTION VII

# APPENDICES

Eastman Wind Ensemble Recording Dates

Eastman Wind Ensemble 45 RPM Singles and Reel-to-Reel Tapes

Frederick Fennell Mercury Records Recording Contracts

Complete Recording Dates of Frederick Fennell [1953-1993]

Where Are They Now?  EWE Personnel - 1952-1962

Study/Performance Essays and Articles by Frederick Fennell

Music Editions/Arrangements/Compositions by Frederick Fennell

# EASTMAN WIND ENSEMBLE RECORDING DATES
## Frederick Fennell, Conductor

| DATE | ALBUM TITLE/*INDIVIDUAL TITLES* | ALBUM NUMBER | |
|---|---|---|---|
| 14 May 1953 | **American Concert Band Masterpieces** | MG 40006/MG 50079 | |
| 21 November 1953 | **Marches by Sousa and Others** | MG 40007/MG 50080 | |
| 12 May 1954 | **La Fiesta Mexicana** | MG 40011/MG 50084 | |
|  | *Tamboo [Cavez]* | Single MG 70678 x 45 | |
| 10 May 1955 | **British Band Classics** | MG 40015/MG 50088/MG 50388/SR 90388 | |
| 20 January 1956 | **Marching Along** | MG 50105/SR 90105 | |
| 6 May 1956 | **Spirit of '76** | MG 50111/SR 90111 | |
| 6 May 1956 | **Ruffles and Flourishes** | MG 50112/SR 90112 | |
| 24 March 1957 | **Hindemith-Schoenberg-Stravinsky** | MG 50143/SR 90143 | |
|  | *Beguine for Band [Osser] Prom Night [Hermann]* | MG 50340/SR 90340 | |
| 19 October 1957 | **March Time** | MG 50170/SR 90170 | |
|  | *A Christmas Festival [Anderson]* | MG 50361/SR 90361 | |
|  | *The Beachcomber [Richardson]* | Only unreleased recording | |
| 2 March 1958 | **Winds in Hi-Fi** | MG 50173/SR 90173 | |
| 3 March 1958 | **Mozart Serenade No. 10, K. 361** | MG 50176/SR 90176 | |
| 21 November 1958 | **British Band Classics, Vol. 2** | MG 50197/SR 90197 | |
| 23 November 1958 | **Hands Across the Sea** | MG 50207/SR 90207 | |
| 3 May 1959 | **American Masterpieces for Concert Band** | MG 50220/SR 90220 | |
| 4 May 1959 | **Diverse Winds** | MG 50221/SR 90221 | |
| 23 October 1959 | **Wagner for Band** | MG 50276/SR 90276 | |
| 24 October 1959 | **Ballet for Band** | MG 50256/SR 90256 | |
| 2 May 1960 | **Sound Off!** | MG 50264/SR 90264 | |
| 13-16 December 1960 | **The Civil War, Volumes 1 & 2** | LPS 2-901/902 | |
| 5 May 1961 | **Sousa on Review** | MG 50284/SR 90284 | |
| 6 May 1961 | **Music of Andrea & Giovanni Gabrieli** | MG 50245/SR 90245 | Recorded at Christ Church, Rochester, New York |
| 6 May 1962 | **Screamers!** | MG 50314/SR 90314 | |

# EASTMAN WIND ENSEMBLE
# SINGLES and TAPE RELEASES
Frederick Fennell, Conductor
Mercury Records

| | |
|---|---|
| 70678X45 | Tamboo - Cavez, F.   Recorded 12 May 1954 - Eastman Theatre - Personnel #2<br>"El Toro" March and Aztec Dance from La Fiesta Mexicana - H. Owen Reed<br>Group listed as Eastman Wind Ensemble.  LP includes "Symphonic" in name. |
| 71238X45 | A Christmas Festival - Anderson.  Recorded 19 October 1957 - Eastman Theatre<br>Personnel list #6.  Sleigh Ride - Anderson, is listed as recorded by EWE.  Recorded by Eastman Rochester POPS Orchestra. |
| 72304X45 | I Ain't Down Yet - Willson; Seventy-Six Trombones - Willson.  Fennell Symphonic Winds.  From SR 90390 "Broadway Marches" |
| EP 1-3285 | Marches [45 EP]  Fairest of the Fair, Hands Across the Sea, Manhattan Beach, Sempre Fidelis.  Group listed as Eastman Symphonic Wind Ensemble |
| EP 1-3286 | Marches [45 EP]  Cheerio, His Honor, Our Director, Glory of the Gridiron<br>Group listed as Eastman Symphonic Wind Ensemble |
| EP 1-5062 | Tunbridge Fair - Walter Piston; George Washington Bridge - William Schuman |
| SR 90340 | Beguine for Band - Glenn Osser.  Recorded 24 March 1957, Hindemith session.<br>Prom Night - Ralph Hermann.  Recorded 24 March 1957, Hindemith session. |
| Un-released | The Beachcomber - Norman Richardson.  Recorded 19 October 1957 at conclusion of "March Time" session.  Only un-released recording. |

# REEL to REEL TAPES

| | |
|---|---|
| MWS5-14 | Marching Along.  List price: $6.95 |
| MS5-13 | Ruffles and Flourishes.  List price: $8.95 |
| MWS5-29 | March Time.  List price: $6.95 |
| ST 90176 | Mozart: Serenade No. in B-flat, K. 361.  List price:  $7.95 |

# FREDERICK FENNELL - MERCURY RECORDS RECORDING CONTRACTS

| RECORDING DATE | ALBUM TITLE | LABEL NUMBER | ENSEMBLE IDENTIFICATION | Album# | Contract # |
|---|---|---|---|---|---|
| 25 October 1956 | Music of Leroy Anderson, I | Mercury SR 90009 | Eastman-Rochester POPS Orchestra | #34 | #1 |
| 25 March 1957 | Hi-Fi Ala Espanola | Mercury SR 90144 | Eastman-Rochester POPS Orchestra | #35 | #2 |
| 3 March 1958 | Music of Leroy Anderson, II | Mercury SR 90043 | Eastman-Rochester POPS Orchestra | #33 | #3 |
| 4 May 1959 | Country Gardens & Other Favorites by Percy A. Grainger | Mercury SR 90219 | Eastman-Rochester POPS Orchestra | #36 | #4 |
| 5 May 1959 | POP Overs | Mercury SR 90222 | Eastman-Rochester POPS Orchestra | #37 | #5 |
| 30 April 1960 | Marches for Orchestra | Mercury SR 90271 | Eastman-Rochester POPS Orchestra | #38 | #6 |
| 26 September 1960 | Frederick Fennell Conducts George Gershwin | Mercury PPS 6006 | Frederick Fennell Orchestra | #48 | #7 |
| 4-5 October 1960 | Frederick Fennell Conducts Victor Herbert | Mercury PPS 6007 | Frederick Fennell Orchestra | #49 | #8 |
| 20-21 November 1961 | Frederick Fennell Conducts Cole Porter | Mercury PPS 6024 | Frederick Fennell Orchestra | #50 | #9 |
| 19 May 1964 | Broadway Marches | Mercury SR 90390 | Fennell Symphonic Winds | #30 | #10 |
| 9 July 1964 | Music of Leroy Anderson, III | Mercury SR 90400 | Fennell Orchestra | #44 | #11 |
| 19-20 July 1965 | Frederick Fennell Conducts the Music of Eric Coates | Mercury SR 90439 | London POPS Orchestra | #45 | #12 |
| 20-21 July 1965 | Frederick Fennell Conducts Carousel Waltz | Mercury SR 90440 | London POPS Orchestra | #46 | #13 |

# COMPLETE RECORDING DATES

| RECORDING DATE | ALBUM TITLE | ALBUM NUMBER |
|---|---|---|
| May 14, 1953 | American Concert Band Masterpieces | 1 |
| November 21, 1953 | Marches | 2 |
| May 12, 1954 | La Fiesta Mexicana | 3 |
| May 10, 1955 | British Band Classics | 4 |
| May 10, 1955 | British Band Classics | 5 |
| January 20, 1956 | Marching Along | 6 |
| May 6, 1956 | The Spirit of '76 | 7 |
| May 6, 1956 | Ruffles and Flourishes | 8 |
| October 25, 1956 | Music of Leroy Anderson, Vol. 1 | 33 |
| March 24, 1957 | Hindemith - Schoenberg - Stravinsky | 10 |
| March 25, 1957 | Hi-Fi Ala Espanola | 35 |
| October 19, 1957 | March Time | 11 |
| March 2, 1958 | Winds in Hi-Fi | 12 |
| March 3, 1958 | Mozart Serenade No. 10 in B-flat, K. 361 | 13 |
| March 3, 1958 | Music of Leroy Anderson, Vol. II | 34 |
| November 21, 1958 | British Band Classics, Vol. II | 14 |
| November 23, 1958 | Hands Across The Sea | 15 |
| May 3, 1959 | American Masterpieces for Concert Band | 16 |
| May 3, 1959 | Gould - West Point Symphony | 166 |
| May 4, 1959 | Diverse Winds | 17 |
| May 4, 1959 | Country Gardens & Other Favorites by Percy A. Grainger | 36 |
| May 5, 1959 | POP Overs | 37 |
| October 23, 1959 | Wagner for Band | 21 |
| October 23, 1959 | Ballet for Band - Wagner | 167 |
| October 24, 1959 | Ballet for Band | 19 |
| April 30, 1960 | Marches For Orchestra | 38 |
| May 2, 1960 | Sound Off! | 20 |
| September 26, 1960 | Frederick Fennell Conducts George Gershwin | 48 |
| October 4, 1960 | Frederick Fennell Conducts Victor Herbert | 49 |
| December 13, 1960 | The Civil War - Its Music and Its Sounds, Volume 1 | 31 |
| December 15, 1960 | The Civil War - Its Music and Its Sounds, Volume 2 | 32 |
| May 5, 1961 | Sousa on Review | 22 |
| May 6, 1961 | Music of Andrea and Giovanni Gabrieli | 18 |
| November 20, 1961 | Frederick Fennell Conducts Cole Porter | 50 |
| May 6, 1962 | Screamers! - A Collection of Exciting Marches from the Circus Ring | 24 |
| May 19, 1964 | Broadway Marches | 30 |
| July 9, 1964 | Music of Leroy Anderson, Volume III | 44 |
| July 19, 1965 | Frederick Fennell Conducts Music by Eric Coates | 45 |
| July 20, 1965 | Frederick Fennell Conducts Carousel Waltz | 46 |
| June 3, 1967 | Promo Recording No. 1 | 96 |
| May 12, 1970 | Promo Recording No. 3 | 97a |
| September 27, 1974 | Our Musical Past - A Concert for Brass Band, Voice and Piano | 52 |
| March 9, 1977 | CBDNA 19th National Conference | 84 |
| August 30, 1977 | American Brass Band Journal - Revisited | 51 |
| April 4, 1978 | The Cleveland Symphonic Winds | 53 |

| Date | Title | # |
|---|---|---|
| December 3, 1978 | Macho Marches | 54 |
| September 26, 1979 | Doc Severinsen Plays Modern Trumpet Concertos | 71 |
| November 18, 1979 | The Cleveland Symphonic Winds | 55 |
| May 24, 1980 | The Compositions of Alec Wilder | 56 |
| March 23, 1982 | Frederick Fennell Conducts the Tokyo Kosei Wind Orchestra | 72 |
| February 22, 1984 | Contest Band Music Selections 1984 | 78 |
| February 28, 1984 | Band Series 1984 - I | 79 |
| February 29, 1984 | Band Series 1984 - II | 80 |
| March 24, 1984 | Fanfare and Allegro | 73 |
| May 1, 1984 | Our Musical Past - Volume 2 | 52a |
| September 28, 1984 | American March Forever | 77 |
| September 28, 1984 | The Best European Marches | 81 |
| October 31, 1984 | La Fiesta Mexicana | 170 |
| December 19, 1984 | Belle of the Ball | 74 |
| December 20, 1984 | Serenata | 75 |
| March 19, 1985 | La Fiesta Mexicana | 76 |
| September 25, 1985 | Toccata and Fugue | 128 |
| November 21, 1985 | The 21st Regular Concert | 171 |
| April 3, 1986 | An American in Paris | 129 |
| April 23, 1986 | Hands Across the Sea | 130 |
| October 15, 1986 | Music for Contest | 172 |
| October 18, 1986 | Music for Contest II | 173 |
| October 22, 1986 | Lincolnshire Posy | 131 |
| November 28, 1986 | Romeo and Juliet | 135 |
| March 24, 1987 | Symphonic Songs for Band | 132 |
| November 25, 1987 | English Folk Songs | 133 |
| February 29, 1988 | Concert Marches for Glory and Tragedy - Classical Music Gallery | 174 |
| December 6, 1988 | Bacchus on Blue Ridge | 137 |
| December 8, 1988 | Seagate Overture | 175 |
| December 8, 1988 | Symphonic Movement | 176 |
| July 13, 1989 | Suite Francaise | 134 |
| October 23, 1989 | The Firebird and Pictures at an Exhibition | 138 |
| December 10, 1989 | Premiere Rhapsodie | 136 |
| April 12, 1990 | Peer Gynt | 139 |
| October 30, 1990 | Mozart - Serenade No. 10 - Serenade No. 12 | 140 |
| January 8, 1991 | Fennell Favorites ! | 177 |
| April 11, 1991 | Hungarian Rhapsody | 141 |
| October 24, 1991 | Piece of Mind - The Contemporary Mix | 142 |
| April 22, 1992 | The Roman Trilogy - Pines, Fountains, Festivals | 143 |
| June 17, 1992 | Trittico | 178 |
| June 17, 1992 | Reference Recordings HDCD Sampler | 179 |
| July 17, 1992 | Introduction | 145 |
| November 4, 1992 | Celebration - Contemporary Mix 2 | 144 |
| April 21, 1993 | Symphonies | 146 |
| May 7, 1993 | Music from Dragon Quest | 147 |
| July 26, 1993 | Dallas Wind Symphony and Organ – Pomp & Pipes | 180 |

# THE EASTMAN WIND ENSEMBLE 1952-1962 - WHERE ARE THEY NOW?
## Alphabetical Order

| INSTRUMENT | NAME | WHERE ARE THEY? |
|---|---|---|
| | | * Known to be deceased |
| Clarinet | Armand Abramson | Professor, Eastern Michigan University, Ypsilanti, MI |
| Oboe | James Alexander | Piano technician, Tulsa, OK |
| Horn | Bette Allison | Instrumental teacher, Montgomery County, MD |
| Trumpet | Manuel Alvarez | Director, University of South Carolina, School of Medicine, Columbia, SC |
| Trombone | Early Anderson | Metropolitan Opera Orchestra, NY |
| Clarinet Contrabass | William Anderson | Associate Dean of Graduate School, Kent State University, OH |
| String Bass | Lawrence Angell | Principal, Cleveland Orchestra |
| Clarinet | Richard Atkins | Humanities Division, Elmira College, Poughkeepsie, NY |
| Trumpet | James Austin | Retired principal, Houston Symphony Orchestra. Associate Professor, University of Houston, TX |
| Clarinet Contrabass | James Badalato | Professor of Theory, Montgomery College, Rockville, MD |
| Trumpet | Rodger Baker | Associate Professor/Program Chair, Rochester Institute of Technology, NY |
| Horn | Gay Banks | Mrs. David Helfrich |
| Harp | Robert Barlow * | |
| Percussion | Ronald Barnett | Associate Professor, University of Maryland, College Park, MD |
| Horn | James Basta | Director of Music, Home Moravian Church, Winston-Salem, NC |
| Clarinet | Charles Bay | Manufacturer of custom clarinet mouthpieces. Formerly with Los Angeles Philharmonic |
| Bassoon | David Beadle | Professor of Bassoon and Music Literature, University of Wisconsin, Stevens Point, WI |
| Percussion | John Beck | U.S. Marine Band; Professor Eastman School of Music; Rochester Philharmonic, timpanist. Rochester, NY |
| Trumpet | Glen Bell | Music Educator, freelance player, Dallas, TX |
| Saxophone | Frank Bencriscutto | Composer, Conductor University of Minnesota Bands, Minneapolis, MN. Retired. |
| Horn | Barry Benjamin | Professor, University of Wisconsin, Milwaukee; adjunct faculty, Northwestern; former member of New York Brass Quintet |
| Horn | Jeff [Carl] Bianchi | Conductor/Music Educator, Fairfax County Schools, Fairfax, VA |

| INSTRUMENT | NAME | WHERE ARE THEY? |
|---|---|---|
| Tuba | Ronald Bishop | Buffalo Philharmonic, San Francisco Symphony, Cleveland Orchestra |
| Horn | Barbara Bloomer | Toronto Symphony |
| Tuba | Roger Bobo | Retired principal - Los Angeles Philharmonic; soloist, conductor |
| Euphonium | Guy Bockman | Retired professor, Tennessee State University, Nashville, TN |
| Flute | Ann Marie Boldt Miller | Teacher, Metaire County Day School |
| Horn | William Bommelje | Associate Professor, University of Tennessee, Knoxville, TN |
| Horn | Aubrey Bouck | Crawford, TX |
| Saxophone | Fred Brenner | |
| Bassoon | John Bridges | Standard Oil of Ohio, Fairport, NY |
| Euphonium | Kenton Briggs | Music Coordinator/Teacher, Homer Central Schools, Homer, NY |
| Oboe | Vivian Brooks Goldstein | Bureau of Indian Affairs, Prewitt, NM |
| Trumpet | William Brower | |
| Bassoon | Alan Brown | Minillas Station, San Juan, Puerto Rico |
| Tuba | Paul Brown | Retired Department Chair, Caledonia-Mumford Central Schools, NY |
| Saxophone | Philip Browne | Conductor and composer; Cal-Poly, Pomona, CA |
| Flute | Elizabeth Bruner Castelvecchi | Private flute instructor, Columbia, CT |
| Flute | Keith Bryan | Professor, University of Michigan, Ann Arbor, MI; Recitalist |
| Clarinet Alto Clarinet | Marshall Burlinghame | Principal librarian, The Boston Symphony Orchestra |
| Percussion | Jane Burnet Varella | Personnel Manager, Principal Percussion, Dayton Philharmonic, Dayton, OH |
| Tuba | Bruce Butler | Dentist, New Orleans, LA |
| Euphonium | Larry Campbell | Professor, Louisiana State University, Baton Rouge, LA |
| Harp | Lauralee Campbell | Michigan State University, Lansing Symphony, Travel agent |
| Bassoon | Richard Campbell | Partner, Williamsport Candy Co., Williamsport, PA |
| Flute | Gerald Carey | Western Illinois State University, Macomb, IL |

| INSTRUMENT | NAME | WHERE ARE THEY? |
|---|---|---|
| Saxophone | Jack Carey | |
| Clarinet | Joseph Carlucci | Retired Conductor Emeritus, Beaumont Symphony Orchestra, Beaumont, TX |
| Horn | Clyde Carpenter | Retired teacher |
| Trumpet | George Cavanagh | Band Director, Department of Music, Purdue University, Fort Wayne, IN |
| Clarinet<br>Alto Clarinet | Paul Cherry | Professor of Music, University of South Dakota, Vermillion, SD |
| Clarinet | Michael Cheskiewicz* | |
| Trombone | Jonathan Clark* | |
| Clarinet | Louis Coccagnia | Teacher, Elmira Free Academy, Elmira, NY |
| Percussion | Frank Cocuzzi | |
| Clarinet<br>Saxophone | Robert Coleman | Saint Louis Symphony Orchestra |
| Saxophone | Donald Coley | Teacher, Brighton Central Schools, Brighton, NY |
| Clarinet | Muriel Colvin | Mrs. Thomas Hohstadt |
| Clarinet | Larry Combs | Principal, Chicago Symphony |
| Horn | Waldo Comfort | Mechanics Auto Parts, Rochester, NY |
| Bassoon<br>Contra Clarinet | Gerald Corey | |
| Saxophone | Ned Corman | Instrumental music director/music entrepreneur, Penfield, NY |
| String Bass | Neil Courtney | Philadelphia Orchestra |
| Horn | John Covert | Faculty, Ithaca College, Ithaca, NY |
| Trombone | Tony DeChario | Retired manager, Rochester Philharmonic; Manager, Honolulu Symphony, Honolulu, HI |
| Saxophone | Rudolph Defelice | Administrator, C.B. Hoober & Son, Intercourse, PA |
| Bassoon<br>Contra | Bruce Degen | Head, Division of Visual/Performing Arts, Simpson College, Indianola, IA |
| Oboe<br>English Horn | Florence Denault Meyers | Buffalo Philharmonic |
| Flute | Joanne Dickinson | Mrs. Peter Tanner; Associate Professor, University of Massachusetts, Amherst, MA |
| Percussion | James Dotson * | |

| INSTRUMENT | NAME | WHERE ARE THEY? |
|---|---|---|
| Saxophone | Robert Dransite | Teacher, Carle Place High School, NY |
| Oboe | Catherine Dufford Paulu* | |
| Oboe<br>English Horn | Blaine Edlefsen | Utah Philharmonic |
| Flute | Barbara Eklund Peterson | Principal, Cleveland Chamber Symphony, Cleveland, OH |
| Clarinet | Charles Ellis-MacLeod | School music director. Ballet conductor |
| Horn | Robert Elworthy * | |
| Percussion | Vivian Emery | Teacher, Boyertown Area School District, PA |
| Harp | Rachel Ewing Corrigan | Harp instructor, Butler University, Indianapolis, IN |
| Trombone | David Fetter | Baltimore Symphony |
| Percussion | Norman Fickett | Detroit Symphony |
| Trombone | Reginald Fink | Professor, Ohio University; Music publisher |
| Clarinet | Joseph Fisher | Retired |
| Oboe | Sandra Flesher | Faculty, University of Oklahoma |
| Percussion | Theodore Frazeur | Professor, State University of New York, Fredonia, NY |
| Clarinet<br>Bass Clarinet | Paul Freeman | Conductor, Chicago Sinfonietta. Extensive recordings catalog |
| Trumpet | Samuel Fricano | Retired conductor U.S. Army Field Band. Conductor, River City Brass, Jacksonville, FL |
| Percussion | John Galm | University of Colorado |
| Clarinet | Robert Gauldin | Eastman School of Music, Chair, Theory, Rochester, NY |
| Alto Clarinet | William Gaver | President, Defem Design-Build, Inc., Brookfield, NH |
| Flute | Donna Geis* | |
| Bassoon<br>Contra | Gerald Gibson | U.S. Government employee, Library of Congress |
| Flute | David Gilbert | Conductor, Greenwich Symphony, Greenwich, CT |
| Percussion | Donald Gilbert | |
| Trombone | Robert Gillespie | Principal, Johannesburg Opera and Symphony, South Africa |

| INSTRUMENT | NAME | WHERE ARE THEY? |
|---|---|---|
| Clarinet Saxophone | Samuel Glenn | Quality Control, Sun Litho, Van Nuys, CA |
| Oboe | Alice Gordon | Teacher, Amarillo Independent Schools, Amarillo, TX |
| Euphonium | Robert Gray | Professor of trombone, University of Illinois; Conductor of University of Illinois Wind Ensemble, Urbana, IL |
| Trumpet | David Greenhoe | Bowling Green State University, OH |
| Bassoon | Theodore Grimes | Teacher, Jacksonville, FL |
| Oboe | Earl Groth * | |
| Flute | Shelly Gruskin | Artist in Residence, College of St. Scholastica, Duluth, MN |
| Clarinet | Peter Hadcock | Buffalo Philharmonic, Boston Symphony. Professor of Clarinet, Eastman School of Music, Rochester, NY |
| Trumpet | John Hall | |
| Bassoon | Richard Hall | Houston Symphony, retired |
| Trombone | Frederick Halt | Buffalo Philharmonic, NY |
| Flute | Michael Hamilton | M.D., Director, Duke University, Diet and Fitness Center, Durham, NC |
| Euphonium | Byron Hanson | Conductor, Interlochen Arts Academy Orchestra, MI |
| Oboe | William Harrod | Cincinnati Symphony |
| Clarinet | William Hartman | |
| Horn | JoAnn Haynes | |
| Horn | David Helfrich | Instructor, Psychology; Pasco Hernando Community College, New Port Richey, FL |
| Saxophone | Fred Hemke | Solo artist. Professor, Northwestern University, Evanston, IL |
| Saxophone | Sydney Hodkinson | Composer, Conductor Musica-NOVA, Eastman School of Music, Rochester, NY |
| Trumpet | Thomas Hohstadt | Conductor, Midland/Odessa Orchestra, TX Retired; author |
| Trumpet | Boyde Hood | Los Angeles Philharmonic |
| Bassoon Contra | Robert Horick | |
| Trombone Euphonium | Donald Hunsberger | Composer/Arranger, Author, Conductor, Eastman Wind Ensemble, Rochester, NY |
| Euphonium | Kenley Inglefield | Professor, Bowling Green State University, Bowling Green, OH |

| INSTRUMENT | NAME | WHERE ARE THEY? |
|---|---|---|
| Saxophone | Frank Jacobsen | |
| Trumpet | David Johnson | Retired, U.S. Marine Band |
| Clarinet | Daniel Johnston | Buffalo Philharmonic, Buffalo, NY |
| Clarinet | Darrell Johnston | Conductor, San Jose City College, CA |
| Clarinet | George Jones | Rutgers University, retired professor, NJ |
| Trumpet | Richard Jones | Principal, Buffalo Philharmonic |
| Percussion | Dennis Kain | Baltimore Symphony, Kettledrums, Baltimore, MD |
| Bassoon | Robert Kalman | Retired, U.S. Marine Band |
| Tuba | William Kearney | Teacher, Amherst Schools, Buffalo, NY |
| Trombone | Stephen Kelleher | |
| Clarinet | Barbara Kessler Goodman | Psychotherapist, Palo Alto, CA |
| Piano | Gary Kirkpatrick | Verdehr Trio |
| Trombone | Peter Kline | Assistant Professor of Music, San Antonio College, TX |
| Clarinet Bass Clarinet | Daniel Kohut | Professor of Music Education, University of Illinois, Urbana, IL |
| Bassoon | Phillip Kolker | Baltimore Orchestra |
| Horn | Eleanor Konzer Lindboe | Private teacher, Malibu, CA |
| Trumpet | Joel Koplin | Investments counselor, Philadelphia, PA |
| Euphonium | Rodger Kramer | Retired teacher of Brass, Birmingham School District, MI |
| Horn | John Krance * | |
| Harp | Lois Kreig | |
| Clarinet | Charles Krusenstjerna | Admissions/Alumni Office, Eastman School of Music, Rochester, NY |
| Oboe | Keith Kummer | Finksburg, MD |
| Organ | Anne Labounsky | Professor of Organ, Duquesne University, PA |
| Horn | Carol Ladrach | Mrs. Robert C. Zajkowski; home maker, Volunteer, Pittsford, NY |

| INSTRUMENT | NAME | WHERE ARE THEY? |
|---|---|---|
| Trumpet | John Landis | Conductor, radio music commentator, WNED-FM, Buffalo, NY. |
| Clarinet | Mary Jane Lang | |
| Clarinet | Rolf Legbandt | Professor of Clarinet, Ball State University, Muncie, IN |
| Percussion | Stanley Leonard | Pittsburgh Symphony Orchestra, Kettledrums |
| Clarinet<br>Alto Clarinet | Jonathan Levine | Midwest Regional Director, American Jewish Committee, Evanston, IL |
| Flute | Susan Levitin | Chicago Ensemble; Sherwood Conservatory of Music, Chicago, IL |
| Harp | Lanalee Litz | |
| Trumpet | William Lockwood | Worldwide Distributor; <u>Teach Yourself Chord Piano</u>, Endicott, NY |
| Clarinet<br>Bass Clarinet | Ralph Long | President, Longs of Newport, Newport Beach, CA |
| Clarinet | Ralph Loomis | Retired principal - U.S. Coast Guard Band. Pacific Gas & Electric Co., Vacaville, CA |
| Saxophone | Larry Loven | |
| Clarinet | Elsa Ludewig Verdehr | Richards Quintet; her own trio; Professor, Michigan State University, East Lansing, MI |
| Trumpet | Albert MacKinnon | New Zealand National Symphony, Wellingham, N.Z. |
| Flute | Donna Maclean Klump | Sacramento, CA |
| Clarinet<br>Alto Clarinet | Philip Macone | |
| Clarinet | Robert Mader | Reverend/Pastor, Bethlehem Lutheran Church, Johnson City, TN |
| Clarinet | James Mandros | Foreign Service Officer, USIA, Washington, DC |
| String Bass | Marie Mann | Mrs. Thomas Stacy |
| Clarinet | George Marge * | |
| Trombone | Perry Martin | Director of Music, Mamaroneck Schools; Conductor, Larchmont Pops Band, NY |
| Percussion | Anthony Matarrese | Woodbridge, VA |
| Clarinet | John Mauro | Instrumental Instructor, Montgomery County Schools, MD |
| Clarinet<br>Contrabass | Lawrence Maxey | Michigan State University, East Lansing, MI |
| Horn | Zora McCann | |

| INSTRUMENT | NAME | WHERE ARE THEY? |
|---|---|---|
| Tuba | Joseph McEnulty | |
| Percussion | Thomas McMillan | Fine Arts Coordinator, Trenton, MI Schools |
| Euphonium | Harold McNeil | Houghton College, School of Music, NY |
| Trombone | Donald Miller | Buffalo Philharmonic |
| Euphonium | Thomas Miller | Regional Representative; African-American Labor Center, Washington, DC |
| Horn | Janet Miller Sheldon | Real Estate Broker, VA |
| Clarinet | Henry Miyamura | Music Director, Hawaii Youth/University of Hawaii, Honolulu, HI |
| Trumpet | Ralph Montgomery | Chairman, Greenville College Music Department, Greenville, IL |
| Saxophone | Kenneth Murley | Retired Professor, Toccoa Falls College, GA |
| Trombone | Robert Norden | New York, NY |
| Horn | Richard Norem | Louisiana State University, Baton Rouge, LA |
| Trombone | George Osborne | Rochester Philharmonic |
| Saxophone | Donald Panhorst | Edinboro University, PA, Retired |
| Oboe | Jonathan Parkes | Rochester Philharmonic |
| Trumpet | Daniel Patrylak | Former assistant to the Director, Eastman School of Music; Dean, University of Connecticut/Music |
| Tuba | Daniel Perantoni | Professor, Arizona State University. Solo artist, Tempe, AZ |
| Clarinet | Roland Persson | English teacher, Pinole Valley High School, Pinole, CA |
| Percussion | Gordon Peters | Chicago Symphony; former conductor of Chicago Civic Orchestra |
| Percussion | Mitchell Peters | Los Angeles Philharmonic, Kettledrums |
| Clarinet Saxophone | Thomas Peterson | Cleveland Orchestra |
| Trombone | Peter Phillips | Freelance musician, Delaware Water Gap, PA |
| Bassoon | Ronald Phillips | Cleveland Orchestra |
| Clarinet | Theodore Pizzarello | |
| Trombone | Porter Poindexter | Freelance musician, New York, NY |

| INSTRUMENT | NAME | WHERE ARE THEY? |
|---|---|---|
| Percussion | James Preiss | Manhattan School of Music, NY |
| Trombone | Ray Premru | Retired, Philip Jones Brass Ensemble ; Philharmonia/England. Professor Oberlin College Conservatory; Composer |
| Clarinet | Donald Puluse | Berkeley College, Marblehead, MA |
| Horn | Jack Reed | Associate Dean, Oklahoma City University, OK |
| Bassoon | Vernon Reed | Conductor, California State University, San Jose, CA |
| Saxophone | Albert Regni | New York Philharmonic |
| Trombone | David Richey | Rochester Philharmonic |
| Trumpet | Barbara Ricksecker | Mrs. Barbara Martinson; retired librarian and music teacher |
| Oboe English Horn | Bernard Rubenstein | Conductor, Tulsa Philharmonic, OK |
| String Bass | Armand Russell | Composer in Residence, University of Hawaii, Honolulu, HI |
| Clarinet Bass Clarinet | Daniel Sandidge | Arranger, conductor; White Sulphur Springs, WV |
| Trumpet | Erwin Sapiro | Williamsburg, VA |
| Trumpet | Maurice Sapiro | Music teacher, North Haven Public Schools, New Haven, CT |
| Oboe | Sharon Sauser Kane | Musician/designer |
| Tuba | Charles Schaffer* | |
| Trumpet | Richard Schaffer | Houston Symphony, TX |
| Clarinet | Joseph Scharbo | Retired music educator; Bellmore Merrick Schools, NY |
| Trumpet | Donald Schmaus | Music supervisor, Lake Brantley, FL |
| Horn | Kenneth Schultz | Saint Louis Symphony |
| Horn | Norman Schweikert | Chicago Symphony |
| Clarinet | Robert Seath | |
| Horn | Stephen Seiffert | Systems Analyst; QL Systems, Ltd. Kingston, Ontario, Canada |
| Flute | Gretel Shanley | Freelance player; Trainer: Suzuki Association of the Americas; Bed & Breakfast owner, Tidioute, PA; Worker for Peace. |
| Horn | Robert Sheldon | Curator, Dayton C. Miller Flute and Instrument Collections, Library of Congress |

| INSTRUMENT | NAME | WHERE ARE THEY? |
|---|---|---|
| Trumpet | Roger Sherman | Pittsburgh Symphony |
| Trombone | George Shroyer | Studio musician, Hollywood, CA |
| Trumpet | Paul Shull | Retired, Manhattan, KS |
| Clarinet Contrabass | Frank Sidorfsky | Kansas State University, Manhattan, KS |
| Saxophone | Robert Silberstein | JFK Center for Performing Arts, Washington, DC |
| Clarinet Alto Clarinet | Thomas Slattery | Retired conductor, Coe College; private businessman |
| Trombone | Lester Slezak | Minister Counselor, Department of State, Washington, DC |
| Trumpet | Gary Smith | Saint Louis Symphony |
| Clarinet | Jerry Neal Smith | Professor of Music, University of Oklahoma, Norman, OK |
| Clarinet Alto Clarinet | Michael Smith | |
| Clarinet | Daniel Sparks | |
| Horn | Herbert Spencer | Professor, Bowling Green State University, OH |
| Clarinet | Mary Anne Spencer | |
| Piano | Robert Spillman | Professor of Piano, University of Colorado, Boulder, CO |
| Oboe English Horn | Thomas Stacy | New York Philharmonic |
| Clarinet | Jerry Steinhagen | Milwaukee, WI |
| Clarinet Saxophone | Noel Stevens | Retired, Tampa, FL |
| Oboe | Daniel Stolper | Michigan State University, Lansing Symphony, Richards Quintet, Interlochen Arts Center |
| Flute | Philip Swanson | Former Dean of Music, University of Redlands, CA |
| Horn | Esther Sweigart Rosenthal | President, Point Roberts Industries, Los Angeles, CA |
| Kettledrums | Peter Tanner | Professor of Music, University of Massachusetts, Amherst, MA |
| Saxophone | Eugene Tettamanti | House musician, Riviera Hotel, Las Vegas, NV |
| Clarinet Bass Clarinet | Leslie Thimmig | University of Wisconsin, Madison, WI |
| Percussion | Joel Thome | Conductor, Orchestra of Our Time, New York, NY |

| INSTRUMENT | NAME | WHERE ARE THEY? |
|---|---|---|
| Trumpet | John Thyhsen | Professor, Glassboro State College, Glassboro, NJ |
| Trumpet | Stephen Toback | Music teacher, New Rochelle Board of Education, New Rochelle, NY |
| Clarinet<br>Bass Clarinet | Paul Tomasick* | |
| Organ | Andrea Toth | Mrs. Andrea C. Haines. Jaeger & Haines, Inc., Fayetteville, AR |
| Flute | Joanna Tousey | Tuscon Symphony; Flutist with Go for Baroque |
| Clarinet | Dorothy Trojan Tomasick* | |
| Oboe<br>English Horn | Joe Turner | Baltimore Symphony |
| String Bass | Elizabeth Twaddell Ferrell | Baltimore Symphony |
| Piano | Clair W. Van Ausdall | Editor-in-Chief; Chamber Music America, NY |
| Horn | Linda VanSickle Smith | Staff Therapist; Pastoral Counseling Center, Dallas, TX |
| Clarinet | Winston Vitous | |
| Saxophone | David Ward | Composer; U.S. Naval Academy Band, Annapolis, MD |
| Clarinet | Richard Webster | Professor of Music, University of Toledo, OH. Retired |
| Clarinet | Mitchell Weiss | New York studio player |
| Saxophone | Gerald Welker | Conductor, University of Alabama Bands, Tuscaloosa, AL |
| Percussion | Kenneth Wendrich | Executive Director, W.O. Smith, Nashville Community Music, TN |
| Bassoon | Glen Williams | Coordinator, Graduate Music Studies, Brigham Young University, Provo, UT |
| Clarinet<br>Contrabass | Lawrence Williams | Bellingham Public Schools, Bellingham, WA |
| Oboe | Dean Wilson | |
| Flute | Doris Wilson Sellards | Principal, Kansas City Symphony, MO |
| Harp | Marjorie Winey | Albany Symphony, NY |
| Clarinet | William Wohlmacher | Professor of Music, California State University, Hayward, CA |
| Percussion | John Wyre | Founding member of NEXUS |
| Tuba | Donald Zale * | |

| INSTRUMENT | NAME | WHERE ARE THEY? |
|---|---|---|
| Tuba | Robert Zale | Director of Music, Gates-Chili Central Schools, NY |
| Oboe | Martha Zepp Salzman | Internist in Early Music, Butler University, Indianapolis, IN |
| String Bass | Robert Zimmerman | Principal, Rochester Philharmonic |
| Clarinet | Eugene Zoro | Professor, Western Washington State University, Bellingham, WA |

# THE EASTMAN WIND ENSEMBLE 1952-1962 - WHERE ARE THEY NOW?
## Score Order

| INSTRUMENT | NAME | WHERE ARE THEY? |
|---|---|---|
| Flute | Ann Marie Boldt Miller | Teacher, Metaire County Day School |
| Flute | Elizabeth Bruner Castelvecchi | Private flute instructor, Columbia, CT |
| Flute | Keith Bryan | Professor, University of Michigan, Ann Arbor, MI; Recitalist |
| Flute | Gerald Carey | Western Illinois State University, Macomb, IL |
| Flute | Joanne Dickinson | Mrs. Peter Tanner; Associate Professor, University of Massachusetts, Amherst, MA |
| Flute | Barbara Eklund Peterson | Principal, Cleveland Chamber Symphony, Cleveland, OH |
| Flute | Donna Geis* | |
| Flute | David Gilbert | Conductor, Greenwich Symphony, Greenwich, CT |
| Flute | Shelly Gruskin | Artist in Residence, College of St. Scholastica, Duluth, MN |
| Flute | Michael Hamilton | M.D., Director, Duke University, Diet and Fitness Center, Durham, NC |
| Flute | Susan Levitin | Chicago Ensemble; Sherwood Conservatory of Music, Chicago, IL |
| Flute | Donna Maclean Klump | Sacramento, CA |
| Flute | Gretel Shanley | Freelance player; Trainer: Suzuki Association of the Americas; Bed & Breakfast owner, Tidioute, PA; Worker for Peace. |
| Flute | Philip Swanson | Former Dean of Music, University of Redlands, CA |
| Flute | Joanna Tousey | Tuscon Symphony; Flutist with Go for Baroque |
| Flute | Doris Wilson Sellards | Principal, Kansas City Symphony, MO |
| Oboe | James Alexander | Piano technician, Tulsa, OK |
| Oboe | Vivian Brooks Goldstein | Bureau of Indian Affairs, Prewitt, NM |
| Oboe English Horn | Florence Denault Meyers | Buffalo Philharmonic |
| Oboe | Catherine Dufford Paulu* | |
| Oboe English Horn | Blaine Edlefsen | Utah Philharmonic |
| Oboe | Sandra Flesher | Faculty, University of Oklahoma |
| Oboe | Alice Gordon | Teacher, Amarillo Independent Schools, Amarillo, TX |

| INSTRUMENT | NAME | WHERE ARE THEY? |
|---|---|---|
| Oboe | Earl Groth * | |
| Oboe | William Harrod | Cincinnati Symphony |
| Oboe | Keith Kummer | Finksburg, MD |
| Oboe | Jonathan Parkes | Rochester Philharmonic |
| Oboe<br>English Horn | Bernard Rubenstein | Conductor, Tulsa Philharmonic, OK |
| Oboe | Sharon Sauser Kane | Musician/designer |
| Oboe<br>English Horn | Thomas Stacy | New York Philharmonic |
| Oboe | Daniel Stolper | Michigan State University, Lansing Symphony, Richards Quintet, Interlochen Arts Center |
| Oboe<br>English Horn | Joe Turner | Baltimore Symphony |
| Oboe | Dean Wilson | |
| Oboe | Martha Zepp Salzman | Internist in Early Music, Butler University, Indianapolis, IN |
| Bassoon | David Beadle | Professor of Bassoon and Music Literature, University of Wisconsin, Stevens Point, WI |
| Bassoon | John Bridges | Standard Oil of Ohio, Fairport, NY |
| Bassoon | Alan Brown | Minillas Station, San Juan, Puerto Rico |
| Bassoon | Richard Campbell | Partner, Williamsport Candy Co., Williamsport, PA |
| Bassoon<br>Contra Clarinet | Gerald Corey | |
| Bassoon<br>Contra | Bruce Degen | Head, Division of Visual/Performing Arts, Simpson College, Indianola, IA |
| Bassoon<br>Contra | Gerald Gibson | U.S. Government employee, Library of Congress |
| Bassoon | Theodore Grimes | Teacher, Jacksonville, FL |
| Bassoon | Richard Hall | Houston Symphony, retired |
| Bassoon<br>Contra | Robert Horick | |
| Bassoon | Robert Kalman | Retired, U.S. Marine Band |
| Bassoon | Phillip Kolker | Baltimore Orchestra |
| Bassoon | Ronald Phillips | Cleveland Orchestra |

| INSTRUMENT | NAME | WHERE ARE THEY? |
|---|---|---|
| Bassoon | Vernon Reed | Conductor, California State University, San Jose, CA |
| Bassoon | Glen Williams | Coordinator, Graduate Music Studies, Brigham Young University, Provo, UT |
| Clarinet | Armand Abramson | Professor, Eastern Michigan University, Ypsilanti, MI |
| Clarinet Contrabass | William Anderson | Associate Dean of Graduate School, Kent State University, OH |
| Clarinet | Richard Atkins | Humanities Division, Elmira College, Poughkeepsie, NY |
| Clarinet Contrabass | James Badalato | Professor of Theory, Montgomery College, Rockville, MD |
| Clarinet | Charles Bay | Manufacturer of custom clarinet mouthpieces. Formerly with Los Angeles Philharmonic |
| Clarinet Alto Clarinet | Marshall Burlinghame | Principal librarian, The Boston Symphony Orchestra |
| Clarinet | Joseph Carlucci | Retired Conductor Emeritus, Beaumont Symphony Orchestra, Beaumont, TX |
| Clarinet Alto Clarinet | Paul Cherry | Professor of Music, University of South Dakota, Vermillion, SD |
| Clarinet | Michael Cheskiewicz* | |
| Clarinet | Louis Coccagnia | Teacher, Elmira Free Academy, Elmira, NY |
| Clarinet Saxophone | Robert Coleman | Saint Louis Symphony Orchestra |
| Clarinet | Muriel Colvin | Mrs. Thomas Hohstadt |
| Clarinet | Larry Combs | Principal, Chicago Symphony |
| Clarinet | Charles Ellis-MacLeod | School music director. Ballet conductor |
| Clarinet | Joseph Fisher | Retired |
| Clarinet Bass Clarinet | Paul Freeman | Conductor, Chicago Sinfonietta. Extensive recordings catalog |
| Clarinet | Robert Gauldin | Eastman School of Music, Chair, Theory, Rochester, NY |
| Alto Clarinet | William Gaver | President, Defem Design-Build, Inc., Brookfield, NH |
| Clarinet Saxophone | Samuel Glenn | Quality Control, Sun Litho, Van Nuys, CA |
| Clarinet | Peter Hadcock | Buffalo Philharmonic, Boston Symphony. Professor of Clarinet, Eastman School of Music, Rochester, NY |
| Clarinet | William Hartman | |
| Clarinet | Daniel Johnston | Buffalo Philharmonic, Buffalo, NY |

| INSTRUMENT | NAME | WHERE ARE THEY? |
|---|---|---|
| Clarinet | Darrell Johnston | Conductor, San Jose City College, CA |
| Clarinet | George Jones | Rutgers University, retired professor, NJ |
| Clarinet | Barbara Kessler Goodman | Psychotherapist, Palo Alto, CA |
| Clarinet<br>Bass Clarinet | Daniel Kohut | Professor of Music Education, University of Illinois, Urbana, IL |
| Clarinet | Charles Krusenstjerna | Admissions/Alumni Office, Eastman School of Music, Rochester, NY |
| Clarinet | Mary Jane Lang | |
| Clarinet | Rolf Legbandt | Professor of Clarinet, Ball State University, Muncie, IN |
| Clarinet<br>Alto Clarinet | Jonathan Levine | Midwest Regional Director, American Jewish Committee, Evanston, IL |
| Clarinet<br>Bass Clarinet | Ralph Long | President, Longs of Newport, Newport Beach, CA |
| Clarinet | Ralph Loomis | Retired principal - U.S. Coast Guard Band. Pacific Gas & Electric Co., Vacaville, CA |
| Clarinet | Elsa Ludewig Verdehr | Richards Quintet; her own trio; Professor, Michigan State University, East Lansing, MI |
| Clarinet<br>Alto Clarinet | Philip Macone | |
| Clarinet | Robert Mader | Reverend/Pastor, Bethlehem Lutheran Church, Johnson City, TN |
| Clarinet | James Mandros | Foreign Service Officer, USIA, Washington, DC |
| Clarinet | George Marge * | |
| Clarinet | John Mauro | Instrumental Instructor, Montgomery County Schools, MD |
| Clarinet<br>Contrabass | Lawrence Maxey | Michigan State University, East Lansing, MI |
| Clarinet | Henry Miyamura | Music Director, Hawaii Youth/University of Hawaii, Honolulu, HI |
| Clarinet | Roland Persson | English teacher, Pinole Valley High School, Pinole, CA |
| Clarinet<br>Saxophone | Thomas Peterson | Cleveland Orchestra |
| Clarinet | Theodore Pizzarello | |
| Clarinet | Donald Puluse | Berkeley College, Marblehead, MA |
| Clarinet<br>Bass Clarinet | Daniel Sandidge | Arranger, conductor; White Sulphur Springs, WV |
| Clarinet | Joseph Scharbo | Retired music educator; Bellmore Merrick Schools, NY |

| INSTRUMENT | NAME | WHERE ARE THEY? |
|---|---|---|
| Clarinet | Robert Seath | |
| Clarinet<br>Contrabass | Frank Sidorfsky | Kansas State University, Manhattan, KS |
| Clarinet<br>Alto Clarinet | Thomas Slattery | Retired conductor, Coe College; private businessman |
| Clarinet | Jerry Neal Smith | Professor of Music, University of Oklahoma, Norman, OK |
| Clarinet<br>Alto Clarinet | Michael Smith | |
| Clarinet | Daniel Sparks | |
| Clarinet | Mary Anne Spencer | |
| Clarinet | Jerry Steinhagen | Milwaukee, WI |
| Clarinet<br>Saxophone | Noel Stevens | Retired, Tampa, FL |
| Clarinet<br>Bass Clarinet | Leslie Thimmig | University of Wisconsin, Madison, WI |
| Clarinet<br>Bass Clarinet | Paul Tomasick* | |
| Clarinet | Dorothy Trojan Tomasick* | |
| Clarinet | Winston Vitous | |
| Clarinet | Richard Webster | Professor of Music, University of Toledo, OH. Retired |
| Clarinet | Mitchell Weiss | New York studio player |
| Clarinet<br>Contrabass | Lawrence Williams | Bellingham Public Schools, Bellingham, WA |
| Clarinet | William Wohlmacher | Professor of Music, California State University, Hayward, CA |
| Clarinet | Eugene Zoro | Professor, Western Washington State University, Bellingham, WA |
| Saxophone | Frank Bencriscutto | Composer, Conductor University of Minnesota Bands, Minneapolis, MN. Retired. |
| Saxophone | Fred Brenner | |
| Saxophone | Philip Browne | Conductor and composer; Cal-Poly, Pomona, CA |
| Saxophone | Jack Carey | |
| Saxophone | Donald Coley | Teacher, Brighton Central Schools, Brighton, NY |
| Saxophone | Ned Corman | Instrumental music director/music entrepreneur, Penfield, NY |

| INSTRUMENT | NAME | WHERE ARE THEY? |
|---|---|---|
| Saxophone | Rudolph Defelice | Administrator, C.B. Hoober & Son, Intercourse, PA |
| Saxophone | Robert Dransite | Teacher, Carle Place High School, NY |
| Saxophone | Fred Hemke | Solo artist. Professor, Northwestern University, Evanston, IL |
| Saxophone | Sydney Hodkinson | Composer, Conductor Musica-NOVA, Eastman School of Music, Rochester, NY |
| Saxophone | Frank Jacobsen | |
| Saxophone | Larry Loven | |
| Saxophone | Kenneth Murley | Retired Professor, Toccoa Falls College, GA |
| Saxophone | Donald Panhorst | Edinboro University, PA, Retired |
| Saxophone | Albert Regni | New York Philharmonic |
| Saxophone | Robert Silberstein | JFK Center for Performing Arts, Washington, DC |
| Saxophone | Eugene Tettamanti | House musician, Riviera Hotel, Las Vegas, NV |
| Saxophone | David Ward | Composer; U.S. Naval Academy Band, Annapolis, MD |
| Saxophone | Gerald Welker | Conductor, University of Alabama Bands, Tuscaloosa, AL |
| Horn | Bette Allison | Instrumental teacher, Montgomery County, MD |
| Horn | Gay Banks | Mrs. David Helfrich |
| Horn | James Basta | Director of Music, Home Moravian Church, Winston-Salem, NC |
| Horn | Barry Benjamin | Professor, University of Wisconsin, Milwaukee; adjunct faculty, Northwestern; former member of New York Brass Quintet |
| Horn | Jeff [Carl] Bianchi | Conductor/Music Educator, Fairfax County Schools, Fairfax, VA |
| Horn | Barbara Bloomer | Toronto Symphony |
| Horn | William Bommelje | Associate Professor, University of Tennessee, Knoxville, TN |
| Horn | Aubrey Bouck | Crawford, TX |
| Horn | Clyde Carpenter | Retired teacher |
| Horn | Waldo Comfort | Mechanics Auto Parts, Rochester, NY |
| Horn | John Covert | Faculty, Ithaca College, Ithaca, NY |

| INSTRUMENT | NAME | WHERE ARE THEY? |
|---|---|---|
| Horn | Robert Elworthy * | |
| Horn | JoAnn Haynes | |
| Horn | David Helfrich | Instructor, Psychology; Pasco Hernando Community College, New Port Richey, FL |
| Horn | Eleanor Konzer Lindboe | Private teacher, Mailbu, CA |
| Horn | John Krance * | |
| Horn | Carol Ladrach | Mrs. Robert C. Zajkowski; home maker, Volunteer, Pittsford, NY |
| Horn | Zora McCann | |
| Horn | Janet Miller Sheldon | Real Estate Broker, VA |
| Horn | Richard Norem | Louisiana State University, Baton Rouge, LA |
| Horn | Jack Reed | Associate Dean, Oklahoma City University, OK |
| Horn | Kenneth Schultz | Saint Louis Symphony |
| Horn | Norman Schweikert | Chicago Symphony |
| Horn | Stephen Seiffert | Systems Analyst; QL Systems, Ltd. Kingston, Ontario, Canada |
| Horn | Robert Sheldon | Curator, Dayton C. Miller Flute and Instrument Collections, Library of Congress |
| Horn | Herbert Spencer | Professor, Bowling Green State University, OH |
| Horn | Esther Sweigart Rosenthal | President, Point Roberts Industries, Los Angeles, CA |
| Horn | Linda VanSickle Smith | Staff Therapist; Pastoral Counseling Center, Dallas, TX |
| Trumpet | Manuel Alvarez | Director, University of South Carolina, School of Medicine, Columbia, SC |
| Trumpet | James Austin | Retired principal, Houston Symphony Orchestra. Associate Professor, University of Houston, TX |
| Trumpet | Rodger Baker | Associate Professor/Program Chair, Rochester Institute of Technology, NY |
| Trumpet | Glen Bell | Music Educator, freelance player, Dallas, TX |
| Trumpet | William Brower | |
| Trumpet | George Cavanagh | Band Director, Department of Music, Purdue University, Fort Wayne, IN |
| Trumpet | Samuel Fricano | Retired conductor U.S. Army Field Band. Conductor, River City Brass, Jacksonville, FL |

| INSTRUMENT | NAME | WHERE ARE THEY? |
|---|---|---|
| Trumpet | David Greenhoe | Bowling Green State University, OH |
| Trumpet | John Hall | |
| Trumpet | Thomas Hohstadt | Conductor, Midland/Odessa Orchestra, TX Retired; author |
| Trumpet | Boyde Hood | Los Angeles Philharmonic |
| Trumpet | David Johnson | Retired, U.S. Marine Band |
| Trumpet | Richard Jones | Principal, Buffalo Philharmonic |
| Trumpet | Joel Koplin | Investments counselor, Philadelphia, PA |
| Trumpet | John Landis | Conductor, radio music commentator, WNED-FM, Buffalo, NY. |
| Trumpet | William Lockwood | Worldwide Distributor; <u>Teach Yourself Chord Piano</u>, Endicott, NY |
| Trumpet | Albert MacKinnon | New Zealand National Symphony, Wellingham, N.Z. |
| Trumpet | Ralph Montgomery | Chairman, Greenville College Music Department, Greenville, IL |
| Trumpet | Daniel Patrylak | Former assistant to the Director, Eastman School of Music; Dean, University of Connecticut/Music |
| Trumpet | Barbara Ricksecker | Mrs. Barbara Martinson; retired librarian and music teacher |
| Trumpet | Erwin Sapiro | Williamsburg, VA |
| Trumpet | Maurice Sapiro | Music teacher, North Haven Public Schools, New Haven, CT |
| Trumpet | Richard Schaffer | Houston Symphony, TX |
| Trumpet | Donald Schmaus | Music supervisor, Lake Brantley, FL |
| Trumpet | Roger Sherman | Pittsburgh Symphony |
| Trumpet | Paul Shull | Retired, Manhattan, KS |
| Trumpet | Gary Smith | Saint Louis Symphony |
| Trumpet | John Thyhsen | Professor, Glassboro State College, Glassboro, NJ |
| Trumpet | Stephen Toback | Music teacher, New Rochelle Board of Education, New Rochelle, NY |
| Trombone | Early Anderson | Metropolitan Opera Orchestra, NY |
| Trombone | Jonathan Clark* | |

| INSTRUMENT | NAME | WHERE ARE THEY? |
|---|---|---|
| Trombone | Tony DeChario | Retired manager, Rochester Philharmonic; Manager, Honolulu Symphony, Honolulu, HI |
| Trombone | David Fetter | Baltimore Symphony |
| Trombone | Reginald Fink | Professor, Ohio University; Music publisher |
| Trombone | Robert Gillespie | Principal, Johannesburg Opera and Symphony, South Africa |
| Trombone | Frederick Halt | Buffalo Philharmonic, NY |
| Trombone Euphonium | Donald Hunsberger | Composer/Arranger, Author, Conductor, Eastman Wind Ensemble, Rochester, NY |
| Trombone | Stephen Kelleher | |
| Trombone | Peter Kline | Assistant Professor of Music, San Antonio College, TX |
| Trombone | Perry Martin | Director of Music, Mamaroneck Schools; Conductor, Larchmont Pops Band, NY |
| Trombone | Donald Miller | Buffalo Philharmonic |
| Trombone | Robert Norden | New York, NY |
| Trombone | George Osborne | Rochester Philharmonic |
| Trombone | Peter Phillips | Freelance musician, Delaware Water Gap, PA |
| Trombone | Porter Poindexter | Freelance musician, New York, NY |
| Trombone | Ray Premru | Retired, Philip Jones Brass Ensemble ; Philharmonia/England. Professor Oberlin College Conservatory; Composer |
| Trombone | David Richey | Rochester Philharmonic |
| Trombone | George Shroyer | Studio musician, Hollywood, CA |
| Trombone | Lester Slezak | Minister Counselor, Department of State, Washington, DC |
| Euphonium | Guy Bockman | Retired professor, Tennessee State University, Nashville, TN |
| Euphonium | Kenton Briggs | Music Coordinator/Teacher, Homer Central Schools, Homer, NY |
| Euphonium | Larry Campbell | Professor, Louisiana State University, Baton Rouge, LA |
| Euphonium | Robert Gray | Professor of trombone, University of Illinois; Conductor of University of Illinois Wind Ensemble, Urbana, IL |
| Euphonium | Byron Hanson | Conductor, Interlochen Arts Academy Orchestra, MI |
| Euphonium | Kenley Inglefield | Professor, Bowling Green State University, Bowling Green, OH |

| INSTRUMENT | NAME | WHERE ARE THEY? |
|---|---|---|
| Euphonium | Rodger Kramer | Retired teacher of Brass, Birmingham School District, MI |
| Euphonium | Harold McNeil | Houghton College, School of Music, NY |
| Euphonium | Thomas Miller | Regional Representative; African-American Labor Center, Washington, DC |
| Tuba | Ronald Bishop | Buffalo Philharmonic, San Francisco Symphony, Cleveland Orchestra |
| Tuba | Roger Bobo | Retired principal - Los Angeles Philharmonic; soloist, conductor |
| Tuba | Paul Brown | Retired Department Chair, Caledonia-Mumford Central Schools, NY |
| Tuba | Bruce Butler | Dentist, New Orleans, LA |
| Tuba | William Kearney | Teacher, Amherst Schools, Buffalo, NY |
| Tuba | Joseph McEnulty | |
| Tuba | Daniel Perantoni | Professor, Arizona State University. Solo artist, Tempe, AZ |
| Tuba | Charles Schaffer* | |
| Tuba | Donald Zale * | |
| Tuba | Robert Zale | Director of Music, Gates-Chili Central Schools, NY |
| String Bass | Lawrence Angell | Principal, Cleveland Orchestra |
| String Bass | Neil Courtney | Philadelphia Orchestra |
| String Bass | Marie Mann | Mrs. Thomas Stacy |
| String Bass | Armand Russell | Composer in Residence, University of Hawaii, Honolulu, HI |
| String Bass | Elizabeth Twaddell Ferrell | Baltimore Symphony |
| String Bass | Robert Zimmerman | Principal, Rochester Philharmonic |
| Harp | Robert Barlow * | |
| Harp | Lauralee Campbell | Michigan State University, Lansing Symphony, Travel agent |
| Harp | Rachel Ewing Corrigan | Harp instructor, Butler University, Indianapolis, IN |
| Harp | Lois Kreig | |
| Harp | Lanalee Litz | |

| INSTRUMENT | NAME | WHERE ARE THEY? |
|---|---|---|
| Harp | Marjorie Winey | Albany Symphony, NY |
| Percussion | Ronald Barnett | Associate Professor, University of Maryland, College Park, MD |
| Percussion | John Beck | U.S. Marine Band; Professor Eastman School of Music; Rochester Philharmonic, timpanist. Rochester, NY |
| Percussion | Jane Burnet Varella | Personnel Manager, Principal Percussion, Dayton Philharmonic, Dayton, OH |
| Percussion | Frank Cocuzzi | |
| Percussion | James Dotson * | |
| Percussion | Vivian Emery | Teacher, Boyertown Area School District, PA |
| Percussion | Norman Fickett | Detroit Symphony |
| Percussion | Theodore Frazeur | Professor, State University of New York, Fredonia, NY |
| Percussion | John Galm | University of Colorado |
| Percussion | Donald Gilbert | |
| Percussion | Dennis Kain | Baltimore Symphony, Kettledrums, Baltimore, MD |
| Percussion | Stanley Leonard | Pittsburgh Symphony Orchestra, Kettledrums |
| Percussion | Anthony Matarrese | Woodbridge, VA |
| Percussion | Thomas McMillan | Fine Arts Coordinator, Trenton, MI Schools |
| Percussion | Gordon Peters | Chicago Symphony; former conductor of Chicago Civic Orchestra |
| Percussion | Mitchell Peters | Los Angeles Philharmonic, Kettledrums |
| Percussion | James Preiss | Manhattan School of Music, NY |
| Kettledrums | Peter Tanner | Professor of Music, University of Massachusetts, Amherst, MA |
| Percussion | Joel Thome | Conductor, Orchestra of Our Time, New York, NY |
| Percussion | Kenneth Wendrich | Executive Director, W.O. Smith, Nashville Community Music, TN |
| Percussion | John Wyre | Founding member of NEXUS |
| Piano | Gary Kirkpatrick | Verdehr Trio |
| Piano | Robert Spillman | Professor of Piano, University of Colorado, Boulder, CO |

| INSTRUMENT | NAME | WHERE ARE THEY? |
|---|---|---|
| Piano | Clair W. Van Ausdall | Editor-in-Chief; <u>Chamber Music America</u>, NY |
| Organ | Anne Labounsky | Professor of Organ, Duquesne University, PA |
| Organ | Andrea Toth | Mrs. Andrea C. Haines. Jaeger & Haines, Inc., Fayetteville, AR |

\* Known to be deceased

# STUDY/PERFORMANCE ESSAYS and ARTICLES by FREDERICK FENNELL

| Author | Title | Publication | Date |
|---|---|---|---|
| Bennett, Robert Russell | Suite of Old American Dances [Study/Performance Essay] [SPE] | The Instrumentalist | September 1, 1979 |
| Chance, John Barnes | Variations on a Korean Folk Song [SPE] | BD Guide | September 1, 1989 |
| Fennell, Frederick | Civil War Music | Selmer Bandwagon | |
| Fennell, Frederick | Modern Use of Percussion | Modern Music | July 1, 1946 |
| Fennell, Frederick | Band as a Medium of Musical Expression | Etude | May 1, 1948 |
| Fennell, Frederick | Listen! | A Tempo - Eastman | November 1, 1950 |
| Fennell, Frederick | Eastman's New Wind Ensemble | Music Journal | September 1, 1952 |
| Fennell, Frederick | Symphonic Winds: Eastman Ensemble seeks to encourage them | New York Times | July 26, 1953 |
| Fennell, Frederick | Time and the Winds | G. Leblanc Co. | October 1, 1954 |
| Fennell, Frederick | The Eastman Wind Ensemble and the American Composer | Pan Pipes | January 1, 1955 |
| Fennell, Frederick | Men of Note | The Instrumentalist | April 1, 1955 |
| Fennell, Frederick | History of an Experiment in Wind Instruments | Music Journal | January 1, 1957 |
| Fennell, Frederick | The American Musical Heritage | Music Educators Journal | February 1, 1957 |
| Fennell, Frederick | The Silent Statistic | The Instrumentalist | June 1, 1957 |
| Fennell, Frederick | Popcorn, Mosquitoes & Music | Hi-Fi & Music Review | August 1, 1958 |
| Fennell, Frederick | Know your Conductors | International Musician | October 1, 1958 |
| Fennell, Frederick | Ruffs, Ratamacues and Paradiddles | Hi-Fi Review | February 1, 1959 |
| Fennell, Frederick | Hardy Perennial: Band in the Open | Musical America | July 1, 1961 |
| Fennell, Frederick | Hanson at Sixty-five | Pan Pipes | June 1, 1962 |
| Fennell, Frederick | Man's Greatest Achievement | Music Journal | April 1, 1967 |
| Fennell, Frederick | The Civil War: Its Music and Its Sounds, Part I | Journal of Band Research | March 1, 1968 |
| Fennell, Frederick | As I See It | School Musician | August 1, 1968 |
| Fennell, Frederick | The Civil War: Its Music and Its Sounds, Part II | Journal of Band Research | September 1, 1968 |
| Fennell, Frederick | The Civil War: Its Music and Its Sounds, Part II, continued | Journal of Band Research | March 1, 1969 |
| Fennell, Frederick | The Wind Ensemble - Inception from Long Distilled Thoughts | The Instrumentalist | February 1, 1972 |
| Fennell, Frederick | How I Discovered Music | The Instrumentalist | October 1, 1973 |
| Fennell, Frederick | Basic Band Repertory | The Instrumentalist | September 1, 1975 |

| Composer/Author | Title | Source | Date |
|---|---|---|---|
| Fennell, Frederick | Testimonial to Albert Austin Harding [1958] | CBDNA/MENC | January 1, 1977 |
| Fennell, Frederick | The American Music Heritage [1956] | CBDNA/MENC | January 1, 1977 |
| Fennell, Frederick | The Band as a Medium of Musical Expression [1952] | CBDNA/MENC | January 1, 1977 |
| Fennell, Frederick | The Band's Service to Music as an Art [1947] | CBDNA/MENC | January 1, 1977 |
| Fennell, Frederick | The Eastman Wind Ensemble [1952] | CBDNA/MENC | January 1, 1977 |
| Fennell, Frederick | Calisthenics of Conducting | The Instrumentalist | November 1, 1978 |
| Fennell, Frederick | Albert Austin Harding - A Tribute During the Centennial | The Instrumentalist | December 1, 1980 |
| Fennell, Frederick | Percussion from the Podium | School Musician | December 1, 1980 |
| Fennell, Frederick | What Happens to our Students? | The Instrumentalist | March 1, 1981 |
| Fennell, Frederick | In Memory: A Tribute given to ABA convention | School Musician | April 1, 1981 |
| Fennell, Frederick | The Silent Art | Music Educators Journal | December 1, 1981 |
| Fennell, Frederick | Sousa! - Still A Somebody | The Instrumentalist | March 1, 1982 |
| Fennell, Frederick | Irish Tune from County Derry and Shepherd's Hey  [SPE] | Carl Fischer -reprint | September 1, 1982 |
| Fennell, Frederick | The Sousa March: A Personal View - Perspectives on J. P. Sousa | Library of Congress | June 1, 1983 |
| Fennell, Frederick | Classic Marches for Concert Band [Band Bulletin] | Carl Fischer | September 1, 1983 |
| Fennell, Frederick | Basic Band Repertory  translated into Japanese by Toshio Akiyama | Kosei Publishing Co. | January 1, 1985 |
| Fennell, Frederick | Time and the Winds, translated into Japanese by Machiko Kumabe | Kosei Publishing Co. | July 1, 1985 |
| Fennell, Frederick | Frederick Fennell - Lifetime Listener - Part I | The Instrumentalist | October 1, 1986 |
| Fennell, Frederick | Frederick Fennell - The Eastman Years - Part II | The Instrumentalist | December 1, 1986 |
| Fennell, Frederick | Frederick Fennell - Growing as a Conductor - Part III | The Instrumentalist | April 1, 1987 |
| Fennell, Frederick | The Wind Ensemble  [with Wm. Francis McBeth] | Delta Publications | September 1, 1988 |
| Fennell, Frederick | Basic Band Repertory [compilation from INSTRUMENTALIST] | The Instrumentalist | January 1, 1989 |
| Fennell, Frederick | Frederick Fennell on the Marching Band | BD Guide | May 1, 1989 |
| Fennell, Frederick | I Really Do Love Marches | BD Guide | March 1, 1990 |
| Fennell, Frederick | The Band's Music, Volume One [from BAND and BD GUIDE] | BD Guide | January 1, 1992 |
| Fennell, Frederick | The Band's Music, Volume Two [from BAND and BD GUIDE] | BD Guide | January 1, 1992 |
| Fennell, Frederick | Bands and A.A. Harding at Interlochen | BD Guide | March 1, 1992 |

| Composer/Author | Title | Source | Date |
|---|---|---|---|
| Grainger, Percy A. | *Irish Tune from County Derry and Shepherd's Hey* [SPE] | The Instrumentalist | September 1, 1978 |
| Grainger, Percy A. | *Lincolnshire Posy, Part I* [SPE] | The Instrumentalist | May 1, 1980 |
| Grainger, Percy A. | *Lincolnshire Posy, Part II* [SPE] | The Instrumentalist | September 1, 1980 |
| Grainger, Percy A. | *Lincolnshire Posy, Part III* [SPE] | The Instrumentalist | October 1, 1980 |
| Grainger, Percy A. | *Ye Banks and Braes O' Bonnie Doon* [SPE] | The Instrumentalist | September 1, 1981 |
| Grainger, Percy A. | *Children's March* [SPE] | The Instrumentalist | December 1, 1982 |
| Grainger, Percy A. | *Country Gardens* [SPE] | The Instrumentalist | January 1, 1983 |
| Grainger, Percy A. | *Colonial Song* [SPE] | The Instrumentalist | March 1, 1983 |
| Grainger, Percy A. | *The Immovable Do* [SPE] | The Instrumentalist | May 1, 1983 |
| Grainger, Percy A. | *Molly on the Shore* [SPE] | The Instrumentalist | October 1, 1983 |
| Grainger, Percy A. | *Hill-Song No. 2* [SPE] | The Instrumentalist | February 1, 1984 |
| Hanson, Howard | *Chorale and Alleluia* [SPE] | BD Guide | September 1, 1990 |
| Holst, Gustav | *First Suite in E-flat for Military Band, Op. 28a* [SPE] | The Instrumentalist | April 1, 1975 |
| Holst, Gustav | *Hammersmith* [SPE] | The Instrumentalist | May 1, 1977 |
| Holst, Gustav | *Second Suite in F for Military Band, Op. 28b* [SPE] | The Instrumentalist | November 1, 1977 |
| Holst, Gustav | *A Moorside Suite* [SPE] | BD Guide | January 1, 1989 |
| Jacob, Gordon | *William Byrd Suite* [SPE] | The Instrumentalist | September 1, 1975 |
| Persichetti, Vincent | *Divertimento for Band* [SPE] | BAND/BD Guide | September 1, 1984 |
| Persichetti, Vincent | *Symphony For Band [Symphony No. 6]* [SPE] | BD Guide | September 1, 1987 |
| Schuman, William | *George Washington Bridge* [SPE] | BD Guide | March 1, 1993 |
| Wagner, Richard | *Elsa's Procession to the Cathedral* [SPE] | BAND/BD Guide | November 1, 1984 |
| Williams, R. Vaughan | *Folk Song Suite* [SPE] | The Instrumentalist | June 1, 1976 |
| Williams, R. Vaughan | *Toccata Marziale* [SPE] | The Instrumentalist | August 1, 1976 |

# MUSIC EDITIONS/ARRANGEMENTS/COMPOSITIONS by FREDERICK FENNELL

| | | |
|---|---|---|
| Alford, Kenneth J. | Army of the Nile | Boosey & Hawkes 1986 |
| Alford, Kenneth J. | Colonel Bogey | Boosey & Hawkes 1982 |
| Alford, Kenneth J. | Mad Major, The | Boosey & Hawkes 1983 |
| Alford, Kenneth J. | Vanished Army, The | Boosey & Hawkes 1984 |
| Bach, J. S. | Ricacare a 6 - The Musical Offering BWV 1079  [trans. Clark McAlister] | Ludwig Music 1986 |
| Bach, J. S. | Toccata and Fugue in D minor BWV 565  [arr. Fujita] | Kosei Publishing |
| Bagley, E. E. | National Emblem | Carl Fischer 1981 |
| Bennett, Harold | Military Escort | Carl Fischer 1980 |
| End, Jack | Blues for a Killed Kat | Ludwig Music 1987 |
| Fennell, Frederick | Hail Sinfonia March  [Manuscript] | Eastman School of Music 1935 |
| Fennell, Frederick | Palestra | Carl Fischer 1937 |
| Fennell, Frederick | Spirit of Youth March, The  [Manuscript] | Interlochen |
| Fennell, Frederick | Tally-Ho !  [arr. John Kinyon] | Remick Music 1963 |
| Fennell, Frederick | The Drummer's Heritage [Spirit of '76 & Ruffles and Flourishes] | Carl Fischer 1956 |
| Fillmore, Henry | Americans We | Carl Fischer 1979 |
| Fillmore, Henry | His Honor | Carl Fischer 1978 |
| Fillmore, Henry | Klaxon, The | Carl Fischer 1983 |
| Fillmore, Henry | Rolling Thunder | Carl Fischer 1982 |
| Fucik, Julius | Florentiner March, The | Carl Fischer 1980 |
| Ganne, Louis | March Lorraine | Carl Fischer 1989 |
| Gounod, Charles | Petite Symphonie, Op. 90 | Ludwig Music 1985 |
| Grafulla, C.S. | Washington Grays | Carl Fischer 1982 |
| Grainger, Percy A. | Lincolnshire Posy  [full score edition] | Ludwig Music 1987 |
| Grieg, Edvard | Funeral March for Rikkard Nordrak [trans. Jan Eriksen] | Ludwig Music 1989 |
| Halvorsen, Johan | Entry March of the Boyars, Op. 17 | Ludwig Music 1991 |
| Klohr, John | Billboard March, The | Carl Fischer 1984 |
| Massenet, Jules | Meditation from Thais  [arr. Harding] | Neil Kjos |
| Mozart, Wolfgang A. | Serenade No. 10 in B-flat | Ludwig Music 1993 |
| Mozart, Wolfgang A. | Serenade No. 12 in C minor | Ludwig Music 1993 |
| Rauski, Joseph H. | Le Regiment de Sambre et Meuse | Carl Fischer 1984 |

| Composer | Title | Source |
|---|---|---|
| San Miguel, Mariano | La Oreja de Oro [The Golden Ear] | Ludwig Music 1984 |
| Sbrocia, B. di | La Banda Nascente | Neil Kjos 1987 |
| Sousa, John Philip | Black Horse Troop, The | Sam Fox 1974 |
| Sousa, John Philip | Bullets and Bayonets | Ludwig Music 1989 |
| Sousa, John Philip | Corcoran Cadets, The | Ludwig Music 1986 |
| Sousa, John Philip | Daughters of Texas | John Church/Presser 1986 |
| Sousa, John Philip | El Capitan March | John Church/Presser 1987 |
| Sousa, John Philip | Fairest of the Fair, The | John Church/Presser 1978 |
| Sousa, John Philip | Gallant Seventh, The | Sam Fox 1972 |
| Sousa, John Philip | Glory of the Yankee Navy, The | John Church/Presser 1984 |
| Sousa, John Philip | Golden Jubilee, The | Sam Fox 1971 |
| Sousa, John Philip | Hands Across the Sea | Theodore Presser 1982 |
| Sousa, John Philip | King Cotton | Theodore Presser 1983 |
| Sousa, John Philip | Manhattan Beach March | John Church/Presser 1980 |
| Sousa, John Philip | Minnesota March | Sam Fox 1968 |
| Sousa, John Philip | New Mexico March | Sam Fox 1970 |
| Sousa, John Philip | Nobles of the Mystic Shrine | Sam Fox 1972 |
| Sousa, John Philip | Pride of the Wolverines, The | Sam Fox 1973 |
| Sousa, John Philip | Riders For the Flag | Sam Fox 1968 |
| Sousa, John Philip | Rifle Regiment, The | Ludwig Music 1985 |
| Sousa, John Philip | Sabre and Spurs | Sam Fox 1972 |
| Sousa, John Philip | Washington Post March, The | Carl Fischer 1983 |
| Strauss, Richard | Allerseelen [All Souls' Day]  arr. Albert O. Davis | Ludwig Music 1985 |
| Strauss, Richard | Serenade in E-flat, Op. 7 | Ludwig Music 1985 |
| Teike, Carl | New Comrades | Theodore Presser 1979 |
| Ventre, Frank | Wings of Victory | Sam Fox |
| Wagner, Richard | Invocation of Alberich  [arr. Cailliet] | Sam Fox |